RHETORIC AND GUNS

RHETORIC AND GUNS

EDITED BY
LYDIA WILKES, NATE KREUTER,
AND RYAN SKINNELL

UTAH STATE UNIVERSITY PRESS
Logan

© 2022 by University Press of Colorado

Published by Utah State University Press
An imprint of University Press of Colorado
245 Century Circle, Suite 202
Louisville, Colorado 80027

 The University Press of Colorado is a proud member of the Association of University Presses.

The University Press of Colorado is a cooperative publishing enterprise supported, in part, by Adams State University, Colorado State University, Fort Lewis College, Metropolitan State University of Denver, Regis University, University of Alaska Fairbanks, University of Colorado, University of Denver, University of Northern Colorado, University of Wyoming, Utah State University, and Western Colorado University.

∞ This paper meets the requirements of the ANSI/NISO Z39.48–1992 (Permanence of Paper)

ISBN: 978-1-64642-214-2 (paperback)
ISBN: 978-1-64642-215-9 (ebook)
https://doi.org/10.7330/9781646422159

Library of Congress Cataloging-in-Publication Data

Names: Wilkes, Lydia, editor. | Kreuter, Nate, editor. | Skinnell, Ryan, 1978– editor.
Title: Rhetoric and guns / edited by Lydia Wilkes, Nate Kreuter, and Ryan Skinnell.
Other titles: Rhetoric & guns
Description: Logan : Utah State University Press, [2022] | Includes bibliographical references and index.
Identifiers: LCCN 2021050438 (print) | LCCN 2021050439 (ebook) | ISBN 9781646422142 (paperback) | ISBN 9781646422159 (ebook)
Subjects: LCSH: Rhetoric—Social aspects—United States. | Rhetoric—Political aspects—United States. | Firearms—Social aspects—United States. | Firearms in popular culture—United States. | Mass shootings—United States. | Gun control—United States.
Classification: LCC P301.5.S63 R4824 2022 (print) | LCC P301.5.S63 (ebook) | DDC 810.9/356—dc23/eng/20220111
LC record available at https://lccn.loc.gov/2021050438
LC ebook record available at https://lccn.loc.gov/2021050439

The University Press of Colorado gratefully acknowledges the support of the University of Georgia and San Jose State University toward this publication.

Cover illustration © GB_Art/Shutterstock

To the victims of gun violence

CONTENTS

ACKNOWLEDGMENTS

I want to offer my boundless gratitude to Nate Kreuter and Ryan Skinnell for their contributions to this book from its beginning at the 2018 Rhetoric Society of America conference. This book would not have been possible without their insights, perspectives, guidance, care, and good humor. I also thank Trish Roberts-Miller for pointing me toward Nate and Ryan as coeditors and for being one of the first contributors to this book. They and other early contributors—Brian Ballentine, Lisa Corrigan, Rosa Eberly, Kendall Gerdes, and Craig Rood—imparted momentum to this project, and I am enduringly grateful for their willingness to invest in it. My sincere thanks to Catherine Squires for providing her perspective on this topic in the afterword, without which this book would be (even more) incomplete. The generosity, kindness, and love circulating in the discipline of rhetoric and its close cousins, composition and communication, continue to overawe me. I also offer thanks to Rachael Levay at Utah State University Press for her enthusiasm about this book and careful shepherding of it through the publication process, and to the two anonymous reviewers whose feedback greatly improved the final manuscript. Finally, I want to thank my mentors in rhetoric—too numerous to name here for fear of accidentally excluding someone—for their guidance and encouragement, and my father, Ronald Wilkes, for teaching me gun safety and responsible gun ownership and operation within a hunting tradition from a young age. These literacies intertwined with the staccato bursts of many kinds of spectacular gun violence to generate this project.

—LYDIA WILKES

Foremost I would like to thank Lydia, who conceived this project, understood its importance before anyone else, and saw the potential for our field to contribute to the nation's collective understanding of a distinctly American and distinctly enduring problem. Like Lydia, I grew up around guns, both enjoying them and in awe of them. Unlike me, Lydia saw, as if she had crosshairs upon it, how the discipline of rhetoric might target the problem of American gun violence, which is unique in the world. Without Ryan this project would have misfired early. His expertise, his publishing experience, and his generosity of intellect have all been essential to this book. Without him, Lydia and I would have wandered like lost hunters, tired, hungry, our quarry long ago escaped. We all owe a debt to Patricia Roberts-Miller, who played matchmaker between the three of us. I owe her a particular debt, because she allowed me the use of her and her husband's ranch when I was a graduate student in Texas: to hunt, to teach fellow nerds how to shoot and, most important, to escape for a few weekends a year the stresses of graduate school. Our contributors have been amazing—to work with, for sure, but most of all for the ideas they have brought forth. As a scholar, I do not know if I agree with every argument presented in this volume, but I am impressed by the rigor and the insights the writers offer. Most of all I am humbled by their concern for their fellow citizens, their fellow humans, and their desire for a safer, more just future. I also want to thank the University of Georgia's Willson Center for Humanities for its support. Finally, I would like to thank Rachael Levay, who believed in this project before it was worthy of faith.

—Nate Kreuter

First and foremost, I want to thank Lydia and Nate for being outstanding collaborators. This has not been an easy project—not least because of the inexorable march of world events—and I am grateful for their camaraderie and vision along the way. Likewise, the contributors. They've taught me a lot, some of which I never wanted to know, but all of which I'm thankful to have learned from such smart, thoughtful people. When Lydia first invited me to coedit this book, she mentioned that Trish Roberts-Miller had recommended me as a good editor. I'm beyond flattered by the recommendation and grateful to Trish for getting me connected to this project. I hope I've lived up to the recommendation. I also want to thank San José State University and SJSU's College of Humanities and the Arts for financially supporting this project. Finally, I want to thank Rachael Levay for shepherding this project through the process. There's no quantifying the importance of Rachael's investment in and support of this book, and she's quickly become a model for what I think great editors should aspire to.

—Ryan Skinnell

RHETORIC AND GUNS

Introduction

RHETORIC AND GUNS

Nate Kreuter, Lydia Wilkes, and Ryan Skinnell

Disparate people in disparate times have viewed massive, state-sponsored violence (war) as, alternately, a continuation or a breakdown of language. Quite famously (or infamously), Prussian cavalry officer and military strategist Carl von Clausewitz declared that "war is a mere continuation of policy by other means" (1984, 87). Contemporary Canadian novelist Margaret Atwood has echoed a version of this thought, writing through a character in one novel that "war is what happens when language fails" (1998, 43). The discipline of rhetoric is generally good at theorizing and explaining the rhetorical failures that might lead states into conflict. Rhetoricians have spent much time studying rhetoric and war in the past century. Early twentieth-century English rhetorician I. A. Richards, for instance, defined rhetoric as "a study of misunderstanding and its remedies" (1964, 3), while the later twentieth-century American rhetorician Wayne Booth argued, apropos the 9/11 attacks, that "the only real alternative to war is rhetoric" (cited in Lunsford et al. 2016, 5). If violence occurs when rhetoric fails, then we need to study the rhetoric of that end point and how it is misunderstood.

The notion of war being the consequence of failed rhetoric is powerful, and maybe even mostly true. But in the United States, hot wars, particularly post-Vietnam, have had decreasing prominence in most people's daily lives.[1] At the same time, other forms of violence—specifically gun violence—have emerged as central to the fabric of Americans' daily lives. Unfortunately, the discipline has done less to help us understand the private violence of individuals within a distinctly US context. This is not to say rhetoricians haven't done any work in this direction, but rhetoric as a discipline has not yet systematically addressed the American gun crisis, wherein 100 people die at the muzzles of firearms each day (Brady 2019).[2] In part we think this is because of the commonplace that violence is a "failure of language." This volume stands alongside other

https://doi.org/10.7330/9781646422159.c000

recent scholarship on embodied aspects of rhetoric and violence, and with it we hope to move the discipline of rhetoric not only to study the failures of language that lead to violence but to examine how violence itself serves an ultimate rhetorical function, in addition to the physical and psychological damage that it inflicts.[3]

Despite the fact that tens of thousands of Americans die every year as a result of guns, victims of gun violence are obviously very different from states that enter into armed conflict. In negotiations between states, violence is always a potential outcome. It is, in fact, a constitutive threat in many state negotiations. But in most interactions we have with friends, neighbors, students, strangers on the bus, and so on, the expectation that we are "negotiating" to "prevent violence" is nonsensical. Consequently, aphorisms suggesting the "failure" of rhetoric/language to explain war simply don't often apply to victims of crime, domestic violence, race- or gender-based violence, suicide, accidents, or mass shootings. There is often no language or rhetoric that exists specifically to prevent private gun violence comparable to the way it exists to head off war. Addressing that rhetorical reality is another one of the central goals of this book. Both rhetoric and violence are exertions of power, and our discipline has much work to do to understand the intersections of rhetorical power, the rhetorically disempowered, and violence.[4] Does violence, for example, become a rhetoric of choice for the domestic abuser or white supremacist because of other rhetorical failures, or is violence for them an ultimate rhetorical act, the most forceful means of delivering their point? Ta-Nehisi Coates, writing about the guns owned by his father, a member and local captain of the Black Panther Party, observes, "The guns seemed to address this country . . . in its primary language—violence" (2015, 30). If the idea of considering violence as itself a rhetorical expression makes us uncomfortable, it should. The discomfort indicates necessary work, inquiry demanded of us by a society that has found no solutions for its internal violence.

RHETORICAL GUNS

At its most basic level, the American gun crisis has two origins, one rhetorical and one material. The rhetorical origin centers around a constitutional right to bear arms and a vocal, well-organized, predominately white constituency of Americans that resists interpretations of the Second Amendment that might restrict or regulate gun ownership. Before it was codified as an individual right in the Constitution, the right to bear arms was employed as a collective right by government-controlled militias to "officially invade and occupy Native land" (Dunbar-Ortiz 2018, 18). From its beginning, gun ownership and use has been inextricably tied to gendered and racialized violence perpetrated primarily by white male European settler-colonists against Black, Indigenous, People of Color (BIPOC). This foundational gendered, racialized violence enacted through firearms has never ceased. Since contact, firearm-based murders of Indigenous women and girls have been imperial, colonial, or federal policy (Adamski 2020). Firearm-based lynchings of Black people (Ore 2019), domestic assaults and murders of women of color across the United States (Squires 2016), and the torture and murder of poor women of color in Ciudad Juárez (Lozano 2019), alongside the endless litany of names-turned-hashtags through law enforcement's deadly force, bear witness to a rhetorically authorized history and present of gendered, racialized gun violence unique to the United States. As Coates writes, the fact that this violence falls most heavily on Black bodies is not a flaw in the system but "an intended result of policy" (2015, 17).

From this gendered, racialized rhetorical origin, a gendered, racialized material reality extends. Hundreds of millions of guns circulate in the United States, passing predominately through the hands of white men. One credible estimate puts the number at 393 million, or 70 million more firearms than citizens in the country (Ingraham 2018). It is easier in the United States to purchase a firearm than it is to open a bank account or vote. Given their material abundance and the ease of acquiring them, guns are readily available to enable accidental deaths, suicides, domestic murders, homicides, and mass shootings. So, guns circulate materially, and gun violence exists, circulates, affects, and is affected by rhetoric and language in a manner differentiated by gender and race and other identity markers.

Whether or not we can directly affect the material circumstances, rhetoricians—people who study argument, language, and pedagogy for a living—have a responsibility to investigate the relationship of rhetoric and guns more thoroughly than we have as a discipline up to this point. Guns and gun violence occupy a unique rhetorical space in the twenty-first-century United States, one characterized by silent majorities (e.g., most gun owners), vocal minorities (especially the firearm industry and gun lobby), and a stalemate that fails to stem the tide of the dead. How Americans talk about, deliberate about, and fight about guns is vital to how guns are marketed, used, and regulated. However, rhetorical studies where guns are concerned is not terribly different from studies regarding American culture more generally. Guns are ever present, they exercise powerful functions, but they are commonly talked about in more oblique, unsystematic ways than they would seem to demand.

The chapters in this book are intended to contribute to more sophisticated understandings about guns, about the violence guns are capable of inflicting, about the violence guns sometimes do inflict, about the ways Americans talk about guns, and certainly about misunderstandings. It is about the nexus of rhetoric and firearms in this particular moment when the United States is experiencing acute crises related to firearms. Violent crime is down nationally, but firearms still facilitate thousands of murders each year. Self-inflicted violence in the form of suicides, committed primarily with guns, is rising nationally, especially among young men. Domestic violence reaches its most tragic crescendos in a nation where firearms are readily available and present in a high percentage of American homes. Mass shooting events, while still statistically rare, are now common enough to have established their own genres of news coverage within the media outlets that report them (Squires 2016). And, as we noted above, racialized and gendered violence proceed apace, as they have from long before the birth of this country.

There is widespread consensus that gun violence in America constitutes a crisis. At the same time, there are very different rhetorical responses to the crises of violent crime, suicide, domestic violence, and mass shootings. Some Americans advocate for large-scale controls on guns and gun rights to affect their availability and use, but not all Americans agree that the gun crises warrant changes to existing gun laws or legislative curtailments of Second Amendment rights. Some people argue, for instance, that a "good guy with a gun" will thwart the violence of the mass shooter, the violent criminal, or the homicidal spouse, and they therefore advocate for more guns and better availability. Arguments about what guns do, what individuals do, what laws do, and what the government can or should do are complicated, as are the people who advocate for any given position about guns. Often such arguments are wrapped up in questions of identity, community, and constitutional protections, which further complicate how Americans deliberate about guns and gun rights (see, e.g., Kelly 2020).

Guns played pivotal roles in the events shaping 2020 as the most tumultuous year yet for the United States in the twenty-first century. In the late spring, as the country struggled to balance personal freedom and public safety in response to the COVID-19 crisis, predominantly white right-wing militia groups intimidated the Michigan legislature, almost certainly affecting the body's policy choices, and without any consequences for those who toted arms into the legislative space. In

October, also in Michigan, fourteen members of a white nationalist militia, the Wolverine Watchmen, were arrested by the FBI for plotting to kidnap Governor Gretchen Whitmer (Cooter 2020). Predominantly white right-wing groups, armed with military-grade weapons and paramilitary gear, deployed themselves to multiple Black Lives Matters protests in the summer, ostensibly to "protect private property," but actually in an attempt to intimidate a new generation of civil rights protesters. Some of these confrontations turned deadly. Just a few months before George Floyd's murder in police custody in May, Ahmaud Arbery was gunned down in Georgia while jogging, the victim of a modern lynching perpetrated by a former law enforcement officer, his son, and another man, who lanced Arbery with racial epithets before running him down with their truck and gunning him to death on a residential street in his own hometown. Arbery's murder, of course, bore sickening echoes of Trayvon Martin's 2012 slaying. Except for the specific people involved, there's no meaningful sense in which Arbery's and Martin's killing, or any other number of racialized shootings, are isolated incidents. Such acts are of course violence—often explicitly gendered and/or racialized violence—but their rhetorical origins and rhetorical effects as specifically entangled in gun violence have only begun to draw the systematic attention of the discipline.

The complexity of gun rhetorics is still further complicated by evolutions in the broader contexts in which such rhetorics circulate. One factor we see as a dangerous trend percolating through American society is the dismissal of the conclusions of experts altogether. Nationally we are experiencing a crisis, in that expertise and experts go widely unvalued; and experts are regularly contradicted by amateurs with little or no expertise but whose counterarguments are nonetheless treated as equal to those of the experts by credulous media and naive publics, fueled by social media (see, e.g., Ceccarelli 2011; Hartelius 2010; Nichols 2017; Rice 2020). Gun debates give us one important example. Never has the nature of American gun violence been better understood. Yet never has that understanding mattered less, as arguments about regulation often refuse to engage research in ways that support meaningful deliberation.

Another factor is the reanimation of an old cultural friction between rural and urban Americans, who once again seem to be splitting and separating along a series of ideological lines—a split that has accelerated since the 2016 presidential election (Rodden 2019). The urban/rural divide animates rhetorically powerful—if usually dangerously erroneous—arguments about education, wealth, motivation, identity, who counts as a "real American," and who is worthy of participating in self-governance. Rhetoric about guns and about the urban/rural divide commonly reinforce one another, even when they do not appear to be explicitly linked.

Finally, we exist in a moment when it is easy to see that violence facilitated by guns is sometimes itself a rhetorical act—rhetoric with guns that is also rhetoric about them. How can we understand the mass shooting at Emanuel African Methodist Church in Charleston, South Carolina, in 2015, for example, as anything other than a rhetorically motivated (in part) attack by an avowed racist? How can we understand assertions from mass shooters around the world that their attacks are motivated by efforts to start race or cultural wars? Or assertions from men who vengefully target women? Certainly not as rhetoric/language being an obstacle to war. Since the mass shooting at Columbine High School in 1999, media pundits have been quick to designate school attacks perpetrated by the schools' own pupils as forms of "speaking out" wherein in the message is carried not through the vibrations of speech nor the scratches of writing, but out of the barrel of gun. Two decades after Columbine—arguably the most influential mass shooting in modern American history—the prevalence of guns-as-rhetoric is as prominent as ever. We needn't rehearse further the ways in which acts of violence are, in addition to everything else that they might be, also rhetorical acts—perhaps the ultimate rhetorical acts.

The nexus we are attempting to describe here, as is surely apparent, is every bit as complex, convoluted, and concerning as massive, state-sponsored violence or organized public violence. We do not expect to solve these problems with this book. Rather, we hope to deepen the care with which rhetoric scholars understand, engage with, and act in relation to rhetoric and guns. As such, the essays collected here take on a variety of complex issues from a multiplicity of complex perspectives.[5]

GUN RHETORIC(S)

Given the challenges of characterizing the multifaceted rhetorical situation at large and even the variety of views within this book, we have come to think of the essays collected here in terms of stasis theory. The classical model of stasis theory posits between four and six standard procedural stases—or potential points of disagreement requiring resolution. The stases provide a powerful heuristic for understanding the potential for argument about a given situation. In the classical model, the stases are existence, definition, value, policy, cause, and action. Sometimes the stases are presented as conjecture, definition, quality, and policy.

There are other ways of labeling the "core" stases, but in all iterations stasis theory contains the idea that issues are decided by moving through a series of steps that begins with the question "Does the thing exist?" and ends with the question "What, if anything, should we do about it?" In the formal model, developed in the ancient tradition primarily for court proceedings, interlocutors are compelled by the authority of law or a judge to argue at the same stasis point and progress through the stases systematically. This ensures that rhetorical adversaries engage one another at the same, relevant points of contention. Such a system, though, is not how public policy debate or public opinion formation proceeds. In these realms there are no rules, no systems or judges to compel constituencies to argue along the same plane of stasis.

Stasis theory need not always be as rigid as the formulation of its classical model, though. One powerful heuristic quality of stasis theory is that it allows us to see ways people disagree, and sometimes the reasons why. A person or group in favor of greater gun regulation, for instance, might argue at the stasis of policy, saying, "We need to forbid the sale of assault weapons." A common tactic of those who oppose such policies is to drag the debate in a more preliminary stasis of definition, arguing, for example, that we cannot regulate "assault weapons" because we have no definition of what constitutes an assault weapon. When two parties are arguing about different stases, there is no prospect of them arriving at a compromise because they are arguing about different things. When we ask if two people or parties are arguing at the same stasis, then, we're really just asking if they are arguing about the same thing. If they are, a resolution or compromise is possible, though by no means guaranteed. If they are not even arguing at the same stasis point, resolution is practically impossible. For people who want to help advance public deliberation about guns and gun violence, understanding stases is a powerful tool for understanding who is arguing about what at any given time, and for moving arguments into at least the same stasis.

In this volume we see rhetoricians taking on the problems of gun ownership and gun violence at a host of different stasis points (though authors do not characterize their arguments as such).

In her chapter "The Only Thing That Stops a Bad Guy with Rhetoric Is a Good Guy with Rhetoric" (chapter 1), Patricia Roberts-Miller opens the volume by diagnosing the anti-deliberative tendency toward demagoguery in the so-called gun debate: legitimate disagreements about gun policy are depoliticized and made into issues of identity and motive, of good guys and bad guys. Both the NRA and mainstream media coverage maintain a zero-sum battle between two groups inaccurately framed as supporting either unrestricted access to and use of guns or an outright ban on gun ownership. Roberts-Miller notes that as "a gun owner opposed to the NRA's policies," she is in a category the NRA's rhetoric doesn't allow. But as long as rhetoric from the NRA and mainstream media reinforces a win or lose contest on the basis of misconstrued identity and motive rather than policy, there can be little movement beyond a tug-of-war between two group identities.

The rhetorical means by which Second Amendment rights activists on the internet amass and exert force on public discussions of gun policy are the focus of Nate Kreuter's chapter, "Muzzle Velocity, Rhetorical Mass, and Rhetorical Force" (chapter 2). Kreuter analogizes the physics and chemistry of firearms' operations to extend the concept of rhetorical velocity by theorizing rhetorical mass and rhetorical force and examining how they propel debates over gun policy. Kreuter's analogies help explain why a well-organized minority of "anti-regulation interlocutors are apparently more rhetorically effective within the American political/rhetorical landscape than their counterparts who advocate on behalf of sensible gun regulations."

Like Kreuter, Brian Ballentine targets the firearms industry's relentless development of ever-greater muzzle velocity in "Hunting Firearms: Rhetorical Pursuits of Range and Power" (chapter 3). Ballentine applies Kenneth Burke's theory of entelechy to question what the "end of the line" might be for gun manufacturers and users, given the constant push to increase a firearm's "killing power." As a hunter, Ballentine focuses on variations in firearm restrictions that deer hunters encounter from state to state, even as states and hunters hold in common the ethical principle of "fair chase." Discussing the stasis of firearms' value in the context of fair chase, Ballentine reveals the complexities and complications of gun use by hunters as ever-more-lethal firearms make their way to market without any "end of the line" identified by gun makers or users.

Lisa M. Corrigan shares Ballentine's concern with firearms as technologies in her chapter, "The Gun as (Race/Gender) *Technê*" (chapter 4), though her interest lies with functions of guns in the contexts of white supremacy and anti-Black racism. Corrigan analyzes how a "duty to retreat" was made into Stand Your Ground laws that codify "the gun's *technê* [as] one premised on both whiteness and property." Two primary effects of this racial *technê* are "a fundamental assertion of ontological Being for white people" and an "erasure or anti-Being for people of color (particularly Black people) in the United States." Guns exist and affect existence in very different ways according to race and gender differences, as white men are accorded the possessive power to stand their ground while white women and people of color must retreat or risk death.

Ian E. J. Hill echoes Corrigan's interest in guns as technologies that affect people in radically different ways dependent on positionality. In "The Rhetoric of Open Carry: Living with the Nonverbal Presence of Guns" (chapter 5), Hill examines the paradoxical effects of open carry (the nonverbal presence of guns) in public spaces. Discussing the Black Panther Party's "defensive use of open carry" to protect their communities from governmental authorities also carrying guns, Cliven Bundy's armed standoff with federal workers, and other examples, Hill shows that "when guns are visible, they convey multiple meanings and messages depending on the political and social power possessed by different populations." Open carry, then, simultaneously conveys "the threat of violence and the promise of protection" in relation to personal security.

In his chapter "The Activism Gap and the Rhetoric of (Un)Certainty" (chapter 6), Craig Rood takes up the "gun control paradox," or the phenomenon of broadly supported firearms restrictions like universal background checks continually failing to become law, which reflects the "activism gap" between gun rights and gun reform supporters. Rood examines the role played by (un)certainty in motivating action among both groups, noting that "moral clarity and urgency" about gun reform "become clouded by appeals to uncertainty, complexity, and incrementalism," such as those made by President Obama after the Sandy Hook Elementary School shooting. In contrast, rhetoric from the NRA attempts to shift the stasis from policy to cause by introducing uncertainty about a gunman's motives into discourse while leveraging a simple message about gun rights to produce certainty among gun rights activists. Rood closes with three options "as a framework for interpretation and invention" for gun reform activists to increase certainty and decrease uncertainty in their rhetoric and thereby help enact popular reforms.

Lydia Wilkes, in her chapter "This Is America on Guns: Rhetorics of Acquiescence and Resistance to Privatized Gun Violence" (chapter 7), examines acquiescence to gun violence, a mood of helpless half acceptance of the inevitability of gun violence, in discursive commonplaces like "thoughts and prayers" and technologies like body armor marketed to civilians as one explanation for the "gun control paradox." These rhetorics of acquiescence make gun violence seem uncontestable. While acquiescence may describe the national mood of those committed neither to gun rights advocacy and activism nor gun control advocacy and activism, Wilkes also examines resistance to rhetorics of acquiescence from clergy members, NRA members and, most notably, the March for Our Lives organization, which was started by teenage survivors of the 2018 shooting at Marjory Stoneman Douglas High School in Parkland, Florida. Wilkes argues that March for Our Lives' social media and grassroots activism, which has already boosted youth voter turnout, can gather enough rhetorical mass to shift discourse from acquiescence to activism.

Bradley Serber also takes up March for Our Lives' rhetoric in his chapter "'The Last Mass Shooting': Anticipating the End of Mass Shootings, Yet Again" (chapter 8), in which he focuses on the group's Twitter handle and hashtag, @NeverAgainMSD and #NeverAgain, and their promise to be "the last mass shooting." Serber explores the benefits and risks of this rhetorical framing and argues that "perpetually anticipating the end of mass shootings" through commonly used phrases like "not one more" ultimately "sets up a never-ending cycle of heartbreak" because gun violence has only increased in spite of these passionate declarations. Serber suggests that March for Our Lives emphasize modest, attainable policy goals, as they do in their ten-point agenda for gun control, rather than the unattainable rallying cry of "never again."

Kendall Gerdes analyzes the long-standing debate over campus carry in Texas in her chapter "Campus Carry, Academic Freedom, and Rhetorical Sensitivity" (chapter 9). Gerdes shows how student activism and anti-Black racialized fear drove both a ban on campus carry in the 1960s and a revival of campus carry in 2016. That revival is tied to broader efforts to "normaliz[e] the presence of guns in every quarter of ordinary life," which chills free speech and academic freedom on campus, according to a lawsuit filed by UT professors. Gerdes reveals a connection between two supposed antagonists: academic freedom and student sensitivity. Defending academic freedom requires recognition of "the sensitive nature of our classrooms" in which "sensitivity to affection in language . . . makes it possible for us to study, teach, and learn."

In his chapter "National News Coverage of White Mass Shooters: Perpetuating White Supremacy through Strategic Rhetoric" (chapter 10), Scott Gage uses recent theoretical work to demonstrate the ways in which the national media has become complicit in reinforcing white supremacy. As he demonstrates, the tropes through which white mass shooters are covered by mass media outlets lean toward reinforcing racist framings of shootings, sometimes even by overtly repeating racist talking points and "laundering" them through the coverage generated by respected news outlets. Far from neutral, media coverage plays a significant role in shaping how the public reacts to mass shooting events and where it places responsibility for such shootings.

Matthew Boedy drills down into the rhetorical framing of gun rights within the white evangelical Christian ideology espoused by Turning Point USA, a college student political organization that campaigns for gun rights. In "Guns and Freedom: The Second Amendment Rhetoric of Turning Point USA" (chapter 11), Boedy shows how the organization constitutes freedom through its interpretation of the Second Amendment as divinely inspired and appeals to conservative Christian beliefs about gender to encourage more women to own guns. Turning Point effectively uses its totalized construction of freedom to target its political opponents through, for example, the Professor Watchlist. Finding himself on the list for opposing campus carry in Georgia in a public forum, Boedy muses about the tense situation inflamed by Turning Point's rigid rhetoric.

Nathalie Kuroiwa-Lewis continues the collection's examination of guns on campus with an analysis of the Civilian Marksmanship Program's information sheet "Air Rifle Marksmanship for Youth" in her chapter "Hiding Guns in Schools: The Rhetoric of US Mass Shootings" (chapter 12). The Civilian Marksmanship Program is a nationwide high school program sponsored by the JROTC (Army Junior Reserve Officer Training Corps) and the NRA: its members at Marjory Stoneman Douglas High School included both the gunman and students who died protecting their peers. Kuroiwa-Lewis applies psychic numbing and rhetorical silence as analytical lenses to argue that the information sheet frames air rifle marksmanship as a safe, inclusive sport that deters "potential negative interest" in guns. Minimizing the social effects of gun violence and emphasizing the recreational benefits of air rifle marksmanship, the information sheet attempts to separate guns from gun violence.

In "A Non-Defensive Gun: Violence, Climate Catastrophe, and Rhetorical Education" (chapter 13), Ira Allen considers the *topos* of a "defensive gun," from the genocidal origins of the Second Amendment to its function as the background condition of contemporary spectacles of gun violence, including but hardly limited to mass shootings. The notion of a "defensive gun" elides or even excuses violence done in the name of (self) defense as morally permissible. Allen ruminates on the consequences for us of disavowing the moral justification of "defensive gun violence," particularly in a moment when we are moving inexorably toward climate catastrophe and the remaking of new worlds that will inevitably involve gun violence. And he calls on us to return again to rhetorical education as a way to imagine possible ways of being in a darker, hotter future world.

The final chapter, "Talking Together about Guns: TTAG and Sustainable Publics" (chapter 14), by Peter Buck, Bradley Serber, and Rosa Eberly, presents itself in an unconventional form. Rather than functioning analytically, the chapter is an edited transcription of the authors' conversation about their own experiences as academics who have lived and worked in proximity to both gun violence and anti-violence activism. The chapter details the ways in which guns, gun violence, activism, and anti-regulation backlashes have converged and shaped the academic and community work of the authors. The chapter is both a testament to how real these issues are for working rhetoricians and a manifestation of the theory they are discussing. Not merely theoretical, guns and the violence that they both threaten and deliver are, as the dialogue shows, tangible realities. The stakes become even higher for rhetoricians and fellow academics who dare to confront gun violence and its sources, as this chapter and several others in the volume demonstrate.

We struggled with how to organize this book. There are clear resonances across chapters. Corrigan, Gage, and Wilkes (among others) focus centrally on race and white supremacy, for example. Ballentine, Kreuter, Rood, and Kuroiwa-Lewis (among others) directly take up questions of firearm technology. Boedy, Roberts-Miller, Serber, and Buck, Serber, and Eberly (among others) investigate interventions in public discourse. And Allen, Gerdes, and Hill (among others) ruminate on deeply embodied reactions to guns and gun violence. At the same time, nearly every chapter could fit comfortably into any other category. Race and white supremacy, technology, interventions in public discourse, and material embodiment are predominant themes in this book, as are activism, politics, media, family and community, hunting and sport, education, and more. Every chapter engages meaningfully in a number of these issues in ways that thwarted our efforts to make tidy groupings. In short, we opted not to break the book into sections. The chapters are organized, then, in what seemed to us to demonstrate a version of continuity—chapter 3, for example, foregrounds technology, and chapter 4 takes up questions of *techné*. The connections are not always quite so obvious, but we see the chapters connecting in a sort of loose daisy chain of themes, even as they all take up similar—and sometimes the same—issues. We have tried to make connections clear across chapters with citations to relevant works in the volume while trying not to overwhelm the reader by citing every resonance we see. Ultimately, we tried to help readers see the volume as we intend it, but the chapters can be read in any order without compromising the integrity of the whole volume.

The one exception is Catherine R. Squires's afterword, which we've placed at the end for obvious reasons. We asked Dr. Squires to write for this book not to sum up its importance (though we hope it is important); rather, we specifically requested her to envision the book's motivating potential for future avenues of research. Having read her work, especially *Dangerous Discourses* (2016), we are acutely aware of some limitations of this book. Our contributors' engagements with race are considerable, for example, but our engagements with gender are somewhat more limited. There are undoubtedly plenty of other aspects of the subject this volume does not explore. Those limitations belong to us as editors, not to the contributors and other people who made this book possible. When we invited Dr. Squires to write the afterword, we asked her to highlight those limitations as she sees fit because we want to ensure the discussions we're hoping to initiate don't immediately devolve into narrow echo chambers of like-minded agreement. She took our prompt in directions we could not have imagined, and for that we are immeasurably thankful. The relationship of rhetoric to guns is complicated. It would be counterproductive to suggest otherwise. And Dr. Squires's afterword has helped us see around corners we didn't even realize existed, a benefit we hope readers will likewise appreciate.

One more word about the contributors. A central premise of this volume is that scholars familiar with gun ownership, gun policy, and gun violence are uniquely positioned to offer insight into the rhetorical nature of America's gun culture and epidemic of mass shootings. Although not all of our contributors fit this profile, many of them do, and all of them have some personal investment in the issues. We have, therefore, asked them to be explicit about their positionality because we think it adds to the exigency of these chapters and to the power of the analysis. We do not come to these issues idly. In any case, the essays collected here indicate how essential it is that rhetoricians apply their expertise to public policy debates (which is not always natural for scholars, even though our discipline arguably originated in such debates), and in particular to the various cultural and policy discussions that surround firearms in the United States. This book builds on existing scholarship about guns to make the case that better understanding rhetorics of guns and gun violence can help Americans understand how to make better arguments about them in the world.

When all is said and done, we hope this book will give our readers an enhanced understanding of rhetoric's relationship to guns from the authors' efforts to analyze rhetoric about guns, guns in rhetoric, and guns as rhetoric, particularly as the issues relate to specific instances of guns in US culture in media coverage, political speech, and marketing and advertising. *Rhetoric and Guns* also extends rhetoricians' sustained interest in rhetoric's relationship to violence, brutality, and atrocity.[6] It contributes to ongoing discussions about how rhetoric informs attitudes about and potential changes to the rhetorical environment and public deliberation about current issues. The goal is to intervene in discussions about rhetoric and guns—hopefully with the ultimate effect of reducing gun violence, but at the very least to introduce new lines of thought and action in discussions about guns in America. In other words, we see this as an early step, not a final word. As such, *Rhetoric and Guns* seeks to advance a more focused, systematic treatment of rhetoric's relationship to guns, gun culture, and gun violence until such investment is rendered moot.

NOTES

1.   This is not to diminish the very real effects of war in Americans' lives at least since the United States invaded Afghanistan and Iraq in 2001 and 2003, respectively. Those effects have been widespread and often devastating, particularly for military service personnel with multiple deployments (sometimes into double digits) and families who have sent children to war. On average, twenty veterans completed suicide each day in 2014, more than two-thirds by firearm (Office of Suicide Prevention 2016, 4). But for most Americans, the perceptible, daily effects of war have faded (e.g., Engels and Saas 2013; Ohl 2015; Simons and Lucaites 2017; Stahl 2009) so much so that Andrew Bacevich, foreign policy critic and former army lieutenant colonel, claimed in 2010 that war is part of "the wallpaper of national life" (23).

2.   For crucial rhetorical research into gun violence, see Brummett 2018; Cryer 2020; Downs 2002; Dubisar 2018; Duerringer 2015; Duerringer and Justus 2016; Eberly 2018; Hogan and Rood 2015; Rood 2018, 2019; Squires 2016; Watts 2017; and Worsham 1998.

3.   For other recent scholarship, see, e.g., Eatman 2020; Eberly 2018; Haynes 2016; Lozano 2019; and Watts 2017.

4.   Though rhetoric scholars Crosswhite (2013), Engels (2015), and Stormer (2013), for example, have treated the intersection of rhetorical power and violence, their scholarship does not emphasize the resistance tactics and strategies of those who are rhetorically disempowered or how violence differentially secures or threatens people in relation to their embodiment. Recent scholarship by Lozano (2019), Ore (2019), and Squires (2016)—and this volume—attends to the intersections of rhetorical power, the rhetorically disempowered, and violence.

5.   One thing we want to be absolutely clear about, given our aims, is that the chapters in this book do not present a unified vision of how to understand or address gun rhetorics. The individual authors do not necessarily see eye to eye about these issues, and no chapter is representative of all the contributors' shared beliefs. Ordinarily, we would not feel the need to state this outright, but given the charged nature of guns and rhetoric, we felt it necessary to be explicit.

6.   See, e.g., Eatman 2020; Eberly 2018; Haynes 2016; Hogan and Rood 2015; Lozano 2019; Miller 2005; Ore 2019; and Worsham 1998.

REFERENCES

Adamski, Mallory. 2020. "NIWRC Releases Statement on 2020 National Day of Awareness for Missing and Murdered Native Women and Girls." National Indigenous Women's Resource Center. https://www.niwrc.org/news/niwrc-releases-statement-2020-national-day-awareness-missing-and-murdered-native-women-and.

Atwood, Margaret. 1998. *The Robber Bride*. New York: Anchor Books.

Bacevich, Andrew J. 2010. *Washington Rules: America's Path to Permanent War*. New York: Henry Holt.

Brady Campaign to Prevent Gun Violence. 2019. "Key Gun Violence Statistics." https://www.bradyunited.org/key-statistics.

Brummett, Barry. 2018. "Notes from a Texas Gun Show." In *Inventing Place: Writing Lone Star Rhetorics*, edited by. Casey Boyle and Jenny Rice, 211–19. Carbondale: Southern Illinois University Press.

Ceccarelli, Leah. 2011. "Manufactured Scientific Controversy: Science, Rhetoric, and Public Debate." *Rhetoric & Public Affairs* 14 (2): 195–228.

Clausewitz, Carl von. 1984. *On War*. Princeton, NJ: Princeton University Press.

Coates, Ta-Nehisi. 2015. *Between the World and Me*. New York: Spiegel & Grau.

Cooter, Amy. 2020. "Lessons from Embedding with the Michigan Militia—5 Questions Answered about the Group Allegedly Plotting to Kidnap a Governor?" *The Conversation*, October 9. https://theconversation.com/lessons-from-embedding-with-the-michigan-militia-5-questions-answered-about-the-group-allegedly-plotting-to-kidnap-a-governor-147876.

Crosswhite, James. 2013. *Deep Rhetoric: Philosophy, Reason, Violence, Justice, Wisdom*. Chicago: University of Chicago Press.

Cryer, Daniel A. 2020. "The Good Man Shooting Well: Authoritarian Submission and Aggression in the 'Gun-Citizen.'" *Rhetoric Society Quarterly* 50 (4): 254–67.

Downs, Douglas. 2002. "Representing Gun Owners: Frame Identification as Social Responsibility in News Media Discourse." *Written Communication* 19 (1): 44–75.

Duhisar, Abby M. 2018. "Mothers against Gun Violence and the Activist Buffer." *College English* 80 (3): 195–217.

Duerringer, Christopher M. 2015. "Dis-honoring the Dead: Negotiating Decorum in the Shadow of Sandy Hook." *Western Journal of Communication* 80 (1): 79–99.

Duerringer, Christopher M., and Z. S. Justus. 2016. "Tropes in the Rhetoric of Gun Rights: A Pragma-Dialectic Analysis." *Argumentation & Advocacy* 52 (3): 181–98.

Dunbar-Ortiz, Roxanne. 2018. *Loaded: A Disarming History of the Second Amendment*. San Francisco: City Lights Books.

Eatman, Megan. 2020. *Ecologies of Harm: Rhetorics of Violence in the United States*. Columbus: Ohio State University Press.

Eberly, Rosa. 2018. *Towers of Rhetoric: Memory and Reinvention*. Intermezzo. http://intermezzo.enculturation.net/05-eberly.htm.

Engels, Jeremy. 2015. *The Politics of Resentment: A Genealogy*. University Park: Pennsylvania State University Press.

Engels, Jeremy, and William O. Saas. 2013. "On Acquiescence and Ends-Less War: An Inquiry into the New War Rhetoric." *Quarterly Journal of Speech* 99 (2): 225–32. http://dx.doi.org/10.1080/00335630.2013.775705.

Hartelius, Johanna E. 2010. *The Rhetoric of Expertise*. Lanham, MD: Lexington.

Haynes, Cynthia. 2016. *The Home Sick Phone Book: Addressing Rhetorics in the Age of Perpetual Conflict*. Carbondale: Southern Illinois University Press.

Hogan, J. Michael, and Craig Rood. 2015. "Rhetorical Studies and the Gun Control Debate: A Public Policy Perspective." *Rhetoric & Public Affairs* 18 (2): 359–71.

Ingraham, Christopher. 2018. "There Are More Guns Than People in the United States, According to a New Study of Global Firearm Ownership." *Washington Post, June 19*. https://

www.washingtonpost.com/news/wonk/wp/2018/06/19/there-are-more-guns-than
-people-in-the-united-states-according-to-a-new-study-of-global-firearm-ownership/.

Kelly, Casey Ryan. 2020. *Apocalypse Man: The Death Drive and the Rhetoric of White Masculine Victimhood.* Columbus: Ohio State University Press.

Lozano, Nina Maria. 2019. *Not One More! Feminicidio on the Border.* Columbus: Ohio State University Press.

Lunsford, Andrea, Michal Brody, Lisa Ede, Beverly Moss, Carole Clark Papper, and Keith Walters. 2016. *Everyone's an Author, with Readings.* New York: Norton.

Miller, Richard E. 2005. *Writing at the End of the World.* Pittsburgh: University of Pittsburgh Press.

Nichols, Tom. 2017. *The Death of Expertise.* New York: Oxford University Press.

Office of Suicide Prevention. 2016. *Suicide among Veterans and Other Americans 2001–2014.* Washington, DC: US Department of Veterans Affairs. https://www.mentalhealth.va .gov/docs/2016suicidedatareport.pdf.

Ohl, Jessy. 2015. "Nothing to See or Fear: Light War and the Boring Visual Rhetoric of US Drone Imagery." *Quarterly Journal of Speech* 101 (4): 612–32.

Ore, Ersula J. 2019. *Lynching: Violence, Rhetoric, and American Identity.* Jackson: University Press of Mississippi.

Rice, Jenny. 2020. *Awful Archives: Conspiracy Theory, Rhetoric, and Acts of Evidence.* Columbus: Ohio State University Press.

Richards, I. A. 1964. *The Philosophy of Rhetoric.* New York: Oxford University Press.

Rodden, Jonathan. 2019. *Why Cities Lose: The Deep Roots of the Urban-Rural Political Divide.* New York: Basic Books.

Rood, Craig. 2018. "'Our Tears Are Not Enough': The Warrant of the Dead in the Rhetoric of Gun Control." *Quarterly Journal of Speech* 104 (1): 47–70.

Rood, Craig. 2019. *After Gun Violence: Deliberation and Memory in an Age of Political Gridlock.* University Park: Pennsylvania State University Press.

Simons, Jon, and John L. Lucaites, eds. 2017. *In/visible War: The Culture of War in Twenty-First Century America.* Tuscaloosa: University of Alabama Press.

Squires, Catherine R., ed. 2016. *Dangerous Discourses: Feminism, Gun Violence, and Civic Life.* New York: Peter Lang.

Stahl, Roger. 2009. "Why We 'Support the Troops': Rhetorical Evolutions." *Rhetoric & Public Affairs* 12 (4): 533–70.

Stormer, Nathan. 2013. "On the Origin of Violence and Language." *Quarterly Journal of Speech* 99 (2): 182–90.

Watts, Eric King. 2017. "Postracial Fantasies, Blackness, and Zombies." *Communication and Critical/Cultural Studies* 14 (4): 317–33.

Worsham, Lynn. 1998. "Going Postal: Pedagogic Violence and the Schooling of Emotion." *JAC: A Journal of Composition Theory* 18 (2): 213–45.

1

THE ONLY THING THAT STOPS A BAD GUY WITH RHETORIC IS A GOOD GUY WITH RHETORIC

Patricia Roberts-Miller

In March 2018, several friends on social media shared a *Scientific American* blog post titled "Why Are White Men Stockpiling Guns?" The post begins by pointing out that "three percent of the population now owns half of the country's firearms" and poses the question "So, who is buying all these guns—and why?" It goes on to cite various studies about gun owners in order to argue that "the kind of man who stockpiles weapons or applies for a concealed-carry license meets a very specific profile." That "profile" is that these white men are "anxious about their ability to protect their families, insecure about their place in the job market, and beset by racial fears." The article characterizes gun owners as irrational, racist, trying to "regain their masculinity," men whose "attachment to guns was based entirely on ideology and emotions" (Smith 2018). What is very unclear in the blog post is any logical connection between the specific statistic of 3 percent of the American population owning a disproportionate amount of guns and the characteristics of gun owners in general (an association not merited by the studies cited). That association enables characterizing gun owners as a homogeneously irrational, impaired, fearful, and ideologically motivated. In other words, an out-group. And furthermore, that out-group (a political and ideological construct) is both constituted and signaled by the material condition of owning a gun. This post irrationalizes the opposition.

What I want to suggest in this chapter is that this blog post epitomizes far too much of our public (and private) discourse about guns. What should be policy argumentation about the many issues regarding gun ownership and use is deflected to demagoguery, thereby transmogrifying the complicated array of policy options and opinions to a zero-sum existential battle between Us (rational, ethical, good) and Them (irrational, ideologically motivated, and bad) (see also Rood's chapter 6 in

https://doi.org/10.7330/9781646422159.c001

this volume). Instead of seeing our world as a lot of people at different places on a spectrum of policy options and commitments (a presentation of disagreement that makes fundraising and mobilizing support more complicated), demagoguery about *the* gun debate says there is no point in arguing with others about policy—*the* opposition is so malevolent, irrational, and mindless—so our goal should be the political (and perhaps literal) extermination of the Other.

Paradoxically, this demagoguery about our options regarding gun ownership, storage, and use—that there are two sides, and it is a question of identity (gun owners versus non–gun owners)—does not equally benefit "both sides," but singularly benefits the most extreme position advocated by figures like Wayne LaPierre of the NRA. To reduce policy argumentation about guns to the motives and identities of "gun owners" versus others is to grant the most demagogic aspect of extreme rhetoric like LaPierre's: that gun ownership constitutes membership in a homogeneous group whose univocal interests are represented by the NRA.

While I don't want to make the argument that "both sides" engage in demagoguery (since that's accepting the premise of there being two sides, the premise that enables the demagoguery), it's true that this demagogic approach is central to the rhetoric of groups like the National Rifle Association and Gun Owners of America. They reduce the available positions and commitments on gun laws to two identities: those who are anti-gun and gun owners. They thereby deflect from policy questions to relationship to guns: people who are opposed to guns, and people who own guns. It doesn't make sense to be anti-*gun*, and very few people (if anyone) are opposed to the *gun*—they're opposed to private gun ownership, open carry, concealed carry, private ownership of certain kinds of weapons, unlimited individual gun ownership. They're opposed to policies about guns, what people do with guns, the consequences of NRA policies. The very term irrationalizes the opposition by shifting the stasis from policy to an irrational motive.

Since my point is that public argumentation about gun ownership and availability is displaced by demagoguery, I should first explain what that means. There are four rhetorical steps in demagoguery. First, an issue is rhetorically divided into two (and only two) positions, which are represented by two rhetorically constructed groups: Us (in-group) and Them (out-group). As an aside, I should mention that in social group theory, the in-group is not the group in power; it's the group we're in. So, for the NRA or Gun Owners of America, the "in-group" is the imagined group identity of "gun owners"; for the author of the *Scientific American* blog post, the imagined group identity of "gun owners" is the out-group.[1] The second step in demagoguery is characterizing the rhe-torically constructed in-group as nuanced, rational, and *essentially* good, and the out-group as mindless, irrational, and *essentially* bad. Thus, the most extreme members of the out-group can be taken as representative of the out-group as a whole, but the most extreme members of the in-group can be dismissed as nonrepresentative exceptions. Third, policy is derived from identity, so the question in demagoguery is which group is better, and it's assumed that, from that determination of essential good-ness, we can know which policy is better (ours, of course). Fourth, we are in a battle for existence with *them*, so any arguing about policy, any attempt to compromise (let alone deliberate) with *them* is trucking with the devil. We shouldn't communicate with *them* at all, but use all of our rhetoric to mobilize the in-group to action.

Since I'm saying that we should resist the assumption that policy affili-ation necessarily and inevitably derives from identity, I should probably engage in full disclosure about my identity. Because of Texas common property laws, I'm a gun owner (I own quite a few, actually). My father owned guns, and I've shot them from time to time. My son and husband shoot with some frequency, and my husband has spent a fair amount of time hunting. (Full disclosure on full disclosure: my father also hunted, but he was really bad at it.)

Some of my favorite people really like guns. They don't *need* all the guns they own, in that they don't imagine themselves shooting an intruder or rattlesnake, but they like them. I don't really like shooting very much (at least not loud guns). While my son and husband shoot at targets, I tend to wander off and shoot out-of-focus pictures of birds. I like birds.

I also like books. So I collect them, including books I don't really need. I know people who like cars, vinyl albums, or teaspoons in the same way. I have the complete works of Wilkie Collins because I like reading them. I could get them from the library, and maybe someday I could get them on Kindle, but I take pleasure in having them here so I can pick one up at any time (and I don't like reading on digital devices). I have a lot of books I never read (such as the Eichmann trial's prosecu-tor's memoirs of the trial, in Hebrew, which I can't read). Collectors are like that. I collect books; some people collect guns.

One might argue that guns are different in that no one is likely to get killed with one of my volumes of Wilkie Collins (I don't really think someone could die of boredom from some of his worse stories, although it might sometimes seem that way). That's true, and certainly there is a difference between collecting books and collecting, say, plague viruses.

If what you are collecting is potentially dangerous, then it's reasonable to put limits on what you can collect, who can collect it, how that collection is stored, and how that collection is used. Because so many people die from others owning cars (in 2016, 38,748 people died from car accidents), we regulate car ownership and use (Xu et al. 2018, 14). I believe that, since a similar number of people die from guns (in 2016, 38,658 people), it would be reasonable to regulate guns as much as we do cars (Xu et al. 2018, 12). The NRA, however, is opposed to any such regulation.

I am a gun owner opposed to the NRA's policies—but that puts me in a category neither the *Scientific American* nor the NRA admits exists. Take, for instance, Wayne LaPierre's 2013 op-ed in the *Daily Caller*, "Stand and Fight." That editorial relies on a perfect binary of "us" and "them." He associates "us," gun owners, with the following identities and traits: Americans, prudent, lawful, decent, responsible, ordinary citizens, law-abiding, freedom lovers, genuine grassroots, survival, patriots, army of freedom. While LaPierre acknowledges that not all gun owners are members of the NRA, his op-ed assumes and asserts that his rhetorically constructed category of "gun owners" is identical to those who "support the NRA stance regarding gun ownership and availability": "We know that responsible gun ownership exemplifies what is good and right about America." Opposed to these patriots is a set of associations for "them": violent criminals, drug gangs, kidnappers, Obama and his cronies, flagrant violation of law, terrorists, Bloomberg, gun prohibitionists, corrupt politicians, anti-gun media, gun-ban lobbies, George Soros, England, enemies of freedom, coming siege.

In other words, LaPierre is relying on the rhetorical strategy that Ernesto Laclau (2005) calls "equivalential chains" and Chaïm Perelman and Lucie Olbrechts-Tyteca (1969) call "paired terms." Laclau argues that populist reason works by equivalential chains—the demands of various people who are identified as "the people" perceive "an accumulation of unfulfilled demands" as essentially equivalent (73). Laclau's example is that clean water is much like good wages is much like good schools (73), except, of course, they aren't (75). What connects good schools and good wages is that they are goods for the disenfranchised. Laclau says, "The consolidation of the equivalential chain [is] through the construction of a popular identity which is something qualitatively more than the simple summation of the equivalential links" (77). That is, the in-group.

There is a second step, the division into "two camps" (Laclau 2005, 75), that Laclau didn't follow up in his discussion of equivalential chains, but it's important. Equivalential chains aren't just about who we are—they're about who we are not. That insight is similarly acknowledged, but also not really pursued, in Perelman and Olbrechts-Tyteca's explanation of dissociation in *The New Rhetoric* (1969). Perelman and Olbrechts-Tyteca note that arguments rely on paired terms—sets of binaries in which positive terms are assumed to be associated with one another as in-group values, policies, or attributes (equivalential chains, in Laclau's terms) and opposed to related negative terms associated with out-group values, policies, or attributes. To extend Laclau's example, good wages (in-group policy goal) are associated with clean water and contrasted to poor wages. So, clean water is to unsafe water as good wages are to poor wages.

clean water		good wages
————————	::	————————
unsafe water		poor wages

In LaPierre's editorial, not only are the "us" terms associated with one another in equivalential chains (ordinary citizens are equivalent to gun owners are equivalent to patriots), but each "us" term is the exact opposite of some term associated with "them."

Good Americans		gun owners		NRA		law-abiding
———————	::	———————	::	———————	::	———————
Obama and cronies		gun prohibitionists		Obama, Bloomberg, Soros		violent criminals

prudent, decent, responsible		ordinary citizens		patriots		genuine grassroots
———————	::	———————	::	———————	::	———————
flagrant violation of law		corrupt politicians		terrorists		gun-ban lobbies

freedom lovers
:: ———————
enemies of freedom

LaPierre doesn't explicitly say that Obama and his cronies are terrorists or violent criminals, and the connection is *very* tenuous. The connections among the positive terms are similarly tenuous (such as NRA being a genuinely grassroots organization). The connections that LaPierre's argument makes aren't *logically* argued; they're *associatively* connected. And they are associatively disconnected from the terms associated with the out-group.

This strategy of argument is common. Amy Gershkoff and Shana Kushner noted this associative rhetoric in the Bush administration's pro-Iraq invasion rhetoric. As they say:

> President Bush never publicly blamed Saddam Hussein or Iraq for the events of September 11, but by consistently linking Iraq with terrorism and al Qaeda he provided the context from which such a connection could be made. Bush also never publicly connected Saddam Hussein to Osama bin Laden, the leader of al Qaeda. Nevertheless, whether or not Bush connected each dot from Saddam Hussein to bin Laden, the way language and transitions are shaped in his official speeches almost compelled listeners to infer a connection. (2005, 525)

While Bush couldn't make the connection between Iraq, bin Laden, and 9/11 *logically*, he could make it *associatively*. And, unhappily, people often make decisions on the basis of such associations—what Milton Lodge and Charles Taber call "processes of unconscious valence affect" (2013, 22). They say, "Evaluations that conform to a simple, bipolar structure, in which liking for a concept (for example, pro-choice) implies disliking of a second concept (pro-life), tend to elicit stronger I-E [implicit-explicit] correlations as well as increasing the speed, consistency, and efficiency of processing" (63). In other words, people make evaluations based on paired terms.

Lodge and Tabor argue that people rely on "identifications," which are "associative knowledge structures in long-term memory with varying chronic and momentary accessibility" (2013, 96). The accessibility of identifications is "influenced by the momentary accessibility of other identifications" via "*a congruent identifications effect* such that priming an in-group will increase the accessibility of all in-group identifications and inhibit out-group identifications, while priming an out-group will facilitate the accessibility of all out-group identifications" (96–97; emphasis in original). That is, priming the various concepts associated with the in-group will inhibit any impulse to identify with out-group concepts—invoking "freedom," "patriotism," or "ordinary citizens" will increase the sense of identification with the other in-group concepts (gun ownership, the NRA), while inhibiting identification with out-group concepts (Obama, gun prohibition).

LaPierre's proposed solution to the threats presented by the out-group is more commitment to the NRA, and more guns. In his conclusion, he says, "We will not surrender. We will not appease. We will buy more guns than ever. We will use them for sport and lawful self-defense more than ever" (2013).[2] LaPierre, and NRA rhetoric more generally, presumes and reinforces a binary between this MOAR GUNZ (to cite an old meme) policy and banning all guns, so the policy options available to us as a nation are reduced to two: NO GUNZ or MOAR GUNZ. That false binary is then depoliticized by making it not a policy issue at all, but a binary of group identity.

This is savvy rhetoric. A depressing amount of scholarship shows that voters make decisions on the basis of identification with the presentation of a group rather than policies—people will vote against their policy agenda in order to vote with an identity (see especially Levendusky 2013 and Mason 2018). Were Americans to debate policy rather than identity, and not as a binary, the NRA would almost certainly not be as successful as it currently is at enacting gun policies that are tremendously unpopular, even with gun owners (as I discuss below). Thus, to the extent that public discourse about guns reduces the complicated array of policy options into a binary of identity (people who want unlimited guns versus people who want to ban guns), the NRA triumphs.

Unhappily, much anti-NRA rhetoric and even supposedly nonpartisan coverage of the issues of gun violence/ownership accepts, reinforces, and promotes precisely the frame (anything related to guns can be reduced to a choice between binary identities) that inhibits reasonable discussion. It does so by talking about "the" or "a" gun debate, referring to "both sides," trying to be "fair" by saying "both sides engage in demagoguery," accepting the NRA's representation of itself as speaking for all gun owners, describing the conflict about policy in terms of identities ("gun owners" versus "gun control advocates"), bungling information about guns, or accepting the binary paired terms of the NRA stance and just flipping them. This reduction of a complicated set of issues to a simple choice between two identities depoliticizes an issue by taking it out of the realm of policy deliberation and into partisanship (it's striking that people talk of "politicizing" an issue when they mean "treating an issue in purely partisan terms").

There is not "*a* gun debate"—there are many arguments about many different policy options. There are not "two sides"—so there is no possibility of "both sides" doing anything. And attitudes about guns do not come down to identity, let alone a binary of identities.

In regard to gun violence, there are multiple—different—problems, and we need to stop conflating them. For instance, consider the problem of mass killings. These incidents are almost always either aspirational claims for fame (e.g., Columbine High School), metastatic domestic violence (e.g., the Mercy Hospital shooting), or violence as the natural extension of eliminationist rhetoric (e.g., the shooting at the Knoxville Unitarian Universalist Church). David Neiwert has pointed out that the

Knoxville murderer's manifesto was "largely a distillation" of the many books by reactionary pundits that the murderer owned. It was a political act (2009, 3). Neither the Columbine nor Mercy Hospital murderers had a political agenda. Thus, the identities and motives even of this one kind of killing are not unitary, and it's unlikely that one single policy will solve all of them.

As long as we think about issues of gun ownership and gun violence in terms of pro- or anti-gun, we're not going to have a productive *policy* debate—because if we treat all gun violence as the same, it's easy for someone to point out that *this* proposal (say, mental health checks) would not have prevented *that* incident of gun violence. J. Michael Hogan and Craig Rood bemoan the current public discourse regarding gun violence:

> We need an honest, open, and robust debate over guns and gun violence—the sort of debate that empowers the American people to make informed judgments and take political action. We need a debate that marshals the best expertise and engages a wide variety of stakeholders, from gun manufacturers and law enforcement agencies, to hunters and sport shooters, educators, parents, and victims' rights groups. And we need journalists to mediate that debate with a renewed commitment to social responsibility and the public good. (2015, 360–61)

That renewed commitment should involve a rejection of the "two sides" model as well as the notion that policies can be argued as identities. Debates about policies regarding who can own guns, what kinds of guns people can own, how they can be modified, under what circumstances guns should be confiscated, whether and how that ownership should be recorded, when and where they can be carried, and so on should be *policy* argumentation. They should not be, as they currently are, truncated into an unanswerable question as to which of the two sides is made up of better people. Nor should the debate be framed as "gun owners" versus "gun control advocates," since those are not—despite the NRA's best rhetorical efforts—mutually exclusive categories.

Most gun owners either support more restrictive policies on guns or support existing levels of restrictions. Gun ownership and supporting MOAR GUNZ are not synonymous. As a 2017 Pew Research Center survey shows:

> Overwhelming majorities of Republicans and Republican-leaning independents and Democrats and Democratic leaners (89% each) say mentally ill people should be barred from buying guns. Nearly as many in both parties (86% of Democrats, 83% of Republicans) favor barring gun purchases by people on federal watch lists. And sizable majorities also favor

> making private gun sales and sales at gun shows subject to background checks (91% of Democrats, 79% of Republicans). (Parker et al. 2017)

Perhaps most interesting, 88 percent of those surveyed said that gun laws should be what they currently are (31 percent) or stricter (57 percent). Even when broken down further, the survey does not support the NRA equation of gun owners and MOAR GUNZ: among Republican or Republican-leaning gun owners, 13 percent say gun laws should be stricter and 61 percent say they're about right. Among Democrat or Democrat-leaning gun owners, 64 percent say laws should be stricter, and 26 percent say they're about right. Thus, despite LaPierre's claims about gun owners' support for no restrictions, most gun owners support restrictions on gun ownership and use.

The NRA, as in LaPierre's editorial, responds to gun violence by appealing to the "responsible gun owners." This is an interesting substitution—of people for practices—and yet possibly a slip that might be used to get to better arguments about policies. What is a "responsible gun owner"? What practices do such owners follow that are responsible? If we can move the issue from their simply being good people to their observing good practices, then we are headed toward a set of policies to which responsible gun owners wouldn't object, since they're actually engaged in those practices—perhaps locking up guns appropriately, for instance.

If our country argues policies rather than identities, the NRA will lose. If the NRA can keep the argument focused on a false binary of gun owners versus gun prohibitionists, and on the issue of motives, it will succeed. Thus, to the extent that the media (and pro-restriction rhetoric) rely on that false binary and consequent motivism, they help the NRA.

Some years ago, Doug Downs elegantly showed that media do present gun owners as irrational. Downs analyzed representation of gun owners "in a 75,000-word corpus of newspaper stories, editorials, and letters to the editor" (2002, 45). He found that media representation of gun owners persistently and consistently presented them unfavorably: "Selfish, incompetent, dangerous, unreasonable on self-defense—one might as well call gun owners irresponsible. That is, in fact, the most frequent characterization of owners in this corpus, sometimes in precisely those terms but often . . . through insinuation and pre-supposition" (59). Downs argues that this characterization of gun owners marginalizes them, and "amplifies the very polarization it should seek to attenuate" (69). I would take the point further.

Earlier, I argued that LaPierre's piece exemplifies NRA rhetoric's reliance on binary paired terms—identifications that are presumed to be connected laterally, while in a binary relationship to other terms: one group is American and the other un-American; one is brave, the other cowardly; one is rational, the other irrational. What much anti-NRA and mainstream coverage does is accept the set of binary paired terms and simply flip the privilege instead of dissociating terms or deconstructing the binaries.

Two sets of paired terms ubiquitous in identity-based arguments about gun policies are afraid/brave and rational/irrational. A common theme in the MOAR GUNZ argument is that "the opposition" (anyone who disagrees with "us") is acting from a position of irrational fear about guns, and their position can, therefore, be dismissed. And it's true that policies advocating restrictions on gun ownership and use do have bases in fears—fear of a disgruntled student, fear of a firefight. But the MOAR GUNZ position is also a profoundly fear-ridden one. LaPierre's argument in "Stand and Fight" is that Obama's weakness and financial irresponsibility will mean a collapse of the government, in which there will be mass looting and no police. The MOAR GUNZ position appeals to fear of criminals (often coded as people of color; see especially Filindra and Kaplan 2016), fear of losing guns, fear of liberals, fear of the government. It's a very fearful argument. For instance, the argument at my own university in favor of concealed carry in classrooms relies heavily on the fear/fantasy of a campus shooter. Thus, it makes no sense to pretend that "one side" was fearful and "the other" was not, nor that the fears of "one side" were rational assessments of danger and those of "the other" side were not—it was the same fear. That someone advocates a policy out of fear is *not* a reason to refuse to engage their argument or dismiss their position from consideration; it's a reason to argue their policy, and not their motives.

That isn't to say that identities are completely irrelevant in policy deliberation, but that identity is simply one datum. And identity that presumes a complicated issue can be reduced to a zero-sum battle between two groups is always going to harm deliberation. But it is possible for the question of identity to be one that enhances democratic fellowship, even if it does little for policy deliberation. Projects such as "Hands across the Hills" (in which people from very different communities come together for structured dialogues) often end without a change in policy beliefs, but with less demonization of the Other. In one of the programs, people from liberal Leverett, Massachusetts, met with people from conservative coal country (Letcher County, Kentucky). One participant wrote that the divisive issues of the 2016 election hadn't disappeared by the time they met together, "but our common concerns—wanting a steady good living, a future for our children and grandchildren—were in the fore-ground" (Dunn and Clayton 2018).

Elsewhere I've argued that we are in a culture of demagoguery in which all policy issues are depoliticized by being reframed as a zero-sum battle between two identities (see Roberts-Miller 2017, 2019a, 2019b). Important to that depoliticizing is the rhetorical strategy of "inocula-tion," a concept not discussed enough in our field. Inoculation is a kind of preemptive refutation, when a rhetor presents an audience with an opposition argument the audience might hear, and also refutes the argument—the idea is that the audience will be more resistant because they will recognize the opposition argument and be primed to remem-ber the refutation (for a summary, see Compton and Pfau 2005). In a culture of demagoguery, inoculation is not so much preemptive refuta-tion as preemptive straw man: an audience is presented with a weak version (or active misrepresentation) of "the" opposition argument (a move that depends on the issue already having been broken into a binary) with the goal of making the in-group feel that they shouldn't even listen to any member of "the" opposition—that is, to any disagree-ment. And, in a culture of demagoguery, motivism is one of the more straightforward ways to inoculate the in-group.

In short, a complicated issue is broken into two sides (the in- and out-group), and "the other side" is represented as having *no* legitimate point of view at all—their position is irrational, the consequence of bad motives, and therefore should not even be heard. Furthermore, it doesn't need to be heard—their stance on this one issue (gun owner-ship and availability) can be used to infer their stances on all other issues. This is a disturbing way for people to participate in democratic decision-making. Bradford Vivian puts it elegantly:

> Defining the fact that others hold competing beliefs or opinions from oneself as a symptom of deep moral failing, corrupted intelligence, or even evil can provide an important precondition of authoritarian governance. A zeal for equating a contrasting political affiliation with essential threats to the nation (as great as, if not greater than, threats posed by foreign adver-saries) may transform institutions designed for democratically mediating among pluralistic values and agendas into undemocratic agencies of non-cooperation and nondeliberative accruals of power. (2018, 434)

This is not to say that we must assume goodwill and good intentions on the part of every political figure, rhetor, or interlocutor. There are peo-ple engaged in bad-faith argumentation. But it does mean we should not assume that disagreement with an in-group policy is all we need to know in order to believe that someone's political views are the consequence of bad intentions.

Characterizing gun owners as irrational and irresponsible yahoos whose views on gun policy can be dismissed because of their motives confirms the NRA presentation of gun policy debates as *really* a zero-sum contest between two groups. The NRA does *not* speak for gun owners. The NRA represents gun owners as fanatically committed to having all the guns carried in all the places—and to the extent that non-NRA media represent gun owners that same way, they are doing NRA work. I am not saying that "both sides" engage in demagoguery about guns, but that any "side" that frames any issue related to guns as a binary of gun owners versus non–gun owners is engaged in demagoguery. Identity is not policy, and if we hope to deliberate well about guns, we'd be wise to argue about the latter rather than the former.

NOTES

1. I'm not claiming that identity is irrelevant to political discourse. We can't talk about politics without talking about identities. I am saying that it's fallacious to assume that policy preferences regarding guns *necessarily* and *inevitably* derive from identity. If we assume that our political landscape is usefully described as left versus right, that gays and African Americans are inevitably on the left, and that leftists are hostile to gun ownership, then we cannot understand organizations like Pink Pistols (Rauch 2000) that promote gun ownership and concealed carry among gays, or people like Robert Williams, the Black civil rights activist who formed an NRA chapter in Monroe, North Carolina, in 1957 to arm African Americans.

2. That last sentence is particularly troubling—what, exactly, does it mean to use guns for "lawful self-defense more than ever"? Is he suggesting that people now use guns for self-defense when they might have used something else previously? Since the piece is called "Stand and Fight," is he calling for more kinds of "self-defense" such as happened with Trayvon Martin?

REFERENCES

Compton, Joshua, and Michael Pfau. 2005. "Inoculation Theory of Resistance to Influence at Maturity: Recent Progress in Theory Development and Application and Suggestions for Future Research." In *Communication Yearbook* 29, edited by Pamela J. Kalbfleisch, 97–145. New York: Routledge.

Downs, Douglas. 2002. "Representing Gun Owners: Frame Identification as Social Responsibility in Discourse." *Written Communication* 19 (1): 44–75. https://doi.org/10.1177/074 108830201900103.

Dunn, Sharon, and John J. Clayton. 2018. "Connecting with Coal Country: What I Learned Visiting Kentucky with Hands across the Hills." *Hands across the Hills.* https://www.handsacrossthehills.org/single-post/2018/05/25/Connecting-with-Coal-Country -What-I-learned-visiting-Kentucky-with-Hands-Across-the-Hills.

Filindra, Alexandra, and Noah J. Kaplan. 2016. "Racial Resentment and Whites' Gun Policy Preferences in Contemporary America." *Political Behavior* 38 (2): 255–75. https://doi.org/10.1007/s11109-015-9326-4.

Gershkoff, Amy, and Shana Kushner. 2005. "Shaping Public Opinion: The 9/11-Iraq Connection in the Bush Administration's Rhetoric." *Perspectives on Politics* 3 (3): 525–37. https://doi.org/10.1017/S1537592705050334.

Hogan, J. Michael, and Craig Rood. 2015. "Rhetorical Studies and the Gun Debate: A Public Policy Perspective." *Rhetoric and Public Affairs* 18 (2): 359–72. https://doi.org/10.14321/rhetpublaffa.18.2.0359.

Laclau, Ernesto. 2005. *On Populist Reason*. New York: Verso.

LaPierre, Wayne. 2013. "Stand and Fight." *Daily Caller*, February 13. https://dailycaller.com/2013/02/13/stand-and-fight.

Levendusky, Matthew. 2013. *How Partisan Media Polarize America*. Chicago: University of Chicago Press.

Lodge, Milton, and Charles S. Taber. 2013. *The Rationalizing Voter*. New York: Cambridge University Press.

Mason, Lilliana. 2018. *Uncivil Agreement: How Politics Become Our Identity*. Chicago: University of Chicago Press.

Neiwert, David. 2009. *The Eliminationists: How Hate Talk Radicalized the American Right*. Sausalito: Polipoint.

Parker, Kim, et al. 2017. "America's Complex Relationship with Guns." *Pew Research Center*. https://www.pewsocialtrends.org/2017/06/22/the-demographics-of-gun-ownership.

Perelman, Chaïm, and Lucie Olbrechts-Tyteca. 1969. *The New Rhetoric: A Treatise on Argumentation*. Translated by John Wilkinson and Purcell Weaver. Notre Dame: University of Notre Dame Press.

Rauch, Jonathan. 2000. "Pink Pistols." *Salon*, March 14. https://www.salon.com/2000/03/14/pistol/.

Roberts-Miller, Patricia. 2017. *Demagoguery and Democracy*. New York: Experiment.

Roberts-Miller, Patricia. 2019a. "Demagoguery, Charismatic Leadership, and the Force of Habit." *Rhetoric Society Quarterly* 49 (3): 233–47.

Roberts-Miller, Patricia. 2019b. *Rhetoric and Demagoguery*. Carbondale: Southern Illinois University Press.

Smith, Jeremy A. 2018. "Why Are White Men Stockpiling Guns?" *Scientific American*. https://blogs.scientificamerican.com/observations/why-are-white-men-stockpiling-guns.

Vivian, Bradford. 2018. "On the Erosion of Democracy by Truth." *Philosophy & Rhetoric* 51 (4): 359–72. https://doi.org/10.5325/philrhet.51.4.0416.

Xu, Jiaquan, et al. 2018. "Deaths: Final Data for 2016." In *National Vital Statistic Reports: From the Centers for Disease Control and Prevention, National Center for Health Statistics, National Vital Statistics System* 67 (5). https://www.cdc.gov/nchs/data/nvsr/nvsr67/nvsr67_05.pdf.

2

MUZZLE VELOCITY, RHETORICAL MASS, AND RHETORICAL FORCE

Nate Kreuter

In February 2013 I learned firsthand of the force generated by the rhetorical velocity of so-called Second Amendment rights advocates. In the wake of the Newtown shootings, my home state (at the time) of North Carolina was considering legislation that would have allowed licensed handgun owners to carry weapons on university campuses, including into the classrooms where I taught. I wrote an essay for *Inside Higher Ed* in which I reflected, as both a gun owner and a college professor, upon my feelings about guns entering into the instructional spaces that I occupied professionally (Kreuter 2013). The timing of the column was not coincidental. I wrote it in part as a response to the legislation under consideration in my state, but also as a reflection forced upon me by the then recent mass shooting at Sandy Hook Elementary School and responses to the shooting. In this sense, the column was kairotic, timely, responding to a newer and darker evil as the mass shooting phenomenon reached into the lives of an even younger set of victims. At the time, both pro– and anti–gun regulation groups were active, mobilizing (in the rhetorical sense) and on edge. Calls for legislation to regulate gun ownership were louder and more widespread than at any other point in my lifetime. Similarly, anti-regulation constituents were on full defensive, trotting out familiar arguments as well as creating wild conspiracy theories, most notably the cruel and defamatory claims of right-wing radio host Alex Jones that the Newtown shooting was a hoax, and the parents of its child victims were "crisis actors" staging a fictional grief over fictional murders (Demick 2017). This environment, with its loud calls for regulation and desperate defenses against regulation, was the rhetorical moment within which my own article was published.

As I explain below, there were consequences for writing that column that I didn't fully anticipate (see also Boedy's chapter 11 in this volume). In addition to referencing a personal experience, writing that column

https://doi.org/10.7330/9781646422159.c002

was also illustrative, I now see, of some important concepts that constitute the gun debate more generally. In this essay I use the example of my own experience of writing about guns and control to illustrate (1) the explanatory power of "rhetorical velocity" for understanding how anti-regulation rhetoric moves through the public sphere; and (2) an extension of rhetorical velocity to "rhetorical mass" and "rhetorical force," a set of physical analogies that at least partially explain why anti-regulation interlocutors are apparently more rhetorically effective within the American political/rhetorical landscape than their counterparts who advocate on behalf of sensible gun regulations.

Before I turn to that argument, though, I think it is important to clarify for an audience of rhetoricians some facts about firearms and how they operate. A failure by some gun control advocates to understand the technical aspects of firearms technologies has undermined their rhetorical efforts (see also Ballentine's chapter 3 in this volume). Accordingly, it's worth our time to reflect upon what actually happens when a trigger is depressed and a gun fires. The physics of how firearms actually operate also serve as metaphors through which we can understand the rhetorical forces that drive contemporary American gun policy debates.

The fundamentals of how a firearm launches its projectile have changed little since the mid-nineteenth century. When the weapon's trigger is pulled, a hammer is released and smashes into the metal body of a cartridge. The end of the cartridge contacted by the hammer contains a primer, a chemical package capable of igniting upon sudden, forceful impact, which in turn ignites the gunpowder in the cartridge. With no other way to release its explosive forces, the combusting gunpowder propels the bullet at the end of the cartridge out and down the barrel of the gun. Those are the basics. Of course, technology has advanced, and modern firearms and cartridges have improved dramatically since the first contained metal firearms cartridges were introduced shortly after the American Civil War. But the fundamental concept of using a controlled explosion to propel a projectile remains the same.

Because the mechanics of how a physical movement (the impact of the hammer) initiates a chemical reaction (the firing of the primer) into a second chemical reaction (the ignition of the propellant) into a final mechanical movement (the firing of the bullet) are so fundamental, firearms and ammunition manufacturers have focused on increasingly subtle technical improvements: physical properties of the firing chamber, projectile shape/aerodynamics, and the chemical properties of cartridge primers and propellants in order to increase muzzle velocity.

Since the Second World War, one of the primary areas of firearms research and development for both military and civilian markets has focused on muzzle velocity. In case the term is not self-evident, *muzzle velocity* is a measure of the speed at which a bullet exits the business end, or muzzle, of a firearm. Muzzle velocity is a measure of kinetic energy—the greater a weapon's muzzle velocity, the greater its killing power. If someone throws a baseball at your chest you might get hurt, but you probably won't die. If someone launches the same baseball at your chest from a cannon, your chest will turn to a mush of dispersed flesh and you're dead. The baseball and your chest share the same physical properties in both scenarios. All that has changed is the velocity of the baseball. Speed kills. Mass kills. Speed plus mass really kill. Somewhat euphemistically, the gun industry refers to the force generated by a bullet's combined mass and velocity as "stopping power," which is actually an attempt to quantify a firearm's and specific ammunition's combined ability to kill. In some firearms literature, shooting enthusiast magazines and such, "stopping power" was previously referred to as "killing power," but the older, more frank term has largely given way to the more sanitized term. Such a shift in nomenclature is itself instructive—collectively, firearms manufacturers and shooting enthusiasts of all stripes are sensitive to the ways in which language frames public thinking about firearms, and thus also frames anti- and pro-firearms regulation efforts.

Not only has muzzle velocity been a focus of manufacturers, so too have consumers become obsessed with the variables and properties that influence the speed with which a bullet leaves a firearm, and thus also the speed with which it impacts its target. Consumers have essentially been trained by firearms manufacturers and the sizeable firearms aficionado media outlets to desire high muzzle velocities from their firearms and ammunition. In practical terms, "stopping power" is a way the firearms industry has quantified a weapon and bullet's combined ability to stop an oncoming attacker. The idea the industry sells when it focuses on stopping power is that a more powerful weapon provides its owner greater protection. In determining stopping power, ammunition tests will typically measure the muzzle velocity of the projectile at the barrel of the gun and then at a preset downrange distance, such as 1,000 feet. Once the muzzle velocity or downrange velocity of the projectile is known, stopping power (or force) at each point can be calculated through simple math, assuming that the mass of the projectile (bullet) is known.

Pick any firearms monthly magazine—and there are dozens upon dozens of them—and you will no doubt find in every issue one or several reports from an ammunition or testing editor, in which he (it's always a "he") reports on his experiments with a new line of ammunition, several cases of which the manufacturer has sent to him, gratis, precisely so that he can test it and sing its praises in the publication, thereby aiding the manufacturer in selling more of the new or newly reformulated cartridges to a consumer group that has been trained to lust for ever increasing muzzle velocities, ever increasing killing power. As an example, see Joseph von Benedikt's editorial, "Get the Most out of the 30.06," published April 1, 2019, on the *Shooting Times* magazine's website. The article is an extended analysis of the kinetic properties of various factory ammunition loads for the 30.06 rifle, a common hunting rifle. A typical paragraph reads:

> Let's push the range farther. At 500 yards the traditional Core-Lokt bullet from the .300 Win. Mag. is down to 1,836 fps and 1,347 ft-lbs of energy, while the modern ABLR from the .30-06 zips along at 2,035 fps and packs 1,746 ft-lbs of wallop. That's fully as much speed and considerably more authority than the magnum-fired Core-Lokt bullet had at just 400 yards. Clearly, modern bullets trounce traditional designs.

The .30-06 Springfield cartridge, originally a military round, has been around for over 100 years. The round is still popular for hunting, and also pulled duty as the ammunition used in the M-1 Garand (the primary rifle of US infantry troops during and shortly after World War II). When first developed, a 220 grain .30-06 round could achieve a muzzle velocity of 2,700 feet per second. As modern gunpowder has been chemically improved, the same bullet with the same mass and fired from the same weapon can achieve a muzzle velocity of over 3,200 feet per second with off-the-shelf ammunition, and even greater, more deadly speeds when bullets, powder, and primer are custom loaded into cartridges by professionals or highly skilled amateurs. Put more simply, modern chemistry in the form of more efficiently burning, more compact gunpowder has increased the killing power of cartridges, improving them to the point that grandpa's old deer rifle can now fire a bullet not only capable of cleanly killing a deer, but also of piercing a police officer's tactical ("bulletproof") vest. Similar developments concerning the optimization of the shape of the bullet have also increased the muzzle velocity weapons can achieve by improving the aerodynamics of the projectile (Benedikt 2019).

It cannot be stated too plainly—one reason that firearms deaths are increasing is that muzzle velocity has increased. Ammunition is more deadly now than it was forty years ago. Certainly, the styles of guns available (with quick rates of fire and high-capacity magazines), as well as the broad availability of those guns also increase the dangers posed by firearms. But an increase in the deadliness of ammunition—an industry-wide pursuit of higher and higher muzzle velocities—makes individual shooting incidents more deadly, and makes inexperienced wielders of firearms more capable than previously of producing deadly shooting results.

The actual impact of the bullet is not the only thing that puts your life at risk. A byproduct of the bullet's velocity is that the AR-15 bullet, for example, travels so fast that when it impacts human flesh a shock wave is created that extends well beyond the path, or channel, of the bullet itself, dispersing kinetic energy through the areas around the impact point/channel and damaging surrounding organs and tissue that the bullet did not even directly contact (Sher 2018). In the case of the AR-15 and other so-called high-velocity firearms, speed kills. The astounding velocity of a round fired from an AR-15 has much more killing power not primarily because of its mass (the mass of the bullets fired by an AR-15 is similar to or even less than the mass of rounds fired by other weapons that are less frequently used in mass murder events), but because of the velocity produced by the explosion that occurs in the firearm's chamber. Many hunting rifles, for example, fire much more massive bullets than those the AR-15 fires, but with much less velocity, rendering them somewhat less deadly. Because of its ability to destroy flesh outside of the wound channel, the AR-15 is considered unsuitable by many for hunting—it destroys too much meat.

Ultimately, though, killing power is generally determined by two factors: the mass of the projectile and the velocity at which the projectile is traveling. There are limits to how much mass can exist in a bullet. Bullets are sized precisely for their firearms, which, along with restraints in the properties of natural materials (the densities and strengths of various metals), limits the maximum mass that a bullet can have. The second constraint on the potential mass of a bullet is in the chemistry of the gunpowder that propels the bullet, and to an extent is also limited by the aerodynamics of the projectile itself. A more massive bullet requires a larger, more powerful explosion in order to propel it at the same speed as a less massive projectile. Only so much gunpowder can be fit into a cartridge, and the powder can only produce so strong of an explosion before it creates the risk of exploding the firearm's entire chamber and injuring or killing the firearm's operator. And the aerodynamics of the bullet can only be improved so much. Drag and gravity are inevitable.

The AR-15, implicated in many recent mass-shooting events, is a somewhat unusual weapon in that instead of balancing bullet mass and muzzle velocity, it utilizes a relatively unmassive projectile but sends it downrange at a very high speed. In the case of the AR-15, stopping/killing power is derived more from a high velocity than it is from a high mass, at least relative to other rifle rounds. This difference, seemingly small, factors largely in the gun control debate and specifically in the possible regulation of the AR-15 and other so-called assault weapons.

The NRA, for instance, regularly uses technical details about how firearms actually operate as details with which to discredit media outlets and derail regulation debates. For example, in his immediate response to the massacre at Sandy Hook Elementary School, NRA vice president Wayne LaPierre remarked in a prepared speech, "The media call semi-automatic firearms 'machine guns'—they claim these civilian semi-automatic firearms are used by the military, and they tell us that the .223 round is one of the most powerful rifle calibers when all of these claims are factually untrue. They don't know what they're talking about!" (2012). His claim that the .223 round fired by the AR-15 is not powerful is technically true, because power in firearms is a product (in the mathematical sense) of the mass and velocity of the bullet it fires. But the statement is intentionally misleading, because the AR-15 is a particularly deadly weapon not because of its power, but because of velocity. The point is that the AR-15 is a very deadly—an especially deadly—weapon. LaPierre's attempt to call out the media on technical grounds is dishonest and misleading, and entirely typical of how some advocacy groups leverage their technical knowledge of how firearms function to derail larger policy discussion.

So here we are in 2021 in the United States, wherein firearms are widely available and technology has advanced to the point of making guns more deadly than they once were. Nevertheless, politically, a significant portion of the electorate resists any efforts to regulate or restrict access to such firearms and ammunition. For rhetoricians, it's necessary to ask why. The physical processes enacted by firearms do much, by way of analogy, to explain the functionality of rhetoric related to the so-called gun control debate, and specifically help to explain how "rhetorical velocity" and "rhetorical force" influence public policy. Indeed, it is worth asking if something(s) in public discourse has also increased the deadliness of guns. The concepts of rhetorical velocity and rhetorical force, in particular, provide part of an explanation.

There are analogues for both "muzzle velocity" and "stopping power" in rhetorical theory. These analogues, what Ridolfo and DeVoss (2009) call "rhetorical velocity" and what I call "rhetorical force," give us a way to understand gun regulation debates and policies in the United States. Perhaps coincidentally, the anti-regulation groups that in recent decades have dominated gun regulation (by preventing meaningful regulation just about altogether) operate, rhetorically speaking, very similarly to how firearms themselves operate. An explicit understanding of how rhetorical velocity and rhetorical force are brought to bear on gun regulation policy debates in the United States provides an opportunity for intervention, a means of mitigating the rhetorical force of anti-regulation groups through a change in the rhetorical tactics of those citizens who support sensible firearms regulation.

Ridolfo and DeVoss developed the concept of rhetorical velocity in their article "Composing for Recomposition: Rhetorical Velocity and Delivery." They define their term at its most basic level in the following manner:

> The term *rhetorical velocity*, as we deploy it . . . , means a conscious rhetorical concern for distance, travel, speed, and time, pertaining specifically to theorizing instances of strategic appropriation by a third party. In thinking about the concept, we drew from several definitions:
> 1. Rapidity or speed of motion; swiftness.
> 2. *Physics*: A vector quantity whose magnitude is a body's speed and whose direction is the body's direction of motion.
> 3. The rate of speed of action or occurrence. (2009)

In the time since Ridolfo and DeVoss developed the term, rhetorical velocity has come to be understood as a means of explaining the movement of specific language, the movement of utterances, particularly in the fast-moving media of internet-based communications platforms. Utterances, like bullets, have velocities. Some travel slowly; some misfire and do not travel at all. Ridolfo and DeVoss's concept of rhetorical velocity is also, though, intended to explain the reappropriation of utterances, and the ways in which rhetors may design some speech and writing specifically to be repeated, to be recited or re-cited by others, and thus carried forward into ever-more-distant rhetorical spaces, in order that the utterance can continue to perform its rhetorical work, expanding its audiences along the way (see Boedy's chapter 11 in this volume). Sometimes the properties of rhetorical velocity shift the utterance's message as well, shoving it into new spaces, in front of unanticipated (by the original rhetor) audiences.

The concept of rhetorical velocity allows us to understand, for example, how a social media meme achieves currency by tapping into a moment of *kairos* and then propagating through social networks, achieving new lives and new rhetorical functions as it is recited and re-cited in online spaces, and then modified and parlayed by subsequent rhetors. The rhetors, in this hypothetical example, that give the meme rhetorical force (a quality that I'll explain shortly) are not only the meme's original creator, but also its propagators, who endorse the meme in one fashion or another when they share/cite it within their own social media circles. So, too, does the concept of rhetorical velocity explain how and why the meme will just as suddenly lose currency, as its tropes become dated, overshared, or the context within which it was created and initially shared shifts. Rhetorical velocity explains not only the speed of an utterance's movement but also the abruptness of its stoppage. A speed of zero is still a speed.

Rhetorical velocity, as an explanatory concept, is particularly valuable for understanding the nature of anti-regulation gun rhetoric. While American arms manufacturers have focused on incremental increases in muzzle velocity, the industry and its affiliated lobbying groups have simultaneously become masters of rhetorical velocity (see Ballentine's chapter 3 in this volume), leveraging a wide array of rhetorical mechanisms and allies in their efforts to keep guns laws liberal (or loose—liberal in a classical, laissez-faire sense) and prevent restrictive gun legislation, even when the prospect of such legislation is widely popular with the American public.

The National Rifle Association, in particular, has become masterful in its ability to leverage rhetorical velocity in the wake of mass shooting events and counter any pressures that might be brought to bear on policy makers to increase firearm regulation. Take, for example, two press releases issued by the NRA's Institute for Legislative Action (its lobbying arms and grassroots sectors, comprised of its most politically active and committed members) in the wake of a 2019 mass shooting at an El Paso, Texas, Walmart. These press releases were pushed both to media outlets and to the NRA membership, and provided key terms and talking points for those who wish to carry the NRA's party line.

The first press release, issued on August 4, 2019, and titled "NRA Statement on Texas, Ohio Tragedies," reads in its entirety:

> Our deepest sympathies are with the families and victims of these tragedies, as well as the entire communities of El Paso and Dayton. On behalf of our millions of members, we salute the courage of the first responders and others offering their services during this time.
>
> The NRA is committed to the safe and lawful use of firearms by those exercising their Second Amendment freedoms. We will not participate in the politicizing of these tragedies but, as always, we will work in good faith to pursue real solutions that protect us all from people who commit these horrific acts. (National Rifle Association 2019a)

The first paragraph of the release issues expected sentiments of grief for victims and their families, as well as support for the first responders who had to deal with the crisis. The second paragraph, however, is far more politically inflected. It immediately associates the Second Amendment with freedom, creating a cognitive distance from the violence that is also enabled by a potentially too liberal (in the classical sense) interpretation of the Second Amendment. It also provides an essential deflection, characterizing any policy debate that might follow the El Paso shooting as "politicizing." In addition to a statement of the NRA's position, this is also a cue to members, a reminder to characterize any legislation that is proposed to narrow the parameters of gun ownership as "politicized." By copying its membership on such press releases, as it does through a variety of communications channels, the NRA almost instantly is able to communicate its talking points for a given situation to its membership. Using such framing to disseminate talking points to constituents is not new. What makes the NRA particularly effective, though, is the high level of organization within its membership network and its ability to provide such statements almost instantly when events call for such framing and possible legislation must be preempted.

The second press release to follow the recent El Paso shooting, also disseminated to the press and throughout the NRA's membership network, was focused upon Walmart's voluntary corporate decision, after El Paso, to stop selling "assault weapons" and high-capacity magazines. The release, issued again throughout the NRA's member network, was dated September 3, 2019, and in its entirety reads:

> The strongest defense of freedom has always been our free-market economy. It is shameful to see Walmart succumb to the pressure of the anti-gun elites. Lines at Walmart will soon be replaced by lines at other retailers who are more supportive of America's fundamental freedoms. The truth is Walmart's actions today will not make us any safer. Rather than place the blame on the criminal, Walmart has chosen to victimize law-abiding Americans. Our leaders must be willing to approach the problems of crime, violence and mental health with sincerity and honesty. (National Rifle Association 2019b)

The statement opens by willfully ignoring the fact that Walmart's voluntary decision to restrict which firearms it sells *is itself* a function of the free market in action. The statement then proceeds to roll out key phrases for its membership to deploy as national attention, and more calls for regulation, followed the El Paso tragedy. The statement characterizes Walmart not as a free market actor, but as itself a victim that has "succumbed" to—and this is one of the key phrases being propagated to constituents—"anti-gun elites." The evidence-less conflation of those who support greater gun regulation with "elites" is a calculated and cynical rhetorical move on the NRA's part, intended to mobilize its majority working-class and majority rural membership in viewing regulation efforts as the product of moneyed, culturally distant Americans. The statement characterizes anti-regulation Americans as victims, paints Walmart as sympathetic to criminals, and ends by arguing that efforts to regulate firearms are insincere and dishonest. Constituents are provided with clear phrases and framings through which to propagate and defend the NRA position. Again, what makes the release effective is not the genius of its content, but the organizational efficiency and speed, rhetorical velocity, with which the talking points are delivered from the central lobbying offices of the NRA down to the grassroots level. The size of the NRA's membership converts rhetorical velocity into what I'll call "rhetorical force," as a large mass of Americans begin repeating the tropes that the NRA has propagated to them.

The NRA is able to generate an enormous amount of rhetorical force as it pressures policy makers to prevaricate or obstruct when gun control legislation is suggested or introduced. Part of what makes the NRA such a politically effective lobbying organization is its ability to mobilize its membership, primarily through email but also telephone and mail campaigns, to exert political pressure on their own elected representatives with breathtaking speed. The NRA is an effective political lobbying organization within the American political system because it has learned how to generate enormous rhetorical force.

In my 2013 *Inside Higher Ed* column discussed above, I had an "opportunity" to experience the grassroots responses orchestrated by the NRA and more fringe anti-regulation groups. I did not realize when I wrote the essay that I was bringing upon myself the full force of the anti-regulation crowd, did not realize that I would feel, viscerally, the effects of both rhetorical velocity and rhetorical force. In the column, I reflected upon my personal conflict as both a gun owner and hunter and my role as a professor who didn't (and doesn't) want guns, even legally carried ones, present in his classroom. The column was less a call to action than perhaps a melancholy reflection upon just how screwed up our national priorities were/are, even in the wake of a killing that stole twenty-seven lives at an elementary school. The venue where my column was published, *Inside Higher Ed*, is essentially a trade publication aimed at professionals working in higher education, a niche readership, and its articles do not typically garner much attention outside of higher-education professional circles. In other words, the rhetorical velocity of its articles typically plummets when those articles move outside the readership of academic professionals and graduate students who tend to care most about higher-ed news and policy.

Not so with this particular article, one of dozens I have written for *Inside Higher Ed* over a period of years. That particular column, humbly titled "On Guns in My Classroom," garnered significantly more attention than anything else I have ever written for any venue. At one point, traffic and links to it threatened to overwhelm the *IHE* servers, and comments on the piece had to be frozen or blocked in order to give editors an opportunity to curate them and weed out threatening content. Early in the day that it was published, *IHE* founding editor Scott Jaschik cautioned me to keep a low profile because he was receiving outraged and borderline threatening messages from anti-regulation visitors to the site. I hesitate to call these folks "readers" of *Inside Higher Ed,* because they weren't comprised of the site's typical readership, and the nuances of their traffic are instructive as to the power of both rhetorical velocity and, as I'll get to in a moment, rhetorical force.

My article generated a staggering number of comments on the *IHE* site, and who knows how many others commented, as it was shared in social media circles by both my supporters and detractors. An even larger number of comments were submitted to *IHE,* but never published, in all cases due to their violations of *IHE* comment policy. These flagged comments fell primarily into two categories: those that threatened violence against me, and those that encouraged me to commit violence against myself, comments suggesting, both implicitly and explicitly, that I should kill myself. So-called Second Amendment activists were explicitly advocating that I turn one of my own guns upon myself. I was, however, very much motivated when I wrote my essay by an urge precisely *not* to be killed, not to die at the business end of a firearm. Of course, such comments are not intended to be persuasive, but instead to intimidate. Of the comments that did make it through the curation process, most are unworthy of dignifying by citing them. Their content is predictable for anyone who has participated in online, largely anonymous discussions of guns and gun control. The critical comments, which certainly constitute the majority of the comments on the article, question my sanity, call me naive, and trot out standard tropes about law-abiding gun carriers versus predatory criminals. The tropes themselves are tired—but what is interesting for our purposes is how the trolls found their way to the article.

Forensically, I now know that one reason for the concentrated attack on my column by academic outsiders, commenters who wouldn't ordinarily have read *IHE,* is from an analysis, provided to me, of the sources of readership and commenters for the article. In the wee hours of the morning of its automated publication on the *IHE* site, usually around 3 a.m. in those days, the article was linked to by a Second Amendment advocacy group in Colorado in one of their message boards. My article had likely come to the attention of the message board operator through a Google Alert or another automated system that scrapes the internet for key terms important to the person monitoring the alert account. From "Second Amendment activists" interactions with my column began to snowball.

The concept of rhetorical velocity as Ridolfo and DeVoss define it is particularly useful for understanding how a column like the one I wrote can elicit such a charged and immediate response, even from interlocutors it wasn't aimed at, and then disappear from related discourse just as quickly. But rhetorical velocity doesn't totally explain the force the Second Amendment activists exerted in response to my essay. We need also an extension of rhetorical velocity, because speed alone does not fully explain the mechanisms that drive discussion of contested issues like gun regulation. Rhetorical mass, I contend, interacts with rhetorical velocity to produce rhetorical force. Together, these physics-inspired rhetorical mechanisms explain why particular utterances in particular moments propagated by particular people can be particularly effective.

If rhetorical velocity represents a rate at which an utterance moves, then rhetorical force is another quality of rhetorical energy we can conceptualize through a metaphor of physics. In physics, force equals mass times acceleration ($F = M \times A$). (In physics, acceleration is understood to be a velocity that is in a state of change, either accelerating or decelerating.) We can use the formula from physics as a metaphor to understand how utterances exert force, and how such exertions accumulate or lose their force. As the formula makes clear, an increase in either or both mass and acceleration will result in an increase in force. If we accept the Ridolfo and DeVoss definition of acceleration (their articulation of rhetorical velocity), then we need also to understand what constitutes mass, in the rhetorical sense. We might define it in two ways. First, it might be an accounting of the number of utterances. Ten thousand citizens crying out for the same thing might easily have more mass than ten citizens crying out for the opposite thing. But are all citizen voices equal? Decidedly not. Not usually, anyway. So rhetorical mass might be thought of in other terms as well. The voices of regular old citizens generally don't have the same mass as celebrity or political voices. For better or worse, a celebrity's position on an issue may carry significantly more weight than the voices of thousands of nonfamous citizens who share the same perspective. And I say this not to be macabre, but the parent of a six-year-old shooting victim, because of the trauma and our empathy and the general feeling that six-year-olds ought not to die in shootings, may then prove more rhetorically massive than the voice of someone who has not suffered a similar loss. In a society that—because of historical and ongoing systemic racism—does not value Black lives in the same way that it values white lives, we might have an explanation for why, so often, violence visited upon Black bodies does not generate the same rhetorical force as violence visited on white bodies. It is a perverse and uncomfortable observation that, unlike physics, which is mathematically clear, rhetorical mass, and thus also rhetorical force, shift in relation to the societal pathologies where they are put in motion. Such shifts in rhetorical mass, with resulting changes to the rhetorical force generated around particular political positions, may shift public policy debates. Such is exactly what was feared by the NRA after the Newtown massacre.

Because our society does not treat people equally, victims of violence, those whose bodies fall to the ground upon being shot, are not treated equally in a rhetorical sense, either. The outrage over white children dying together in Newtown was greater than it is over the steady drip of Black children's deaths in routine acts of public violence. That such public rhetorical reactions are different further exposes the inequities of our society. Tragically, rhetorical force also gives us a pseudo-quantitative concept through which to observe the stark dramatic inequalities in how our culture reacts to white men and Black men carrying guns in public, and the similarly dissimilar reactions to gunshots felling bodies of our nation's white children and its Black children.

Rhetorical mass is a way, as some readers might already be recognizing, of describing shifts in ethos, or a certain type of societal-cultural standing. Rhetorical mass explains why the ethical appeals of a parent who has not lost a child in a shooting might not equal in terms of forcefulness the ethical appeals of a parent stricken by grief over the preventable shooting death of his or her child. In this way, rhetorical mass offers us a conceptual way, a quasi-method, to understand the different values afforded to different types of individual rhetors, as well as a way to understand the collective and cumulative effects (or force) of utterances proffered by groups of rhetors and how those utterances create rhetorical effects within distributions of time.

Rhetorical velocity and rhetorical mass combined to create a very particular anti-regulation rhetorical force in the comments on my *IHE* article. First, an algorithmic net had captured my column, which had been published in a forum unlikely to be frequented by most Second Amendment activists. Then, the algorithm quickly distributed an alert to a human network of Second Amendment defenders. Finally, the human network of activists began bombarding the column with their comments and reposting their critiques of my own critique to firearms-related message boards. An incredibly large number of gun rights activists (large rhetorical mass) concentrated their vitriol on my column with incredible speed (rhetorical velocity) in a way that essentially overwhelmed the comments on my column (both actually and rhetorically), and almost even overwhelmed the *IHE* servers—generating, in other words, an enormous amount of rhetorical force. After the article was initially linked in the Colorado "gun rights" advocacy forum, other anti-regulation websites began to link to my column and editorialize upon it, as well as to conduct armchair psychological profiling of me. I won't dignify these articles by citing them directly, but I will note that they endure, that the twisted speculations of uninformed, semi-literate online trolls persist as artifacts of my own digital legacy. If you google my name you can find and read them. While their rhetorical force is all but destroyed now, some of their mass endures, though not as it did when I was untenured and feared that the rantings of anonymous threatening "Second Amendment advocates" might affect my tenure case at a provincial institution in a conservative state. All of which is to say, the metaphors linking physics and rhetoric, so smartly initiated by Ridolfo and DeVoss, do much to explain the rhetorical dysfunction surrounding gun policy debate in the United States.

The events surrounding my own pro-regulation column again illustrate the extended conceptual metaphor of rhetorical force. What was notable in the response to my column was not only the velocity (acceleration) of responses, but their mass as well. So many Second Amendment advocates flooded the *IHE* comments section that day that a reader going back archivally and examining them might be forgiven for arriving at the erroneous conclusion that the average reader of higher-ed trade publications is a highly motivated, politically engaged member of the circles that view "defense" of the Second Amendment as one of their primary political objectives. In other words, a likely specious correlation. The sheer mass of my critics overwhelmed the typical commenter population, and that mass in turn generated secondary posts in other firearms venues, where authors unknown to me (and typically writing anonymously) continued their critiques of both my column and my person. This response is indicative of Second Amendment activism more generally. The gun industry, and especially the NRA, is particularly skilled at and built for such rapid, overwhelming comment campaigns. They exert enormous rhetorical force by efficiently leveraging the rhetorical mass of their membership and allies. How else can we explain the failures of popular legislation regulating firearms after mass shooting events?

Rhetorical force also explains how and why those who advocate for greater regulation of firearms suffer in large part due to their relative lack of organization, which results in an inability to leverage rhetorical mass and to generate rhetorical force. When their advocacy is delivered piecemeal, in dribs and drabs by self-motivated individuals, even an equal number of comments and phone calls lacks the rhetorical force of a coordinated comment/call campaign in which the comments arrive more or less simultaneously. In other words, 1,000 phone calls to a policy maker that arrive in a single day arguing against gun regulation generate much more rhetorical force than 1,000 phone calls demanding tighter regulation of firearms arriving over the course of a month. Even though more Americans might support reasonable gun legislation than oppose it, the mass of Americans amenable to such legislation appears small and weak—not because it is small and weak, but because it is disorganized.

An analogy from the physical world is again instructive. If you are standing outside a two-story building and someone on the roof drops a penny onto your head, you will be annoyed, and your head may smart a tad, but you're not likely to be injured. If that same ruffian throws 100,000 pennies at you by the handful, they will be annoying and sound scary, but still probably no grave harm will be done. But if our hooligan takes his 100,000 pennies, binds them up into a bunch, and throws them onto your head, you will be grievously injured or even killed. The total mass thrown at you is the same and travels at the same rate, drawn by the same forces of gravity, but the end effects are entirely different. Rhetorical force operates similarly. When mass is compiled into a tight bundle, it is more capable of generating force, in the rhetorical sense.

This same scenario that occurs—again, in a rhetorical sense—when pro-gun (usually organized by the NRA) and pro-regulation forces mobilize after a mass shooting event. Those who are pro-regulation are, in comparison to the NRA, relatively unorganized. Their 100,000 phone calls and emails to policy makers are 100,000 ineffectual pennies thrown separately from the roof. Whereas the pro-gun forces, organized into a unit, targeting the very crown of the policy maker's head, arrive en masse and with enormous and deliberatively destructive force. Within my framing of rhetorical force, utterances are not equal, even when they might be present in equal numbers and are offered by equally credible rhetors. So, it is not just the speed with which the NRA mobilizes that is rhetorically effective, but also its ability to concentrate a critical mass of responses within a tight temporal and spatial window. The rhetorical effect, the rhetorical force, is understandably overwhelming for many policy makers.

Understanding how rhetorical velocity and rhetorical mass come together to make rhetorical force is invaluable for people who want to understand the dynamics of gun control debates in America. If you can change velocity or mass, you can also change force. If losing a child increases the rhetorical mass of a parent's utterances on gun control, then we begin to see why particular lobbies and allies of pro-gun groups immediately attack and seek to dismiss the utterances of such interlocutors. They work to amplify the velocity of their messages. And so we see conspiracy theorists, such as Alex Jones and his Infowars media group, attacking the credibility of the parents of mass shooting victims, and spinning elaborate, confusing conspiracies about mass shooting events, all in order to moderate and reduce the amount of rhetorical force that survivors and their loved ones are able to generate in the kairotic, emotionally laden moments that immediately follow mass shooting events. Alex Jones and his media network—for all their conspiracy theory fuckery—are experts at wielding rhetorical velocity, leveraging rhetorical mass, and manipulating rhetorical force. Not only does Infowars—which was born on AM radio and matured on the internet—generate enormous rhetorical velocity through its immediate responses to current events such as mass shootings, it also packages its conspiracy theory talking points as perfect bytes for recitation by its listeners and readers, thus conscripting its audience to move from passive consumers of pro-gun, anti-government talking points into propagators of those same utterances. The NRA follows a similar strategy of delivering talking points to its constituents and mobilizing them en masse.

Masterful though they are at preventing changes to gun legislation, however, Jones and the NRA illustrate an equally important point for people who would argue for different gun laws in America. If rhetorical mass and rhetorical velocity are contingent, rather than absolute qualities, then the force they exert can be changed through rhetorical work. But doing so requires a better understanding of how velocity, mass, and force work so that they can be acted on in productive ways.

REFERENCES

Benedikt, Joseph von. 2019. "Get the Most out of the 30.06." *Shooting Times.* https://www.shootingtimes.com/editorial/get-the-most-out-of-the-30–06/359132.

Demick, Barbara. 2017. "In an Age of 'Alternative Facts,' a Massacre of Schoolchildren Is Called a Hoax." *Los Angeles Times,* February 3. https://www.latimes.com/nation/la-na-sandy-hook-conspiracy-20170203-story.html.

Kreuter, Nate. 2013. "On Guns in My Classroom." *Inside Higher Ed*, February 6. https://www.insidehighered.com/advice/2013/02/06/essay-prospect-politicians-allowing-guns-college-classrooms.

LaPierre, Wayne. 2012. "NRA: Full Response from Wayne LaPierre in Response to the Newtown Shootings." *Guardian*, December 21. https://www.theguardian.com/world/2012/dec/21/nra-full-statement-lapierre-newtown.

National Rifle Association. 2019a. "NRA Statement on Texas, Ohio Tragedies." https://www.nraila.org/articles/20190804/nra-statement-on-texas-ohio-tragedies.

National Rifle Association. 2019b. "NRA Statement on Walmart's Decision to Change Firearms Policy." https://www.nraila.org/articles/20190903/nra-statement-on-walmarts-decision-to-change-firearms-policy.

Ridolfo, Jim, and Dànielle Nicole DeVoss. 2009. "Composing for Recomposition: Rhetorical Velocity and Delivery." *Kairos*. http://kairos.technorhetoric.net/13.2/topoi/ridolfo_devoss/velocity.html.

Sher, Heather. 2018. "What I Saw Treating the Victims from Parkland Should Change the Debate on Guns." *Atlantic*, February 22. https://www.theatlantic.com/politics/archive/2018/02/what-i-saw-treating-the-victims-from-parkland-should-change-the-debate-on-guns/553937/.

3

HUNTING FIREARMS
Rhetorical Pursuits of Range and Power

Brian Ballentine

Years ago, during the week-long gun season for deer in Ohio, I was walking slowly through freshly fallen snow into a field with a south-facing slope where deer would bed in the tall grass in the later afternoon sun. A doe stood up quickly and began running diagonally away from me toward the field's edge. In this moment, I can't say for certain how the deer knew I was there. Even though it was cold, I was sweating from walking up the hillside in the snow, so perhaps the wind swirled and blew my scent to the hiding deer. Perhaps I moved too quickly or the snow creaked too loudly under my boots. Regardless, my part in the moment was the role of the hunter: I aimed at the deer through the scope on the 12-gauge shotgun and fired. The "left to right" of the shot was on target but well short of the deer; it only kicked up snow. I located the deer in the scope again and fired, but the shot was still short of the animal. The third shot threw up snow right underneath the running deer. Confident I now had the deer in range, I squeezed the trigger a fourth time, only to hear the click of an empty gun. The deer bounded safely into the woods. That was the last time I shot at a moving deer, let alone a running one. I share this story here not to question my choice to shoot but instead to serve as a backdrop for beginning to understand guns as advanced technological agents whose use and effectiveness are influenced by varying rules and regulations when these technologies are used for hunting. As both a technology and an agent, guns are bound up in complex networks of other actors, rules, regulations, and codes that may shape and guide their use.

There are two core theoretical components that undergird this chapter's discussion of guns as technological agents. The first borrows from Kenneth Burke and his treatment of entelechy, a term that for Burke would ultimately stand in for humankind's relentless drive to actualize the maximum potential of any technological advancement. Critical to the discussion here, Burke notes that our pursuit of these advancements

https://doi.org/10.7330/9781646422159.c003

is often to the detriment of humanity. The second employs tenets of new materialism, specifically Jane Bennett's understanding of it that treats all objects, animate and inanimate, as having their own vibrancy and agency. For Bennett, all things possess "a kind of vitalism, an enchanted materialism" (2010, 447). Her work places objects, or what she calls "actants," into complex relationships, or "assemblages," with one another. With the aid of Bennett's brand of new materialism, we can view the above hunting scenario as an entanglement of hunters, guns, deer, snow, wind, sound, sweat, and clothing, but also of hunting rules and regulations as well as ethical codes of conduct. Entelechy serves as a useful frame for analyzing some of the many significant advancements in firearm range and power (see Kreuter's chapter 2 in this volume). The interconnectedness of Bennett's "vibrant matter" means that guns are one of many actants within complex networks. As all objects have agency, new materialism relieves us of the reductive arguments often used to exculpate guns and gun violence (i.e., "Guns don't kill people; people kill people"). As employed here, new materialism helps expand and complicate our rhetorical analyses of firearm technology. In other words, for the purposes of hunting, guns *do* kill deer, and this chapter works to reveal how the entelechial drive behind the technical advancements of some of these entangled objects, policies, and codes help or hinder hunting.

ENTELECHY AND PUSHING TECHNOLOGY TO THE "END OF THE LINE"

Willfully or not, hunters and their weaponry often enter the public debates surrounding American gun culture without enough detail to contextualize the many varying gun regulations already in place to control hunting practices. Those practices are set at the state level and include inconsistencies in regulating whether a hunter could, for example, pursue a deer with an assault-style weapon versus a weapon with a far more limited range, such as a shotgun. Both guns are a form of technology, and technology, according to Charles Bazerman, "as a human-made object, has always been part of human needs, desires, values, and evaluation, articulated in language and at the heart of rhetoric" (1998, 383). This volume contends with many of the intersections of rhetoric and guns, and this chapter aims to unpack some of the complexities of firearms as technology. Among the benefits of this approach is that "rhetorical studies of technology should help us understand the wide dissemination, diverse applications, and cultural potency of technology as a shaper of our minds and lives" (Miller 1998, 310). As manifestations of technology, firearms certainly do shape us, as they have arguably divided contemporary American culture as much as they have transformed it. Our current cultural divisions over gun regulation makes common ground on civilian gun ownership difficult, if not impossible, to come by (see Rood's chapter 6 in this volume).

A great deal of rhetoric and technology scholarship reflects on communication technology, especially the ways in which networked, digital technologies alter both how we communicate and the communications themselves (Selber 2010). But firearms, when considered as technological artifacts, are rhetorical, too, and "technology, like rhetoric, can push and pull at us" (Miller 2010, ix). The destructive capabilities of technological advancements in modern firearms are read in this chapter through a Burkean lens and his evolving theory of entelechy. He adapted the term from Aristotle to capture what Burke described as a "principle of perfection" where humankind strives toward extreme optimization and ultimate efficiency, including technological innovations that contain the power to bring about our own demise (Burke 1963, 510). Burke came to fear what Hill has described as "the relentless entelechial demand for technological progress at the expense of humaneness and the environment" (Hill 2009). Burke lived through the development and multiple detonations of the atomic bomb—in a very real sense the entelechial fulfillment of taking something to "the end of the line" (Burke 1974, 314). On the day the United States bombed Nagasaki, Burke wrote to his childhood friend Malcolm Cowley, "There seems now no logical thing to do but go on tinkering with this damned thing until they have blown up the whole damned world" (Burke and Cowley 1990, 268). The parallel drawn here is not just the destructive capabilities of both bombs and guns (no doubt there is a huge distinction in scale), but also the relentless "tinkering" within the firearms industry that has led to stunning advancements in the effective range and power of civilian firearms, including those that are legal for hunting.

Breaking down Aristotle's entelechy (*entelecheia*), Stan Lindsay recalls its biological or natural origins with a metaphor of a plant seed. The "final cause," end goal, or *telos* of the seed, to grow roots, sprout, and become a plant, is already preprogrammed within it. As a term, *entelechy* attempts to signal the telos (*tel*) inherently within (*en*) the processes (*y*) possessed or had by (*ech*) the seed (Lindsay 1999, 268). In *A Grammar of Motives*, Burke casts Aristotle's entelechy as "the striving of each thing to be perfectly the kind of thing it was" (1969, 249). But, as Burke moves entelechy from the realm of the biological into the symbolic, he lets in "the implicit freedom of human action" (Lindsay 1999, 269). As symbol-using animals, humans are compelled to action that strives for perfection. Perfection for the firearm industry and hunters who use its products means not so much a specific, well-defined metric but an expectation of year after year advancements. I would argue, too, that hunters are then conditioned by this rhetorical, entelechial push for continued increases in a firearm's range and power to expect those advancements. As discussed later, the entelechial drive has a constitutive dimension on firearms manufacturers, who are compelled to push the limits of range and power. Burke's "Definition of Man" contains perhaps his more famous discussion on this entelechial push, noting first that we are "goaded by the spirit of hierarchy (or moved by the sense of order) and rotten with a sense of perfection" (1963, 507). The "principle of perfection" that Burke derives from Aristotle's *entelekheia* moves beyond the telos inherent within a biological organism.

In what may read like unbridled entelechy, this chapter provides brief overviews of the range and power of now-common hunting firearms including semiautomatic firearms like the AR-15, shotguns, and what many might consider standard center-fire, bolt-action, or lever-action hunting rifles. Hunters wielding the technological advancements found in the firearms discussed in this chapter are held in check, at least partially, by state regulations and the guiding principle of fair chase. Fair chase requires that hunters don't have undue advantage over the animals they are pursuing but, as will be discussed, what exactly constitutes "fair chase" is open to interpretation. In a Burkean sense, *fair* and *ethical* are terms that compose hunters' "terministic screen" through which they base their actions (Burke 1966, 44–45). They are also invisible actants influencing a hunter's behavior. Ultimately, I argue that these two forces, one a set of legal rules hunters are required to follow like any other law, and the other an ethical position that helps shape a code of conduct or moral responsibility while pursuing animals, do little to contain the "relentless" advancement of gun technology for hunters and the hunting community. The human desire to "tinker" with guns and their ammunition shows no signs of abating, and the range and capacity of hunting firearms continue with the same relentlessness Burke came to expect. The next section discusses how these advancements become enmeshed in Bennett's assemblages of other vibrant actants.

ENTELECHY AND LINKS TO NEW MATERIALISM

Rhetoricians have exemplary models of identifying and reflecting on engineering and technological advancements, including Bazerman's remarkable book tracing Edison's development of electrical power and lighting (1999). Beyond the new technical developments coming out of Edison's labs, Bazerman also asks us to consider how the advancements in lighting and electricity "emerge as part of the drama of human meanings" (2). That drama sets the advancement of technological "goods" alongside the ways in which "people have come to attribute values to goods and how they have come to demand particular products and services" (143). Edison was more than a maker of light bulbs; Bazerman's book captures the sociopolitical and legal drama surrounding Edison's inventions and Edison the inventor. His ethos as the Wizard of Menlo Park can't be disentangled from his many patent applications or, for example, his participation and stake in debates to pursue direct current (DC) versus alternating current (AC). Even with the value of electric light long since established, innovations in the industry continue apace as longer-lasting bulbs, LED technology, and different brightness and white light color spectrum values come on the consumer market. The market for light and the electrical connectivity that makes it possible have had their own entelechial push.

Our country's electrical grid happens to be the foundation of Bennett's "The Agency of Assemblages and the North American Blackout," where she argues that the grid is a complex assemblage of electrical networks that includes nonhuman components such as "electrons, trees, wind, [and] electromagnetic fields" (2005, 446). Following Gilles Deleuze and Bruno Latour, she argues that these components, or "actants," cluster together in "ad hoc groupings of diverse elements, of vibrant materials of all sorts" (Bennett 2010, 23). While Bennet is interested in locating agency across and through an assemblage, she makes clear that "power is not equally distributed" and actants within the assemblage may or may not be operating toward a shared goal (2005, 445). The 2005 article is later folded into her book *Vibrant Matter* (2010), which traces in more detail the evolution of her materialist ontology, with roots in Bergson, Driesch, and Kant. All three had versions of vitalism (including Driesch's take on entelechy) that Bennett artfully unpacks to form her "kind of thing-power" (2010, 18). Bennett specifically values Kant's theories that reveal "an impersonal, ahistorical agency, an impetus that 'drives' men on" (69). Bennett offers the important distinction between the "desire of the craftsperson to see what a metal can do, rather than the desire of the scientist to know what a metal is" (60). She notes that "not all vitalisms are alike," and indeed she distances herself from vitalism that bends toward essentialism and hinges on a religious conception of a soul or some other spiritual power. Bennett's work is careful, too, to "avoid anthropocentricism and biocentrism" and instead allow for "material vitality" (61). Ultimately, the list of actants in Bennett's grid assemblage is massive and yet still incomplete: "To the vital materialist, the electrical grid is better understood as a volatile mix of coal, sweat, electromagnetic fields, computer programs, electron streams, profit motives, heat, lifestyles, nuclear fuel, plastic, fantasies of mastery, static, legislation, water, economic theory, wire, and wood—to name just some of the actants" (25).

Conceptualizing firearms as actants enmeshed in an assemblage or assemblages of various kinds is another avenue for understanding entelechy within US gun culture, specifically hunting practices. As noted in this chapter's introduction, hunters, firearms, clothing, wind and other weather conditions, trees, and of course deer are but a few in an assemblage constructed from a hunting season. Again, different policies and regulations in play have agency, too. For example, gun season for deer hunters comes at different calendar times of the year depending on the state. Wisconsin's season traditionally opens the Saturday before Thanksgiving and runs for nine days, while Ohio's season begins on the Monday after Thanksgiving and extends for seven days. Tracing actants and their many frictions in a deer season assemblage could be a book-length project. In the scenario at the start of the chapter, I was hunting in Ohio with a shotgun, not a more versatile, longer-range weapon such as a high-power, bolt-action rifle or even an assault-style rifle. The following section examines the rise in popularity of assault-style weapons as a model case of a Burkean entelechy that has pushed the limits of the range and power of these "actants."

THE ARMALITE RIFLE, OR "AR"

Writing in an issue of *Poroi* dedicated to "inventing the future: rhetoric of science, technology, and medicine," John Lynch and William Kinsella state, "Rhetorical studies of technology (or technologies) ideally encourage us to identify and reflect upon the moments of decision in technological development writ large" (2013, 3–4). Such a reflection is necessary for this chapter, but an attempt to recount the history of the development of the AR-15, even briefly, contains several key "moments of decision" that require examination. Not surprisingly, the development of the modern version of the AR-15 is part of military history. The company Armalite began developing firearms in the 1950s, and its practice has been to designate all its weapons as "AR," for Armalite rifle (Armalite n.d.). The "AR" initials do not, therefore, stand for "assault rifle" or "automatic rifle"—a misunderstanding journalists have had to correct (Peters 2016). It is true, though, that "AR" has come to stand in as a generic term for similarly styled semiautomatic guns now manufactured by dozens of companies (Myre 2018). In 1956, army officials approached Armalite about developing a smaller, lighter-weight version of one of the company's existing rifles, the AR-10, as a replacement for other rifles then in use by the military. Due to economic and engineering challenges, Armalite sold its patents for the AR-10 and AR-15 to Colt, another famous firearms manufacturer, which would eventually complete the development of the AR-15 (Bartocci 2012). The long and at points tragic development of the AR-15 into what would become the US military's M-16 combat rifle is beyond the scope of the chapter but is chronicled in *Gun Digest* (Bartocci 2012). The primary distinction between the two weapons is the ability of the military-grade weapon, the M-16, to fire on full automatic. That is, a solider can hold down the gun's trigger and the weapon will continue to fire. The AR-15 is a semiautomatic weapon, meaning that the trigger needs to be squeezed to fire, then released and squeezed again to fire again. Essentially, the gun will fire only as quickly as the user can pull and release the trigger. Unlike in a bolt-action or lever-action rifle, there is no need to manually rechamber a round of ammunition to continue firing. The decades of "tinkering" that have refined the workings of military (fully automatic) and civilian (semiautomatic) firearms represent technological developments worthy of our field's attention. That is, as scholars we should "examine the choices that we have made during the creation and dissemination of any given technology, which we can hopefully revise or redesign" (Lynch and Kinsella 2013, 4).

Firearms manufacturers in addition to Armalite and Colt, including Daniel Defense, DPMS, Ruger, Sig Sauer, and Smith & Wesson, among others, have reengineered and redesigned their civilian offerings of semiautomatic, assault-style weapons. The manufacturers listed here sell their versions of the AR-15 starting at about $500, with more expensive models selling for $2,000 or more. Most of the higher-priced models advertise the different components of the gun, including the upper and lower receivers, the bolt carrier group, and barrel as "mil-spec," or made with a level of quality that meets military specifications. Claiming "mil-spec" standards no doubt helps catch the eye of a civilian consumer but just meeting those standards does not necessarily slow the entelechial push to innovate the AR platform. Frank DeSomma, an aerospace engineer and the president of Patriot Ordnance Factory (POF-USA), started his AR company in a garage in 2002. His company is credited with being the first in many years to bring significant innovations to the AR platform, including how the firearm cycles rounds of ammunition. DeSomma's innovations are also known to manage heat more efficiently; the guns remain cooler than other ARs after firing the same number of rounds. According to DeSomma, his competitors "were just building the same gun with another widget on it." At a tradeshow in 2004, DeSomma's new designs were "laughed at," but they were selling "like hot cakes" by 2012 (Tactical-Life 2014). In 2017, he and his company accepted a major industry award—Firearm of the Year—for a new AR the company calls the Revolution. The gun was reportedly the clear winner in an otherwise crowded field because it "possesses all the accuracy of a heavier, harder-kicking, bolt-action rifle in a trim, lightweight, autoloading package" (American Rifleman 2018). In other words, companies like DeSomma's are setting new standards and expectations for AR range, power, and overall improved performance.

ARISTOTLE'S FOUR CAUSES, *TECHNÊ*, AND VITALISM

The work of engineers like DeSomma, or any artisan, could be viewed as purely a form of rhetorical *technê*. Productive knowledge, or the "reasoned state of capacity to make," as technê has been classically understood, exists in a fluid relationship with its counterpart *epistêmê* (Aristotle 1998, 141). The "state of capacity to demonstrate" of episteme is the scientific knowledge waiting to be discovered, revealed, and shown (141). According to Chad Wickman, "Aristotle differentiates between science [*epistêmê*] and art [*technê*] on the basis of being and coming into being" (2012, 25). Aristotle's technê and the art of bringing an object into being are tied to his four causes of being: the material, efficient, formal, and final. The material is what an object is made of, the efficient is the source or the agent that brings the object into being, the formal is the object's conceptualized or abstracted design structure, and the final is the purpose of the created object and the object itself. An AR could arguably be understood as an achievement of both science and art, with its four causes alloys and synthetic polymers (material), a gunsmith or design engineer (efficient), the schematics or blueprints for the AR (formal), and an automatic or semiautomatic AR that shoots farther, flatter, and more efficiently (final). In her "The Gun as (Race/Gender) *Technê*" (chapter 4 in this volume), Lisa Corrigan clarifies that "debates about technê are about craft, applied practice, or what we call praxis." She invokes Heidegger to create a connection between technê and instrumentality, or the process of using a particular technology.

For Corrigan, it is within this connection that we see the "disciplining human relationship to the technology as that technology reveals truths about us." In other words, our development (our tinkering) and use define who we are. Of course, our use of a thing or another actant constitutes an entanglement with it. If understood only through the lens of technê, advancements in firearm performance can neglect the vitalism of entelechy.

Revisiting the example of the seed, if its final cause is to grow roots, sprout, and become a plant, the blueprint or formal cause already contained within it serves as the driving or entelechial force to move the process ahead. According to Byron Hawk, in biological examples, the "formal cause creates the self-motivation to strive toward its final completion, to play out its potential" (2007, 124). A larger mission of Hawk's *A Counter-History of Composition* is to separate out romanticism, expressivism, and vitalism in order to undo their conflation, which has resulted in a devaluing of vitalism as crucial to invention. Indeed, "Compositionists use vitalism as a term that denotes an 'anything-goes' approach to writing and thinking, as an ahistorical category that subsumes multiple divergent practices, and as an assumed negative counterpart to the preferred rhetorical practices that establishes a binary between rhetoric and poetics" (3). To save vitalism from unwanted associations, Hawk returns to scholars of Aristotle writing before it was something to be avoided. Richard Hughes's "The Contemporaneity of Classical Rhetoric" (1965) draws a clear line between vitalism and Aristotle's entelechy. He states, "By vitalism I mean that assumption, ubiquitous in Aristotle's writings, springing from his concern for entelechy, that all the arts are generative" (quoted in Hawk 2007, 123). For Hughes and subsequently for Hawk, vitalism is not just rhetorical, it is foundational for invention and how an object moves from conception or plan to completion. Burke moved entelechy out of the realm of the biological into the symbolic and Hawk exhibits no reservations regarding vitalism's prominent role in both nature and art: "The basic logic of entelechy is that the overall configuration of any situation, including both natural and human acts and forms, combines to create its own conditions of possibility that strive to be played out to completion" (126). Reading Hawk reinforces for rhetoric and composition scholars the importance of entelechy and vitalism, and his work complements Bennett's notion of "thing power" when we read some of Hawk's concluding claims, such as his statement that "the system generates its own thriving" (150). The acknowledgment of a larger enmeshed "system" or assemblage in which humans endeavor to take a concept to "the end of the line" necessitates recognizing the popularity of the AR platform with both hunters and non-hunters alike, which continues even amid a complex cultural and political landscape.

POLITICS AND AR POWER

In his 1980 article "Do Artifacts Have Politics?" Langdon Winner reminds readers that "physical arrangements of industrial production, warfare, communications, and the like have fundamentally changed the exercise of power and the experience of citizenship" (122). But Winner steps away from attributing the push for all technological innovation as socially derived or determined. Instead, he opens the door for a perspective that "identifies certain technologies as political phenomena in their own right" (123). Clearly, advancements in civilian firearms, in particular as they relate to the AR platform, do not exist in a vacuum, nor are they free from our country's political landscape. The Clinton administration was able to pass legislation that banned all "assault-style" weapons from 1994 to 2004 (Myre 2018). After the ban lapsed, assault-style weapons were popular again and gunmakers were able to capitalize on different political climates to increase sales, including the possible threat of reinstated gun restrictions during the Obama administration. Following the 2016 presidential election, the political threat of gun restrictions disappeared and the firearms market experienced a drop in sales that was termed a "Trump slump" (Elinson and McWhirter, 2018). However, at the time of this writing, the country remains in a state of political, economic, and cultural instability due, in part, to a global pandemic and our country's response to it. While the pandemic has slowed manufacturing output for many industries, including the firearms industry, the country's current climate means assault-style weapons sales and gun sales in general spiked in 2020. Reporting that citizens are "fearful that the pandemic could lead to civil unrest," the *New York Times* documented that in March 2020, Americans bought more than 2 million guns, making it the "second-busiest" month for gun sales ever recorded (Collins and Yaffe-Bellany 2020). In fact, a record 21 million guns were sold in 2020, and according to *CBS News*, 2021 sales could "slightly surpass" last year's number. The pandemic no doubt continues to drive sales, but renewed discussion of gun control legislation in Congress is "undeniably a factor that drives sales" (Gandel 2021).

Even with the brief slump in sales in 2016, since the assault weapons ban lapsed in 2004, the AR-15 has gone on to be the most popular rifle in the United States. The National Rifle Association's David Keene (2013) attributes the success "in part to the fact that it is a semiautomatic version of the rifle used by the men and women of the military. Nearly half of AR owners are veterans, law enforcement officers, or both." He goes on to say that his daughter, a military veteran, owns only one gun—an AR-15. He also claims that "AR 15s are good for hunting" and notes, "The standard AR is illegal in most states for deer and big game hunting because it is not considered powerful enough to reliably put down deer-sized or larger game, but is used for coyote, wolf and feral pig hunting in many states." Writing in *Slate*, Justin Peters (2016) contends that "the AR-15 is not ideal for hunting . . . Though it can be used for hunting, the AR-15 isn't really a hunting rifle. Its standard .223 caliber ammunition doesn't offer much stopping power for anything other than small game." The word *standard* in Peters's claim requires attention. The standard 5.56 ammunition round is a 55-grain bullet; despite its ability to shoot accurately in excess of 500 yards, it is too lightweight and, as will be discussed, typically too fragile to adequately penetrate and ethically kill deer or other larger game animals. It is important to note that assault-style weapons chambered in 5.56 will also shoot .223 ammunition. The reverse, however, is not true (Massaro 2018).

But advancements in AR-15 ammunition, including heavier-grain bullets, are just the beginning of the "tinkering" with this semiautomatic platform that has changed the hunting viability of the gun. Hornady, a popular ammunition manufacturer and well-known innovator whose engineers have pushed the capabilities of standard ammunition rounds, offers the Hornady Black, a 75-grain bullet the company advertises as suitable for deer (Hornady n.d.a). In a 2016 *Time* magazine article, "Here Are 7 Animals Hunters Kill Using an AR-15" (Drabold), feral goats and pigs, coyotes, deer, and even elk are shown as having been killed (hunters generally prefer the term *harvested*) with a variety of configurations of the AR platform. Technically, the elk was harvested with a larger AR-10 platform shooting a larger-caliber bullet such as a .308. However, the deer was shot with a larger, .270 bullet that the hunter was able to use thanks to a few relatively simple modifications to his AR-15. An AR-15 is remarkably customizable; without getting into an excessive amount of detail, its primary components, an upper and lower receiver and the gun's barrel, can be disassembled and mated with other parts with ease. To convert the standard AR-15 shooting the 5.56/.223 bullet to shooting a .270 bullet the hunter would need a separate barrel, bolt (or a separate upper receiver), and separate magazines for the different bullets (Butler 2017). Recognizing the popularity of such modifications for higher-caliber ARs, manufacturers are moving into the market. A cover story in a recent issue of *Deer & Deer Hunting* magazine showcases "7 Black Rifles Built for

Whitetails" (Meitin 2019). "Black rifle" and "modern sporting rifle" are common terms AR enthusiasts use for the firearm in order to deflect the negative connotations that come with "AR" or "assault rifle." The author concludes, "ARs are no longer considered a political statement, but mainstream hunting tools for the average hunter" (66).

While a scholarly project researching the rhetoric at work as military-derived, semiautomatic weapons moved into the civilian market does not exist, the popularity and the entelechial push to keep advancing the capabilities of these firearms and their respective ammunition is clearly present. The patented technologies that made the AR platform a success for Colt expired years ago, and each year gun and ammunition companies compete to have their wares shoot farther, flatter (less arc or bullet drop as the projectile travels in a straight line), and more accurately, and do the damage the bullets are engineered to do.

INVISIBLE ACTANTS: STATE RULES AND REGULATIONS

Semiautomatic weapons—or, again, what are commonly reported as AR-15 assault-style weapons—are in fact legal for hunting in all fifty states, but the species hunters are permitted to pursue with those rifles vary from state to state (Snyder 2017). States such as Ohio, for example, limit hunting with an AR-15 to smaller game and are a popular choice for predator hunters in pursuit of coyotes. For deer, hunters may only use shotguns with single-ball or slug ammunition (10-, 12-, 20-gauge and .410) or rifles taking straight-walled cartridges (a minimum of .357 to a maximum of .50 caliber), all of which limit the effective range of the hunter. State regulations in Ohio also restrict the number of bullets a hunter may have in his or her firearm while in the field. Specifically, "Shotguns and straight-walled cartridge rifles can be loaded with no more than three shells in the chamber and magazine combined" (Ohio Department of Natural Resources 2018, 13). In the opening anecdote of this chapter, the shotgun I was hunting with was out of ammunition and didn't have a fourth shot because I was complying with this state regulation. This is a significant restriction, considering that AR-15s are often sold with 30-round magazines and common hunting shotguns will hold five shotgun shells.

Despite the literal origins of the name "shot" gun, deer hunters in Ohio are not permitted to load shotguns with shot pellets, including heavy-grade buckshot designed to take down deer at shorter ranges. Advancements in shotgun ballistics have also come a long way. When slug ammunition (a single ball of lead) was introduced for shotguns, it

Figure 3.1. Side view of a 12-gauge (left) and a 20-gauge (right) shotgun shell.

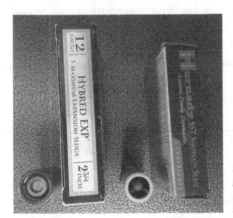

Figure 3.2. Top view of a lead 12-gauge shotgun shell with a blunt end (left) and a 20-gauge shotgun shell with a newer-style ballistic tip (right).

was fired out of a smoothbore shotgun barrel that provided plenty of power but poor accuracy and range. Manufacturers engineered rifled barrels (spiraling within the barrel that makes the bullet twist or spin for greater accuracy) for shotguns and even manufactured shotgun slugs with grooves on the slug itself to generate spin. They have since developed "ballistic tip" ammunition that makes shotgun projectile look and behave more like regular bullets rather than the more blunt-ended "slugs." Figure 3.1 shows an older 12-gauge shell and a newer 20-gauge shell, both legal for deer in Ohio. Figure 3.2 is a top view of the shells, showing differences in the 12-gauge slug and the 20-gauge projectiles.

Figure 3.3. Left to right: a .30-06 round, a .45-70 round, a 12-gauge shotgun shell, and a 20-gauge shotgun shell.

For context, when I started hunting more than twenty years ago, a 12-gauge, smoothbore shotgun loaded with slug ammunition was reliable out to fifty yards and seventy-five yards was considered far (as with all conversations about firearms in the hunting community, one would not need to search to find someone willing to dispute those yardages). By contrast, Hornady advertises its new 12-gauge, 300-grain slugs, which "feature the flattest trajectory on the market," claiming that they drop just 6.7 inches at two hundred yards (Hornady n.d.b). In other words, "Modern-day slug guns resemble their centerfire counterparts in looks and efficiency—capable of accuracy only dreamed of a decade or two ago" (Carpenter 2019, 64). Straight-walled cartridges also shoot heavy, shorter-range bullets and, like shotguns, traditionally have plenty of power to ethically harvest a deer. Figure 3.3 shows several rifle and shotgun shells used for hunting in different states. The .30-06 is legal for hunting in states like Pennsylvania, West Virginia, and Wisconsin, but not in others such as Ohio. The straight-walled .45-70 and the shotgun slugs are all legal in Ohio and could be used in other states, too, although the hunter would be giving up the superior range of the .30-06.

In contrast to the straight-walled casings, .223/5.56 and other rounds traditionally chambered for the AR-10 or AR-15 have a contoured shoulder where the casing tapers up and around the bullet. Figure 3.4 shows the larger .30-06 next to the smaller .223 and 5.56 rounds fired from an AR-15. Major advancements in ballistics and bullet construction reflect further tinkering that continues to push the effective ranges of all of these firearms and their projectiles.

There are books and guides for hunters dedicated to the many differences in range, capacity, and caliber, and certainly no shortage of debate

Figure 3.4. Left to right *a .30-06, a .223, and a 5.56.*

about the optimal hunting firearm and firearm calibration (Van Zwoll 2012). Different firearms can have substantially different effective ranges, and here "effective" is not understood just in terms of how far a projectile will travel but the range at which the projectile can effectively dispatch an animal. The National Shooting Sports Foundation hosts its annual SHOT Show each year, and reviews of the latest advancements from the firearms industry include ammunition: "Ammunition has gotten so much better in recent years, you might think that engineers have run out of room for improvement. Nope. The new ammo on hand at the 2019 SHOT show proves they're not done innovating" (Mann and Bourjaily 2018). Even with this cursory overview of firearm technology, from ammunition to the guns themselves, it becomes clear that new levels of efficiency are being reached each year.

FAIR CHASE AND ETHICAL HUNTING

Setting aside lengthy debates over the ethics of hunting as a practice and animal rights in general (Bronner 2008; Singer 1975; Swan 1995), there is consensus within the hunting community that animals should not be made to suffer unnecessarily and are entitled to a quick, ethical kill. State-sponsored hunter safety training programs reinforce this message. In Ohio, first-time license buyers must complete a hunter safety course that "is designed to instill a code of ethics and responsibility, as well as provide instruction on guns and how they work, types of ammunition, gun handling," and aspects of managing game after it has been shot (Ohio Department of Natural Resources 2018, 36). That focus on ethics is present at the national level, too. The Boone and Crockett Club, the "oldest wildlife conservation organization in North America," founded in 1887 by Theodore Roosevelt and George Bird Grinnell, "pioneered and established the principles of responsible, ethical, and sustainable use hunting known as Fair Chase" (Boone and Crockett Club. n.d.a). As defined by the club, the concept of fair chase "is the ethical, sportsman-like, and lawful pursuit and taking of any free-ranging wild, native North American big game animal in a manner that does not give the hunter an improper advantage over such animals" (Boone and Crocket Club n.d.b). Defining the boundaries of what constitutes "improper advantage" is, as described above, in part done by each state. That is, the type of firearm hunters are permitted to use will dictate how close they need to get to an animal to make an ethical shot. When I hunt deer in Wisconsin, I use a high-power, bolt-action rifle such as a .30-06 that shoots, in my case, a 155-grain bullet much farther and with a flatter trajectory than a shotgun or rifle using a straight-walled cartridge (see figure 3.3). When I hunt deer in Ohio, high-powered, necked cartridges like the .30-06 or other popular rounds (.243, .270, .308, 6.5mm, 7mm) are illegal, so I use a shotgun or lever-action rifle taking a straight-walled cartridge (see figure 3.2).

Why does one weapon offer improper advantage in one state and not the other? Some would argue that the flatter terrain of midwestern and western states makes it difficult to get closer to animals like deer, so longer-range rifles are necessary for success. The reverse of that argument doesn't seem to hold true, however, as states with more mountainous terrain like Pennsylvania and West Virginia do allow high-power rifle hunting. In states like Ohio that have a mixture of topography, a claim is often made for safety, especially considering that for a state of its size it has several major cities, including Cleveland, Columbus, Cincinnati, and Dayton. If public hunting land is available too close to cities, "the danger from errant bullets in populated areas is deemed too great" (Van Zwoll 2012, 3). Safety should be paramount, but it is too easy to find discrepancies between states to make cohesive claims regarding safety or terrain. For the purposes of this chapter, the significance is that the shotgun that was initially deemed legal, not affording an improper advantage, will continually increase in range and power in the coming years. The entelechial push remains persistent, if not relentless. The same certainly holds true for high-powered, necked cartridges, where there is even more opportunity for improvements.

While not within the scope of this chapter, there is much for rhetoricians studying technology to consider regarding other hunting advancements that may cross the line of improper advantage. Some states have already taken measures to ban drones for scouting and locating deer. When Michigan imposed the ban, it had the dual purpose of preventing hunters from using drones to their advantage and prohibiting animal activists from using drones to harass hunters while hunting (Oosting 2015). Other advancements in camouflage, scent control, range finding optics, smartphone apps to track weather conditions, including changes in wind direction and speed, all improve a hunter's chances of success. This chapter has also not touched on advancements in archery products, including the new popularity (and increased legality) of crossbows that can double the effective range of a standard compound bow. These technologies are rich opportunities for rhetoricians.

CLOSING

As the scholars cited in this chapter have noted, it remains critical that we continue our work to better understand the rhetorical nature of our technologies—especially, I would add, those technologies that are lethal and yet legal. Addressing what he sees as the common arhetorical and therefore "unacceptable" definitions of technology, Dave Clark notes that arhetorical approaches to technology mean that we can't imagine how "the tools themselves or their creation," rather than humans, are things capable of introducing "questions of ideology, morality, and ethics" (2010, 88). In other words, an arhetorical approach closes off the witnessing of our entelechial push for increased range and power as well as the vibrancy of a firearm as an actant. Although not writing specifically about guns, Clark adds, "We do, of course, have some baseline, cultural agreements about what technologies should be allowed (we cannot, as of today, buy a grenade launcher at WalMart)" (88). While this remains true, the shotgun I used for hunting years ago has a fraction of the range and power of current firearms.

I would argue that attempting to define the technology of firearms for hunting is more complicated because the value system by which the guns are judged is situated within the context of fair chase. That is, a semiautomatic firearm that shoots farther, with greater accuracy, and with less recoil, therefore providing easier target reacquisition, does not necessarily make it the superior hunting tool when considered within a certain ethical frame. The lethality, legality, and use of assault-style weapons remain issues in the public spotlight that continue to face scrutiny,

including in the form of satire. For example, an editorial cartoon by
Pulitzer Prize–winning artist Mike Luckovich (2012) shows a hunter
reclining in a chair in a room surrounded by taxidermied animals. The
animals have large holes, even chunks, taken out of them. There are
four orange and black disembodied legs, presumably of a tiger, standing on a pedestal and a wall-mounted deer's head with only portions of
a nose, eye, and antlers remaining. The caption over the man's head
reads, "I hunt with assault weapons." The cartoon at once argues the literal overkill of assault-style weapons employed in the act of hunting and
the absurdity of needing to fire multiple high-power rounds at an animal target when the assumption is that the animal would be claimed as
trophy, food, or both. The continued advance and our entelechial push
for increases in the range and power of firearms reveal much about us
as humans, including our willingness to tolerate and even enable what
are arguably absurd legal increases to range and power.

REFERENCES

American Rifleman Staff. 2018. "2018 American Rifleman Golden Bullseye Awards." https://www.americanrifleman.org/articles/2018/3/21/2018-american-rifleman-golden-bullseye-awards/.
Aristotle. 1998. *Nichomachean Ethics.* Translated by David Ross. Oxford: Oxford University Press.
Armalite. n.d. "History." https://armalite.com/history.
Bartocci, Christopher R. 2012. "The AR-15/M16: The Rifle That Was Never Supposed to Be." *Gun Digest,* July 16. https://gundigest.com/reviews/the-ar-16m16-the-rifle-that-was-never-supposed-to-be.
Bazerman, Charles. 1998. "The Production of Technology and the Production of Human Meaning." *Journal of Business and Technical Communication* 12 (3): 381–87.
Bazerman, Charles. 1999. *The Languages of Edison's Light.* New Baskerville, MA: MIT Press.
Bennett, Jane. 2005. "The Agency of Assemblages and the North American Blackout." *Public Culture* 17 (3): 445–65.
Bennett, Jane. 2010. *Vibrant Matter: A Political Ecology of Things.* Durham, NC: Duke University Press.
Boone and Crockett Club. n.d.a. "About B&C Club." https://www.boone-crockett.org/about/about_overview.asp?area=about.
Boone and Crockett Club. n.d.b. "Fair Chase Statement." https://www.boone-crockett.org/huntingEthics/ethics_fairchase.asp.
Burke, Kenneth. 1963. "Definition of Man." *Hudson Review* 16 (4): 491–514. https://doi.org/10.2307/3848123.
Burke, Kenneth. 1966. *Language as Symbolic Action: Essays on Life, Literature, and Method.* Berkeley: University of California Press.
Burke, Kenneth. 1969. *A Grammar of Motives.* Berkeley: University of California Press.
Burke, Kenneth. 1974. "Why Satire, with a Plan for Writing One." *Michigan Quarterly Review* 13 (4): 320–30.
Burke, Kenneth, and Malcolm Cowley. 1990. *The Selected Correspondence of Kenneth Burke and Malcolm Cowley, 1915–1981.* Edited by Jay Paul. Berkeley: University of California Press.

Butler, Brandon. 2017. "How to Set Up an AR-15 for Hunting." *Realtree*, May 12. https://www.realtree.com/guns-and-shooting/articles/how-to-set-up-an-ar-15-for-hunting.

Bronner, Simon J. 2008. *Killing Tradition: Inside Hunting and Animal Rights Controversies.* Lexington: University Press of Kentucky.

Carpenter, Tom. 2019. "A Slug Gun Hunter's Journey." *Deer & Deer Hunting* 42 (10): 61–4.

Clark, Dave. 2010. "Shaped and Shaping Tools: The Rhetorical Nature of Technical Communication Technologies." In *Digital Literacy for Technical Communication: 21st Century Theory and Practice*, edited by Rachel Spilka, 85–102. New York: Routledge.

Collins, Keith, and David Yaffe-Bellany. April 1, 2020. "About 2 Million Guns Were Sold in the US as Virus Fears Spread." *New York Times*, April 1, 2020. https://www.nytimes.com/interactive/2020/04/01/business/coronavirus-gun-sales.html.

Drabold, Will. 2016. "Here Are 7 Animals Hunters Kill Using an AR-15." *Time*, July 6. http://time.com/4390506/gun-control-ar-15-semiautomatic-rifles/.

Elinson, Zusha, and Cameron McWhirter. Aug. 30, 2018. "The 'Trump Slump': With a Friend in the White House, Gun Sales Sag." *Wall Street Journal*, August 30, 2018. https://www.wsj.com/articles/the-trump-slump-with-a-friend-in-the-white-house-gun-sales-sag-1535640346.

Gandel, Stephen. 2021. "Gun Sales Hit All-Time High amid Flurry of Mass Shootings." *CBS News*, April 21, 2021. https://www.cbsnews.com/news/gun-sales-on-pace-to-hit-new-record-in-2021/.

Hawk, Byron. 2007. *A Counter-History of Composition: Toward Methodologies of Complexity.* Pittsburgh: University of Pittsburgh Press.

Hill, Ian. 2009. "'The Human Barnyard' and Kenneth Burke's Philosophy of Technology." *The Kenneth Burke Journal* 5 (2). https://www.kbjournal.org/ian_hill.

Hornady. n.d.a. "Hornady Black." https://www.hornady.com/ammunition/rifle/5.56-nato-75-gr-interlock-hd-sbr-black#!/.

Hornady. n.d.b. "Hornady SST Slugs." https://www.hornady.com/ammunition/shotgun/12-ga-sst-300-gr-ftx-slug#!/.

Keene, D. 2013. "The AR-15: The Gun Liberals Love to Hate." *Human Events: Powerful Conservative Voices*. http://humanevents.com/2013/01/02/the-ar-15-the-gun-liberals-love-to-hate/.

Lindsay, Stan. 1999. "Waco and Andover: An Application of Kenneth Burke's Psychotic Entelechy." *Quarterly Journal of Speech* 85 (3): 268–84.

Luckovich, Mike. 2012. "Mike Luckovich's Editorial Cartoons," December 28. Cartoonist Group. http://www.cartoonistgroup.com/store/add.php?iid=91831.

Lynch, John A., and William J. Kinsella. 2013. "The Rhetoric of Technology as a Rhetorical Technology." *Poroi* 9 (1): 1–6. https://doi.org/10.13008/2151-2957.1152.

Mann, Richard, and Phil Bourjaily. 2018. "Best New Ammo from the 2019 Shot Show." *Field & Stream*, January 24. https://www.fieldandstream.com/best-new-ammo-from-2019-shot-show.

Massaro, Philip. 2018. "5.56 NATO vs. .223 Rem.: What's the Difference?" *NRA Shooting Illustrated*, July 28, 2018. https://www.shootingillustrated.com/articles/2018/7/28/556-nato-vs-223-rem-whats-the-difference/.

Meitin, Patrick. 2019. "7 Black Rifles Built for Whitetails." *Deer & Deer Hunting* 43 (1): 62–68.

Miller, Carolyn. 1998. "Learning from History: World War II and the Culture of High Technology." *Journal of Business and Technical Communication* 12 (3): 288–314.

Miller, Carolyn. 2010. Foreword to *Rhetorics and Technologies: New Directions in Writing and Communication*, edited by Stuart Selber, ix–xii. Columbia: University of South Carolina Press.

Myre, Greg. 2018. "A Brief History of the AR-15." *NPR*, February 28, 2018. https://www.npr.org/2018/02/28/588861820/a-brief-history-of-the-ar-15.

Ohio Department of Natural Resources. 2018. *Ohio Hunting and Trapping Regulations, 2018–2019.* http://wildlife.ohiodnr.gov/portals/wildlife/pdfs/hunting/2018-19%20 Ohio%20Hunting%20Regs_Web.pdf.

Oosting, Johnathan. 2015. "Michigan Bans Drone Hunting, Hunter Harassment with New Laws Signed by Gov. Rick Snyder." *Michigan Live.* https://www.mlive.com/lansing -news/2015/04/michigan_bans_drone_hunting_hu.html.

Peters, Justin. 2016. "The NRA Claims the AR-15 Is Useful for Hunting and Home Defense. Not Exactly." *Slate.* https://slate.com/news-and-politics/2016/06/gun-control-ar-15 -rifle-the-nra-claims-the-ar-15-rifle-is-for-hunting-and-home-defense-not-exactly.html.

Selber, Stuart A., ed. 2010. *Rhetorics and Technologies: New Directions in Writing and Communication.* Columbia: University of South Carolina Press.

Singer, Peter. 1975. *Animal Liberation.* New York: HarperCollins.

Snyder, Myles. 2017. "Game Commission Won't Allow Semiautomatic Rifles for Big Game." *ABC News.* https://www.abc27.com/news/game-commission-wont-allow-semiautomatic -rifles-for-big-game_20180313093128103/1037166241.

Swan, James A. 1995. *In Defense of Hunting.* San Francisco: Harper San Francisco.

Tactical-Life. 2014. "Mr. Patriot Ordnance: A Chat with Frank DeSomma." https://www .tactical-life.com/firearms/mr-patriot-ordnance-a-chat-with-frank-desomma/.

Van Zwoll, Wayne. 2012. *Deer Rifles and Cartridges: A Complete Guide to All Hunting Situations.* New York: Constable & Robinson.

Wickman, Chad. 2012. "Rhetoric, Technê, and the Art of Scientific Inquiry." *Rhetoric Review* 31 (1): 21–40. doi: 10.1080/07350198.2012.630953.

Winner, Langdon. 1980. "Do Artifacts Have Politics?" *Daedalus* 109 (1): 121–36.

4

THE GUN AS (RACE/GENDER) *TECHNÊ*

Lisa M. Corrigan

On November 17, 1871, a group of Union army veterans led by William C. Church and George W. Wingate founded the National Rifle Association (NRA), whose mission was to train men to be better marksmen. Church, a former reporter for the *New York Times*, supported strong gun control, but after the turn of the twentieth century the organization's mission began to evolve toward more permissive ecology around gun ownership and usage in ways that have substantially shaped racial violence. Since the 1970s, as a response to civil rights legislation and the emergence of Black Power politics, the NRA has pushed for more extremist views on gun ownership and use of force. The increasing hostility to government regulation in the 1970s amplified the NRA's message, particularly in its work to repeal the Gun Control Act of 1968 as a response to the assassinations of President John F. Kennedy, Martin Luther King Jr., and presidential candidate Robert F. Kennedy.[1]

After the election of Ronald Reagan in 1980, the NRA's role in public life shifted dramatically as the organization began to exert itself in Washington to challenge norms around gun ownership and usage. Alexander DeConde notes that Reagan "quickly became the first [president] to assume openly what appeared to many as the role of popular spokesman for such an organization," boasting "of his ties to the National Rifle Association" (2001, 213). Working with the NRA to weaken and then eventually dissolve the Bureau of Alcohol, Tobacco, and Firearms (BATF), Reagan underfunded and undercut the organization, allowing it to exist only as a weak enforcement of gun laws without the teeth or resources it needed. Additionally, in 1981, after Republicans took over the Senate and South Carolina senator Strom Thurmond became chair of the Judiciary Committee, it became hard for Senator Ted Kennedy to block the NRA's anti–gun control efforts (Davidson 1998, 54). Attorney General Edwin Meese ushered in legal conservatives from the Federalist Society and conservative think tanks, seeking out

https://doi.org/10.7330/9781646422159.c004

judicial nominees committed to originalism in their constitutional perspectives, particularly on the Second Amendment. During this period, the NRA sought to expand individual gun ownership by weakening gun control and by expanding gun sales.[2]

By 2000, the NRA's lobbying efforts prompted a major shift in the Department of Justice after the Supreme Court's decision in *Bush v. Gore* and after George W. Bush's presidential inauguration. Bush's attorney general, John Ashcroft, wrote a memorandum to the NRA announcing a major policy shift in the administration.[3] Where the Department of Justice (DOJ) had historically endorsed the idea that the Second Amendment primarily protected the existence of militias, Ashcroft's memo, written in response to the Fifth Circuit's case *United States v. Emerson* (2001), echoed the NRA's interpretation of the Second Amendment as an almost unabridged individual's right to bear arms, though it was tempered by an affirmation of some "reasonable restrictions" on this right. Fundamentally, the Ashcroft memorandum exacerbated confusion surrounding the phrase "reasonable restrictions" in *Emerson*, but the existence of this individualist interpretation is not surprising given the tremendous donations the NRA contributed to the Bush campaign, accounting for nearly one-third of all outside group donations to the campaign fund. Likewise, the NRA spent heavily on key Senate races to provide Bush with a comfortable majority to expand its vision of the Second Amendment as a constitutional guarantee of the individual's right to bear arms (Winkler 2011, 59; *Los Angeles Times* 2001).

The NRA's coziness with Reagan had marked a profound political and rhetorical change in the operationalization of the Second Amendment that allowed for broader interpretations of lethal self-defense in the 1980s. By the time of George W. Bush's election in 2000, the NRA's influence in Washington had prompted a radical departure from the "duty to retreat" doctrine (Light 2017, 47). "Duty to retreat" generally meant that a gun owner had a responsibility to avoid the possibility of injury or death in the pursuit of self-defense. Defended most famously in Richard Maxwell Brown's *No Duty to Retreat: Violence and Values in American History and Society* (1991), the end of the duty to retreat doctrine changed the relationship between gun owners and victims of gun violence. Light documents how this shift was an extension of the post-Reconstruction era's "white backlash in response to Black male citizenship and enfranchisement," which "represented the convergence of sex panic and race panic" (2017, 47). The DOJ's change in stance on self-defense with lethal force coupled with the kinds of race and sex panic that have motivated racial politics, especially in the South since Reconstruction, paved the way for new legislation called Stand Your Ground (SYG) laws. "On their surface, SYG laws provide legal justification and criminal immunity to *any* person who uses deadly force in self-defense" (8). In addition, SYG laws emphasize "each person's right to defend one's self and property from criminal violation" (8). In tandem with its support of Bush's campaign and key Senate races, the NRA's dismissal of duty to retreat was coupled with its pressure on then governor of Florida, Jeb Bush, who signed the first Stand Your Ground bill in 2005 to undermine the duty to retreat doctrine and expand the use of lethal force.

To understand the effects of this rhetorical and political shift in gun control policy, I use Martin Heidegger's essay "The Question Concerning Technology" ([1954] 2013) to provide a reading of the gun as a form of *technê* (or technology) in American public discourse, particularly after the advent of Stand Your Ground laws. I suggest that in reading the gun as a technê, we see how the rhetorical and material move from the duty to retreat to stand your ground demonstrates what Heidegger calls "a mode of revealing"—in this case, of a relationship between the gun owner and his or her gun (see also Ballentine's chapter 3 in this volume). First, I use Heidegger's arguments regarding technê to understand how the meme of the gun functions as both an instrumentality and a poetics. I then turn to Cheryl Harris's (1993) work to chart how the gun operates as a racialized and gendered technê and to uncover how the gun's technê is one premised on both whiteness and property (see also Gage's chapter 10 in this volume). In this case, the gun reveals *how* whiteness "gets things done," what Heidegger calls "instrumentality," and how it forms part of the basis of our knowledge of both whiteness and sex/gender. Finally, I conclude with an assessment of the gun's technê as a fundamental assertion of ontological Being for white people and as a tool of erasure or anti-Being for people of color (particularly Black people) in the United States. I do this through an analysis of Stand Your Ground laws to understand how these laws undermine Black political participation by asserting the gun as an a priori instrumentality where the gun is an extension of *whiteness as property*.

My interest in this racialized and gendered relationship between technê and the gun began with my work against bills in the Arkansas state legislature supporting open carry on college campuses between 2011 and 2019. These bills were part of a larger national strategy by the NRA, much of which is chronicled in Stephen K. Boss's *Guns and College Homicide: The Case to Prohibit Firearms on Campus* (2019).[4] As one of three founders of Arkansans against Guns on Campus and the statewide architect of the opposition to those bills, our innovative digital lobbying (especially on Twitter) and our success in amending and defeating these bills led to invitations for me to consult on campus gun bill opposition in Texas, Missouri, Florida, Indiana, and Nebraska. Additionally, in 2019, our organization unseated the Arkansas legislator sponsoring the campus gun bills. Since much of my academic work concerns anti-Black violence, political assassinations, and police brutality, this theoretical assessment of technê fills in some gaps in my previous work to document how the gun itself functions as an extension and protection of whiteness.[5]

TECHNÊ AND INSTRUMENTAL DISCOURSE

The relation between *epistêmê* and *technê* defines much philosophical thought, ranging from Xenophon to Plotinus. Here, the Greeks debated the distinction(s) between theory and practice that have created our base of knowledge. Where the epistêmê is primarily understood as knowledge (as opposed to public opinion, or doxa/δόξα) and the epistemic is concerned with *how* we know what we know, debates about technê are about craft, applied practice, or what we call praxis. In "The Question concerning Technology" ([1954] 2013), Heidegger takes up the Greek debates to articulate two interrelated points central to understanding how technology operates. The first concerns technê and its relationship to instrumentality (the process by which a technology is used) and the second concerns its role in the arts as a part of *poiesis* (or poetry), where a maker brings into existence a new idea or social good through a process he calls "bringing forth." For Heidegger, technê's importance lies in its ability to reveal truths about *knowledge.* Modern technology "is a means to an end. That is why the instrumental conception of technology conditions every attempt to bring man into the right relation to technology. Everything depends on our manipulating technology in the proper manner as a means" (5). Heidegger adds, "Technology itself is a contrivance, or, in Latin, an *instrumentum*" (5). In this sense, instrumentality is an essential component of the technological because it is about disciplining human relationship to the technology as that technology reveals truths about us: our desires, ambitions, goals, and relation to others.

Heidegger's writing on the instrumentality of technology emerges against the backdrop the first and second Industrial Revolutions: large-scale machinery, steam and water power, mechanized factories, machine tools, and the rise of factory farming. The widespread use of electricity succeeded these innovations, revolutionizing production and increasing consumption. Here, cradled in the Industrial Revolution, "the empire of guns" was forged (Satia 2018). Documenting the manufacturing of guns central to the development of industrial capitalism, Priya Satia showcases just how the demand for personal firearms and military munitions provided the rationale for a massive modern arms industry on the European continent and in the United States to help expand and consolidate empire at the turn of the twentieth century. The use of technology, according to Heidegger, was what defined humans, particularly in this period of rapid technological expansion.

But if instrumentality is so crucial in defining the technological, then mastery is paramount in understanding how technology shapes us. Heidegger explains, "We will master [technology]. The will to mastery becomes all the more urgent the more technology threatens to slip from human control" (1954, 5). This notion of mastery is central to understanding the relationship, especially in the United States, between white people (men) and their guns. For Heidegger, the central understanding of mastery pivots on the relationship between instrumentality and causality. Heidegger explains, "What technology is, when represented as a means, discloses itself when we trace instrumentality back to fourfold causality" (6). For clarity's sake I will enumerate the four major causes that scaffold causality: (1) the *causa materialis*, the material, the matter out of which, for example, a silver chalice is made; (2) the *causa formalis*, the form, the shape into which the material enters; (3) the *causa finalis*, the end, for example, the sacrificial rite in relation to which the chalice required is determined as to its form and matter; (4) the *causa efficiens*, which brings about the effect that is the finished, actual chalice, in this instance, the silversmith (6).

In thinking through technology as matter, form, sacrificial rite, and artist/maker, Heidegger understands technology as a process through which relations are forged. In the case of the gun, its causa materialis is obviously the previous metals from which it is shaped. The causa formalis is physically the kind of gun that the metal is fashioned into, but ontologically it is the shape of terror or strength. The causa finalis is certainly death, for the gun is meant to kill. Its function is to procure death. And its causa efficiens is the gun owner/potential killer. In considering the relationship between instrumentality and causality, it seems that when Heidegger asks about causal character, he is asking for the essence of the technology as the space of interrogation for its relationship to humankind. Mastery of the gun in the "empire of guns" is what defines the human.

Technological mastery was a hallmark of the Third Reich and the Allied war machine. And while Heidegger is often philosopher non grata in the academy (see Cohen 2009; Horn 2009) due to the Third Reich's use of his work and his support of Nazism, it is precisely the connections that he made among technology, Aryan whiteness, and power that are salient for an analysis that sees technê as always already *white* (see Rothman 2014; Zielinski 2016).[6] That is, *whiteness* is perhaps the most important framework for understanding technê as the production of power through nationalism or empire, particularly in the West, because whiteness is what the Third Reich was attempting to control and (re)produce through explicitly anti-Semitic violence, philosophy, and pseudoscience.[7] Heidegger's description of the instrumentality of technê sees technology as human activity that defines humanness in particularly white ways, both toward and against people, objects, tools, and art. In Heidegger's own defense of National Socialism as an ideal (even long after World War II had ended), his original discussion of agricultural technology was tremendously indifferent to suffering, as this passage from "The Question concerning Technology" demonstrates: "Agriculture is now a mechanized food industry, in essence the same as the manufacturing of corpses in gas chambers and extermination camps, the same as the blockade and the starvation of nations, the same as the production of hydrogen bombs" ([1954] 2013, 15; see also Rockmore 1991, 214; Gordon 2014). This comparison between factory farming and gas chambers demonstrates a supreme indifference to human suffering at the hands of technology designed to promote "metaphysical racism," as Tom Rockmore has argued (1991, 242).

Heidegger's extended discussion of the "calculative Jew" stereotype has been largely critiqued as the racial mode of engagement with technologies designed to repress Jewish Germans (most notably in Wendland 2018, 160–61). Rockmore adds, "Heidegger's failure to denounce, or even to acknowledge, Nazi practice can be interpreted as an oblique resistance to the practice consequence of his theoretical inquiry" (1991, 241). Heidegger's discussion of this relationship between dominance and technology is strikingly silent on the genocide of the Holocaust, demonstrating Heidegger's complete, in Rockmore's words, "inability to comprehend the Holocaust through his theory of technology" (241). Heidegger, then, is an important midcentury touchstone for understanding how white masculinity can't or won't see its production/usage of technology as instrumental in creating racial hierarchies demarcated by the violent tools of the age of machines: guns, gas chambers, and bombs. Heidegger's technologies provided the contours of whiteness and empire in the middle of the twentieth century in ways that the handgun or the assault weapon do today.

Where Harris cites "whiteness as the unspoken center" of debates about racial policies like "affirmative action" (1993, 1715), I argue that the same is true for gun policies. As a technology of self, the gun highlights whiteness as a mode of instrumentality because whiteness itself *is* property. As a legacy of slavery and both de jure and de facto racial segregation, Harris writes, the concept of a "protectable property interest in whiteness" is pervasive in discourse surrounding gun ownership, permitting, and usage that found legal footing in the pursuit of escaped slaves (1715). Mark Lause's (2005) history of the NRA's political lobbying on the expansion of slavery, liberal homesteading laws, and fugitive slave catching demonstrates how whiteness was an essential feature of the NRA's positions on slavery and property. Harris suggests that equal protection jurisprudence, while opposing Jim Crow, nonetheless reinforced whiteness as property, Blackness as property-less, and Black people as property, particularly as extrajudicial lynching attempted to contain Black political participation after Reconstruction. Although Harris uses *Plessy v. Ferguson* and *Brown vs. Board of Education* to elucidate how status property and modern property law have emerged as racial constructs, I'm interested in analyzing Stand Your Ground laws to understand how gun ownership is a similarly central place where property, whiteness, and violence converge to shape the contours of modern citizenship.

STAND YOUR GROUND LAWS AND HEIDEGGERIAN TECHNÊ

After the election of George W. Bush in 2000, the legislative strategy of the NRA heavily promoted the adoption of Stand Your Ground laws. The NRA's Institute for Legislative Action (NRA-ILA) defines SYG laws thus: "Stand Your Ground laws, correctly understood, focus on the narrow issue of whether and to what extent a person who would otherwise have a right to self-defense forfeits that right by not first attempting to flee the confrontation" (2014). Stand Your Ground laws emerge from the rhetorical space where whiteness *is* property, particularly in southern states where racial animus has been part of the old and new plantation economies and where nineteenth-century gun culture calcified around slave catching. As an extrajudicial model of punishment, Stand Your Ground laws allow the gun owner to kill on sight anyone threatening them or their property. As Steve Martinot has argued, white democratic exclusion "originates in a paranoia, a sense of white solidarity, and a valorization of disenfranchising violence" (2010, 129). As the NRA expanded its presence in American life throughout the twentieth century, it embraced frontier masculinity in the face of Reconstruction, early women's suffrage momentum, and immigration. As Scott Melzer (2009) has documented in his expansive history of the NRA, white masculinity was an *organizing principle* of the NRA as it responded to the changing norms of citizenship, nationalism, and civic participation. In fact, the imperative to interpolate *the nation itself* as a white space is a colonial practice, what Aileen Moreton-Robinson (2015) has called "the white possessive," which I see as a practice of understanding all positive technological advancement as the product of whiteness, with white people the technological beneficiaries. Cheryl Harris explains, "Rights in property are contingent on, intertwined with, and conflated with race." She adds, "Whiteness and property share a common premise—a conceptual nucleus—a right to exclude"; after Jim Crow ended and segregation was legally prohibited, those privileges marked "whiteness as property evolved into a more modern form through the law's ratification of the settled expectations of relative white privilege as a legitimate and natural baseline" (1993, 1714). Built from property ownership, privilege and domination are modes of power that create and destroy identity, particularly racial identity.

The first Stand Your Ground law was passed in Florida in 2005 after tremendous NRA pressure on Governor Jeb Bush. "Over a nine-year period, the organization gave more than $73,000 in campaign donations to the 43 Florida legislators who backed the law," wrote Andy Kroll. "That money was buttressed by intense lobbying activity and additional funds spent by the NRA in support of the bill's introduction and passage" (2012).

Passage of the SYG law in Florida revolved around the case of James Workman. Workman, a white seventy-seven-year old retiree who was living with his wife in his RV after Hurricane Ivan destroyed his Florida home, shot and killed a man who reportedly invaded his RV during the night. The man, Rodney Cox, was a white man from North Carolina and a Federal Emergency Management Agency worker who had been dispatched during the relief effort. According to news reports, the NRA used the Workman case as a lightning rod, in effect pushing for greater license to kill in the name of self-defense and substantially increasing the number of justifiable homicides in the states that have passed SYG laws since (Lave 2013). The confluence of environmental catastrophe, racial panic, and white gun ownership propelled the case in the public imaginary.

While the Florida law has been a hotbed of controversy, particularly since the 2012 killing of Black teenager Trayvon Martin, SYG laws have historically been de facto, especially in the South, where the geography of race has been marked by the transition from plantation economy to prison-industrial complex. SYG laws have increased the number of homicides in Florida exponentially since their passage. For example, a study released in August 2013 by the Urban Institute reported that prior to the introduction of Stand your Ground laws, only 9 percent of white-on-Black shootings were considered justified (Rowman). Since 2005, however, in states that have adopted SYG laws, 17 percent of white-on-Black shootings were adjudged justified. This compares to only 1 percent of Black-on-white shootings in the same places. Indeed, after the passage of SYG laws in Florida, 73 percent of those individuals killing a Black person walked away with *no penalty*. This compares to 59 percent of those killing a white person (Martin 2012). And, in Florida alone, homicides increased 22 percent in the decade after SYG passed (Rapaport 2017). The data demonstrates how changes in the NRA's doctrinal interpretation of the Second Amendment affected laws about gun ownership and usage, suggesting that the gun functions as a modern technê of whiteness, as gun owners claim self-defense in targeting people of color, especially Black people.

Rhetorically central to the normalization of the gun as a technê of whiteness (and masculinity) has been the "Good Guy with a Gun" narrative (see also Roberts-Miller's chapter 1 in this volume). NRA vice president Wayne LaPierre's assertion that "the only thing that stops a bad guy with a gun is a good guy with a gun" circulates as a defining rhetorical shift in SYG discourse.[8] This is, in part, because the shift from "duty to retreat" to "stand your ground" is a predictive one; it asks the gun owner to take up a position before an encounter even happens. Stand Your Ground laws offered the notion that he who is "right" (i.e., always the gun owner) should not have to retreat from those that challenge him, calcifying white gun ownership as white (and male) truth. From a Heideggarian perspective, this is precisely how the gun works as technê: it overdetermines how the technology defines the self in relation to others. Harris argues that "the law has accorded 'holders' of whiteness the same privileges and benefits accorded holders of other types of property," in this case, holders of guns and gun permits (1993, 1731). I argue that inalienable property rights have been conferred upon the gun as a *symbol of whiteness*, but also as a badge of masculinity. In this case, given the rates of gun ownership, guns' status in the courts, and their use (especially in the South) as a tool to secure property and safeguard white generational wealth, the gun functions as a racial and gendered technology. Thus does *gun law* serve to reify white supremacy as the driving force of *property law* and as a rationale for white nationalism (see

Dunbar-Ortiz 2018). The gun becomes the technology that elevates or subordinates rights based on the presence of whiteness and the way in which it is exercised through lethal force.

But this "good [white] guy with a gun" myth is about the production of a future [white] self—articulated through an encounter with one's own gun. Margaret J. Radin explains this kind of relationship, "If an object you now control is bound up in your future plans or in your anticipation of your future self, and it is partly these plans for your own continuity that make you a person, then your personhood depends on the realization of these expectations" (1982, 968n3). This is because personhood is articulated through scaffolding (racializing) privilege and avoiding punishment. "When the law recognizes, either implicitly or explicitly, the settled expectations of whites built on the privileges and benefits produced by white supremacy, it acknowledges and reinforces a property interest in whiteness that reproduces Black subordination" (Harris 1993, 1731). The production and reproduction of Black subordination creates what Achille Mbembe has called "necropolitics," where technological advancement is premised upon Black death as a precondition for the constitution of whiteness (2003). Thus, the erasure of their Black and brown citizenship provides a legal (Dayan 2011) as well as rhetorical strategy capable of depicting Black and brown residents of states with Stand Your Ground laws as legitimate targets of white supremacist violence. The NRA even published a guide for "how to survive the aftermath of a lawful self-defense shooting," suggesting that gun owners are already always potential victims, despite the fact that they are exercising lethal force.[9]

Stand Your Ground laws are important primarily because they bring into focus how the gun functions as a racial technê, demystifying the relationship between instrumentality and causality and highlighting anti-Black disposability as a feature of the nation. As Patricia J. Williams has written:

> The history of the right to bear arms is shaped by exclusionary privilege based on race and gender. It is almost exclusively white men who may "reasonably" carry firearms to protests outside Target or political conventions. It is almost exclusively white men who do not need to retreat from domestic disputes while on ground deemed "theirs." Nonwhites and women, however, are much less likely to be able to walk through the world with assault rifles . . . and not be mowed down for that reason alone—either by police or the idealized citizen-savior. (2018)

The "Good Guy with a Gun" myth ensconces whiteness into the gun's technê as a means of undermining white accountability and Black citizenship.

CONCLUSION

The scholarly studies on Stand Your Ground laws demonstrate that they clearly increase homicide rates, particularly of people of color (Spitzer 2015), and there is no debate among race scholars that SYG laws enshrine anti-Black gun violence as justifiable homicide. But beyond this, a Heideggarian account of the relationship of the gun to SYG laws is useful because it explains why gun ownership and usage is important as the nation "browns," becoming demographically less white (Stavans 2002). It is precisely because the gun is a primary technology through which whiteness and the license to kill can be affirmed that it can be embraced as a way of managing whiteness.

Heidegger's account of technê helps to demystify the processes by which the gun has come to be such a revered and reviled technological force, not because of the gun *itself* but because of what the gun reveals about, in Heidegger's terms, "the essence" of man. A rhetorical and phenomenological account of Stand Your Ground laws as an expression of this essence of man and his gun highlights how the gun creates a stark contrast in permissible orientations toward Being for white people (especially but not only gun owners) and Black people, who are at the mercy of the kinds of justifiable aggression that cannot be and are not disproved in court. This analysis of the gun, evidenced more clearly in Stand Your Ground laws, demonstrates how the gun reveals and conceals power and identity as white men aggressively presence themselves through a biopolitical erasure of Black people.

With the NRA's expansive political power at the turn of the century moving the country away from "duty to retreat" and toward "stand your ground" there is a rhetorical shift not just in how the gun functions as a historically situated technê but also how it is changing in response to ideas about whiteness, as the alt-Right and modern neo-Nazis occupy public space in a way that they haven't since the early twentieth century when Heidegger was writing his early polemics about technê. As white resentment of people of color grows (see Metzl 2019; Sundstrom 2008), legal and rhetorical rationales of white citizen-saviors will enshrine extrajudicial killing as a means of managing white anxiety about loss of privilege in ways that look similar to the SYG debates. Whether the new white supremacists are similar to the old white supremacists is a question fundamentally concerned with technê. Finally, the kinds of discursive turns like those in the SYG debates indicate material shifts in power that are ultimately located within technology and in racialized and gendered technê.

NOTES

The author wishes to thank William K. Reeder for talking through some of the early ideas for this essay.

1.   That act banned all mail-order sales of rifles and shotguns and prohibited most felons, drug users, and people found mentally incompetent to buy guns.

2.   While skirmishes over the Brady Bill in 1988 and the assault weapons ban debates beginning in 1990 helped to invigorate gun control efforts, they ultimately propelled the NRA's lobbying efforts by increasing the profile of the organization and highlighting its perspective that gun control amounts to harassment of gun owners rather than efforts to seriously curb violent crime (Winkler 2011, 36).

3.   Hereafter referred to as the Ashcroft memorandum, this letter praises the decision in *United States v. Emerson*. As Ashcroft explains, "The Department can and will continue to defend vigorously the constitutionality, under the Second Amendment, of all existing federal firearms laws. The Department has a solemn obligation both to enforce federal law and to respect the constitutional rights guaranteed to Americans" (2001).

4.   I'm deeply grateful for the camaraderie and talent of my colleagues Stephen K. Boss and Sidney Burris over these years as well as for the pro bono political talents of Angie Maxwell.

5.   See Corrigan 2016, 2020.

6.   Heidegger's recently published "black notebooks" have demonstrated that his relationship to Nazism was not naive but rather vociferous. See *Open Culture* 2019.

7.   Notably, a similar process was consolidating white hegemony in the United States during World War II as Jim Crow's segregation expanded, Japanese internment camps proliferated, and the atomic bomb was perfected.

8.   This phrase is a meme that was repeated throughout NRA discourse during the Obama administration. See, for example, Overby 2012.

9.   The NRA's Carry Guard program, called "Surviving the Aftermath," asks, "Surviving a Self-Defense Shooting Is only the Beginning. Will You Know What to Do in the Seconds that Follow?" (NRA Carry Guard n.d.)

REFERENCES

Ashcroft, John. 2001. "Memorandum to All United States' Attorneys." Washington, DC: Office of the Attorney General.

Boss, Stephen K. 2019. *Guns and College Homicide: The Case to Prohibit Firearms on Campus.* New York: McFarland.

Brown, Richard Maxwell. 1991. *No Duty to Retreat: Violence and Values in American History and Society.* Norman: University of Oklahoma Press.

Cohen, Patricia. 2009. "An Ethical Question: Does Heidegger Deserve a Place among Philosophers?" *New York Times*, November 9, 2009. https://www.nytimes.com/2009/11/09/books/09philosophy.html?_r=2&em.

Corrigan, Lisa M. 2016. *Prison Power: How Prison Influenced the Movement for Black Liberation.* Jackson: University Press of Mississippi.

Corrigan, Lisa M. 2020. *Black Feelings: Race, Affect, and the Long Sixties.* Jackson: University Press of Mississippi.

Davidson, Osha Gray. 1998. *Under Fire: The NRA and the Battle for Gun Control.* Iowa City: University of Iowa Press.

Dayan, Colin. 2011. *The Law Is a White Dog: How Legal Rituals Make and Unmake Persons.* Princeton, NJ: Princeton University Press.

DeConde, Alexander. 2001. *Gun Violence in America: The Struggle for Control.* Boston: Northeastern University Press.

Dunbar-Ortiz, Roxanne. 2018. *Loaded: A Disarming History of the Second Amendment.* San Francisco: City Lights.

Gordon, Peter E. 2014. "Heidegger and the Gas Chambers." *New York Review of Books,* December 4, 2014. https://www.nybooks.com/articles/2014/12/04/heidegger-and-gas-chambers/.

Harris, Cheryl I. 1993. "Whiteness as Property." *Harvard Law Review* 106 (8): 1709–91.

Heidegger, Martin. (1954) 2013. "The Question concerning Technology." In *The Question concerning Technology and Other Essays,* 3–35. New York: Harper Perennial.

Horn, Heather. 2009. "What to Do with Nazi Philosophers?" *Atlantic,* November 11, 2021. https://www.theatlantic.com/entertainment/archive/2009/11/what-to-do-with-nazi-philosophers/347607/.

Kroll, Andy. 2012. "The Money Trail behind Florida's Notorious Gun Law." *Mother Jones,* March 29, 2012. https://www.motherjones.com/politics/2012/03/nra-stand-your-ground-trayvon-martin/.

Lause, Mark. 2005. *Young America: Land, Labor, and Republican Community.* Urbana: University of Illinois Press.

Lave, Tamara Rice. 2013. "Shoot to Kill: A Critical Look at Stand Your Ground Laws." *University of Miami Law Review* 67 (4): 827–60.

Light, Caroline E. 2017. *Stand Your Ground: A History of America's Love Affair with Lethal Self-Defense.* Boston: Beacon.

Los Angeles Times. 2001. "NRA Gets Money's Worth." https://www.latimes.com/archives/la-xpm-2001-jul-04-me-18459-story.html.

Martin, Susan Taylor. 2012. "Florida 'Stand Your Ground' Law Yields Some Shocking Outcomes Depending on How Law Is Applied." *Tampa Bay Times,* March 29, 2012. http://www.tampabay.com/news/publicsafety/crime/florida-stand-your-ground-law-yields-some-shocking-outcomes-depending-on/1233133.

Martinot, Steve. 2010. *The Machinery of Whiteness: Studies in the Structure of Racialization.* Philadelphia: Temple University Press.

Mbembe, Achille. 2003. "Necropolitics." *Public Culture* 15 (1): 11–40.

Melzer, Scott. 2009. *Gun Crusaders: The NRA's Culture War.* New York: New York University Press.

Metzl, Jonathan. 2019. *Dying of Whiteness: How the Politics of Racial Resentment Is Killing America's Heartland.* New York: Hachette.

Moreton-Robinson, Aileen. 2015. *The White Possessive: Property, Power, and Indigenous Sovereignty.* Minneapolis: University of Minnesota Press.

National Rifle Association Institute for Legislative Action. 2014. "Stand Your Ground." https://www.nraila.org/articles/20140201/stand-your-ground.

NRA Carry Guard. n.d. "Surviving the Aftermath." https://www.nracarryguard.com/aftermath/.

Open Culture. 2015. "Heidegger's 'Black Notebooks' Suggest He Was a Serious Anti-Semite, Not Just a Naïve Nazi." http://www.openculture.com/2015/03/martin-heideggers-black-notebooks-reveal-the-depth-of-anti-semitism.html.

Overby, Peter. 2012. "NRA: 'Only Thing That Stops a Bad Guy with a Gun Is a Good Guy with a Gun.'" *All Things Considered,* NPR, December 21, 2012. https://www.npr.org/2012/12/21/167824766/nra-only-thing-that-stops-a-bad-guy-with-a-gun-is-a-good-guy-with-a-gun.

Radin, Margaret J. 1982. "Property and Personhood." *Stanford Law Review* 34 (5): 957–1015.

Rapaport, Lisa. 2017. "Murders Surge in Florida in Decade After 'Stand Your Ground' Law." *Reuters,* August 14, 2017. https://www.reuters.com/article/us-health-homicides-standyourground/murders-surge-in-florida-in-decade-after-stand-your-ground-law-idUSKCN1AU1QL.

Rockmore, Tom. 1991. *On Heidegger's Nazism and Philosophy*. Berkeley: University of California Press.

Rothman, Joshua. 2014. "Is Heidegger Contaminated by Nazism?" *New Yorker*, April 28, 2014. https://www.newyorker.com/books/page-turner/is-heidegger-contaminated-by-nazism.

Rowman, John K. 2013. "Race, Justifiable Homicide, and Stand Your Ground Laws: Analysis of FBI Supplementary Homicide Report Data." Urban Institute. http://www.ncjrs.gov/App/publications/abstract.aspx?ID=265405.

Satia, Priya. 2018. *Empire of Guns: The Violent Making of the Industrial Revolution*. Stanford: Stanford University Press.

Spitzer, Robert J. 2015. *Guns across America: Reconciling Gun Rules and Rights*. Oxford: Oxford University Press.

Stavans, Ilan. 2002. "The Browning of America." *Nation*, May 30, 2002. https://www.thenation.com/article/browning-america/.

Sundstrom, Ronald R. 2008. *The Browning of America and the Evasion of Social Justice*. Albany: SUNY Press.

United States v. Emerson. 2001. United States Court of Appeals, Fifth Circuit.

Wendland, Adam James. 2018. "Heidegger's New Beginning: History, Technology, and National Socialism." In *Heidegger on Technology*, edited by Aaron James Wendland, Christopher Merwin, and Christos Hadjioannou, 163–87. New York: Routledge.

Williams, Patricia J. 2018. "The 'Ground' in 'Stand Your Ground' Means Any Place a White Person Is Nervous." *Nation*, August 15, 2018. https://www.thenation.com/article/the-ground-in-stand-your-ground-means-any-place-a-white-person-is-nervous/.

Winkler, Adam. 2011. *Gunfight: The Battle over the Right to Bear Arms in America*. New York: Norton.

Zielinski, Luisa. 2016. "In His Own Words," *Paris Review*, October 18, 2016. https://www.theparisreview.org/blog/2016/10/18/in-his-own-words/.

5

THE RHETORIC OF OPEN CARRY
Living with the Nonverbal Presence of Guns

Ian E. J. Hill

In what has become an iconic instance of publicly displaying guns, Bobby Seale and his fellow Black Panthers took their shotguns and rifles inside the California state legislative chambers in 1967 to protest the soon-to-be-voted-upon Mulford Act. There, Seale delivered the group's "first major message to *all* the American people, and *all* the Black people, in particular" (Seale 1970, 149). The Mulford Act in part sought to ban the open carry of loaded long guns in California at a moment when the Black Panthers had become conspicuous for armed community self-defense while seeking "an immediate end to POLICE BRUTALITY and MURDER of Black people" (73). In short, it was time to "pick up some guns and don't be bullshitting" (64). Whether the historical tethering of the symbol of the gun to the Black Panthers is justified given the group's other activities in California and across the United States that had nothing to do with guns, such as voter registration and food distribution, barging armed into the California legislature to protest for Black freedom and against gun control was a novel, audacious spectacle. The presence of guns at the capitol, however, was in no way a novelty. Less conspicuous and not at all audacious that day, owing to the thorough banality of the phenomenon, were the many armed police and security personnel present at the legislative assembly and nearby in Sacramento. The public carrying of firearms by Black Panthers and government authorities were displays of force that compelled differing interpretations of their guns by reminding everyone involved that guns can provide both security and terror, and that guns distribute security and terror differently to different populations (Hill 2019).

The Black Panthers' display of force demonstrated the securitizing, defensive use of open carry as a means of protecting the Black community from the government, and the simultaneous threat posed by firearms to elected government officials, who were already wary

https://doi.org/10.7330/9781646422159.c005

of the Black Panthers' guns. Securitization refers to the identification of a threatened population and the measures taken to mitigate the threat (see also Allen's chapter 13 in this volume). Conversely, the security guards and police who intermediated the presence of the Black Panthers within the capitol—and later confronted them at a gas station after they had left the capitol building—demonstrated that the government's guns meant security for the mostly white California legislature and insecurity for California's Black population. In what now seems like a political contradiction, the Republican-sponsored pro–gun control Mulford Act was quickly passed by California legislators and signed into law by future president Ronald Reagan, banning the Black Panthers from carrying their loaded long guns in public.[1] Yet for a brief moment, the Black Panthers disrupted the status quo of California's racially divided security-insecurity relationship, while also demonstrating that the deep and rich tradition of Black gun ownership and armed self-defense that had developed since the Civil War made American gun ownership pervasive, a tradition claimed, clarified, and expounded by Robert F. Williams's 1962 treatise *Negroes with Guns* (see also Johnson 2014; Cobb 2016; Umoja 2013). In stark fashion, Second Amendment rights and widespread gun ownership empowered both the Black Power movement and structural racism. In sum, it was the public display of guns that precipitated the Black Panthers' and the California government's actions, motivated the writing and enactment of a new law, and imbued the event with symbolic and historical importance. This chapter delves into the carrying and brandishing of firearms in public by focusing on how the visible presence of guns functions rhetorically.

I argue that the visible, embodied, material, and nonverbal public presence of guns, whether in the possession of citizens or security personnel, motivates divergent and paradoxical reactions as the means of threatening violence and the means of securing protection become interchangeable. When people see guns and experience their physical presence, the weapons can convey both danger and safety by provoking feelings that range between extreme terror and securitized ease.[2] Open carry thus rhetorically functions by using intimidation to convey both the threat of violence and the promise of protection.

I use the phrase "open carry" to refer to its typical meaning—the right granted to some citizens to freely possess firearms in public spaces—but I extend the concept to include the rights of government representatives and other authorized institutions' security personnel to openly carry firearms in public. I redefine open carry to include security personnel in order to emphasize the paradoxical tension between arming them and arming citizens, tension that disrupts perceptions of who protects society and who threatens it. Although open carry laws do not authorize security personnel's public displays of firearms, the commonplace phrase "open carry" mobilizes the US population's conflicted collective understanding of guns with respect to the gun control controversy. The security-insecurity paradox, already embedded within the concept of open carry, is vital for understanding, for instance, why the Black Panthers needed armed self-defense, why the US government avoided violent responses to the Cliven Bundy standoffs, the injustice of Tamir Rice's killing by police, and why minority populations feel targeted by law enforcement agencies that are rarely held accountable for their violence. Thus, this chapter considers open carry as a diverse practice that is not restricted to conventional provisions of gun control policy. This loose definition of open carry supports a broad consideration of the legality and illegality of firearms possession and emphasizes the differing potential intentions and results of publicly displaying firearms, from possessing holstered guns to brandishing them for attack or defense, and from keeping them visible as a means of assuring populations of their security to conveying the threat of imminent violence.

Historically, the minor infraction known as "affrighting" demonstrates the interaction of threat and security inherent in public displays of weapons. Affrighting stood in juxtaposition to the colonial-era English common law right of bearing arms for self-defense. Affrighting law applied to the general population and "prohibited carrying a weapon in a way that menaced others," whether a club, a mace, or a gun (Waldman 2014, 33). So, one might carry a gun for self-defense or to scare people—the same gun facilitates both purposes, and therefore possesses the capacity to communicate multiple messages. Brandishing a gun for self-defense is lawful and peace making, while brandishing a gun to menace others is illegal and peace breaking. So rhetorically, the importance of affrighting laws derives from their official mandate that audience responses—the feelings of safety or danger experienced by the people who live in the presence of guns—rather than the intentions of gun owners determine the legality or illegality of the rhetoric of open carry with respect to security and insecurity. And open carry can provoke many other potential reactions in addition to feelings of safety or danger. At minimum, "when people bring rifles into restaurants they inevitably invite controversy" (Lunceford 2015, 336), and open carry incites deliberations about the actions, accidents, and events that test the limits of public policy, and that drive pro-gun and anti-gun activism. Whether illegal or legal, open carry motivates a wide range of emotions, beliefs, and actions, from the inconsequential to the deadly.

Open carry provokes contextual responses centered on the perceived likelihood of violence, so I begin by synthesizing the visual, embodied, and material aspects of nonverbal rhetoric as a type of presence that demonstrates how open carry motivates contradictory, if not paradoxical, responses to the possibility of gunfire. Then, I examine three examples of the rhetoric of open carry in action—the Cliven Bundy standoffs, Tamir Rice's murder, and the increasingly common sight of heavily armed security personnel wherever crowds gather, or what I call militarized open carry. To conclude, I consider how potential benefits of gun control legislation do not limit the rhetoric of open carry when such laws do not pertain to militarized security personnel.

THINKING THROUGH THE VISIBLE, EMBODIED, MATERIAL PRESENCE OF GUNS

Several strands of rhetorical thinking about visuality, embodiment, and materiality facilitate understanding of open carry. These three foci act as counterparts to one another, often functioning in conjunction, especially when visual rhetoric, body rhetoric, and material rhetoric are all considered means of amplifying rhetorical presence (Hill 2004, 27–30; Butterworth 2008, 261–63; Hill 2018, 12–13). Chaïm Perelman and Lucie Obrechts-Tyteca conceptualized rhetorical presence as a way of thinking about how rhetors can act "directly" on an audience's "sensibility" by doing their best to heighten the audience's experience of content, either through vivid description or through bringing an audience into close proximity to physical artifacts (1969, 116). For rhetorical presence, visuality, embodiment, and materiality deemphasize the use of vivid description, and emphasize how rhetoric works in nonverbal ways. Space constraints prohibit a detailed theoretical explanation of visual, embodied, and material rhetorics.[3] Rather, I aim to suggest that focusing on presence unites these rhetorics in straightforward fashion.

The concept of visual rhetoric holds that photographs, art, and all varieties of images, visualizations, and any visually perceivable entities have the capacity to motivate viewers. With or without accompanying words, visuality enhances audiences' perceptive experiences by increasing an object's or image's potential rhetorical force, sometimes to the point of "crowd[ing] out other considerations from the viewer's mind" (Hill 2004, 29). Depending on the vast range of potential scenarios, the sudden appearance of someone carrying a gun in public might compel one's full attention, compel no attention at all, or compel the full range of attention between these two extremes, depending on whether the gun's presence appears dangerous, protective, or ambiguous to those who see it. In the words of Danielle Allen, an image can "render visible democracy's 'public sphere'" as it exists in a particular context (2004, 5), and the presence or absence of guns in public renders a society's gun policies visible. Open carry laws and militarized open carry in part determine which populations see guns in public, and thereby regulate when and where the visible presence of guns might crowd out consideration of any or all other present objects to compel cognizance of security and insecurity in bystanders. Yet the visuality of guns is polysemous. When guns are visible, they convey multiple meanings and messages depending on the political and social power possessed by different populations, since public spheres encompass a cacophony of divergent opinions and beliefs.

Despite this polysemy, seeing a gun compels anticipation about whether its owner will or will not open fire, or if the gun might accidentally discharge, defining a situation's visual experience. Therefore, visual presence likely focuses the viewer's attention on his or her personal security and that of everyone else in the vicinity. If the appearance of a gun is normal or unthreatening, then business likely carries on as usual. But if the appearance of a gun seems incongruous with the situation or outright dangerous, seeing a gun might provoke an about-to-die sensation. In her analysis of photojournalism's circulation of morbid spectacle, Barbie Zelizer proposed that "about-to-die" images of people who are still alive but in life-threatening situations (e.g., pictures of people falling from buildings, standing beside explosions, or about to be executed) tend to provoke a wide range of emotions and thinking in viewers by drawing attention to "what could be" rather than "what is" (2010, 14). Such images force viewers to imagine the likely fate of the people depicted, and provoke hope that, contrary to logic, perhaps those depicted right before death might have survived. The threatening appearance of a gun in public, in contrast, forces people to consider their own death and, like a journalistic image of impending death, open carry can "suggest rather than establish evidence," which "fastens people to the illogical position of knowing more than they see" (309). Open carry can invite an about-to-die realization that might motivate such actions as fight or flight, and thus experiencing open carry takes the about-to-die image and transfers it to those who see weapons in person rather than those who experience a frozen moment of someone else's mortality via photographic representation. Conversely, given the broad range of "as if" scenarios (2), a counterpart—an about-to-be protected experience—occurs when people in the presence of guns believe they are safe.

As indicated by the ways that about-to-die and about-to-be-protected experiences compel feelings of bodily danger or safety, visual presence is interconnected with embodied presence. The concept of body rhetoric advances two general premises that impinge upon one another. First, people use and invoke their own bodies and other peoples' bodies for rhetorical purposes. Bodies are persuasive via the elocutionary skills of voice, countenance, gesture, and posture, as argumentative examples, and as sites where meanings can be manipulated. For example, when mass shooting victims embody death and thereby provide their own persuasive "weight" (Rood 2018), gun control advocates can seize upon the corpses, mobilizing all three of these characteristics of body rhetoric. Second, bodies register rhetorical experiences, mentally, emotionally, in human/nonhuman assemblages, and as an inventory of motivated actions. Arming and disarming bodies increases and decreases the rhetorical presence of the gun-person assemblage by opening up and foreclosing a specific set of potential actions. Guns therefore impinge on embodiment in many ways, including when manifested through armed gestures, as sites of injury, pain, and trauma, and as a type of record of how guns are used for securitization, coercion, and violence. At base, guns fit into hands and are used to influence, injure, or eradicate bodies.

With respect to open carry, whether guns are holstered or drawn, and if drawn, at whom they are aimed, defines and differentiates embodied presence for the gun toter and those who experience someone else's open carry. Brandishing a gun, or holding a gun in a threatening manner, whether for attack or defense, shows how open carry can convert a peaceable body into a violent body, can embody affective states, and can indicate the potential for victimhood that comes with bodily injury. For those at whom guns are brandished, the phenomenon of rhetorical embodiment is straightforward and coercive; feeling threatened and fearing bodily injury, people should run away. This simplistic, plausible formula has been abused by pro-gun advocates who claim that brandishing guns is the most successful means of both self-defense and crime prevention. The commonsense plausibility of this embodied causal argument has led to both statistical abuse, such as unsubstantiated claims that brandishing guns is effective up to 98 percent of the time, and the proliferation of a commonplace reductio ad absurdum wherein "guns sometimes appear akin to magic wands that make criminals disappear" (McDowall 2005, 246, 260). From another perspective, some advocates of open carry have argued that guns, always attached to the body via holster or hand, are such an integral part of their identities that to deny them the right of open carry is a form of discrimination (Collins 2014). Thus, the embodied presence of open carry is tied to the multiple ways that humans become guns in technological assemblages, produce bodily effects from emotions to death, and motivate physical actions.

Owing to the interplay of bodies and technologies, the physical presence of guns draws attention to the rhetorical force of weapons' materiality. The concept of material rhetoric holds that nonlinguistic things have "motivational force unto themselves," regardless of human intervention (Hill 2018, 13). As I wrote elsewhere, "With or without the presence of words about weapons, weapons possess their own rhetorical presence" (13). The presence of guns can define situations so forcefully that sometimes even their absence from known violent contexts can seem like a jarring erasure (Ott, Aoki, and Dickinson 2011). The material presence of firearms functions, at minimum, as a crude tool of rhetorical force regardless of whether gun owners intend to influence others to think or act in certain ways. Thus materiality, in part because of the inscrutability of seemingly mute artifacts, promotes polysemy.

Open carry's material force entails that the presence of guns can perform politics. As Lindsay Livingston noted, "Guns are inherently performative in that they alter the behavior of both those who wield them and those who are confronted by them in public spaces" (2018, 345). Open carry technologically communicates a hierarchical power imbalance between the armed and unarmed, or those armed with less and more sophisticated weaponry, or a potential sharing of power between people with equivalent firepower. Moreover, the potential power imbalances introduced by open carry can bolster the demographic hierarchies that maintain the sociopolitical status quo when the more powerful are armed or more powerfully armed. However, open carry can also disrupt such hierarchies. As an example of the latter, consider how armed Black self-defense organizations utilized open carry during the civil rights movement both as "a means of survival" and as a means to "symbolize" unequal treatment before the law (Umoja 2013, 256). The material presence of guns thus compels people to consider their physical and political relationship to everyone else within a public space, a realization that operationalizes ethical and civil conventions in order to maintain or seize advantage over others. Meanwhile, courts do not usually consider using guns to communicate ideas as protected speech (Horwitz 2016, 112), but materialist and object-oriented scholarship might end up inadvertently abetting those who brandish guns by helping to establish the communicative potential of firearms, a result made plausible by the 2010 *Citizens United v. Federal Election Commission* Supreme Court decision that declared money to be protected free speech. The gun-focused material presence of open carry distributes ease and anxiety, order and chaos, fight and flight, and life and death as guns control the people around them at a moment in history when the materiality of guns is, in the words of Vicaro and Seitz, "most vivid" (2017, 4).

The two main takeaways from the preceding gloss of nonverbal visual, embodied, and material rhetorical presence are the pervasive imbrication of the three critical perspectives, and their pertinence to the rhetoric of open carry. Focusing attention on one of the three tends to draw implicit or explicit attention to the other two, and this overlapping is especially prevalent when engaging with the security-insecurity gap manifested by gun rhetorics. Hence, without making explicit references to obvious instances of visuality, embodiment, and materiality, I now turn to several examples that show how these interrelated strands of rhetorical thinking afford insight into the nonverbal, paradoxical motivational force of open carry.

THE RHETORIC OF OPEN CARRY IN ACTION

Three divergent instances of the rhetoric of open carry—the Cliven Bundy standoffs, the police killing of Tamir Rice, and the more general phenomenon of well-armed security personnel who appear with increasing frequency in public settings—exemplify the entanglement of visual, embodied, and material presence in nonverbal rhetorics of open carry that influence public perceptions of potential violence. Each case demonstrates a different, but still interrelated, component of living in the presence of guns and their motivational forces. The Bundy standoffs demonstrate how the use of open carry by citizens might compel governments to respond with less or equivalent force; Tamir Rice's murder demonstrates the security-insecurity imbalance of governmental responses to different armed populations according to race, racism, and the proclivity to perpetrate asymmetrical violence afforded by patrol weapons; and militarized open carry demonstrates how armed governmental responses to dissent, crime, terrorism, and securitization provoke bystanders' counter-responses. All together, these examples of the rhetoric of open carry illustrate the securitization gaps between different demographic and civic populations.

The Bundy Ranch standoff of April 12, 2014, in the remote ranchlands of Nevada near Bunkerville and its aftermath in Oregon demonstrate the motivational force of public weapons displays. Cattle rancher Cliven Bundy, his family, and like-minded supporters organized the media spectacle as a means of generating public support for Bundy's decades-old conflict with the Bureau of Land Management (BLM). Bundy owed over $1 million in unpaid fees and fines because of his steadfast refusal to abide by federal public land-grazing rules, and the BLM was finally rounding up Bundy's herd. Unwilling to desist from illegal grazing, Bundy called upon his supporters to defend his ranching methods with armed force. Although a federal judge declared "that the United States is entitled to protect the New Trespass Lands against this trespass, and all future trespasses by Bundy" (George 2013, 5), BLM personnel found themselves trapped between two Interstate 15 overpasses and outgunned by well-armed militia snipers perched on the overpasses and in the bushes. While the BLM workers had handguns, it was the high-caliber revolvers, assault rifles, and other long guns of Bundy's crew that defined the outcome of this event.

In the Bundy case, open carry communicated the insecurity of BLM workers and local residents leveraged against the security of ranchers and libertarian militias. In addition to the latter chasing off the BLM and compelling the release of Bundy's herd with their assault rifles and orchestrated armed standoff, the Bundy affair stretched across multiple instances of public armed intimidation. For instance, the day after the Bunkerville standoff, Bundy imagined a national movement, and "called on county sheriffs across the country to 'take away the guns from United States bureaucrats'" (quoted in Makley 2017, 102). Doing so would, of course, necessitate the widespread brandishing of guns to affrighten civil servants. Around the same time, a former Arizona county sheriff who announced both his willingness to die for Bundy's cause and his willingness "to use women as human shields," reasoned that in order "'to show the world how ruthless these people [BLM] are, women needed to be the first ones shot'" (Makley 2017, 2). He thereby contrived a fantastical vision of a public open carry standoff that would, if successful, exemplify Craig Rood's (2018) concept of the rhetorical weight of the dead. Then, in April 2015 armed anti-BLM protesters gathered outside a BLM office in Grants Pass, Oregon, forcing its closure (Makley 2017, 103). At the second major Bundy standoff with federal agents, in Burns, Oregon, during a forty-one-day occupation of the federal Malheur Wildlife Refuge in early 2016, Ammon Bundy and some of his supporters entered a town meeting at a school where the residents of Burns voted against the presence of Bundy and his cohorts. The interloping ranchers entered "packing their firearms, and strategically spread around the room" (105). This attempt to affrighten failed, but the Bundys' open display of firearms at the wildlife refuge kept federal agents at bay for weeks.

Thus, the Bundy affair demonstrated that, at minimum, the rhetoric of open carry encompasses the capacity to force armed federal agents into retreat and procedural inertia. By suggesting that Bundy-ites should imagine the standoff as a response to law enforcement's culpability for the botched Ruby Ridge raid and the massacre of Branch Davidians at Waco, Bundy supporters signaled that the BLM should beware any violent inclinations (Livingston 2018, 344). Second, the Bundy gang's public displays of firearms motivated a long, protracted legal battle, threatened political violence, and eventually, at the Oregon standoff, provoked the police killing of Bundy-ite LaVoy Finicum. However, the slow and mostly nonviolent handling of the Bundy affair raises a third point about the public display of firearms. The race of those who practice open carry in part determines differing responses by the government, and the BLM's reluctance to use violence when dealing with the Bundy Ranch and wildlife refuge standoffs became evidence of both the unequal legal treatment of open carry for different races and their unequal securitization.[4]

The police killing of Tamir Rice in Cleveland in late November 2014 exemplifies the potential insecurity of citizens, and especially Black citizens in the United States, whether they are lawfully and openly carrying weapons or committing misdemeanor gun-brandishing infractions. In this instance, open carry motivated two actions—first, the initial call to 911 by a concerned and affrighted bystander who said Rice was "probably a juvenile" and that the weapon was "probably fake, but you know what, he's scaring the shit out of people" (MacDonald 2015). Then, open carry compelled police officer Timothy Loehmann's extrajudicial street execution of Rice. Therefore, unlike the Black Panthers in 1967 whose open carry communicated a gun-based power equilibrium, Tamir Rice's open carry did not exude the threat level necessary to compel governmental restraint, which amplified the hierarchical power imbalance between Cleveland's armed population and Cleveland's police force. According to Cleveland municipal gun-brandishing law, affrighting with any replica firearm is a first-degree misdemeanor, punishable by a "possible 6 months in jail or a maximum fine of $1,000 or both" for adults (City of Cleveland 1996; Cleveland Municipal Court 2012). Emphatically, what is menacing is in the fright of the beholder, as Rice's gun was just a twelve-year-old's toy.

Loehmann shot Rice from about five feet away beside a recreation center park gazebo where Rice had been playing. A nearby CCTV camera recorded the whole incident. The footage shows Rice playing with his airsoft gun (a type of toy, not a real firearm), aiming at unknown targets beyond the video's frame (*Full Surveillance Video* 2014, 4:15–4:24). He was also making snowballs, stomping in the snow, wandering around, and sitting in the gazebo. Rice was at once both "just a kid with a toy playing in a park" and a Black youth who might not have taken "the talk" about police brutality as seriously as he should have (Lowery 2016, 77), since the barrel's orange tip, which signals a gun's non-lethality, was missing (Cuyahoga County Sheriff's Department 2015). The whole shooting incident unfolded in a matter of seconds; Loehmann shot Rice even before his vehicle had come to a complete stop. Looking at the CCTV footage, it's clear that when the police cruiser careened up and stopped a few feet away from Rice, Rice pulled up his shirt. The graininess of the footage is an issue, and whether Rice had his hand on his gun is not discernable, although the official story is that he pulled the gun. But if his toy gun was stuck in his waistband, his hands seemed to move downward toward it only upon being shot by Loehmann. In the end, the City of Cleveland settled a wrongful death lawsuit filed by Rice's family and later fired Loehmann.

That the weapon that instigated Rice's murder was a toy gun only emphasizes open carry's persuasive force. And it adds insult to injury as it articulates the difficulties of assessing open carry threat levels. Innumerable failures to prosecute instances of police brutality lend credibility to assertions that when people, but notably African Americans, brandish guns, the government tacitly authorizes brutal suppression, if not execution, of those who frighten people with guns in public settings, even when the risk to security is negligible. Regarding the grand jury's clearance of Loehmann and its failure to prosecute the case, Cuyahoga County prosecutor Timothy McGinty blamed Rice for being large for his age, ignoring warnings about playing with a pellet gun in public, and for revealing the toy, while he excused Loehmann for having a "different perspective" (Lowery 2016, 108). Regardless of whether one believes these tone-deaf excuses for police brutality, open carry motivated a street execution. Yet Loehmann was the threat, not Rice. Thus, perceiving Rice's supposed open carry as an existential threat, Loehmann denied the right of open carry to Rice, demonstrating once again the security disparity for different races in the United States.

Within an atmosphere of mass-mediated global terrorism, the perception of guns as existential threats—and as the means of existential protection—also encompasses the conspicuous arming of security personnel in public places, from those standing guard at government buildings, airports, and stadiums to those mobilized to quell protests. In considering the sanctioned armed presence of security personnel, I turn attention toward a general phenomenon of militarized open carry that raises questions about why such displays of force are necessary at peaceable locations when, meanwhile, the US government sent the BLM to confront the well-armed, openly hostile Bundy gang with mere pistols. Wherever large crowds gather in places deemed at risk for terrorist or criminal violence, "warrior cops" (Balko 2013), armed with military surplus equipment designed for waging war and obtained through the US Department of Defense's 1033 Program or Department of Homeland Security funding, protect and serve with tactical gear, tear gas, and assault rifles. Federal decree, or authorized affrighting, rather than state gun control laws, empowers militarized open carry. The militarization of policing entails balancing the force required to stop terrorist attacks with the misuses of an asymmetrical warfare strategy to police political protests and other public places. As exemplified by mass shootings, truck bombings, and vehicular mass homicides, the threat of terrorism can appear to necessitate a reciprocal, escalated public show of governmental security that in turn trains the public to accept such displays of force as conventional. But when the killing power of the guns displayed in public increases as governments transfer the means of soldiering to police departments, often untrained in military tactics, militarized open carry in turn communicates an increased risk for those who feel unsafe around armed strangers. This anxiety is justified. One recent study found that, compared to white men, Black men are 3.2 to 3.5 times more likely to be killed by police, which does not even take into account all of the nonfatal police shootings (Edwards, Esposito, and Lee 2018, 1241). Thus, the public display of open carry by security personnel is an amplified version of individual open carry that can intensify perceptions of danger and safety, and has even "changed the [public] interpretation of policing" (Phillips 2018, 131).

Militarized police provide assurance that civilians are being protected, but nobody can know if a well-armed and well-trained soldier or police officer might transform into a threat, whether owing to governmental authorization, situational fear, or hateful ideology. Furthermore, militarized open carry draws attention to shootings committed at military bases and by former military personnel, as well as the plethora of police killings of unarmed civilians across the United States. At public protests, though, the potential threat posed by open carry becomes even more tangible when a crowd cannot discern if an initial barrage of sonic weapons and tear gas might foreshadow volleys of tank and assault rifle fire, especially in jurisdictions already characterized by police brutality. The growing presence of militarized policing increases the probability that security personnel will use the weapons that they brandish (Lawson 2019). The spectacle of police and the National Guard gathered to confront peaceful protesters of the 2014 police killing of Michael Brown in Ferguson, Missouri, was an ominous public display of weapons. In addition to deploying Lenco-made Bear and Bearcat armored vehicles, a sonic blaster, and tactical body armor, their open carrying of assault rifles visualized why the Black population felt threatened. The appearance of the overarmed police and National Guard heightened the volatile scene and provoked the asymmetrical crowd suppression that ensued. When governments give security personnel weapons to deter violence via their conspicuous display, it is the crowd that needs security, not the government.

At the same time that security personnel depend on open carry as a deterrent to quell crime and terrorism, that presence can also portend confrontation by conveying a specific technological threat level. Militarized open carry invites people to imagine bloody carnage in their communities by drawing attention to the number and technological sophistication of the patrol rifles being displayed (AR-15s, M-16s, and M-4s), as well as inviting consideration of the high level of force possessed by enemies of the state, which militarized open carry is meant to repel (Phillips 2018, 125, 134). Whether a government intends to instill an atmosphere of intimidation is moot when that government provides security personnel with the means to unequivocally communicate both that certain populations are targeted as threats and that the terroristic threat is so pervasive that no one is ever safe in a crowd. The presence of militarized open carry during constitutionally protected dissent signals that the government has authorized oppression, if not injury or killing, of one population, if not of another. It thereby escalates the firepower needed for viable self-defense. Militarized open carry thus indicates the pervasive creep of counterterrorism securitization as it converts more and more soft targets into hard targets.

As demonstrated by the Bundy standoffs, Rice's murder, and militarized policing, the rhetoric of open carry motivates people via visual, embodied, and material rhetorical presence. When people see guns in public places, when their physical and psychological presence is felt, and when guns impinge upon society as a technological force, their conspicuous presence communicates relative levels of securitized danger and safety, depending on factors as diverse as the perceptions of everyday banality, media spectacle, distinctions between legality and criminality, technical firepower, hierarchical social divisions, and governance. Nonverbal rhetorical presence indicates that people who see and feel open displays of firearms contribute as much to the public perception of guns as those who regulate, carry, brandish, and aim them. As one legal scholar put it, "Until reasonable audiences are not intimidated by the possibility of violence, guns and 'free speech' are largely incompatible" (Horwitz 2016, 120). Thus, the transformative political possibilities of open carry rhetoric depend upon how audiences, or those who experience open carry in action, interpret and react to the presence of firearms, feeling more or less safe and more or less threatened around guns.

CONCLUSION

When examined with the synthesized critical apparatus of visual, embodied, and material presence, the rhetoric of open carry reveals the antithetical, if not paradoxical, creation of security for some populations and insecurity for other populations in public places where guns are conspicuous. As examples, the Cliven Bundy standoffs, the murder of Tamir Rice, and militarized open carry demonstrate that the rhetoric of open carry is multifaceted and provokes interrelated responses to and experiences of the public display of firearms that, when gathered together, define the American experience of living in the presence of guns. These particular cases indicate that living with open carry entails negotiating the differing levels of power, publicity, and rights of individual gun owners and different civilian populations leveraged against local, state, and federal governments. Future analysis of the rhetoric of open carry might therefore analyze its motivational force as it manifests between various civilians and civilian populations in situations when governmental forces are not present. Furthermore, attentiveness to how rhetorical presence functions in these examples shows that guns possess nonverbal motivational force, and that gun rhetoric encompasses more than policy discourse and mass-mediated verbal appeals. Rhetoricians and gun policy stakeholders should therefore pay heed to the nonverbal rhetorical force of being in the public presence of firearms, especially if an equitable and just atmosphere of security is the goal. The cases of Bundy, Rice, and warrior cops indicate that current gun laws, including open carry laws, have failed to achieve that goal.

The capacity of any gun control policy to mitigate experiences of security and insecurity caused by open carry, however, is inherently limited when policy is oriented toward the rights of individual citizens and nongovernmental groups, and when official security personnel abide by a different set of open carry protocols and regulations. The potential benefits of gun control legislation, such as reducing gun violence, presume that security personnel will uphold justice when they maintain a visible, if not palpable, armed power imbalance. This power discrepancy indicates the uneasy conceptual alliance of ideologically divergent groups, such as right-wing militias and movements against police brutality, that perceive the government's military capabilities first and foremost as dangerous. Thus, as armed security personnel become more often present at airports, stadiums, and protests, as armed individuals become more or less likely to frequent public places, and as the killing capacities of their firearms and other weaponry increase, the life-and-death stakes of securitization rise and fall for those who must learn to live in the presence of guns.

NOTES

1. A similar scenario unfolded in Texas in the 1960s (see Gerdes's chapter 9 in this volume).
2. When I witness open carry, whether by citizens or government authorities, I automatically think that the chances of getting shot have exponentially increased.
3. For more in-depth overviews of visual, embodied, and material rhetorical theories, see, respectively, Hill and Helmers 2004; Chávez 2018; and Barnett and Boyle 2016. In his analysis of media coverage of the Mother Emanuel Church mass shooter, Gage (chapter 10 in this volume) emphasizes the importance of visual rhetoric for analyzing journalistic coverage of guns and gun violence.
4. Corrigan (chapter 4 in this volume) makes a correlated point about the influence of race in enforcement of stand your ground self-defense laws.

REFERENCES

Allen, Danielle. 2004. *Talking to Strangers: Anxieties of Citizenship since* Brown v. Board of Education. Chicago: University of Chicago Press.

Balko, Radley. 2013. *Rise of the Warrior Cop: The Militarization of America's Police Forces.* New York: Public Affairs.

Barnett, Scot, and Casey Boyle, eds. 2016. *Rhetoric, through Everyday Things.* Tuscaloosa: University of Alabama Press.

Butterworth, Michael L. 2008. " 'Katie Was Not Only a Girl, She Was Terrible': Katie Hnida, Body Rhetoric, and Football at the University of Colorado." *Communication Studies* 59 (3): 259–73.

Chávez, Karma R. 2018. "The Body: An Abstract and Actual Rhetorical Concept." *Rhetoric Society Quarterly* 48 (3): 242–50.

City of Cleveland. 1996. "§ 627.23. Facsimile Firearms." elaws.us. http://cleveland-oh .elaws.us/code/coor_ptsix_ti_ch627_sec627.23.

Cleveland Municipal Court. 2012. "Misdemeanor Criminal Arraignment." Clevelandmuni cipalcourt.org. https://clevelandmunicipalcourt.org/judicial-services/administrative -services/central-scheduling/misdemeanor-criminal-arraignment.

Cobb, Charles E. 2016. *This Nonviolent Stuff'll Get You Killed: How Guns Made the Civil Rights Movement Possible.* Durham, NC: Duke University Press.

Collins, Laura J. 2014. "The Second Amendment as Demanding Subject: Figuring the Marginalized Subject in Demands for an Unbridled Second Amendment." *Rhetoric & Public Affairs* 17 (4): 737–56.

Cuyahoga County Sheriff's Department. 2015. "Synopsis of CCSD Case #15-004 Use of Deadly Force Incident." https://assets.documentcloud.org/documents/2101805/tamir-rice-investigation.pdf.

Edwards, Frank, Michael H. Esposito, and Hedwig Lee. 2018. "Risk of Police-Involved Death by Race/Ethnicity and Place, United States, 2012–2018." *American Journal of Public Health* 108 (9): 1241–48.

Full Surveillance Video Released of Tamir Rice Shot by Police. 2014. *YouTube.com.* https://www.youtube.com/watch?v=sdAYPQd1H1A.

George, Lloyd D. 2013. "United States of America, Plaintiff, v. Cliven Bundy, Defendant, Case No. 2:12-cv-0804-LDG-GWF." *Wikimedia.org.* https://upload.wikimedia.org/wikipedia/commons/8/8e/United_States_v_Bundy_Court_Order_July_2013.pdf.

Hill, Charles A. 2004. "The Psychology of Rhetorical Images." In *Defining Visual Rhetorics*, edited by Charles A. Hill and Marguerite Helmers, 25–40. New York: Routledge.

Hill, Charles A., and Marguerite Helmers, eds. 2004. *Defining Visual Rhetorics.* New York: Routledge.

Hill, Ian E. J. 2018. *Advocating Weapons, War, and Terrorism: Technological and Rhetorical Paradox.* University Park: Pennsylvania State University Press.

Hill, Ian E. J. 2019. "Communication History and Security." In *The Handbook of Communication and Security*, edited by by Bryan Taylor and Hamilton Bean, 25–40. New York: Routledge.

Horwitz, Daniel. 2016. "Open-Carry: Open-Conversation or Open-Threat." *First Amendment Law Review* 15: 96–120.

Johnson, Nicholas. 2014. *Negroes and the Gun: The Black Tradition of Arms.* Amherst, NY: Prometheus.

Lawson, Edward Jr. 2019. "Police Militarization and the Use of Lethal Force." *Political Research Quarterly* 72 (1): 177–89.

Livingston, Lindsay. 2018. "Brandishing Guns: Performing Race and Belonging in the American West." *Journal of Visual Culture* 17 (3): 343–55.

Lowery, Wesley. 2016. *They Can't Kill Us All: Ferguson, Baltimore, and a New Era in America's Racial Justice Movement.* New York: Little, Brown.

Lunceford, Brett. 2015. "Armed Victims: The Ego Function of Second Amendment Rhetoric." *Rhetoric & Public Affairs* 18 (2): 333–46.

MacDonald, Evan. 2015. "911 Caller Was Frightened Tamir Rice Might Shoot Him." *Cleveland.com.* https://www.cleveland.com/metro/index.ssf/2015/06/911_caller_was_frightened_tami.html.

Makley, Michael J. 2017. *Open Spaces, Open Rebellions: The War over America's Public Lands.* Amherst: University of Massachusetts Press.

McDowall, David. 2005. "John R. Lott, Jr.'s Defensive Gun Brandishing Estimates." *Public Opinion Quarterly* 69 (2): 246–63.

Ott, Brian L., Eric Aoki, and Greg Dickinson. 2011. "Ways of (Not) Seeing Guns: Presence and Absence at the Cody Firearms Museum." *Communication and Critical/Cultural Studies* 8 (3): 215–39.

Perelman, Chaïm, and Lucie Olbrechts-Tyteca. 1969. *The New Rhetoric: A Treatise on Argumentation.* Translated by John Wilkinson and Purcell Weaver. Notre Dame, IN: Notre Dame University Press.

Phillips, Scott W. 2018. *Police Militarization: Understanding the Perspectives of Police Chiefs, Administrators, and Tactical Officers.* New York: Routledge.

Rood, Craig. 2018. "'Our Tears Are Not Enough': The Warrant of the Dead in the Rhetoric of Gun Control." *Quarterly Journal of Speech* 104 (1): 47–70.

Seale, Bobby. 1970. *Seize the Time: The Story of the Black Panther Party and Huey P. Newton.* New York: Random House.

Umoja, Akinyele Omowale. 2013. *We Will Shoot Back: Armed Resistance in the Mississippi Freedom Movement.* New York: New York University Press.

Vicaro, Michael P., and David W. Seitz. 2017. "Guns, Crime, and Dangerous Minds: Assessing the Mental Health Turn in Gun Policy Discourse." *Cultural Studies ↔ Critical Methodologies* 17 (2): 1–5.

Waldman, Michael. 2014. *The Second Amendment: A Biography.* New York: Simon & Schuster.

Williams, Robert F. 1962. *Negroes with Guns.* New York: Marzani & Munsell.

Zelizer, Barbie. 2010. *About to Die: How News Images Move the Public.* New York: Oxford University Press.

6

THE ACTIVISM GAP AND THE RHETORIC OF (UN)CERTAINTY

Craig Rood

US debates over gun violence and gun policy are often marked by vehement disagreement. On television, online, and in person, Americans disagree about the causes of and solutions to gun violence. In Robert J. Spitzer's (2012) words, these debates occur "with great fury but astonishing little effect" (14). In *After Gun Violence*, I highlighted that these dysfunctional debates "often consist of talking points and talking past one another. Such talk fails to address the problem while only seeming to drive Americans further and further apart" (Rood 2019, 5).

I was born in North Dakota in 1985, and I grew up in a rural, predominantly white community. Guns played a central role in my childhood (and by guns, I mean BB guns, rifles, and shotguns—not pistols or semiautomatic rifles). I earned my hunter's safety card when I was twelve, though I had been using guns long before then. For me, guns were linked to target shooting and hunting. Today, many of my family members have their own arsenal of guns, and their reasons vary—some hunt, while others see guns as collectibles, a source of protection, recreation, or a political statement. I have chosen not to own or use guns. This choice is primarily a matter of conscience and risk assessment, though I also recognize that this choice is predicated on the privilege and felt sense of safety that comes from my identity (a relatively large, able-bodied, white, heterosexual, cisgender male), occupation (college professor), and location (Ames, Iowa). I have been researching debates over guns and gun violence since 2012, during which time I have tried to understand why productive public deliberation about gun violence and gun policy is often so difficult, and I have explored how better deliberation could help rebuild trust and resolve disagreements.

Although polling suggests that Americans are roughly evenly divided when it comes to the question of whether it is more important to control gun ownership or to protect gun rights, that picture changes when

https://doi.org/10.7330/9781646422159.c006

Americans are asked about specific gun reforms. Some gun reform measures garner nearly universal agreement, including majority support from Democrats and Republicans, gun owners and non–gun owners (Pew Research Center 2013). Yet still there is inaction. In those cases, the key challenge is not to dispel bad arguments, change minds, or achieve mutual understanding. Instead, the challenge is to translate public opinion into political action.

To think through this challenge, I return to 2013. A month after the December 14, 2012, mass shooting at Sandy Hook Elementary School, President Obama proposed three changes in gun policy: requiring "a universal background check for anyone trying to buy a gun," restoring the ban on "military-style assault weapons," and creating a "10-round limit for magazines" (Obama 2013a).[1] While polling from January 2013 indicated that the majority of Americans supported all three measures, universal background checks had the largest amount of approval, enjoying 85 percent support (Pew Research Center 2013). On April 17, 2013, when the US Senate voted on the bill—which was co-sponsored by a Democrat and a Republican—a range of polls showed that public support had remained between 80 and 90 percent (Silver 2013). Yet the bill received only 54 of 100 votes, falling short of the Senate's 60-vote threshold.

After the Senate vote that day, a frustrated Obama spoke from the White House Rose Garden: "I'm going to speak plainly and honestly about what's happened here because the American people are trying to figure out how can something have 90 percent support and yet not happen" (2013b). Indeed, how was that possible? Researchers refer to this mismatch between public opinion and political action as the "gun control paradox" (Cook and Goss 2014, 176). Put simply, how could something with a clear exigency and broad support—and the backing of a newly reelected president—fail to become enacted into law? Pursuing this question can help us understand what happened in 2013, of course, but it can also provide insight about the ongoing problem of gun violence and America's failure to address it.

In that Rose Garden speech, Obama suggested that senators were at fault for not having more courage to resist the gun lobby and the vocal minority of gun owners. But he also placed partial responsibility on gun reform supporters for not doing more: "To change Washington, you, the American people, are going to have to sustain some passion about this." Moving forward, he urged gun reform supporters to put more pressure on elected officials—and if that failed, to elect different officials. He claimed that "those who care deeply about preventing more and more gun violence will have to be as passionate, and as organized, and as vocal as those who blocked these common-sense steps to help keep our kids safe." More people supported universal background checks than opposed them, but the opposition was "better organized. They're better financed. They've been at it longer. And they make sure to stay focused on this one issue during election time" (2013b; see also Kreuter's chapter 2 in this volume).

Obama's explanation points to some of the larger forces that benefit gun rights advocates, including the role that the gun industry and gun lobby play in the political process. Political commentators and academics have extended Obama's analysis. For instance, political commentators Ezra Klein and Evan Soltas (2013) highlight that the Senate is designed so that lower-population states (which tend to be more rural and elect leaders who oppose gun reforms) have equal power with higher-population states (which tend to be more urban and elect leaders who support gun reform). Lilliana Mason (2018), a political scientist, claims that because of heightened political polarization, senators regularly vote along party lines. Mason's analysis highlights that voters and legislators believe in policies, to be sure, but they also want their side to win—and often, they want to see the opposition lose. Identity becomes more important than arguments. Worse, identity leads, and arguments follow; arguments become post hoc rationalizations to justify why "we" are good and right whereas "they" are not (see Roberts-Miller's chapter 1 in this volume). Illustrating her point, Mason refers to the 2013 debate over background checks: "81 percent of Republicans personally supported a law expanding background checks," yet "only 57 percent of Republicans supported the Senate passing a background check bill, an action that would have been a victory for Democrats" (54). These larger forces, among others, create an uneven playing field.

Although such forces are important for understanding the gun control paradox, individual and collective effort still play some role in transforming—or failing to transform—public opinion into political action. Obama saw the need for this effort, calling for "persistence" and for supporters of gun reforms to "sustain some passion" (2013b). Obama is not alone in this assessment. Robert J. Spitzer, a political scientist, pushes this further, highlighting that not all support is equally passionate: "For most people, the gun issue is not a top-tier concern (i.e., is a less salient issue for them), whereas it is for the gun rights community" (Cook, Kopel, and Spitzer 2019, 338). Polling reveals that there is an "activism gap" between gun reform supporters and gun rights supporters. Data from the Pew Research Center in 2013 indicate that gun rights supporters are about "twice as likely as gun control support-ers to have contacted a public official about gun policy (15% vs. 8%)" and that "nearly a quarter (23%) of those who say gun rights should be the priority have contributed money to an organization that takes a posi-tion on gun policy, compared with just 5 percent of those who prioritize gun control." And when it comes to elections, opponents of gun reform have been more likely than supporters of it to both vote and to prioritize the issue of guns when voting (Drutman 2015).

If gun reform groups want to effect gun legislation in ways that reflect public sentiment, one of their key challenges is to close this activism gap.[2] But doing so is neither simple nor easy. First, Philip J. Cook and Kristin A. Goss (2014) highlight that activism depends upon networks of support and material conditions (e.g., time off from work and the ability to travel), which are unevenly distributed.[3] Second, activism also depends on a sense of purpose. Cook and Goss note, for instance, that the gun reform movement has "struggled to find powerful frameworks to inspire people to join" (208). Once people have joined, they need guidance in knowing which actions to take, and they need confidence that their efforts will be worthwhile.

To better understand the activism gap, I examine the rhetoric used in both the gun reform and the gun rights movements. Comparing these two movements reveals an imbalance in how groups and leaders in each side address their supporters. Specifically, there is an imbalance in the kinds of actions that are called for, as well as in the level of confidence that such actions will be worthwhile. Put simply, each side does not provide supporters with the same degree of certainty. Examining this imbalance is crucial for understanding why the activism gap exists—and for imagining how it could be closed.

My argument unfolds in three main moves. First, I set up my analysis by briefly describing certainty and uncertainty as rhetorical constructs. Second, I use this framework of (un)certainty to describe the structure and context of America's gun debate and then analyze the rhetoric of gun reform and gun rights advocates. My analysis focuses on the post–Sandy Hook debate in 2013, though I also point to more recent examples to indicate that my claims are not restricted to that moment. Finally, I claim that the rhetoric of (un)certainty illuminates at least three approaches that gun reform advocates either have taken or might take to help close the activism gap.

THE RHETORIC OF (UN)CERTAINTY

Questions about certainty—whether something is possible and, if so, how to acquire or achieve it—have a long and important history. Rhetoricians typically claim that uncertainty is what makes space for rhetorical activity. In their introduction to *The SAGE Handbook of Rhetorical Studies*, the editors explain, "In the absence of absolute certainty [whether momentarily or existentially], rhetoric is the art (and theory and practice) that can guide humans to make the best decisions possible in any given circumstance" (Lunsford, Wilson, and Eberly 2009, xxi).

But the relationship also goes the other way: rhetorical activity shapes what is regarded as certain or uncertain. Certainty and uncertainty are not objective and natural states—rather, they are deeply subjective and human. And these states do not just happen; they are rhetorically constructed and mobilized. To say that certainty and uncertainty are rhetorically constructed is not to deny the importance of facts, evidence, and reasons. These things matter. But they matter—or are made to matter—to someone in a particular context.

A speaker can establish certainty by relying on "resolute and totalistic language," such as by stating *always* rather than *sometimes* (Hart and Childers 2004, 520). Beyond simple word choices, those claims that are expressed and heard and those that are not can establish certainty or uncertainty. Certainty and uncertainty also depend on the relationship between claims and how frequently they circulate. As the truism goes, a lie repeated often enough—or by the right people in the right context—can make that lie seem true. For example, scholars who study the rhetoric of science have helped illustrate how matters that are nearly certain—such as the efficacy of vaccines or the human causes of global warming—can be cast into doubt (see, e.g., Ceccarelli 2011; Caulfield, Marcon, and Murdoch 2017; Oreskes and Conway 2019). On the flip side, beliefs that are at odds with empirical evidence and scientific consensus—such as the belief that vaccines cause autism—can be cast for some audiences as a matter of certainty. Whether the move is from certainty to uncertainty or vice versa, rhetoric is at work. And as we will see, certainty and uncertainty are often relational, working together like two sides of the same coin. For instance, efforts by the National Rifle Association (NRA) to show that gun reform advocates are wrong are simultaneously efforts to show that gun rights advocates are right—or at least to unite gun rights advocates against their opponents and their wrongness.

I will not claim that certainty is a universal desire or that uncertainty is a universal fear. People's identity and lived experience—including their age, class, gender, race, and sexual orientation—shape whether they expect certainty and perhaps even what it means. But I am operating on the assumption that, in general, certainty and action are linked: people are more likely to act if they are confident that their beliefs are true and that their actions will be worthwhile because they are moral, consequential, or otherwise valuable.

STRUCTURE AND CONTEXT OF THE GUN DEBATE

Gun rights advocates have several advantages over gun reform advocates, not simply because of their greater efforts but because of the structure and context of America's gun debate. For starters, what is commonly called the "gun debate" actually consists of at least two debates—one over gun rights and a second over the causes of and solutions to gun violence. For gun rights advocates, the key question is whether or not the United States should restrict gun access. Gun reform advocates obviously have a view on that question, but that is not their starting place. They are not arguing about the value of restricting gun access for its own sake; instead, they are arguing about the value of restricting gun access as a means—and perhaps the best means—for addressing the problem of gun violence. Thus, gun reform advocates are faced with arguing that (1) gun violence is a problem significant enough to warrant state or federal attention and intervention (rather than no action or individual action), (2) guns bear significant responsibility for the existence of gun violence, (3) particular restrictions on gun possession and use will adequately address the problem of gun violence, and (4) restrictions on gun possession and use do not have negative consequences that could cause more harm than good. Gun rights advocates and gun reform advocates might agree on (1) yet disagree on (2), (3), and (4).

Gun rights and gun reform advocates are not debating whether to support policy X or policy Y. Instead, gun rights advocates argue that there should be no policy change (or if there is, it should be to *remove* restrictions in order to increase gun access), whereas gun reform advocates argue that there should be a policy change. The latter option tends to be more difficult: proposing and defending a policy change is more difficult than critiquing or refusing others' policy proposals. Moreover, those advocating for change (whether to gun policy or anything else) are always at some disadvantage because the status quo enjoys the benefit of inertia—of keeping things as they are. Advocating for changing gun laws is especially difficult because the problem of gun violence is complex; for instance, the sources of and solutions to domestic violence, gang violence, mass shootings, and suicides might not overlap. Given the various types of violence—as well as the diverse range of restrictions and of firearms and accessories—policy solutions are also potentially complex, and they can extend beyond guns to issues such as mental health and economic reform. Each policy option has potential benefits and drawbacks that must be reconciled. Moreover, advocates need to defend solutions that are bold enough to be worth the effort but not so bold as to violate the Second Amendment or repel relatively moderate gun reform supporters.

The structure of the debate means that success and failure look different for gun reform advocates and gun rights advocates, so groups are able to provide their supporters with different degrees of certainty that their actions will be consequential. For example, gun rights groups like the NRA have framed relatively modest gun restrictions as alarming, as if they entail confiscation of all guns from all people (Pfau 2017). And in some cases, gun reform advocates have helped make this story easier to tell.[4] Gun rights advocates who believe that relatively modest gun restrictions are equivalent to a total gun ban see themselves as fighting to keep the guns they already own (and the literal and symbolic power that their guns represent). Thus, losing this policy fight is depicted as having direct and significant consequences.

Gun reform advocates, by contrast, hope that passing gun reform laws will decrease gun violence. This can also be a direct and significant consequence, though it is arguably harder to imagine. Such restrictions would not guarantee that all gun violence would stop, and supporters are left with uncertainty about whether their actions would make a difference. Since murder, suicide, and harm can still happen without guns, policy action to regulate gun ownership and use does not promise the same kind of direct consequence for gun reform advocates as it purportedly does for gun rights advocates. And given that the goal for gun reform advocates is to reduce gun violence, success is gauged by something *not* happening. In general, it is more difficult to measure something that is not happening than something that is (although in communities where gun violence occurs regularly, the recognition of such violence not happening might come more easily). Success can also be hard to imagine for gun reform supporters because of the sheer magnitude of gun violence. According to the Centers for Disease Control and Prevention, in 2017, firearms were used in 14,542 homicides and 23,854 suicides (Kochanek et al. 2019). Reducing those numbers by 1,000—or even 10—is significant progress, but it might not look like it because of the sheer magnitude of gun violence in the United States.

Although the structure of the gun debate itself provides an inbuilt advantage to gun rights advocates, this advantage is especially pronounced because of the context in which these debates occur. In other words, the structure of the debate about gun violence and gun policy—and its relative advantages and disadvantages—would look different if the debate were undertaken in a different time and place or with different people.

Consider just two examples. First, the US political system is currently marked by polarization, mistrust, and inaction. There is widespread cynicism about government and distrust of elected officials, evidenced by astonishing low approval ratings of Congress. From January to April 2013, the time during which Obama pushed for gun reform legislation, congressional approval moved between 14 percent and 15 percent (Gallup n.d.). This cynicism and distrust works doubly to the detriment of gun reform efforts: for gun reform supporters, this widespread attitude suggests that good policies are unlikely to become a reality, so advocating for policy reform is not worth the effort; for gun rights supporters, cynicism and distrust suggest that even if policy change might be desirable and possible, it should be avoided because politicians cannot be trusted to fix America's problems. If current levels of polarization and mistrust improved, then policy change would seem less daunting.

Second, cognitive psychologists and behavioral economists highlight that human beings appear hardwired to privilege the simple and familiar (see Kahneman 2011). And a host of cultural, economic, and technological forces in the twenty-first century keep Americans busy (and at times distracted), making them more amenable to simple slogans than to complex, nuanced proposals. Anti-intellectualism exists, of course, but even people who want to think in deep and complex ways nonetheless experience "choice fatigue" (Gastil and Knobloch 2020, 157). If such forces were different, the expectations for public discourse might also be different. In particular, certainty and complexity might not be so far apart, and certainty and simplicity might be not so close together.

GUN REFORM ADVOCATES

When President Obama introduced his gun reform proposals on January 16, 2013, he noted that "keeping our children safe" is "our first task as a society" (2013a). He argued that we have an obligation to honor children who have become victims of gun violence and to protect those who are at risk of becoming victims. His line of argument is potentially powerful, but, as I noted in an earlier article, "there is a gap between accepting responsibility for others and embracing gun reforms. Gun control advocates need to argue not only that we are responsible for protecting others, but that this responsibility for others entails gun control; it is possible to accept the first step but not the second" (Rood 2018, 64). In that article, I examined gun reform advocates' argument that we are responsible for others. Here, I want to examine their argument that gun reform measures in particular can help us meet that responsibility. In short, the moral clarity and urgency of our obligations to honor past victims and prevent future acts of gun violence have become clouded by appeals to uncertainty, complexity, and incrementalism.

In his speech to introduce gun reform proposals, Obama (2013a) acknowledged that "reducing gun violence is a complicated challenge," conceding that "there is no law or set of laws that can prevent every senseless act of violence completely." But he nonetheless insisted that "if there is even one thing we can do to reduce this violence, if there is even one life that can be saved, then we've got an obligation to try." Notably, he did not claim to have a single answer that would yield drastic results; instead, acknowledging the difficulty of addressing gun violence, he insisted on gradual, incremental progress.

Obama's assessment continued throughout the remainder of his presidency. In a January 7, 2016, *New York Times* op-ed, Obama (2016a) claimed, "The epidemic of gun violence in our country is a crisis," but "if we can meet this moment," then "we will achieve the change we seek" and "leave a stronger, safer country to our children." He knew, however, from his inability to pass gun legislation through Congress, that "reducing gun violence will be hard." He urged readers to think of the campaign against gun violence as akin to other civil rights movements in American history: "It won't happen overnight. But securing a woman's right to vote didn't happen overnight. The liberation of African-Americans didn't happen overnight. Advancing the rights of lesbian, gay, bisexual, and transgender Americans has taken decades' worth of work." He insisted that "meeting this crisis of gun violence will require the same relentless focus, over many years, at every level." Obama's framing, then, encourages readers to see this campaign against gun violence in the tradition of other social movements, and thus recalibrate their expectations for immediate success in order to prepare for a long struggle. This vision of social change seems realistic. Yet it is worth noting that such appeals to incrementalism ask more of activists than the promise that success could be achieved by a simple, quick action.

The rhetoric of uncertainty, complexity, and incrementalism is not unique to Obama. Consider the rhetoric used by gun reform groups in

2019. The mission statement of Moms Demand Action for Gun Sense in America, for instance, claims that these moms are "fighting for public safety measures that can protect people from gun violence" (Moms Demand Action n.d.). The statement references the plural "measures" to indicate that there is not just one simple solution. By directing attention toward a future possibility ("can"), it acknowledges that success is not guaranteed. And by stating that these measures can "protect people from gun violence," it leaves unspecified the scope of how many people will be protected (it does not say "all people").

Other organizations make bolder promises. In its mission statement, Everytown for Gun Safety (n.d.) declares that the organization is "a movement of Americans working together to end gun violence and build safer communities." These bold promises to "end" gun violence can help supporters imagine a hopeful future and motivate them to act. But when supporters wonder how to create this hopeful future, these organizations reaffirm uncertainty by acknowledging the complexity of gun violence and the difficulty of trying to address it. For example, the website of the Brady Campaign to Prevent Gun Violence (n.d.) states, "There is no one solution to end this epidemic of gun violence and no one side has the answer." The website offers the Brady Plan, consisting of twelve different measures for "ending gun violence." As of October 2021, these measures appear under the following headings:

(1) background checks, (2) prohibited purchasers, (3) weapons of war, (4) restrict bump stocks, (5) outlaw ghost & 3D guns, (6) extreme risk laws, (7) fund CDC research, (8) fund urban programs, (9) end family fire, (10) end gun industry immunity, (11) hold ATF accountable, (12) stop shielding data

First, it is unclear whether these all of these measures taken together would be enough to "end" gun violence. This does not mean that these measures are not worthwhile. Instead, my point is that the organization appears to be wrestling with a tension: on the one hand, it makes a bold promise ("ending gun violence") to attract support; yet on the other hand, it offers relatively moderate measures that promise incremental progress toward achieving that goal. Second, it is worth emphasizing that their plan consists of twelve measures. This complex picture arguably reflects the complexity of gun violence. Moreover, this wide range of measures might be necessary for an organization to establish a coalition of supporters who prioritize different aspects of gun violence. But the risk of complexity is that it will foster uncertainty and stall action.

GUN RIGHTS ADVOCATES

A week after the shooting at Sandy Hook Elementary School, the NRA's executive vice president, Wayne LaPierre, spoke. NRA leaders typically do not deliver speeches after mass shootings, but this shooting was different because the Obama administration signaled that it planned to push for gun reforms. Given that the NRA's purported mission is to be "diligent protectors of the Second Amendment" (National Rifle Association n.d.), it is worth noting at the outset that LaPierre's *primary* objective was not to try to explain why gun violence happens or to outline a plan to prevent future violence (although he did do both of those things). Instead, his main intention in that speech was to prevent gun reforms. And one of the ways he did that was by attempting to create doubt about such reforms, thus generating a sense of uncertainty for his opponents and a sense of certainty for his followers. Not only did his rhetoric attempt to thwart policy, it also attempted to shape identity: his supporters were cast as wise and virtuous while his opponents were depicted as unwise and vile.

LaPierre attempted to deflect blame away from guns and disperse it in several directions. He placed blame on the perpetrators of gun violence by calling them "genuine monsters," people "so deranged, so evil, so possessed by voices and driven by demons that no sane person can possibly ever comprehend them" (LaPierre 2012). But he also placed blame on society, directing responsibility to at least these six sources beyond the shooter: politicians for creating gun-free school zones, news media for making mass shooters famous and thus encouraging copycats, legislators for not having a database to track mentally ill people, prosecutors for being soft on criminals and not adequately enforcing existing gun laws, Obama for not making school security a priority, and the entertainment industry for encouraging and profiting from violence through video games, music, and movies.

Although LaPierre returned to blaming the news media and entertainment industry several times, throughout the speech his list of those culpable appeared without a clear sense of hierarchy, thus suggesting equal responsibility. Since he was not invested in a single explanation for the cause of this mass shooting—or gun violence in general—he and his supporters could not be easily rebutted because they could shift from one explanation to another. Even if audiences insisted that guns played some role in the violence, LaPierre's rhetoric attempted to flatten responsibility by suggesting that guns were merely one source of blame among many. In short, he used the causal complexity of mass shootings to instill uncertainty about the source of them, thus weakening the link between guns and mass shootings and diminishing the calls for gun reform.

LaPierre's rhetoric mirrors the strategies Leah Ceccarelli critiques in her analysis of public debates about science. Ceccarelli describes "manufactured scientific controversies" as instances when "rhetors seek to promote or delay public policy by announcing that there is an ongoing scientific debate about a matter for which there is actually scientific consensus" (2011, 195). Although LaPierre was not focused on scientific controversies, similar dynamics seemed to be at work: he attempted to shift the stasis of the dispute from one about policy (what should we do to address the sources of gun violence?) to the more basic question about cause (what are the sources of gun violence?). Gun violence is indeed complex, but rather than grappling with that complexity, LaPierre used it to justify inaction. As part of his strategy, he attempted to conceal the role of guns in gun violence while highlighting other explanations for it. Given LaPierre's institutional position, this strategy is not surprising. But Ceccarelli's analysis of scientific controversies helps us see how LaPierre's invocation of complexity can be a rhetorical trap for his listeners, including those who support gun reform and those who are undecided. Our cultural norm of open-mindedness encourages even skeptical audiences to think, "Well, maybe he has a point." Moreover, our cultural norm of open-mindedness allows anyone who questions LaPierre's assessment to be dismissed as closed-minded (Rood 2019, 137).

Whereas LaPierre invoked complexity to create uncertainty among gun reform supporters, he appealed to simplicity to create certainty among his own supporters. LaPierre asserted that gun reforms have been and will continue to be ineffective, claiming that supporters of gun reforms "perpetuate the dangerous notion that *one more gun ban*—or one more law imposed on peaceful, lawful people—will protect us where 20,000 others have failed." In his telling, gun reform supporters are fools who wrongly believe that more laws will fix our problems; in their foolishness they are perverting justice and hurting good people like "us"—"peaceful, lawful people." While his opponents have "20,000" wrong solutions, LaPierre purports to have the only correct one: "The only way to stop a monster from killing our kids is to be personally involved and invested in a plan of absolute protection. The *only* thing that stops a *bad* guy with a gun is a *good* guy with a gun" (LaPierre 2012). His use of the words *absolute* and *only* presents his solution as obvious, simple, and certain.

Although cloaked in a commonsense appeal, LaPierre's proposal is not as simple and straightforward as he suggested. We might ask, for instance: aren't there other ways to stop a bad guy with a gun? How did that bad guy get a gun in the first place? Why not at least make it more difficult for a bad guy to get a gun, even if such efforts are not always successful? How do we know who is a "good guy" and who is a "bad guy"? Can't a good guy become a bad guy? I could go on, but my point is that LaPierre's depiction not only ignored these questions but denied they might exist. Instead, he offered his supporters the confidence and comfort of a simple, unchanging solution. The NRA website illustrates this point directly in its discussion of the Second Amendment: "In this time of such uncertainty, we must hold fast to the principles of freedom" (National Rifle Association n.d.).

MOVING FORWARD

My primary goal for this research has been diagnostic—to determine how and why the rhetoric of gun reform advocates and gun rights advocates contributes to the activism gap that currently exists. But given the diagnosis that this rhetoric of (un)certainty does contribute to this gap, what is the prescription? How might different rhetoric help gun reform supporters, advocates, and groups close the activism gap (while bearing in mind that rhetoric alone is not responsible for its existence)? My focus on the rhetoric of (un)certainty helps illuminate three approaches for moving forward. To be clear, gun reform advocates have already begun pursuing these three approaches. Thus, I do not claim to have discovered something new; instead, I am claiming that these tactics have gone unnamed and underused. Writing as a rhetorical scholar, not a political strategist, I describe these options as a framework for interpretation and invention rather than as concrete strategies for gun reform leaders, advocates, and supporters.

First, groups and leaders committed to gun reform could increase certainty that their own policies are correct, consequential, and thus worthy of effort. One way to do this is to embrace more aggressive policies that promise a greater impact on reducing levels of gun violence. This might inspire some activists, but it could alienate moderates and further agitate opponents. Another possibility is to increase enthusiasm about gun reforms that already have broad support (e.g., universal background checks). Groups and leaders might do so by presenting empirical research that illustrates and emphasizes the harm caused by failing to pass this legislation and the benefits that will likely accrue if it is passed. Obama (2016b) illustrates this move in a speech delivered on January 5, 2016: "After Connecticut passed a law requiring background checks and gun safety courses, gun deaths decreased by 40 percent—40 percent. Meanwhile, since Missouri repealed a law requiring comprehensive background checks and purchase permits, gun deaths have increased to almost 50 percent higher than the national average." But empirical research and rational argumentation are not the only ways to establish certainty. It can also be fostered by telling stories as well as by creating or invoking identity and affect (Collins, 2014; Vavrus and Leinbach, 2016).

Second, groups and leaders committed to gun reform could increase uncertainty about their opponents' position. One avenue for doing so is to challenge the view that gun regulation and gun rights are at odds. The NRA regularly casts any proposed gun regulation as eradicating the Second Amendment (Rood 2019, 60–66). Reacting to the post–Sandy Hook push for gun reform, LaPierre insisted that regarding the Second Amendment, the NRA is "as 'absolutist' as the Founding Fathers and the Framers of the Constitution" (Pappas 2013). This stance is problematic on both historical and legal grounds. Historians, legal scholars, and political scientists have highlighted that gun rights and gun regulation currently coexist in the United States, and that they have since America's founding (e.g., in history, see Ellis 2018, 160–70; in law, see Winkler 2013; in political science, see Spitzer 2015). Although the Supreme Court's 2008 *District of Columbia v. Heller* decision was seen as a victory for gun rights advocates, even that decision challenged the NRA's absolutist reading of the Second Amendment. Speaking for the 5-4 conservative majority, Justice Antonin Scalia wrote, "Like most rights, the right secured by the Second Amendment is not unlimited"; it is "not a right to keep and carry any weapon whatsoever in any manner whatsoever and [for] whatever purposes." As Obama (2013a) has claimed: "We can respect the Second Amendment while keeping an irresponsible law-breaking few from inflicting harm on a massive scale."

Gun reform proponents could also increase uncertainty about the gun rights position by focusing on how the debate is framed. Gun rights advocates regularly frame the debate as a question about rights: is the right to own and use guns being honored? This debate is important—but given that gun rights and gun regulations can and have coexisted, that question should not be allowed to serve as a debate stopper.[5] If the debate were framed in the terms that gun reform advocates prefer, the key question would focus on addressing gun violence: what can we do to eliminate—or at least reduce—gun violence (and not create more harm than good)? By focusing on that question, gun reform advocates are rhetorically disadvantaged because the answers rely on probabilistic arguments about costs and benefits that promise only incremental progress. But that is not their fault. It is a necessary result of the kind of question they are addressing. Gun reform advocates might pressure their opponents to engage the debate on those terms. That is, they might pressure gun rights advocates to offer solutions that address the problem of gun violence, to subject those proposed solutions to reasonable scrutiny, and to demand that those proposals fulfill their promises. In doing so, gun rights advocates will be pressured to engage the messiness that comes with trying to address the problem of gun violence directly. And when gun rights advocates make proposals involving mental health care or armed self-defense, they should be expected to provide empirical evidence that the implementation of these proposals will work in general (not just in a few isolated cases) and will ultimately do more good than harm.

Given the mistrust that exists in the gun debate and the level of partisanship in general, it is not clear whether gun rights advocates would ever encounter—let alone be persuaded by—such critiques from gun reform advocates. Nonetheless, these critiques might persuade moderates to join the gun reform movement. Moreover, such rhetoric could inspire current gun reform supporters to become advocates by making them feel more confident that the opposition is wrong—and therefore that their own side is right.

A third approach for closing the activism gap is to adjust expectations about certainty and its relationship to advocacy. Echoing his January 16, 2013, speech in which he announced his proposals for gun reform legislation, Obama's April 17, 2013, speech addressing the failed Senate vote directly responded to the charge that "this legislation wouldn't prevent all future massacres." Rather than fight that challenge, Obama conceded it, acknowledging that "no single piece of legislation can stop every act of violence and evil." But, he continued, the lack of perfect success does not mean that partial success is impossible or undesirable: "If action by Congress could have saved one person, one child, a few hundred, a few thousand—if it could have prevented those people from losing their lives to gun violence in the future while preserving our Second Amendment rights, we had an obligation to try" (2013b). Obama, then, was trying to make an argument for moderation, as I noted earlier in this essay. And in a separate essay, I argued that Obama seemed to be trying to "create activists who are paradoxically moderate" (Rood 2018, 64).

But when we look at this speech from another angle, we can see that Obama was also doing something bigger: he questioned the culturally assumed link between certainty and advocacy, knowledge and action. He urged listeners to recalibrate their rhetorical, epistemic, and civic

expectations. The challenge, he suggested, was for gun reform supporters and advocates—indeed, supporters and advocates of all kinds—to
acknowledge doubts yet still be certain enough to act and confident
enough to believe that even small improvements are worthwhile. He
illustrated this point most succinctly in his January 5, 2016 speech:
"We're here today," he explained, "to prove that the vast majority of
Americans, even if our voices aren't always the loudest or most extreme,
care enough about a little boy like Daniel [who was killed at Sandy Hook
Elementary School] to come together and take common-sense steps to
save lives and protect more of our children" (2016b). In Obama's telling, moderates (e.g., "vast majority," not always "the loudest or most
extreme," "common-sense") can, in their own way, still be activists (e.g.,
"we're here," "care enough," "take common-sense steps to save lives").
Moderation and activism need not be a paradox.

Given that Obama's 2013 and 2016 speeches marked Congress's failure to pass gun reform legislation, he seemed to be describing things as
they might be, not as they were (and are). But even if such a shift in public thought and action occurs—even if being certain enough becomes
sufficient to inspire action—gun reform supporters will still need
enough confidence, and perhaps hope, that their efforts will make a difference and that the difference is worth their time and effort. In other
words, understanding the activism gap—let alone addressing it—seems
to require continued attention to the rhetoric of certainty, uncertainty,
and the space between.

NOTES

1. Under the current system, federal law requires a background check to purchase a
   gun from a licensed dealer but not to purchase a gun at a gun show or through
   a private sale. One study estimated that 22 percent of "gun owners who reported
   obtaining their most recent firearm within the previous 2 years reported doing so
   without a background check" (Miller, Hepburn, and Azrael 2017, 233). The proposed legislation would have helped close that loophole.
2. Thanks to editor Ryan Skinnell for this language.
3. Cook and Goss (2014) note that for the gun reform movement, one of the core
   constituencies are "people who have suffered from gun violence or live in fear of
   it." They continue, "Many survivors and family members live in low income communities and lack time, money, and powerful networks that are useful in movement
   building; many would-be advocates also are emotionally depleted by their experience" (208).
4. Michael Waldman (2014) calls the Obama administration's choice to group
   together universal background checks and an assault weapons ban a "strategic
   blunder" because that grouping made it easier for gun rights advocates to depict
   all of Obama's proposals as a ban (156).

5.   Commenting on "rights talk" generally, Mary Ann Glendon (1991) notes that in the United States, rights "tend to be presented as absolute, individual, and independent of any necessary relation to responsibilities." As a result, these traits "promote mere assertion over reason-giving" (12–14).

REFERENCES

Brady Campaign to Prevent Gun Violence. n.d. "About." https://www.bradyunited.org/about.

Caulfield, Timothy, Alessandro R. Marcon, and Blake Murdoch. 2017. "Injecting Doubt: Responding to the Naturopathic Anti-vaccination Rhetoric." *Journal of Law and the Biosciences* 4 (2): 229–49.

Ceccarelli, Leah. 2011. "Manufactured Scientific Controversy: Science, Rhetoric, and Public Debate." *Rhetoric & Public Affairs* 14 (2): 195–228.

Collins, Laura J. 2014. "The Second Amendment as Demanding Subject: Figuring the Marginalized Subject in Demands for an Unbridled Second Amendment." *Rhetoric & Public Affairs* 17 (4): 737–56.

Cook, Philip J., and Kristin A. Goss. 2014. *The Gun Debate: What Everyone Needs to Know.* New York: Oxford University Press.

Cook, Philip J., David B. Kopel, and Robert J. Spitzer. 2019. "Gun Policy Research: Personal Reflections on Public Questions." In *Gun Studies: Interdisciplinary Approaches to Politics,* edited by Jennifer Carlson, Kristin A. Goss, and Harel Shapira, 330–40. New York: Routledge.

District of Columbia v. Heller. 554 US 570 (2008).

Drutman, Lee. 2015. "Here's the Real Reason We Don't Have Gun Reform (It's Not Campaign Contributions)." *Vox,* December 15, 2015. https://www.vox.com/polyarchy/2015/12/3/9841798/gun-lobby-power.

Ellis, Joseph J. 2018. *American Dialogue: The Founders and Us.* New York: Knopf.

Everytown for Gun Safety. n.d. "Who We Are." https://everytown.org/who-we-are/.

Gallup. n.d. "Congress and the Public." https://news.gallup.com/poll/1600/congress-public.aspx.

Gastil, John, and Katherine R. Knobloch. 2020. *Hope for Democracy: How Citizens Can Bring Reason Back into Politics.* New York: Oxford University Press.

Glendon, Mary Ann. 1991. *Rights Talk: The Impoverishment of Political Discourse.* New York: Free Press.

Hart, Roderick P., and Jay P. Childers. 2004. "Verbal Certainty in American Politics: An Overview and Extension." *Presidential Studies Quarterly* 34 (3): 516–35.

Kahneman, Daniel. 2011. *Thinking, Fast and Slow.* New York: Farrar, Straus & Giroux.

Klein, Ezra, and Evan Soltas. 2013. "Wonkbook: The Gun Bill Failed Because the Senate Is Wildly Undemocratic." *Washington Post,* April 18, 2013. https://www.washingtonpost.com/news/wonk/wp/2013/04/18/wonkbook-the-gun-bill-failed-because-the-senate-is-wildly-undemocratic/?utm_term=.8283877275f2.

Kochanek, Kenneth D., Sherry L. Murphy, Jiaquan Xu, and Elizabeth Arias. 2019. "Deaths: Final Data for 2017." *National Vital Statistics Reports* 68 (9). https://www.cdc.gov/nchs/data/nvsr/nvsr68/nvsr68_09-508.pdf.

LaPierre, Wayne. 2012. "NRA Press Conference, December 21, 2012." *New York Times,* December 21, 2012. http://www.nytimes.com/interactive/2012/12/21/us/nra-news-conference-transcript.html.

Lunsford, Andrea A., Kirt H. Wilson, and Rosa A. Eberly. 2009. "Introduction: Rhetoric and Roadmaps." In *The SAGE Handbook of Rhetorical Studies,* edited by Andrea A. Lunsford, Kirt H. Wilson, and Rosa A. Eberly, xi–xxix. Thousand Oaks, CA: SAGE.

Mason, Lilliana. 2018. *Uncivil Agreement: How Politics Became Our Identity*. Chicago: University of Chicago Press.

Miller, Matthew, Lisa Hepburn, and Deborah Azrael. 2017. "Firearm Acquisition without Background Checks: Results of a National Survey." *Annals of Internal Medicine* 166 (4): 233–39.

Moms Demand Action. n.d. "About." https://momsdemandaction.org/about/.

National Rifle Association. n.d. "A Brief History of the NRA." https://home.nra.org/about-the-nra/.

Obama, Barack. 2013a. "Remarks by the President and the Vice President on Gun Violence." *The White House,* January 16. https://obamawhitehouse.archives.gov/the-press-office/2013/01/16/remarks-president-and-vice-president-gun-violence.

Obama, Barack. 2013b. "Statement by the President." *The White House,* April 17. https://obamawhitehouse.archives.gov/the-press-office/2013/04/17/statement-president.

Obama, Barack. 2016a. "Guns Are Our Shared Responsibility." *New York Times,* January 7. https://www.nytimes.com/2016/01/08/opinion/president-barack-obama-guns-are-our-shared-responsibility.html.

Obama, Barack. 2016b. "Remarks by the President on Common-sense Gun Safety Reform." *The White House,* January 5. https://obamawhitehouse.archives.gov/the-press-office/2016/01/05/remarks-president-common-sense-gun-safety-reform.

Oreskes, Naomi, and Erik M. Conway. 2019. *Merchants of Doubt: How a Handful of Scientists Obscured the Truth on Issues from Tobacco Smoke to Climate Change*. New York: Bloomsbury.

Pappas, Alex. 2013. "NRA Leader Criticizes Obama for Attacks on 'Absolutism.'" *Daily Caller,* January 22, 2013. http://dailycaller.com/2013/01/22/nra-leader-criticizes-obama-for-attacks-on absolutism/.

Pew Research Center. 2013. "In Gun Control Debate, Several Options Draw Majority Support: Gun Rights Proponents More Politically Active." *Pew Research Center,* January 14, 2013. http://www.people-press.org/2013/01/14/in-gun-control-debate-several-options-draw-majority-support/.

Pfau, Michael William. 2017. "Bright Lines or Blurred Lines? Universal Background Checks and the NRA Slippery Slope Argument." *Argumentation and Advocacy* 53 (4): 253–70.

Rood, Craig. 2018. "'Our Tears Are Not Enough': The Warrant of the Dead in the Rhetoric of Gun Control." *Quarterly Journal of Speech* 104 (1): 47–70.

Rood, Craig. 2019. *After Gun Violence: Deliberation and Memory in an Age of Political Gridlock*. University Park: Pennsylvania State University Press.

Silver, Nate. 2013. "The Gun Vote and 2014: Will There Be an Electoral Price?" *FiveThirtyEight,* April 23, 2013. http://fivethirtyeight.blogs.nytimes.com/2013/04/23/the-gun-vote-and-2014-will-there-be-an-electoral-price/.

Spitzer, Robert J. 2012. *The Politics of Gun Control*. 5th ed. New York: Routledge.

Spitzer, Robert J. 2015. *Guns across America: Reconciling Gun Rules and Rights*. New York: Oxford University Press.

Vavrus, Mary D., and August Lienbach. 2016. "Postfeminism at the Shooting Range: Vulnerability and Fire-Empowerment in the Gun Women Network." In *Dangerous Discourses: Feminism, Gun Violence, and Civic Life,* edited by Catherine R. Squires, 179–212. New York: Peter Lang.

Waldman, Michael. 2014. *The Second Amendment: A Biography*. New York: Simon & Schuster.

Winkler, Adam. 2013. *Gunfight: The Battle over the Right to Bear Arms in America*. New York: Norton.

7

THIS IS AMERICA ON GUNS
Rhetorics of Acquiescence and Resistance to Privatized Gun Violence

Lydia Wilkes

In the provocative 2018 music video *This Is America*, Childish Gambino, the musical persona of Donald Glover, presents a definition of the United States in which "guns are treated with more respect than human lives" (Tesema 2018). In the video, Gambino alternates between dancing and killing, first dancing his way to a hooded Black man playing the song's opening guitar riff before executing him from behind with a handgun that he "carefully places . . . on a lush pillow held out for him by an eager school-aged black child" (St. Félix 2018). After a Black choir sings the chorus, Gambino, catching an AK-47 thrown to him from off-screen, sprays bullets at the choir, whose members fall limp and bloody to the ground in a disturbing nod to the anti-Black mass shooting at Mother Emanuel AME Church in Charleston, South Carolina. A Black child in a school uniform receives the rifle and, as Doreen St. Félix writes for the *New Yorker*, "then Glover is dancing again—this time, with cars burning and police chaos beyond him." While the video is "fundamentally ambiguous" (St. Félix 2018), it unambiguously treats guns with more respect than human lives. In doing so, *This Is America* accurately defines the nation's centuries-old relationship with gun ownership, use, and violence in which whites, armed to the teeth, waged war against Indigenous peoples to steal their land and then defend it as white territory, both spatially and ideologically, against Indigenous peoples and enslaved Africans rhetorically constructed as savage enemies (Dunbar-Ortiz 2018; Ore 2019). When enslaved Africans, valued only as property, managed to escape plantation violence, white men acting as armed slave patrols, the precursor of police forces, hunted them at the behest of the law (Dunbar-Ortiz 2018). In the video's final scene, Gambino runs for his life in wide-eyed terror, chased by invisible slave patrollers or police or a lynch mob—the same people by different group names. This stark

https://doi.org/10.7330/9781646422159.c007

reminder of the ontological terror imposed on Black people in America is as unambiguous as the privileging of guns over human life. This is not new, not as violence, not as spectacle.

What is new vis-à-vis gun violence in *This Is America* is how it dramatizes the difficulty of sustaining attention in an age of distraction, just as whites are (again) waking up to the notion that our silence is complicity in systemic anti-Black violence, so we are joining movements like Black Lives Matter to enact antiracist policies.[1] The video dramatizes the onslaught of "joy and destruction" juxtaposed in social media—dancing, killing, dancing, killing (St. Félix 2018)—an onslaught that drains human capacities for attention and feeds acquiescence to the epidemic of gun violence as the status quo. Drawing on Jeremy Engels's *The Politics of Resentment*, Craig Rood calls this the "problem of fleeting engagement" (2018, 50). Fleeting engagement marks the United States' collective response to gun violence in an attention economy. According to Engels, when violence recurs, "we are moved, and we move on," rarely dwelling with a violent event long enough to form a more productive rhetorical and political response (2015, 3). Furthermore, in this distracted environment, right-wing politicians and pundits push to continually privatize violence as a depoliticized individual problem caused not by the proliferation of firearms or systemic social problems open to public deliberation but rather by a lone wolf or a bad apple (Engels 2015).

Privatizing violence removes it from the sphere of public rhetoric. Any attempt to discuss gun control policy can be successfully dismissed as an inappropriate politicization of a person's death (Duerringer 2015), and any attempt to connect modern-day lynchings with firearms to historical lynchings with rope can be successfully dismissed as stoking racial division (Ore 2019). Roxanne Dunbar-Ortiz posits that, along with "reverence for the Second Amendment," "the privileging of individual rights over collective rights, not the NRA, [is] the source of the problem with enacting firearms regulations" (2018, 199). Privatizing gun violence, silencing those who would discuss gun control policy as violators of decorum, and privileging individual rights over collective rights forcefully maintain a deadly status quo that, for the most part, garners only fleeting engagement in media environments. When firearm-related deaths remain a daily occurrence and the collective response, underwritten by discourses of privatization, amounts to short-lived "thoughts and prayers," a majority of Americans have acquiesced to gun violence as the status quo. This is America on guns.

This chapter argues that rhetorics of acquiescence in a time of fleeting engagement help perpetuate gun violence by promoting a "glazed over half-acceptance" (Engels and Saas 2013, 227) of gun violence. Rhetorics of acquiescence, developed to characterize post-9/11 war rhetoric, seek neither assent nor dissent but instead "cultivat[e] passivity and numbness" in order to depoliticize war (227). Rhetorics of acquiescence to gun violence have similar effects: they leave people feeling helpless, numb, and unable to act as violence recurs—too exhausted by the onslaught of joy and despair, dancing and killing, to feel capable of action. This chapter will examine some of the many discursive and material rhetorics of acquiescence that sustain gun violence, discourage dissent, and perpetuate the privatization of violence. Discursive rhetorics of acquiescence include the cliché "thoughts and prayers" and the ideologically driven injunction to decorous silence in the aftermath of mass shootings (Duerringer 2015), while material rhetorics range from expensive bullet-resistant clothing and backpacks—body armor for (mostly white) kids from well-resourced homes—to a multimillion-dollar high school redesign based on antiballistic trench engineering from World War I. These examples illustrate the ongoing privatization of gun violence despite its effects on communities. Though prevalent, acquiescence does not stop dissent—it just makes dissent seem too difficult or fruitless to pursue, as energy, numbers, momentum, and rhetorical force are greatest among gun rights advocates and activists who for decades have been better organized and funded than gun control advocates and activists (Rood 2018; see also Rood, chapter 6 in this volume). But like shifting attention, rhetorical force—the suasive impact of differently organized and circulated messages—can be changed by well-organized, savvy rhetors (see Kreuter, chapter 2 in this volume).

Hence this chapter will also examine discursive and material dissent from (or resistance to) the violent status quo from clergy members condemning the appropriation of prayer to a new generation of rhetorically trained activists exemplified by the youth-led organization March for Our Lives. While the gun lobby and a well-organized minority of gun owners have exerted more rhetorical force on the gun debate than the vast majority of Americans, including the vast majority of gun owners, dissenters appeal to ethos in their attempts to gather mass and change the direction of rhetorical force about gun ownership and gun violence, to break the spell of passive numbness—acquiescence—in response to gun violence. As Roxanne Dunbar-Ortiz points out, there is no "gun-control 'movement'" (2018, 198); rather, organizations are scattered like pennies thrown from a roof and hence have little impact on gun regulations (see Kreuter, chapter 2 in this volume). However, children, teenagers, and young adults who grew up after Columbine in militarized schools where they learned to scope out exits "just in case" have been organizing and networking to loudly and repeatedly dissent from a status quo that terrorizes them in public places. If gun clubs and gun shops comprise the grassroots structure of the gun rights movement (Han 2017; Dunbar-Ortiz 2018), student- and youth-led local chapters of gun violence prevention organizations have begun to grow the grassroots coalitions necessary to prevent gun violence as it manifests locally. These organizations seek to shift values back to communalism and change accompanying frames and narratives so that human lives, especially Black lives, are respected (and legally protected) more than guns, privatized violence again becomes a matter of public deliberation, and discourse about gun violence's effects immediately after headline-grabbing shootings again becomes appropriate. As these organizations' discursive and material rhetorics of dissent gather rhetorical mass, speed, and force in the direction of gun safety and gun control, they provide a "glimmer of hope" (Hogan and Rood 2015, 360; Founders 2018) that cultural, political, and policy changes will curtail the widespread gun violence uniquely definitional of the United States of America. This task is enormous and gun rights organizations have a decades-old head start, but the young members of the "school shooting generation" (Founders 2018, 7) frame it as a fight for their lives—for their right to live—and they refuse to acquiesce to dominant narratives or to the terror wrought by pervasive gun violence.

RHETORICS OF ACQUIESCENCE

Rhetorics of acquiescence were first identified by Jeremy Engels and William O. Saas as aspects of post-9/11 war rhetoric that help explain Americans' relationship to endless war in the twenty-first century. They stem from the traditional binary in rhetorical criticism of assent/dissent or for/against. Whereas people in the United States might have been for or against, say, the war in Vietnam, public rhetoric operates differently in a post-9/11 time of endless war. "Overriding the for/against distinction," write Engels and Saas, "is the general feeling of acquiescence in relation to war" (2013, 226). This feeling of acquiescence is "the black oil . . . that now powers the war machine," while assent to war is "something like a 2 percent additive" (226). Rhetorics of acquiescence pervade the rhetorical landscape and aim "at promoting a glazed-over half-acceptance of the inevitability of war, whatever the outcome" (227). They do so by "display[ing] war in such a way that it cannot be contested, constituting a distracted civic body numb to violence" (227).

War continues apace in part because citizens, tranquilized by rhetorics of acquiescence and distracted by the speed of contemporary life, feel that they cannot contest it.

While Engels and Saas focus on public discourse by powerful actors, I extend rhetorics of acquiescence to individuals and groups who (mostly) do not exercise state power but nevertheless affect discourse and deliberation about gun ownership and gun violence. Rhetorics of acquiescence to gun violence feed a mood of continually giving in to gun violence as inevitable, despite sincere assertions by those affected by gun violence of "never again" (see Serber's chapter 8 in this volume). Gun violence continues apace in part because people who neither assent to nor dissent from increasing gun violence *feel* that they cannot contest it.

Crucially, acquiescence as a rhetorical response operates at a remove from vulnerability to violence and hence is available only to those privileged enough to avoid daily exposure to gun violence. Black mothers, for example, have dissented from the status quo of racialized violence at least since Mamie Till demanded an open casket funeral for her son Emmett (Ore 2019), and more recently, Black mothers have organized to prevent gun violence in their communities (see, e.g., Dubisar 2018). But Black women have carried burdens of violence for centuries in the United States. Broad coalitions are also necessary to meet a problem as deeply rooted as gun violence, but too many potential members of these coalitions—"the majority of the population [that] passively supports gun regulations" (Dunbar-Ortiz 2018, 198)—continue instead to acquiesce to gun violence, prompted by discursive and material rhetorics of acquiescence circulating in the United States. Mood and attention, then, are two suasive aspects of firearms-related discourse influencing and influenced by assent, dissent, and acquiescence. While discursive and material rhetorics of acquiescence intertwine, for the sake of clarity I treat rhetorics that register more as discursive in the following section and rhetorics that register more as material in the next.

Discursive Rhetorics of Acquiescence: "Thoughts and Prayers" and Decorous Silence

Discursive rhetorics of acquiescence to gun violence include commonplaces repeated on legacy and social media such as the refrain "thoughts and prayers" and the appeal to decorous silence, both of which indefinitely defer discussion of gun control policies. They do so based on the contention that grief and suffering related to gun violence should adhere to a script and remain private matters rather than be exploited for political gain or cheapened by exposure to the public (Duerringer 2015). In his rhetorical analysis of gun rights commentators' denunciations of eulogies after the mass shooting at Sandy Hook Elementary, Christopher M. Duerringer argues that "any instantiation of decorum . . . is a manifestation of ideology," and these manifestations "provide rhetorical critics with a clear point of entry from which one may work to infer the ideology being offered to an audience" (81). Duerringer derives two ideological justifications for right-wing claims that linking "an innocent person's murder to the cause of gun control policy" inappropriately politicizes that person's death: that the deaths at Sandy Hook "were not of importance for the general public" and that "political discourse inherently cheapens or sullies what ought to be a . . . private process of mourning" (92). These ideologies espouse a radical form of individualism that "disavows significant bonds or relations between individuals" and renounces "the social, identificatory function of rhetoric" (92). These ideologies also underwrite the ritual murmuring of "thoughts and prayers" whenever gun violence captures public attention for a fleeting moment.

As a collective response to gun violence, "thoughts and prayers" exemplifies fleeting engagement and promotes acquiescence to pervasive gun violence as an uncontestable status quo. *Washington Post* columnist Dana Millbank captures this sense in a bitter op-ed in which he cites a litany of "thoughts and prayers" tweets from Republican lawmakers after two mass shootings in August 2019. Millbank claims that " 'thoughts and prayers' has become a meme, a cynical punchline conveying inaction on guns." As one Democratic senator tweeted, "My Republican colleagues cut and paste the words 'thoughts and prayers' into a tweet and then do nothing on gun violence." This response to "thoughts and prayers" as code for inaction circulates often enough that some Republican lawmakers preemptively address it when a mass shooting occurs, as one representative did when he tweeted that "there will be a few that criticize our calls for earnest prayer." "Actually, we criticize prayer in lieu of action," Millbank replies in the op-ed. As a left-wing bearer of this message, Millbank is open to criticism from political opponents. But he is not alone in positing "thoughts and prayers" as a ritualized rhetoric of acquiescence, a response to mass shootings that conveys an intention to "do nothing on gun violence," to acquiesce or give in to the status quo.

Clergy members in mainline Christian denominations have joined in condemning "thoughts and prayers" as code for inaction and have dissented from the status quo of pervasive gun violence by assenting to conversation and a type of rhetorical listening. In 2019 the Presbyterian Church (USA) ordained "its first minister of gun violence prevention," the Reverend Deanna Hollas, a Texan who aims through her supervision of 800 people across fifty states to "creat[e] the cultural change that is needed along with legislation" (Hassan 2019). Hollas also refutes the false dilemma positing prayer and action as mutually exclusive: "While all that we do as Christians should be rooted in worship and prayer, it should not stay there. It is like breathing—worship and prayer is the in-breath, and action is the out-breath." Linking prayer and action, Hollas dissents from the appropriation of prayer as a rhetoric of acquiescence. She also assents to conversation, listening, and compassion in the space of a mainline Christian denomination, arguing that these denominations are "in a unique position to be leaders in bringing conversations about gun violence out of the shadows, as our congregations are one of the few places where people of different political persuasions still gather together voluntarily" (quoted in Hassan 2019). Of course, not all Christian denominations value listening, conversation and, in particular, dissent (see Boedy's chapter 11 in this volume), but mainstream religious spaces provide an increasingly rare opportunity to listen across cultures (Royster 1996) from a non-defensive stance (Ratcliffe 2005).

Just as "thoughts and prayers" registers for some as code for inaction that promotes acquiescence to pervasive gun violence, the appeal to decorous silence as the only appropriate response to mass shootings condemns any speech (like Hollas's) that expresses anything more than sympathy. The National Rifle Association in particular urges decorous silence in response to mass shootings, as Craig Rood has shown in his analysis of President Obama's gun control rhetoric after the shooting at Sandy Hook Elementary. As Obama led the nation in mourning, the NRA's executive vice president, Wayne LaPierre, appealed to decorous silence to condemn Obama's speech: "While some have tried to exploit tragedy for political gain, we have remained respectfully silent" (quoted in Rood 2018, 62). This appeal to decorum asserts that "proper mourning should include no talk of policy" (62), or at least no talk of gun *control* policy, as LaPierre used his speech after Sandy Hook to argue for installing armed guards in schools (*Washington Post* 2012). Speech and action honor the dead only when they lead to more armed "good guys," LaPierre suggests. The only respectful response to mass school shootings, according to the gun lobby, is to acquiesce to the status quo through decorous silence or to assent to, as Patricia Roberts-Miller puts it (chapter 1 in this volume), MOAR GUNZ by supporting the policy of armed guards in schools (or its offspring, arming teachers). As long as the majority of Americans who support gun regulations observe decorous silence or murmur "thoughts and prayers" in response to gun violence, they—we—distracted perhaps by the next catastrophe or viral dance video, continue to acquiesce discursively.

Material Rhetorics of Acquiescence: Militarizing Everyday Life

Material rhetorics also encourage acquiescence to gun violence by providing technological solutions that offer an illusion of safety (but limited actual safety) to those who can afford to purchase them.

Uniquely prevalent in the United States, the public presence of guns and gun violence has ambient rhetorical effects on everyone (see Hill's chapter 5 in this volume), though these effects vary considerably according to factors like location, sex, gender, race and ethnicity, and age (Squires 2016; Kalesan et al. 2018). As Indigenous cultures have long known (e.g., Todd 2016) and Western rhetoricians have recently noted (e.g., Rickert 2013), environments, things, objects, and other nonhumans make available certain comportments with others and the world. While guns show up differently for individuals and groups depending on their past experiences with them (Carter 2017), acquiescence is one of the ambient rhetorical effects of firearms' material ubiquity in the United States. These material rhetorics of acquiescence, as I call them, manifest the mood of giving in to the inevitability of gun violence in civilian spaces via the adoption of military technologies for self-defense and group defense. These military technologies include body armor and antiballistic engineering, and their growing presence further militarizes an already heavily militarized domestic US landscape. As the gun lobby, politicians, and political pundits advocate decorous silence and condemn speech in the aftermath of attention-getting shootings, material rhetorics of acquiescence to gun violence quietly accrue. This is America on guns.

Material rhetorics of acquiescence proliferated with renewed urgency after the 2012 shooting at Sandy Hook Elementary as (mostly white) people worried about themselves or their loved ones getting shot in a public place and sought commercial, technological solutions to the widespread presence of increasingly lethal firearms. By 2019, "bulletproof" backpacks were a back-to-school trend: one Twitter user shared search results for "bulletproof backpack" with the hashtag #ThisisAmerica, evidence of "our sad reality" (Strauss 2019). In addition to referencing Childish Gambino's video, the hashtag suggests that material acquiescence to gun violence defines the United States as a nation (whereas, as

Dunbar-Ortiz [2018] shows, assent to gun violence defined the United States for most of its history).

Alongside "bulletproof" backpacks in the search results appears the Wonder Hoodie. The Wonder Hoodie's ad copy describes it as "the only stand-alone product on the market to seamlessly and discreetly protect all the vital organs" and brags that "this bulletproof hoodie will become a family favorite as it accompanies your child to and from home" (Wonder Hoodie 2019). Wonder Hoodies are available in sizes small enough to fit a six-year-old child, and the company's "growing future program" promises that "when purchasing a bulletproof hoodie for your child, know you can always trade-up for a larger size when they outgrow it (shipping and size surcharge not included)." Finally, the company portrays itself as socially minded, noting that for "every 10 hoodies we sell, we donate 1 to a public-school teacher." This product offers a commercial solution to gun violence constructed as private, a matter for a resourced individual to solve with this item of clothing.

Like the backpacks advertised in the tweet, the Wonder Hoodie touts its "Premium NIJ-IIIA Protection," referring to the National Institute of Justice's Level IIIA test for body armor. Level IIIA body armor stops bullets—from the smaller 9mm and .22 to the larger .44 magnum—that can be fired out of a handgun. However, Level IIIA offers "no rifle ammunition protection" (National Institute of Justice n.d.). It would not stop a 5.56mm/.223 bullet fired from the popular AR-15 platform, a variant of which was used in the shooting at Sandy Hook Elementary and a litany of other widely known shootings since then. The so-called stopping power (actually killing power) of ammunition fired from rifles (see Kreuter's chapter 2 in this volume) is much greater than that of handguns, necessitating additional classes of body armor used by law enforcement and the military. The Wonder Hoodie and its ilk *do* offer protection from bullets fired from handguns, but when it comes to rifle ammunition, they provide an illusion of safety more than protection from harm.

They also further normalize acquiescence among civilians to military technologies in civilian spaces. Some civilians, of course, heartily assent to this militarization while others heartily dissent, but millions of people in the broad middle acquiesce, even as those in the broad middle might also recoil in horror at militarized police responses to protests, such as the police overreaction to protests in Ferguson after Michael Brown's death. Some of these civilians, if they can afford it, might purchase a Wonder Hoodie so they can feel safe going to a church or school or movie theater. Most in the broad acquiescent middle feel helpless and unsure of how they might intervene beyond the ritualized utterance thoughts and prayers, thoughts and prayers. This is America on guns.

Material rhetorics of acquiescence to gun violence are not new but have been accelerating in the past two decades. In the aftermath of the 1999 Columbine High School shooting, metal detectors began to appear at high schools, utilizing the defensive, acquiescent technology of the day to garner an illusory sense of safety. An especially strong example of contemporary material acquiescence to gun violence comes from a high school in western Michigan. Fruitport High School planned a $48 million construction project to apply antiballistic engineering developed during World War I's trench warfare to the high school's hallways in order to "to dampen the killing potential of a mass shooter" (Horton 2019). Alex Horton, an Iraq War infantry veteran and *Washington Post* reporter, explains that World War I's "serpentine trenches" resulted from a "horrifically clear logic": "If enemy soldiers ever breached it, the zigzagging pattern would prevent them from shooting in a straight line down the length of the trench—leaving only a relative few exposed to gunfire or shrapnel." Construction at Fruitport High School includes curved hallways inspired by serpentine trenches "to reduce a gunman's range," as well as "jutting barriers to provide cover and egress, and meticulously spaced classrooms that can lock on demand and hide students in the corner, out of a killer's sight." The school's superintendent attributed the redesign to "the ubiquity of mass shootings in the United States," including school shootings mentioned in this chapter and the 2019 mass shooting at a Walmart in El Paso, Texas. The firm behind the design "also designs prisons . . . [and] wanted to strike a balance between security and a welcoming presence without the pendulum swinging too far in either direction." Prison-like features include a shatter-resistant film on glass, "an educational Panopticon" in the front office with "views of the main approach, the vestibule and some of the hallways," and a switch that allows "all doors to be locked from the front office." This is America on guns.

The militarization of K–12 schools is at least two decades old, but unless the school was initially designed for military use, this militarization did not include the incorporation of military defenses in the school's design and construction. Fruitport High School's design assumes and acquiesces to the eventual presence of a shooter bent on killing as many people as possible with a high-velocity firearm. The popularity of these material rhetorics of acquiescence to gun violence suggests that military-grade firearms in civilian hands call for military-grade body armor on the bodies of children, not for restrictions on civilian ownership of military-grade firearms.

Further, these material rhetorics of acquiescence intensify the ongoing militarization of the United States, most of which is far more quotidian than "bulletproof" backpacks and school redesigns, and hence far less covered by most media. The Black Lives Matter movement emerged from everyday violence against Black people, Black men in particular, that its founders characterize as an extension of the War on Drugs (Khan-Cullors and Bandele 2017). Similarly, March for Our Lives founder Matt Deitsch uses a war frame to describe the group's grassroots activism tour, the Road to Change: "Organizing put an end to the war in Vietnam. Young people organized to stop their friends from coming back in body bags. Today, the war is on our soil, with our weapons, taking our lives. It will take young people organizing to end this war too" (Founders 2018, 204). Founder Alex Wind made a similar point: "We would not need metal detectors and clear backpacks and more weapons in our streets if there weren't weapons of war in the hands of civilians" (174).

Deitsch and Wind suggest that gun violence in the United States amounts to a war, and recent public health research supports this claim. A public health study comparing firearm-related deaths among US school-age children (ages five–eighteen) to *all* deaths among police officers and US military personnel found that an average of 2,500 children died by firearm *every year* between 1999 and 2017 in the United States (Rubenstein et al. 2019). The study's authors write: "It is sobering to reflect that in 2017 there were 144 US police officers who died in the line of duty, fewer than 1000 deaths among active duty military, and 2462 school-age children killed with firearms" (994).

Though school shootings attract media attention, the vast majority of deaths by firearm happen outside of school settings in an obfuscated domestic war, a claim backed by other studies. For example, a study looking at violence in schools between 1992 and 2016 found that less than 3 percent of youth homicides and less than 1 percent of youth suicides happened on a school campus (Musu et al. 2019, 29). A separate study of gun violence between 2009 and 2018 found that mass shootings comprised only 1 percent of each year's firearm-related deaths (Brooks 2019). The vast majority of those deaths happened at the victim's home in relation to domestic violence. Propped up by dominant power structures and falling as it does on people with less power and fewer resources, this "less spectacular everyday gun violence and victimhood . . . rarely garners [much media] attention" compared to mass shootings and school shootings, "but claims many more lives" (Squires 2016, xvi). Indeed, the endless stream of everyday deaths by firearm in the United States—100 people killed each day, 4 of them children (Brady 2019)—receives about as much public attention as the endless stream of non-US civilian deaths in foreign war zones (see Dunbar-Ortiz 2018; Eberly 2018). Gun violence continues apace. This is America on guns.

ACCRUING MASS THROUGH ETHOS AND STYLE: MARCH FOR OUR LIVES

How might the helpless feeling of being unable to contest privatized gun violence be mitigated and support for gun regulations be activated? Gun control advocates and activists have invested a great deal of hope in the young people who formed March for Our Lives after the shooting at Marjory Stoneman Douglas High School. The same groups were equally hopeful that the appeals of parents of young children who died at Sandy Hook Elementary School would have some impact. Brad Serber notes that even the harshest critics of the March for Our Lives founders recognize (and resent) their unique positionality as young adults who retain an association with childlike innocence but can speak quite capably for themselves (see Serber's chapter 8 in this volume); these critics argue that "you're not allowed to disagree or you're attacking a child" and deemed a "bad person" (Sinclair 2018). In other words, the critics acknowledge that ethos resides so strongly with the students from Parkland, Florida, that their opponents have no appropriate ethos from which to disagree, as these young people refuse ideologies that would privatize gun violence and attempt to change the narratives associated with guns in the United States, not only to make the prevention of gun violence a matter of public conversation and policy, but also to sustain attention until gun regulations are established.

The Parkland students and the coalitions they have formed with students across the country have persistently invoked ethos and style in their attempts to accrue rhetorical mass. In their account of the emergence of March for Our Lives from the shooting, the group's teenage founders appeal to their ethos as members of "the school shooting generation" and their sense of owning their story: "*This is not the media's narrative . . . The students of Stoneman Douglas know what happened at Stoneman Douglas, and under no circumstances will you tell our story for us*" (Founders 2018, 7, 5; emphasis in original). Defining themselves a youth-led movement, March for Our Lives members found disparities in gun control knowledge between the state and federal representatives and school-aged activists they met. As founder Matt Deitsch writes, "Around the country, I have met ten-year-olds who know policy better than five-term congressmen" (204). Deitsch took on the task of "coordinating the adults we were bringing in" because adults "had no idea what they were doing in regards to the message we were trying to convey" (207). That message: whereas other gun violence prevention organizations are arranged to sustain themselves over time, "we don't want March for Our Lives to exist; we want this organization to complete a mission and render itself obsolete" (208). And so, March for Our Lives, "inspired by the farmers' movement in California and the Freedom Riders," focuses its grassroots activism on registering new voters, creating coalitions, and "empowering young people . . . to be the leaders in their community" (209). Founder Delaney Tarr captures this focus: "It was cool to meet Bernie Sanders, it was cool to meet John Lewis, but it means a lot more to meet a teenager who says, 'You inspired me to create my own march'" (99).

Over 800 sibling marches occurred around the world when March for Our Lives held its first march in 2018 only six weeks after the shooting (Founders 2018, 182). Almost overnight, the students went from learning about the NRA as an interest group in an advanced placement government class the same day the shooting happened to demanding accountability from their state and federal representatives, inspiring other youth, and committing themselves to making gun control "the voting issue" in "every election, [in] every state, in every city" (151, 158). As Tarr said in her speech during the march, "This is a movement relying on the persistence and passion of its people. We cannot move on" (163). "The march," said Cameron Kasky in his speech, "is not the climax of this movement, it is the beginning" (161). These young people understand the need for "the persistence of voters" (152), especially young voters coming together to form intersectional coalitions and committed to voting out of office politicians who do not fight for gun restrictions (160, 163).

March for Our Lives measures mass in terms of newly registered voters much more so than in tweets and retweets (Founders 2018, 183), yet its members also understand how grassroots activism and digital activism blend and blur, and how they might use style to deliver their message and promote action. Whereas the Wonder Hoodie acquiesces to gun violence as an individual's problem rather than a collective's problem by assuming a defensive posture, clothing designed by young gun control activists redefines patriotism not as owning a gun but as registering to vote. Jammal Lemy, creative director for March for Our Lives, was already designing clothing and donating proceeds "to microfund projects within war-stricken areas" when the then inchoate group asked him to design merch for the march: "They came to me saying that we have to attack the NRA where it hurts," Lemy writes. "The NRA's main defense is patriotism, and we can take that away from them by designing merch that is just as patriotic" (192, 197). Knowing that "most of our phone cameras have QR readers already integrated," Lemy chose to combine the American flag with a QR code linking to the voter registration page on March for Our Lives' website (197). "So imagine," he writes, "being able to register everyone around you in two minutes or less?" (197). Part of the group's initiative to bring voter registration to high schools, the shirt became a "staple," "a conversation piece every place we went . . . [about] youth empowerment and civic engagement" (Huriash 2018).

Through style and ethos, the group can inspire others and in so doing, to accrue rhetorical mass. March for Our Lives registered over 50,000 voters and "spurred a historic youth turnout in the 2018 midterm elections, with a 47 percent increase over the last midterm election and the highest percentage of youth voter turnout ever" (March 2019). While this accretion of mass cannot yet match the funding or organizational power of the rhetorically massive hardline minority of gun owners, gun rights lobbying groups, and the behemoth gun industry, it offers hope for overcoming the "activism gap" among gun control supporters (see Rood's chapter 6 in this volume) and curtailing the upward trajectory of gun fatalities.

GLIMMERING HOPE

Can these young adults sustain attention long enough to shepherd gun control policies through state and federal legislative bodies currently comprised of adults who, as March for Our Lives founders noted, do not understand gun violence very well or treat it with adequate urgency? A definitive answer to this question isn't yet available. However, March for Our Lives appears to be the vanguard of a generation that by and large values life and safety over civilian access to military-grade firearms and firearms accessories. March for Our Lives is also one of many youth-led movements dissenting from a violent status quo. For example, members of the group met with Black students from Chicago and with Tokata Iron Eyes of the Standing Rock Youth Council, a water protector and climate change activist, during the summer of 2018. These young leaders recognize their considerable capacity to accrue rhetorical mass through ethos and style, and they have their lives and senses of safety to gain every time they refuse acquiescence and choose to assent to the public deliberation of policy. They are unlikely to abandon their fight until they accomplish their goal of reducing gun violence to the point that March for Our Lives becomes obsolete. They want a redefined America in which human lives are treated with more respect than guns.

Although the forces of acquiescence strongly influence the mood of public discourse about guns and gun violence, as J. Michael Hogan and Craig Rood (2015) write, "The vast majority of Americans are neither 'gun nuts' nor 'gun haters,' and therein lies a glimmer of hope that something might be done about the epidemic of gun violence in America" (360). The eldest members of the school shooting generation are about twenty years old at the time of this writing. They lead the way by refusing the many rhetorics of acquiescence that sustain a deadly status quo they find "simply unacceptable" (March 2019, 2). Combined with millennials, this generation comprises just under half the US population, representing substantial voting and economic power. Their numbers suggest dire economic consequences for industries that do not display a commitment to social responsibility, something *Forbes* recommended to gun manufacturers after yet another series of high-profile mass shootings during summer 2019 (Cardello 2019). Having exhausted judicial appeals to prevent survivors of gun violence from suing them, gun manufacturers are again legally liable for damage done by their products (Hussey and Williamson 2019). Public health research into gun violence, chilled for nearly two decades by the Dickey Amendment, has begun to appear, though funding is still scarce. The rhetorical force of gun control activist groups like March for Our Lives, which intend to influence as many future elections as possible with their grassroots and social media activism, stands to increase. Hope that the majority of Americans who already (passively) value human lives more than unrestricted access to guns will act to turn that value into policy glimmers brightly on the horizon.

NOTE

1. As a white woman who owns guns solely for hunting as part of a family tradition, I was moved to begin this book and to contribute this chapter not only by repeated mass shootings and the daily realities of gun violence but also by repeated failures on the part of gun regulation proponents to secure the regulations supported by a vast majority of Americans, including a majority of gun owners. I grew up in a home where guns were never fetishized or valued over human life but rather treated as dangerous technologies of potentially lethal violence—part of a family tradition of hunting to eat game meat, yes, but no less dangerous for that. The rhetorical machinations that prevent guns from being regulated like other dangerous technologies (such as cars, which cause about the same number of deaths as guns each year in the United States) motivated me to share more nuanced understandings of rhetorics of gun ownership, use, and violence. I hope present and future activists for gun regulations can make more effective arguments when they are equipped with a robust understanding of firearms as technologies embedded in complex historical, political, and rhetorical circumstances that then inform their use: who can use them, where and how they can be used, what purposes they can be used for, and what legal repercussions accompany their use.

REFERENCES

Brady Campaign to Prevent Gun Violence. 2019. "Key Gun Violence Statistics." https://www.bradyunited.org/key-statistics.

Brooks, Brad. 2019. "More US Children Die in Mass Shootings at Home Than at School: Study." *Reuters*, November 21, 2019. https://www.reuters.com/article/us-usa-guncontrol-children/more-u-s-children-die-in-mass-shootings-at-home-than-at-school-study-idUSKBN1XV185.

Carter, Gregg Lee. 2017. *Gun Control in the United States*, 2nd ed. Santa Barbara: ABC-CLIO.

Cardello, Hank. 2019. "What Big Food Can Teach Gunmakers about Social Responsibility." *Forbes*, August 30, 2019. https://www.forbes.com/sites/hankcardello/2019/08/30/what-big-food-can-teach-gunmakers-about-social-responsibility/.

Dubisar, Abby M. 2018. "Mothers against Gun Violence and the Activist Buffer." *College English* 80 (3): 105–217.

Duerringer, Christopher M. 2015. "Dis-honoring the Dead: Negotiating Decorum in the Shadow of Sandy Hook." *Western Journal of Communication* 80 (1): 79–99.

Dunbar-Ortiz, Roxanne. 2018. *Loaded: A Disarming History of the Second Amendment*. San Francisco: City Lights Books.

Eberly, Rosa. 2018. *Towers of Rhetoric: Memory and Reinvention. Intermezzo*. http://intermezzo.enculturation.net/05-eberly.htm.

Engels, Jeremy. 2015. *The Politics of Resentment: A Genealogy*. University Park: The Pennsylvania University Press.

Engels, Jeremy, and William O. Saas. 2013. "On Acquiescence and Ends-Less War: An Inquiry into the New War Rhetoric." *Quarterly Journal of Speech* 99 (2): 225–32. http://dx.doi.org/10.1080/00335630.2013.775705.

Founders of March for Our Lives. 2018. *Glimmer of Hope: How Tragedy Sparked a Movement*. New York: Razorbill & Dutton.

Gambino, Childish [Donald Glover]. 2018. *This Is America*. YouTube. https://www.youtube.com/watch?v=VYOjWnS4cMY.

Hassan, Adeel. 2019. "'Thoughts and Prayers' Aren't Enough, America's First Gun Violence Minister Says." *New York Times*, July 28, 2019. https://www.nytimes.com/2019/07/28/us/minister-gun-violence-church.html.

Han, Hahrie. 2017. "Want Gun Control? Learn from the N.R.A." *New York Times*, October 4, 2017. https://www.nytimes.com/2017/10/04/opinion/gun-control-nra-vegas.html.

Hogan, J. Michael, and Craig Rood. 2015. "Rhetorical Studies and the Gun Debate: A Public Policy Perspective." *Rhetoric & Public Affairs* 18 (2): 359–72. 10.1080/10570314.2015.1116712.

Horton, Alex. 2019. "A New High School Will Have Sleek Classrooms—and Places to Hide from a Mass Shooter." *Washington Post*, August 22, 2019. https://www.washingtonpost.com/education/2019/08/22/new-high-school-will-have-sleek-classrooms-places-hide-mass-shooter/.

Huriash, Lisa J. 2018. "Stoneman Douglas Grad Wants to Change the World, One Piece of Art at a Time." *Florida Sun Sentinel*, August 31, 2018. https://www.sun-sentinel.com/local/broward/parkland/florida-school-shooting/fl-sb-jammal-lemy-march-for-our-lives-20180831-story.html.

Hussey, Kristin, and Elizabeth Williamson. 2019. "Supreme Court Allows Sandy Hook Relatives to Sue Gun Maker." *New York Times*, November 12, 2019. https://www.nytimes.com/2019/11/12/us/politics/supreme-court-sandy-hook-remington.html.

Kalesan, Bindu, et al. 2018. "Cross-Sectional Study of Loss of Life Expectancy at Different Ages Related to Firearm Deaths among Black and White Americans." *BMJ Evidence-Based Medicine* 24 (2): 55–58. http://dx.doi.org/10.1136/bmjebm-2018-111103.

Khan-Cullors, Patrice, and Asha Bandele. 2017. *When They Call You a Terrorist: A Black Lives Matter Memoir*. New York: St. Martin's.

March for Our Lives. 2019. *Peace Plan for a Safer America.* https://marchforourlives.com/wp-content/uploads/2019/08/MFOL_PeacePlan_2019_-FINAL.pdf.

Millbank, Dana. 2019. "Republicans' Thoughts and Prayers Have Become a Cruel Joke." *Washington Post,* August 5, 2019. https://www.washingtonpost.com/opinions/cue-the-thoughts-and-prayers/2019/08/05/2de2b8d6-b7b8-11e9-bad6-609f75bfd97f_story.html.

Musu, Lauren, et al. 2019. *Indicators of School Crime and Safety: 2018.* Washington, DC: National Center for Education Statistics, US Department of Education, and Bureau of Justice Statistics, Office of Justice Programs, US Department of Justice. https://nces.ed.gov/pubs2019/2019047.pdf.

National Institute of Justice. n.d. "Understanding NIJ 0101.06 Armor Protection Levels." *Justice Technology Information Center.* https://www.justnet.org/pdf/Understanding-Armor-Protection.pdf.

Ore, Ersula J. 2019. *Lynching: Violence, Rhetoric, and American Identity.* Jackson: University Press of Mississippi.

Ratcliffe, Krista. 2005. *Rhetorical Listening: Identification, Gender, Whiteness.* Carbondale: Southern Illinois University Press.

Rickert, Thomas. 2013. *Ambient Rhetoric: Attunements of Rhetorical Being.* Pittsburgh: University of Pittsburgh Press.

Rood, Craig. 2018. "'Our Tears are Not Enough': The Warrant of the Dead in the Rhetoric of Gun Control." *Quarterly Journal of Speech* 104 (1): 47–70. 10.1080/00335630.2017.1401223.

Royster, Jaqueline Jones. 1996. "When the First Voice You Hear Is Not Your Own." *College Composition and Communication* 47 (1): 29–40.

Rubenstein, Alexandra, Sarah K. Wood, Robert S. Levine, and Charles H. Hennekens. 2019. "Alarming Trends in Mortality from Firearms among United States Schoolchildren." *American Journal of Medicine* 132 (8): 992–94.

Sinclair, Harriet. 2018. "*Fox News*' Tucker Carlson: Florida Survivors Being Used as 'Moral Blackmail' in Gun Crime Debate." *Newsweek,* February 21, 2018. https://www.newsweek.com/florida-shooting-tucker-carlson-814418.

Squires, Catherine R. 2016. Introduction to *Dangerous Discourses: Feminism, Gun Violence, and Civic Life,* edited by Catherine R. Squires, xv–xxv. New York: Peter Lang.

St. Félix, Doreen. 2018. "The Carnage and Chaos of Childish Gambino's *This Is America.*" *New Yorker,* May 7, 2018. https://www.newyorker.com/culture/culture-desk/the-carnage-and-chaos-of-childish-gambinos-this-is-america.

Strauss, Valerie. 2019. "'This Is Our Sad Reality': Bulletproof Backpacks are a Big Back-to-School Item." *Washington Post,* August 2, 2019. https://www.washingtonpost.com/education/2019/08/02/this-is-our-sad-reality-bulletproof-backpacks-are-big-back-to-school-item/.

Tesema, Martha. 2018. "All the Things You Might Have Missed in Donald Glover's *This Is America* Video." *Mashable,* May 6, 2018. https://mashable.com/2018/05/06/donald-glover-this-is-america-breakdown/.

Todd, Zoe. 2016. "An Indigenous Feminist's Take on the Ontological Turn: 'Ontology' Is Just Another Word for Colonialism." *Journal of Historical Sociology* 29 (1): 4–22.

Washington Post. 2012. "Remarks from the NRA Press Conference on Sandy Hook School Shooting, Delivered on Dec. 21, 2012 (Transcript, December 21)." https://www.washingtonpost.com/politics/remarks-from-the-nra-press-conference-on-sandy-hook-school-shooting-delivered-on-dec-21-2012-transcript/2012/12/21/bd1841fe-4b88-11e2-a6a6-aabac85e8036_story.html.

Wonder Hoodie. 2019. *Wonderhoodie.com.* https://wonderhoodie.com/.

8

"THE LAST MASS SHOOTING"
Anticipating the End of Mass Shootings, Yet Again

Bradley A. Serber

On February 14, 2018, a nineteen-year-old former student entered Marjory Stoneman Douglas High School in Parkland, Florida. It was Valentine's Day, a day normally reserved for romantic daydreaming that quickly became an all-too-familiar nightmare. Over the course of about six minutes, the shooter fired off more than 100 rounds, killing seventeen students and teachers and injuring seventeen more (Price and McCarthy 2018). Several students who survived the shooting decided that they needed to speak up and take action about what had happened. Shortly after the shooting—and in some cases even during—many of the students spoke out on social media.

One of those students is related to me and my wife. That relative and their parents have given me permission to share that detail, but for the sake of confidentiality and to avoid conflicts of interest, I will not be sharing their name, how they are related, their story, or their politics here. That is not what this chapter is about, but it is an important part of its context (Founders 2018, x, 147). I have been studying and teaching about targeted violence for almost a decade now, but up until the shooting in Parkland, it was always from the perspective of a detached observer. Needless to say, this attack came close to home. I had a bad feeling that it would happen sometime. I hope that having a relative survive a shooting is the closest that it ever gets for me, and I have great sympathy for those for whom targeted violence has come even closer. Writing about targeted violence takes a lot of emotional labor, and on my worst days, thinking of its victims' pain makes it hard to write anything at all.

The Parkland survivors did not waste any time getting organized.[1] Just two days after the shooting, a core group decided to consolidate its social media activism under the Twitter handle @NeverAgainMSD and the hashtag #NeverAgain. Despite previous associations between the

https://doi.org/10.7330/9781646422159.c008

phrase "never again" and the Holocaust, the Parkland students chose to make that phrase central to their movement because, in their words, "it really encapsulated what we wanted to get out of all of our activism: we didn't want anyone to endure the pain and hardships that Parkland had suffered" (Founders 2018, 45; Hogg and Hogg 2018, 102). A few days after the shooting, the group's members organized a two-day trip of about 100 students to Tallahassee to partake in over seventy meetings with state legislators about gun laws (Founders 2018, 69–73). Roughly a month later, on March 24, they organized the protest March for Our Lives in Washington, DC, where they would gather with nearly a million supporters, not to mention over 800 other solidarity protests taking place across the country and even around the world. Then, over the summer, they organized and embarked upon a national tour called "Road to Change."

Although the group has faced criticism from gun rights groups, many gun control advocates looked up to the founders of March for Our Lives for their outspokenness, organizing skills, activism, and eloquence (see also Rood's chapter 6 in this volume). A common theme among the founders was that they wanted to do everything in their power to make sure others did not have to endure what they had. Tired of a seemingly endless string of mass shootings, they declared that they "were not going to allow [their] shooting to become another statistic" (Founders 2018, 46). In a speech she gave at a rally in Fort Lauderdale, Emma González declared, to applause and follow-up sound-bite media coverage, "We are going to be the last mass shooting!" (Velez and Lakshmin 2018). Similarly, during his speech at the March for Our Lives, David Hogg told politicians who refused to stop taking money from the NRA to "get [their] résumés ready" and repeated the words "no more" six times amid a list of grievances regarding gun deaths and politicians' inaction (Hogg 2018). Whether they meant the phrase literally or not, "never again" became the rallying cry of the Parkland students and their supporters.

The Parkland students' activism gained momentum among gun control supporters because it offered them a sense of hope that the responses to this shooting would differ from previous ones. As I discuss in this chapter, there are some good reasons for these students and their supporters to believe that things will, in fact, be different, but there are also good reasons to believe that they will not. To explore both of these positions, I begin by using Craig Rood's (2018) notion of the "warrant of the dead" to explore why and how the rallying cry of "never again" might well come with good intentions and persuasive power. However, that rallying cry also belies important contextual factors about previous mass shootings and material evidence about the nature and causes of gun violence. To reframe public responses to mass shootings, I draw from Joshua Gunn and David Beard's (2000) notion of the "apocalyptic sublime" to suggest that perpetually anticipating the end of mass shootings might be an unhealthy and counterproductive frame (see also Gage's chapter 10 in this volume). As an alternative to the teleological rhetoric of "never again," I conclude by suggesting a humbler possibility that still honors the dead without relying upon the total prevention of mass shootings.

WARRANT OF THE DEAD OR APOCALYPTIC SUBLIME?

The Parkland students' repeated invocations of the phrase "never again" exemplify what Craig Rood calls the "warrant of the dead": "an explicit or implicit claim that the dead place a demand on the living." More specifically, it is the claim that "since they died, we should do X, where X can be almost anything" (2018, 48). Oftentimes gun control advocates will use the warrant of the dead to argue that "since they died from gun violence, we should support gun control legislation," and gun rights advocates invoke it to call for more guns or other alternatives to gun control (48, 63). Part of the impasse around gun laws in the United States comes from the ability of X in the equation to be so variable. Nevertheless, the power of the warrant of the dead lies in the notion that the living have an obligation to honor the dead through a commitment to particular values and actions.

One way to read the #NeverAgain movement, which later became the March for Our Lives, is that the students are grounding their activism in an altruistic version of the warrant of the dead:

WARRANT: When people die, the only or best way to honor them is
   through preventing others from dying how they died ("never again").

DATA: People died in Parkland.

CLAIM: Therefore, we should honor them through prevention.

Although people on all sides of the gun debate regularly frame their work as altruistic, the founders of March for Our Lives happen to be on the side that supports gun control legislation, so they use the corresponding warrant that X = gun control to argue for it. Not all of the students at Marjory Stoneman Douglas High School support gun control—student Kyle Kashuv, for instance, has been particularly outspoken against it—but the ones who started March for Our Lives have promoted an agenda that calls for what they consider "commonsense" gun control measures. Since it is nearly impossible to argue with both the dead and with those who are mourning, the warrant of the dead is quite strong on its own, but because these students personally lived through the shooting at their high school, and because they were close to the victims, their ethos as survivors intensifies its power. An optimistic reading of their activism is that the Parkland students are acting out of good will to ensure that their friends, family members, and teachers did not die in vain.

A less optimistic reading of this activism, however, suggests that their movement inadvertently perpetuates what Joshua Gunn and David Beard (2000) call the "apocalyptic sublime." As they describe it, the apocalyptic sublime is a secular postmodern alternative to religious eschatological predictions of the apocalypse (270). Borrowing from literary critic Frank Kermode, Gunn and Beard distinguish between "imminent" and "immanent" senses of the apocalypse, with the "imminent" referring to apocalyptic visions with a clear ending and the "immanent" referring to a perpetual anticipation of an ending that never arrives. Put another way, imminence is impending but finite; immanence is lurking and infinite. It is always awaiting but never actualized. Immanent apocalyptic rhetoric is thus "marked by ambivalence and confusion" and stuck in a "sense of perpetual transition" (272). As Gunn and Beard (2003) explain, the best exemplar of the apocalyptic sublime is "the mythic Sisyphus, who has no foreseeable end to his labors but rather resigns himself to a dwelling in end-time" (200).

Gunn and Beard argue that such rhetoric is not only apocalyptic but also sublime in the sense that people feel compelled to gawk at natural or anthropogenic disasters, much like highway drivers surveying the wreckage of a car crash. Despite the immanence of the apocalyptic, there is something oddly compelling and perhaps even satisfying about the perpetual anticipation of updates about each new horrific detail. Thus, they explain that "however terrifying or threatening the sublime object may seem, we nevertheless find our experience of it enjoyable" (2003, 276). Whereas the fear of imminence ends, the fear of immanence continues, and we find ourselves perpetually fascinated by it. Every time that Sisyphus's boulder rolls down the hill, he still decides to push it back up again.

In their extended application of the apocalyptic sublime to media coverage of the Columbine High School shooting, Gunn and Beard (2003) further clarify that one of the ways in which the apocalyptic sublime manifests is through mass media coverage of violent events. Skeptical of the mass media as a profit-driven industry, they argue that media companies exploit viewers' strong emotions—fear of the apocalypse and fascination with the sublime—through "the televisual portrayal of continuous crisis," which "keeps the spectator watching, which, in turn, helps to generate money for television stations" (199). Even long after events like Columbine or 9/11 conclude, the media coverage of them continues. Whether because of the spectacle of violence, a fascination with the macabre, a sense of obligation, or a desire for the latest updates, viewers keep watching the news indefinitely despite its gruesome nature and the slow and repetitive coverage of the twenty-four-hour news cycle. The sublime keeps viewers watching violent news despite its apocalyptic nature, but because the media industry thrives on immanence, the story goes on long after the event is over. Even when the story "ends," it never goes away completely as long as it remains in public memory and has the potential to resurface—say, on an anniversary or when the next attack of a similar nature happens.

Building upon Gunn and Beard's work, I argue that after mass shootings, we see a different manifestation of the apocalyptic sublime. In this version, survivors of mass shootings make promises that they will do everything in their power to prevent the next one. As a presumably well-meaning gesture for others and perhaps a coping mechanism for themselves, they use the warrant of the dead to argue "since they died, the only way to honor them is to prevent others from dying in the same way." This warrant commits them to fight for violence prevention, which sounds noble at face value. However, as I will argue here, contextual and material evidence from previous attacks suggests that prevention may not be achievable. If not, then promises of prevention set those who make them and those who believe in them up for two major rhetorical challenges. First, even if those shouting "never again" do not mean the phrase literally, their supporters, who interpret it that way or wish for its actualization, are setting themselves up for retraumatization each time another attack occurs. Second, even if the claim is aspirational rather than literal, stating "never again" explicitly as a rallying cry makes it easy for the movement's critics to dismiss or thwart its agenda by refocusing energy away from its concrete policy proposals and toward their own paternalistic mocking of what they see as an unattainable childish fantasy. As a result, responses to mass shootings grounded in warrants of "never again" participate in a version of the apocalyptic sublime that always anticipates, but never actualizes, and perhaps never can actualize, the end of mass shootings.

I must be clear here that unlike Gunn and Beard's critique of the media industry, I am not implying that the Parkland students or others like them are perpetuating the apocalyptic sublime intentionally or with self-serving motives. Nevertheless, by contributing to the apocalyptic sublime through a warrant of the dead that promises total prevention, they risk retraumatizing themselves or others and undermining their own message each time that promise remains unfulfilled. Comparing and contrasting responses to Parkland and other similar attacks will help demonstrate why.

WHY PARKLAND MIGHT BE DIFFERENT

Despite the recent pattern of mass shootings and the struggles of politicians, law enforcement officials, and others to prevent them, many people had hoped that the Parkland shooting might be different. One reason why is that the movement is being led by young adults. This isn't the first time that people had hoped that a shooting that affected youth would change the gun debate in the United States. Shortly after the Sandy Hook Elementary School shooting, many gun control supporters had hoped that it would mark a "tipping point" for federal, or at least state, gun control legislation. The faces of the twenty children and six adults killed at Sandy Hook were plastered all over the news. Because of the associations of youth with innocence, hope, and potential for the future, it was hard to imagine members of Congress saying no to the families of twenty elementary school children.

Just a few months after the December 2012 shooting, Senator Dianne Feinstein introduced the Assault Weapons Ban of 2013, and Senators Joe Manchin and Pat Toomey introduced a bill for universal background checks (Feinstein 2013; Manchin and Toomey 2013). Both needed sixty votes to pass. The Assault Weapons Ban was defeated by a 40-60 vote and the Manchin-Toomey Amendment by a 54-46 vote. Meanwhile, as Matthew Lysiak (2013) reported in his book about the Sandy Hook shooting, gun legislation at the state level produced mixed results. "During the first six months, five states tightened gun laws," Lysiak reported, and "fifteen states have loosened them" (240). The political and legal polarization here implies that both gun control and gun rights advocates in different states were grounding arguments in different warrants of the dead with the same conclusion: "Since the Sandy Hook victims (and perhaps especially the children) died, we should do X," with X meaning different things to different people, and sometimes meaning not doing anything because the different X's and their proponents were stuck in gridlock with one another.

At the time, gun control supporters were optimistic that the faces and stories of young children and the grief of their parents would convince enough politicians to support gun control in ways that they were not willing to do with previous shootings that affected adults and teenagers. When Congress voted down federal gun control measures and states polarized in opposite directions, that optimism dissipated. Shortly after the shooting at Mother Emanuel AME Church in Charleston, journalist Dan Hodges (2015) issued a viral tweet that read, "In retrospect Sandy Hook marked the end of the US gun control debate. Once America decided killing children was bearable, it was over." To a certain extent, Parkland student David Hogg shares Hodges's skepticism. "We knew the odds were against us," he wrote in the book he coauthored with his sister. "If people could shrug off Sandy Hook and twenty dead first-graders, what chance did we have?" (Hogg and Hogg 2018, 104). Nevertheless, Hogg has been one of the most outspoken among the March for Our Lives organizers, perhaps because he believes that he and his classmates can still accomplish what the Sandy Hook parents couldn't.

Perhaps the most distinctive feature of the Parkland students can be best summarized in the term "young adults." As *young* adults, the Parkland students retain some of the childlike innocence of the victims and survivors at Sandy Hook. As young *adults* (or soon-to-be adults), however, they are old enough to stand up for themselves and speak out about issues that affect them. A number of them even credited their training in debate with teaching them to how to make and defend arguments in ways that would get adults to take them seriously (Gurney 2018). In their own words, the Parkland students acknowledged that the children at Sandy Hook "were too young and the parents were the ones who had to find the courage and voice to speak up for a change in legislation. But the tragedy at Marjory Stoneman Douglas was in many ways the perfect storm, because we were high schoolers" (Founders 2018, 41). Their youth retains some of the childlike innocence of the Sandy Hook victims, but their ability to sound like adults allows them to speak for themselves.

Even some of their harshest critics recognized the challenge of fighting with articulate young adults. *Fox News* host Tucker Carlson, for instance, suggested that politicians and journalists were "using these kids in a kind of moral blackmail where you're not allowed to disagree or you're attacking a child . . . [and] you're a bad person" (Sinclair 2018). In a liminal space between childhood and adulthood, the Parkland students occupy a unique position that is difficult to challenge. Not only do they enjoy the benefits of young adulthood, but when older adults challenge them, it only makes the older adults look like bullies.

The Parkland students are able to leverage their position as young adults, but they are also cognizant of the violent context in which they have grown up. As one of the organizers, Cameron Kasky, despondently put it, he and his classmates are part of "the school shooting generation"—those born after the Columbine High School shooting who grew up with regular active shooter training drills (Founders 2018, 7). Whereas they differ from the Sandy Hook students because they are old enough to speak for themselves, they differ from the Columbine and Virginia Tech students because of the frequency and salience of other school shootings that happened before the one at their high school. Not only are they around the right age, they also seem to have come of age at the right time.

The timing also seems right because these students grew up around digital technology that allows them to reach broad audiences instantaneously. Many of these students credit their abilities to speak up and to reach large audiences to being digital natives. "Our generation has grown up with new information readily available at our fingertips," they say. "Despite some of its negative effects on our culture, social media has let us access important data with ease, allowing us to be more informed than ever" (Founders 2018, 39). A few of them expressed surprise at how quickly and how widely their messages spread. They came up with the @NeverAgainMSD page the night after the shooting, and by the next night it had 300,000 followers and was the #2 trending hashtag on Twitter (Founders 2018, 17, 45). Similarly, Hogg noted that "Emma [González] didn't even have a Twitter account before Valentine's Day, but eleven days later she had more followers than the NRA" (Hogg and Hogg 2018, 118). It is difficult to imagine the Parkland students being able to organize and spread their messages so widely prior to the age of social media.

One of the biggest reasons why gun control supporters might expect the aftermath of the Parkland shooting to be different, however, is that the students have taken their activism off of social media in order to make changes offline as well. For instance, together they have drafted and advocated for the "Parkland Manifesto," a ten-point political agenda:

1. funding gun violence research
2. digitizing records from the Bureau of Alcohol, Tobacco, and Firearms (ATF)
3. instituting universal background checks
4. banning high-capacity magazines
5. banning assault weapons
6. funding violence intervention programs

7. instituting extreme risk protection orders (ERPOs) to remove guns from individuals who might pose a threat

8. disarming domestic abusers

9. passing federal gun trafficking laws

10. requiring safe storage and mandatory theft reporting (Founders 2018, 215–18)

In their pursuit of these agenda items, they already have helped fight an assault weapons ban overturn in Massachusetts and supported new legislation in New York, Vermont, Illinois, Maryland, and their home state of Florida (Hogg and Hogg 2018, 124–26). Moreover, they helped convince Dick's Sporting Goods to stop carrying assault weapons and encouraged large companies like Hertz, Delta, and MetLife to cut their ties to the NRA (108, 124). Already hurting from a $55 million revenue loss between 2016 and 2017, the NRA even acknowledged in a 2018 lawsuit against the New York State Department of Financial Services that its primary insurance carrier, Lockton, dropped its insurance liability coverage within two weeks of the Parkland shooting and declared that it was "unwilling to renew coverage at any price" (*National Rifle Association* 2018, 18). For gun control advocates, these are some big changes in a short amount of time. Despite the many obstacles in their way, the Parkland students have still accomplished many things that other young adults, and even some older ones, have not.

WHY PARKLAND MIGHT BE MORE OF THE SAME

Despite some of the Parkland students' accomplishments, they have learned the hard way that not everyone agrees with their assessment of their agenda as "commonsense reforms" (Founders 2018, 215). Cameron Kasky and Chris Grady described learning, on their way to Tallahassee just days after the shooting, that the Florida House of Representatives had rejected a motion to consider new gun laws. "The fact that they voted down even having a debate about the bill on the floor felt like a slap in the face on the drive up," they recalled. "It was rough" (84). Class President Jaclyn Corin said that once they arrived and met with legislators, state senators "sent thoughts and prayers to Parkland, but promised no action" and that "there was a common thread in every meeting we took—avoiding a real conversation about guns" (76). She added that "my peers and I advocated for placing more psychologists in schools—something almost all people can agree on," but that Governor Rick Scott "proceeded to cut mental health funding after our visit" (77). To be sure, Scott later signed into law the Marjory Stoneman Douglas High School Public Safety Act, which banned bump stocks and raised the minimum age to purchase a firearm to twenty-one, but that same act also included a provision called the Coach Aaron Feis Guardian Program, which allows schools to arm trained teachers if both the school district and sheriff agree (*Marjory Stoneman* 2018). Corin noted that Broward County, where Parkland is, "decided against the program," but expressed her concern that "other communities in the state now have the option to put *more* guns in their schools" (Founders 2018, 77–78). Even in their home state of Florida, new gun legislation was hard to pass, incremental, and controversial, as it would prove to be in other states as well.

As was the case after Sandy Hook, gun rights and gun control advocates have sparred over what kinds of gun laws to enact to try to prevent, or at least mitigate, mass shootings. In May 2018, a little over a month after the March for Our Lives rally, other high school students across the United States held another rally, a smaller but not insignificant one, called Stand for the Second, in which they defended Second Amendment rights and alternatives to gun control (Livingston 2018). In the months following the Parkland shooting, some states did tighten their gun laws, but others, like Tennessee, Oklahoma, and Nebraska, loosened them by enacting "Stand Your Ground" laws, expanding concealed carry, and keeping gun permits out of state public records. Others, like Colorado, Ohio, and South Carolina, remained in stalemates with divided state legislatures (Foley 2018). The continued division over gun laws after the Parkland shooting led Michael Hammond, the legislative counsel for Gun Owners of America, to say, "It's exactly what happened after Newtown: The anti-gun states became more anti-gun and the pro-gun states became more pro-gun" (Foley 2018). The nation is still quite polarized on the issue.

Meanwhile, despite González's hope that Parkland would "be the last mass shooting," the reality is that it has not been. David and Lauren Hogg (2018) even acknowledge this, noting a shooting later that February in which "a man in Detroit who had just gotten out of a hospital where he was being treated for hallucinations shot and killed his daughter, her mother, his cousin, and two people who just happened to be there" (128). Following that shooting in Detroit, other mass shootings have taken place at the YouTube headquarters in San Bruno, California, a Waffle House in Antioch, Tennessee, another high school in Santa Fe, Texas, a newspaper in Annapolis, Maryland, a synagogue in Pittsburgh, Pennsylvania, and a bar in Thousand Oaks, California, to name a few from the first year after the Parkland shooting. Even in the Parkland students' home state of Florida, theirs has not been the last mass shooting. Others include one at a video game convention in Jacksonville, a yoga studio in Tallahassee, and a bank in Sebring.

These other incidents prompted journalist Rick Hampson (2018) to ask of the Parkland students, "The last mass shooting? In a nation with about one a day?" The complex definitional question of what constitutes a "mass shooting" is as much a political one as it is a practical one (Borchers 2017). Defining a mass shooting raises questions about how many people must be shot and under what circumstances in order to constitute a "mass" shooting and whether those people need to be killed or merely shot. Hampson appears to be using a broad definition of "mass shootings," which includes incidents in which multiple people are shot, regardless of whether they are injured or killed. His framework differs from the FBI definition of "mass murder by firearms," which restricts the term to "a multiple homicide incident in which four or more victims are murdered—not including the offender(s)—within one event, and in one or more geographical locations relatively near one another" (Krouse and Richardson 2015, 2). Regardless of who gets to define what constitutes a mass shooting and how to count them, their frequent occurrence, even if not a daily one, backs Hampson's critique of the Parkland students: "Their hashtag motto [#NeverAgain] summed up their hope and their hubris." As catchy and hopeful as a phrase like #NeverAgain might be, it sets a high standard that is easy for skeptics to jump on in order to label the movement as a whole as a failure despite its partial but significant pragmatic successes.

The Parkland students are not alone in either the hope or the hubris that Hampson describes. The mission statement of Sandy Hook Promise is to "prevent gun-related deaths due to crime, suicide and accidental discharge so that no other parent experiences the senseless, horrific loss of their child" (Sandy Hook Promise 2019). Similarly, after the attack in Isla Vista (#YesAllWomen) that killed his son, Richard Martinez (2014) gave a passionate speech in which he declared "not one more" should die from gun violence. That phrase became not only a trendy hashtag on social media but also the slogan on the front of 2.4 million postcards that he and members of Everytown for Gun Safety sent to politicians all over the country (Menezes 2015). Not only has Parkland not been "the last mass shooting," but survivors from other attacks that preceded it also tried to promise that Parkland would never happen.

Unfortunately, there are also several reasons to believe that there will be other attacks coming beyond the ones that have happened since

Parkland. First, the best estimates of gun sales and background checks indicate that, since 2015, the United States has had more guns than people (Ingraham 2015). Second, among the over 300 million guns already in circulation are many that can fire multiple rounds per second, meaning that mass shootings can happen within a matter of minutes or even seconds. Like the shooter at Parkland, the shooter at Sandy Hook fired off over 150 rounds in about five minutes (Lysiak 2013, 84). In Tucson, the shooter fired over thirty rounds in only fifteen seconds (Smith and Hollihan 2014, 586). Third, other incidents show substantive evidence of what Loren Coleman calls the "copycat effect," meaning that many of these attacks are not spontaneous but instead are calculated acts in which shooters researched previous attacks in order to plan their own and determine how to make them more deadly (Coleman 2004; Meloy et al. 2015; Follman 2015). Fourth, as I have argued elsewhere (Serber 2016), a narrow focus on guns, as opposed to a broader focus on what Fein, Vossekuil, and Holden (1995) call "targeted violence" carried out with other weapons, misses the point that not all attacks involve guns—or only guns. All of this suggests that "never again" likely will give way to "repetition, yet again."[2]

THE LAST MASS SHOOTING, YET AGAIN

My concern with the particular warrant of the dead rhetoric behind "never again" and the apocalyptic sublime is that the material reality of repeated school shootings contradicts the symbolic rhetoric of "never again." The inconsistency between the two sets up a never-ending cycle of heartbreak. In both Holocaust and mass shooting prevention efforts, promises of "never again" have given way to repetition.[3] This is not to say that efforts to prevent or mitigate genocide, mass shootings, and other kinds of violence are not worthy endeavors or that activists should stop working toward them, but rather that they should be cautious of how they frame their pursuit of those goals in order to avoid retraumatizing themselves or others or coming across as insincere or unrealistic. With a broader understanding of the nature and causes of mass shootings and different expectations about what they can and cannot control, the Parkland students and their supporters might instead focus not on prevention, but rather on perseverance and pragmatism.

One of the dangers of "never again" rhetoric is that whenever it gives way to "again," it does not take much to retraumatize those who had hoped to honor the dead by preventing more deaths. The same Emma González who declared that Parkland would be "the last mass shooting" also has described how little it takes for something to retraumatize her: "One of my friends finds an old picture or video of someone who died; another shooting happens. I hear helicopters or one too many unexplained bangs or pops in one day, and it all starts to slip" (Founders 2018, 34). She insists, consistent with the "never again" warrant of the dead, that "without a radical change in America's priorities and in our gun laws, our protests will have been in vain" (Hogg and Hogg 2018, 129). When the expectations are framed as all or nothing, anything short of all can feel like Sisyphus's boulder not only rolls back down the hill every time he gets it close to the top, it also crashes into Sisyphus on the way down. That seems like no way for young adults, or others who look to them for hope, to live.

The rhetoric of prevention makes it seem like anything short of completely stopping mass shootings once and for all dishonors the dead. It also plays into the apocalyptic sublime by being overly optimistic about a future that may never come. Any setback to the plan of prevention can be demotivating and immobilizing. If enough preventative efforts fail, they risk becoming imminent in the sense that people might give up on those efforts, thereby giving them a finite ending. The apocalyptic sublime, however, is immanent. It sustains its own energy. Matching that energy requires a rhetoric not of prevention, but rather of perseverance. The Parkland students, and others like them, already tap into that rhetoric when they focus on what they do have control over in their own situation, that is, staying #MSDStrong, rather than what they may not have control over in other situations.

Meanwhile, another alternative to the rhetoric of prevention is the rhetoric of pragmatism. The rhetoric of total prevention makes even small setbacks feel like failures. It also opens up critiques that those who call for change are being unrealistic, disingenuous, or naively optimistic. Pragmatism acknowledges that there is usually some give-and-take in politics. It recognizes that even if schools and other public spaces might never be completely safe, there are concrete steps that activists and politicians can take to make them much safer. It encourages celebrating large and small victories rather than mourning anytime that anything goes wrong. Pragmatism also leaves open the possibility for local politics and the recognition that what may work in Florida may not work in Kansas or Arizona. For that matter, what works in Parkland may not be what works in Miami or Jacksonville. If #NeverAgain perpetuates the apocalyptic sublime, then perhaps promoting and celebrating smaller, more concrete and attainable goals, like the Parkland students' ten-point agenda, is a way to break the cycle.

With all of this in mind, perhaps the best resources that the Parkland students have at their disposal are their status as young adults, their argumentation and debate skills, and their access to digital and traditional megaphones. Part of what seems to have worked about @NeverAgainMSD and March for Our Lives is that the students are in the same place and around the same age and the shooting is still fresh in public memory. As one of the movement's founders, Delaney Tarr, explains it, "The core of this movement is and always will be with young people, instead of people who are older" (Founders 2018, 100). However, with the first-year class—who were both the youngest students at Marjory Stoneman Douglas at the time of the shooting and the ones most directly targeted by it—graduating in Spring 2021, they now have gone their separate ways and pretty soon will no longer be young adults.

Although the nation will remember this shooting, it will remember the other ones that happened before and after it as well. Like the Sandy Hook shooting before Parkland, the 2019 shootings in El Paso and Dayton, for instance, both led to similar cries of "never again" (*El Paso Times* 2019; Whaley 2019). The "never again" warrant of the dead might seem optimistic and well intentioned, but it easily gives way to the apocalyptic sublime. However, there are alternative rhetorics to the rhetoric of prevention. Rather than feeling immobilized and retraumatized, those who focus on perseverance can remind themselves of what they have been through already and stay strong even when things get tough. Similarly, rather than feeling defeated by legal and political decisions that did not turn out the way they had hoped, those who focus on pragmatic victories can celebrate the changes that they were able to bring about. By replacing the rhetoric of prevention with the rhetorics of perseverance and pragmatism, the Parkland students and their supporters might instead see their efforts not as a series of "failures" measured against an unreasonable bar of success, but rather as their best efforts to live by their values and to honor the memories of their loved ones. If #NeverAgain operates within the logic of the apocalyptic sublime, then perhaps maintaining an attitude of persistence in spite of setbacks and promoting and celebrating smaller, more concrete and attainable goals are ways to break the cycle of anticipating the end of mass shootings again and again.

NOTES

1.   My relative is *not* one of the official Founders of March for Our Lives, whose work
      I draw upon heavily here.

2. The subtitle of this essay comes from a tongue-in-cheek National Communication Association conference panel that Joshua Gunn has participated in on at least six separate occasions, entitled "Repetition, Yet Again." Although I do not wish to make light of mass shootings, the concept of repetition paired all too well with his and David Beard's work on the apocalyptic sublime.
3. For more on the former, see Power 2002.

REFERENCES

Borchers, Callum. 2017. "The Squishy Definition of 'Mass Shooting' Complicates Media Coverage." *Washington Post*, October 4, 2017. https://www.washingtonpost.com/news/the-fix/wp/2017/10/04/the-squishy-definition-of-mass-shooting-complicates-media-coverage/.

Coleman, Loren. 2004. *The Copycat Effect: How the Media and Popular Culture Trigger the Mayhem in Tomorrow's Headlines.* New York: Gallery Books.

El Paso Times, December 29, 2019. "As El Paso Heals from Mass Shooting, We Must Lead in Declaring Never Again." December 29, 2019. https://www.elpasotimes.com/story/opinion/editorials/2019/12/29/walmart-el-paso-shooting-city-must-lead-opinion/2755962001/.

Fein, Robert A., Bryan Vossekuil, and Gwen A. Holden. 1995. "Threat Assessment: An Approach to Prevent Targeted Violence." Washington, DC: US Department of Justice. https://www.ncjrs.gov/pdffiles/threat.pdf.

Feinstein, Dianne. 2013. *S.150—113th Congress (2013–2014): Assault Weapons Ban of 2013.* https://www.congress.gov/bill/113th-congress/senate-bill/150/text.

Foley, Ryan J. 2018. "No Widespread Changes in Gun Laws After Recent Shootings." *Associated Press*, September 26, 2018. https://apnews.com/384667155bbd4b2dbe48e3315cad9cdb.

Follman, Mark. 2015. "Inside the Race to Stop the Next Mass Shooter." *Mother Jones* (November/December). http://www.motherjones.com/politics/2015/09/mass-shootings-threat-assessment-shooter-fbi-columbine.

Founders of March for Our Lives. 2018. *Glimmer of Hope.* New York: Penguin.

Gunn, Joshua, and David E. Beard. 2000. "On the Apocalyptic Sublime." *Southern Communication Journal* 65 (4): 269–86.

Gunn, Joshua, and David E. Beard. 2003. "On the Apocalyptic Columbine." *Southern Communication Journal* 68 (3): 198–216.

Gurney, Kyra. 2018. "They Debated Gun Control in Class Last Fall. Now, They Debate Lawmakers on TV." *Tampa Bay Times*, February 23, 2018. https://www.tampabay.com/florida-politics/buzz/2018/02/23/they-debated-gun-control-in-class-last-fall-now-they-debate-lawmakers-on-tv/.

Hampson, Rick. 2018. "After Parkland Shooting: A Day-by-Day Fight over Guns in America." *USA Today*, December 26, 2018. https://www.usatoday.com/story/news/2018/12/26/parkland-school-shooting-10-months-gun-control-united-states/2310683002/.

Hodges, Dan. 2015. "In retrospect Sandy Hook marked the end of the US gun control debate. Once America decided killing children was bearable, it was over." Twitter, June 19, 2015. https://twitter.com/dpjhodges/status/611943312401002496?lang=en.

Hogg, David. 2018. *March for Our Lives Speech. YouTube.com*, March 24, 2018. https://www.youtube.com/watch?v=kwpTPkQVJao.

Hogg, David, and Lauren Hogg. 2018. *#NeverAgain: A New Generation Draws the Line.* New York: Random House.

Ingraham, Chris. 2015. "There Are Now More Guns Than People in the United States." *Washington Post*, October 5, 2015. https://www.washingtonpost.com/news/wonk/wp/2015/10/05/guns-in-the-united-states-one-for-every-man-woman-and-child-and-then-some/.

Krouse, William J., and Daniel J. Richardson. 2015. "Mass Murder with Firearms: Incidents and Victims, 1999–2013." Washington, DC: Congressional Research Service. https://fas.org/sgp/crs/misc/R44126.pdf.

Livingston, Michael. 2018. "Students Stage Another Walkout over Guns—This Time in Favor." Los Angeles Times, May 2, 2018. https://www.latimes.com/nation/la-na-student-walkouts-second-amendment20180502-story.html.

Lysiak, Matthew. 2013. Newtown: An American Tragedy. New York: Simon & Schuster.

Manchin, Joe III, and Pat Toomey. 2013. S.Amdt.715 to S.649—113th Congress (2013–2014). https://www.congress.gov/amendment/113th-congress/senate-amendment/715/text.

Marjory Stoneman Douglas High School Public Safety Act. 2018. https://www.flsenate.gov/Session/Bill/2018/7026/BillText/er/pdf.

Martinez, Richard. 2014. Not One More. YouTube.com, May 24. https://www.youtube.com/watch?v=bZGKstCRDu0.

Meloy, J. Reid, Kris Mohandie, James L. Knoll, and Jens Hoffman. 2015. "The Concept of Identification in Threat Assessment." Behavioral Sciences and the Law 33 (2–3): 213–37.

Menezes, Ryan. 2015. "A Fight against Guns; Father of Isla Vista Victim Is to Attend State of the Union Address. 'This, for Me, Is Personal,' He Says." Los Angeles Times, January 20.

National Rifle Association of America v. Andrew Cuomo, Maria T. Vullo, and the New York State Department of Financial Services. 2018. US District Court for the Northern District of New York.

Power, Samantha. 2002. A Problem from Hell: America and the Age of Genocide. New York: Basic Books.

Price, Wayne T., and John McCarthy. 2018. "Step by Step: How the Parkland School Shooting Unfolded." Florida Today, February 17, 2018. https://www.floridatoday.com/story/news/2018/02/17/minute-minute-how-parkland-school-shooting-unfolded/345817002/.

Rood, Craig. 2018. "'Our Tears Are Not Enough': The Warrant of the Dead in the Rhetoric of Gun Control." Quarterly Journal of Speech 104 (1): 47–70.

Sandy Hook Promise. 2019. "About Us." http://www.sandyhookpromise.org/about.

Serber, Bradley A. 2016. "Reaction Rhetorics: Targeted Violence and Public Security." PhD diss., Pennsylvania State University.

Sinclair, Harriet. 2018. "Fox News' Tucker Carlson: Florida Survivors Being Used as 'Moral Blackmail' in Gun Crime Debate." Newsweek, February 21, 2018. https://www.newsweek.com/florida-shooting-tucker-carlson-814418.

Smith, Francesca Marie, and Thomas A. Hollihan. 2014. "'Out of Chaos Breathes Creation': Human Agency, Mental Illness, and Conservative Arguments Locating Responsibility for the Tucson Massacre." Rhetoric & Public Affairs 17 (4): 585–618.

Velez, Mandy, and Deepa Lakshmin. 2018. "Florida's Teen Survivors Refuse to Stay Silent: 'We Are the Change': Marjory Stoneman Douglas High School Students Like Emma González Are Turning Their Grief into Action." Daily Beast, February 20, 2018. https://www.thedailybeast.com/floridas-teen-survivors-refuse-to-stay-silent-we-are-the-change.

Whaley, Nan. 2019. "We Owe It to Mass Shooting Victims to Take Action on Gun Control." Washington Post, August 23, 2019. https://www.washingtonpost.com/opinions/daytons-mayor-we-owe-it-to-mass-shooting-victims-to-take-action-on-gun-control/2019/08/23/1377167e-c51c-11e9-9986-1fb3e4397be4_story.html.

9

CAMPUS CARRY, ACADEMIC FREEDOM, AND RHETORICAL SENSITIVITY

Kendall Gerdes

Trigger warning: this chapter contains somewhat detailed descriptions of gun violence and suicide on college campuses.

INTRODUCTION

On August 1, 2016, fifty years to the day after Charles Whitman shot and killed sixteen people on the campus of the University of Texas at Austin and injured thirty-one others, a law passed by the Texas state legislature allowing concealed handguns to be carried by licensed holders onto public university campuses took effect. The Texas State Capitol, less than two miles from the UT Austin Tower, did not seem to remark the occasion—or the irony. In fact, the official view was that "the campus carry legislation going into effect the same day of the 50th anniversary is a coincidence" (Eberly 2016). Of course, this statement is denotatively true: the date of the two events merely coincides; at least at one level, this response from the Texas state legislature's office of external relations is merely begging the question. One way to understand the legislature's willful ignorance is as part of a long history of conflict and even antagonism between the University of Texas and the state government (Burr 1988; Nelson et al. 2013; *Daily Texan* Editorial Board 2013; Somers and Phelps 2018, 8), but it may also be understood as part of a larger national trend of provocations to university communities orchestrated by the gun lobby and aimed at normalizing the presence of guns in every quarter of ordinary life.

In 2016, students at the University of Texas organized a unique and headline-getting protest for the first day of class after the campus carry law's implementation, under the cheeky and rhyming name "Cocks Not Glocks" (Timmons 2016a). In what might seem like a bit of a non

https://doi.org/10.7330/9781646422159.c009

sequitur, students strapped dildos to their backpacks, putting the new campus carry law into conversation with an older Texas state blue law prohibiting the open display of sex toys. By lampooning the law that criminalizes sexuality but permits deadly weapons, the idea was to invoke the issues of censorship, free speech and, in the campus setting, academic freedom. The argument protesters aimed to circulate was that openly carrying the sex toys in contravention of the law was harmless, but the concealed carry of handguns on campus in *compliance* with the law presented a far more serious threat to the safety and well-being of the campus community (Dart 2016).

Some months before the campus carry law in Texas (known as Senate Bill or SB 11) went into effect, three professors at UT Austin brought a lawsuit against the state and the university officials responsible for implementing the law (Waller 2018). The professors alleged that SB 11 violated, among other constitutionally protected rights, their First Amendment right to academic freedom (*Glass et al.* 2016). After a judge in Texas dismissed the lawsuit, the professors escalated their complaint to the Fifth US Circuit Court of Appeals in New Orleans (McGill 2018).

This chapter examines the public debate over campus carry laws, from the 1960s Texas law banning guns on campus to the contemporary student organization advocating to bring guns back. It connects the resonance of the 1966 Tower shooting to contemporary moments of gun violence and related provocations on the UT campus, and argues that this context is key to understanding the relationship between campus carry and academic freedom. The debate unfolds in media focused on higher education, such as online magazines like the *Chronicle of Higher Education* and *Insider Higher Ed,* as well as in student newspapers and on public or social media platforms where faculty as well as outsiders editorialize about the policies. Faculty, staff, and students who oppose campus carry laws have frequently been described in terms now quite familiar to virtually anyone who's paid attention to other campus debates in recent years: they're just too sensitive. Claims about the hypersensitivity of students in particular have been in circulation now for several years on a range of campus issues, perhaps most notably trigger warnings, an issue on which student survivors of trauma have been accused of infringing on the academic freedom of their instructors by asking for notice when course material is likely to retraumatize them (for more on trigger warnings, see Gerdes 2019; Orem and Simpkins 2015; Carter 2015).

In fact, the polysemy of the word *trigger* has itself created a bit of extra overlap between the campus carry debate and the trigger warnings debate as campus issues. About a month after the new gun law took effect, someone deposited shell casings on bulletin boards in several UT campus buildings, quite literally in the shadow of the Tower. The casings had small notes tucked inside that read "TRIGGERED?" (Hall 2016; see also Gerdes 2019). I will return to this incident for further discussion a little later on. The Parlin building, where the first casings were found, is home to the Department of Rhetoric and Writing.[1] In 1966, Austin police officer Billy Speed was shot and killed just in front of the Parlin building, near the now-former site of the Jefferson Davis statue (*Texas Standard* 2016).

Usually, arguments about sensitivity interface with other campus issues through critics who claim that students' sensitivity poses a threat to the academic freedom of the faculty. But in the case of the campus carry debate, faculty as well as students who oppose guns on campus *on the grounds of academic freedom* and free speech are the ones targeted by accusations of sensitivity. In the rare case of a contemporary campus issue where academic freedom and sensitivity appear to be aligned rather than opposed, critics' arguments against sensitivity circulate without apparent concern for academic freedom. The UT professors' lawsuit and the debate over campus carry in Texas demonstrates that the strength of attacks on sensitivity in higher education is enough to overwhelm some critics' attachment to the values of free speech and academic freedom. Austin is an especially charged site for debate over campus carry because the university itself is represented synecdochally in images as well as casual speech by the Tower, the building that Charles Whitman used in 1966 as a sniper's perch to perpetrate the first mass shooting on a college campus in American history.

I begin my analysis of the debate over campus carry policies in Texas with a short history of campus gun policies in the state. I argue that the state's ban on guns on campus in the late 1960s was not a response to the Tower shooting, as one might suppose, but to student activism, especially Black student organizing that took place both before and after the Tower shooting. I then analyze the echo of racist fear underwriting Texas gun laws today, drawing on a sociological study of members of the campus gun advocacy group Students for Concealed Carry on Campus. Texas has more than once changed its campus gun laws in response to student activism, but whether it was barring guns or bringing them back, the policy changes were connected with racialized fears, and pointedly *not* with the headline-dominating school shootings, from the UT Tower to Virginia Tech, that gun advocates purported to understand as their exigence. I conclude by examining how arguments presented in the *Glass* case illuminate the condition of rhetorical sensitivity necessary to academic freedom.

A SHORT HISTORY

It's widely known as both stereotype and caricature that the gun culture in Texas is especially strong. Romantic (and likely apocryphal) stories about the Tower shooting contend that armed bystanders and even professors returned Whitman's fire, though even if true such bravado seems to have neither slowed nor stopped him. Yet the strength of Texas gun fantasies like these may help to explain why the governor's report on the Tower shooting included no recommendations to ban guns from campus (Timmons 2016b). It's as if banning guns didn't cross anyone's mind in 1966. Perhaps the fantasy of heroic bystanders occluded consideration of a gun ban. Nevertheless, the year after the shooting, the Texas state legislature did try to ban guns from campus dormitories (the 1967 session was the first after the Tower shooting). But Whitman didn't live in a dorm, or keep guns there. To understand the attempt to ban guns from dorms, we have to understand more of the context the legislature was responding to at the time.

In the years immediately before the Tower shooting, civil rights activism effected major changes at universities across the country, including at UT. In 1963, in response to student protests outside its November meeting site, the UT Board of Regents ruled for the removal of racial restrictions throughout the campus (Burr 1988, 14), and university-owned housing was racially integrated the following year. In 1965, student newspaper the *Daily Texan* published an editorial calling for solidarity among Black students and the development of "a racial consciousness" (Burr 1988, 25). In 1966, the year of the UT Tower shooting, the Black Panther Party for Self-Defense was founded at Merritt College in Oakland, California. In addition to establishing community programs, such as free breakfasts and health clinics, the Black Panthers laid claim to the right of using guns as tools of self-defense, explicitly contesting the American norm that reserves this right for mainly white men. Their influence was felt in student and activist groups across the country.

The year after the Tower shooting, in April 1967, the chairman of the Student Nonviolent Coordinating Committee, Stokely Carmichael (later known by the name Kwame Ture), gave a speech on the UT campus in which he "spoke about the Black power movement and criticized the 'white racist press' for its unfair reporting" (Burr 1988, 25; see also Hatch 2019). In May 1967, a dorm at Texas State University in Houston was the scene of a violent police raid, widely reported at the time as a Black student riot. A police officer was killed by a bullet later determined to be ricochet from Houston police gunfire (LaRotta 2017). Four hundred eighty-eight students were arrested, but the "TSU Five," who were charged with inciting the riot, were released due to insufficient evidence. In the 1967 legislative session, the ban on guns in dorms failed, but the legislature did pass a law allowing campus security officers to be recognized as sworn police officers, permitting them to carry guns on campus (Pennie 2017, 58).

Meanwhile, in Austin, Black student organizations garnered public attention by focusing on the failure of the university to recruit Black athletes. In 1968, only a few months after the assassination of Martin Luther King Jr., the student group Afro-Americans for Black Liberation helped established two new programs in Afro-American studies at UT (Burr 1988, 26). Black students were gaining ground in the fight for civil rights on campus. After a controversial meeting of leaders from Students for a Democratic Society in March 1969 (Segalman and Segalman 1969), UT police were concerned about "the presence of armed white and Black radicals on campus" (Timmons 2016b). By the time the state legislature met again in 1969, it was ready to enact a total campus ban on guns (Timmons 2016b). An Institute for Public Affairs report on the sixty-first legislative session described the bill as a "response to a growing concern about campus violence," noting (strangely, given the incident at TSU two years earlier) that "Texas has thus far been spared any militant student unrest" (1970, 28).

The timing of legislative action to ban guns on campus is coincidental. It coincides not only with the Tower shooting, which seems to have caused barely a ripple of reflection about the role of guns on campus, but also with the growing solidarity and mobilization for social action among Black students across the state and the nation. The timing of the ban, situated in the context of campus politics in the late 1960s, suggests that it wasn't the Tower shooting that catalyzed the Texas legislature to ban guns, but radical student activism. The question of allowing guns on campus has historically been not only a *provocation to* student activism, it has historically also been a *response to* the activism of Black students (see also Corrigan's chapter 4 and Gage's chapter 10 in this volume).

A PERSISTENT THEME

It's said that history repeats itself. In the case of campus guns laws in the state of Texas, history also reversed itself. The legislature disarmed the campus because it was afraid of the possibility of armed and organized Black students in the 1960s; but in the 2010s, the legislature rearmed the campus in response to the agitating and organizing of white students. Perhaps because the incidence of campus shootings has only become more frequent and spectacular since the turn of the millennium, it would be easy to think that those college students who do support campus carry laws are concerned about their ability to protect themselves in, as we now casually call it, an active shooter situation.[2] To be sure, some have made that claim—though research into the beliefs and arguments advanced by student advocates for campus carry contradicts it. Evidence also contradicts the realism of the belief that a good guy with a gun is the only thing that can stop a bad guy with a gun. Setting aside for the moment the few recent times that active shooters have been slowed down or disrupted by the intervention of unarmed civilians—often by veterans or young people with military commitments ahead of them (Britzky 2019)—recall that when a shooter opened fire on the Umpqua Community College (UCC) campus in Oregon in 2015, a state that did then and does now allow concealed carry on campus, US Air Force veteran John Parker Jr. told news media that he and other armed veterans who were with him chose not to pursue the shooter because "we could have opened ourselves up to be potential targets ourselves, and not knowing where SWAT was, their response time, they wouldn't know who we were. And if we had our guns ready to shoot, they could think that we were bad guys" (Boggioni 2015). Like many other recent active shooter incidents, the UCC incident ended when the shooter died by suicide. Perhaps advocates of campus carry laws believe that in the midst of such violence and uncertainty they'd somehow make smarter tactical decisions than trained vets like Parker.

Such self-certainty unwarranted by facts or experience would not be inconsistent with the other beliefs of campus carry advocates. For his dissertation research at Texas A&M University in 2014, sociologist Todd Couch conducted thirty interviews with members of the contemporary group Students for Concealed Carry on Campus (SCCC). Couch found a widespread and "very intense pro-white/anti-other racial framing guiding much of SCCC membership" (2014, ii). Couch asked his interview subjects how they got involved with the group and to describe their beliefs about concealed carry on campus, their personal carrying practices, and their history with firearms as well as their desire to obtain a concealed handgun license (CHL). At the close of his interviews, Couch also asked his subjects to describe the demographics of their SCCC chapters. When asked about the racial homogeneity of their chapters, Couch's respondents often became incoherent, pausing for a long time or searching for words (79). If they claimed that their group only reflected the demographics of the larger campus community, Couch confronted them with recent demographic information about their campus, which consistently demonstrated far more diversity than respondents had claimed that there was. In these instances, respondents expressed disbelief, and urged the interviewer to check his facts. They described their (failed) attempts to get women and people of color to join the groups, and even claimed *their group* was discriminated against *because* its membership consists mainly of white men.

This persecution-complex perspective was not held unanimously, however. The only two women who agreed to be interviewed for Couch's research did describe their SCCC chapters as having a "good ol' boy vibe," but they actually seemed to pride themselves on being able to tolerate the pervasive sexist and racist jokes, attributing such joking to boys being boys (2014, 80). In contrast, the military veterans who were interviewed commented openly on the overt racism of SCCC members. On veteran respondent commented, "I came to see that the kids here were just concerned about not getting robbed by minorities. That's all they would talk about" (87). The veterans who participated in Couch's study were so put off by the other members' racism that they hesitated to recommend the group to others, and it seems all of the veteran participants had stopped attending or had left the group altogether by the time interviews took place (81–88).

Couch's findings confirm the investment of SCCC members in white supremacy far beyond denialism or dim awareness of the racial homogeneity of their groups. Couch's respondents consistently testified to their fears of racialized others as the main motivation for their desire to carry concealed handguns, not only on campus specifically but as part of an undifferentiated right to carry at all times. One interviewee directly disclosed, "We're not concerned so much about school shootings. The likelihood of that sort of thing is pretty slim. Those aren't the people we're really concerned about. We're more interested in individual self-defense. When I'm walking home at night there are always these . . . well just to be honest Black guys outside the store by my house" (2014, 55–56). Couch elicited this comment from his respondent over the phone; Couch, a multiracial Black man, sometimes met his interview subjects in person, sometimes spoke with them by videoconference, and sometimes spoke with them over the phone. He organized their comments into categories ranging from hard racial framing like the comment I have quoted above to soft or socially permitted racial framing, such as fear of and complaints about immigration, or about crime in predominantly Black neighborhoods, to color-blind racial framing, where the dynamic of race is minimized or denied, as in the fumbling responses to Couch's demographic inquiries. Couch notes that hard racial framing only appeared in interviews conducted at a distance without cameras (51).

Couch's study demonstrates that anti-Black and anti-immigrant racism broadly informs the views of students who are organized in favor of campus carry across the country. Some respondents openly articulated their racialized fears as part of a culture war in which white American masculinity is viewed as under attack not only by men of color, but by feminists and LGBT people as well as gun control advocates (2014, 57–58). Although respondents tended to displace assertions of white vulnerability onto women, saying they want to carry at all times in order to be able to protect their girlfriends, wives, or daughters, their attachment to guns enables respondents to repair their masculinity by disavowing the very fantasy of vulnerability that underwrites their desire for guns. As Couch points out, the fear of being victimized is articulated as an assertion that carrying a gun enables one to choose *not* to be a victim (109).

Couch concludes with a clarion call for campus administrators to consider how the implementation of campus carry laws will affect their students of color, "since they are the group/individuals framed by most of the members of SCCC as threatening and warranting the loosening of gun control to allow for firearms on campus" (2014, 127, 133). I would add that other people of color who are members of the campus community, including staff as well as faculty of color, are disproportionately exposed to the possible negative impacts of an armed campus environment in which they are viewed, especially by gun advocates, as not belonging (see Ore 2017). A poll conducted of registered Texas voters in March 2016 found that "the majority of Black (79%) and Latino voters (66%) oppose[d] allowing concealed handgun licensees to carry handguns on public university campuses, while less than half of White voters (47%) opposed" the policy (Cokley 2016, 2). A statement issued by UT's African American and African Diaspora Department, noting the commonplace nature of threats and harassment targeting Black faculty, argues that "in the presence of firearms the probability that bullets will find us is higher than for any other campus population" (quoted in Somers and Phelps 2018, 12).

How deeply animating is the fear of racialized others in the history of guns and the University of Texas? In *Towers of Rhetoric: Memory and Invention* (2018), Rosa Eberly briefly recounts arguments that put the UT Tower shooting in this precise context:

> In addition to Whitman's family stress and substance abuse, historian Doug Rassinow, in his book *The Politics of Authenticity*, argued persuasively that Charles Whitman was also a racist, inflamed by white supremacists,

who chose his victims not randomly but for specific reasons. Rassinow describes Whitman as "a student with strongly racist views and apparently with ties to the Minutemen." . . . TimeLife's *True Crime: Mass Murderers* quotes anecdotes reported by Whitman's friends of his bullying African American students and international students.

These claims belie the narrative, which now commonly attaches to many a modern-day mass shooting, that the motives of such violence are mysterious and unknowable. In 2016, to commemorate the Tower shooting fifty years on, *The Texas Standard* radio program created an online multimedia documentary, catachrestically named *Out of the Blue*.[3] The title is a misnomer, though it fits a widely held public narrative. Understanding the UT Tower shooting as a random act of violence enabled the widespread and long-lived denialism about the central role white masculinity played in this violence. The smiling portrait of the shooter in coat and tie, refrains about his military service and his youthful achievement of the Eagle Scout rank—the image of the shooter as an all-American boy (at age twenty-five) was constructed and recirculated *because* of what it elided: aggrieved whiteness; wounded masculinity; violence that at least began as targeted, first, against the women in the shooter's life.[4] After the Columbine shooting in 1999, both Orlando Patterson (1999) and Gloria Steinem (1999) identified this same denialist dynamic at work in contemporary popular media coverage. When white masculinity, however aggressively dysfunctional, is normalized and venerated in American culture, its role in the spectacular violence of mass shooting is mystified.

Students for Concealed Carry on Campus was formed the day after the Virginia Tech shooting in 2007, but whether this means the group is a response to fear about students' vulnerability to campus shootings or strategic opportunism ought to be viewed as an open question. Journalist Adam Weinstein argues in a 2015 article that the conservative Blackwell Leadership Institute helped train campus leaders and paid organizers to seed SCCC chapters across the country (see also Somers and Phelps 2018, 3). According to Weinstein's reporting, campus carry activism is part of a larger right-wing strategy in which state bills like SB 11, even when they don't pass, can be used to identify moderate Republicans vulnerable to primary challengers. Strategists are aware that securing changes in state law is not the only effect of debating campus carry legislation around the country. Such debates can be used to inflame racist and xenophobic passions, and to drag the right wing of American politics further and further to the right.

AFTERMATH AT UT IN 2016

After SB 11 took effect in Texas, the *New York Times* interviewed, among other stakeholders at the University of Texas, a graduate student who chose to meet the writer and photographer in the campus library because he lived with housemates whom he thought wouldn't like his view on guns. Whether or not he should have disclosed to his housemates that he kept firearms in the house they shared, the student clearly violated the new law by displaying his gun for the photographer to document while he was in the campus library (Philipps 2016; see also Timmons 2016a). Published just three days after the start of fall classes, the *NYT* photo documents a student who is licensed to carry a concealed handgun violating the *concealed* stipulation of the law. Presumably, the library in question is the main Perry-Castañeda Library, where, less than six years prior, an armed student who had walked to the library from across campus, firing random shots on his way but not apparently targeting others, died by suicide on the top floor. When the campus went into a more than three-hour lockdown while SWAT teams investigated classrooms and campus buildings, concerned by conflicting reports that there might be a second shooter (there wasn't), the UT chapter of SCCC had to cancel its on-campus venue for a lecture by the author of a specious book called *More Guns, Less Crime* (Goldberg 2010).[5] I doubt that the graduate student who displayed his weapon to the *NYT* photographer was aware of this resonance: the fact that the last known time a student bore a firearm into that campus library, he had terrorized the campus community and then died there. I can tell you that as both a rhetorician and a graduate of the University of Texas, I am tuned into such resonances, and I hope that sharing them here—drawing a line between many moments connected to the same *topos*—will make the affective and psychological landscape of that topos more legible. That this resonance, or we might say coincidence, is lost on some does not mean it isn't exerting an affective force. As Avital Ronell has argued, "There is a zone of undecidability that invests the difference between knowledge and ignorance" (2002, 118).[6] Perhaps the topos remembers and makes its history felt.

The grad student's casual violation of the new campus carry law was not the only breach in the responsible gun behavior that the law's advocates had promised. I turn back now to the shell casings found in Parlin Hall and other nearby buildings in September 2016. There were at least three. The first one found was placed atop a bulletin board, above a flyer for the group Gun Free UT advertising the group's Peace Zone workshop. The flyer was defaced with text reading: "In the land of the pigs, the butcher is king. oink . . . oink . . . oink . . ." Some readers may think that the note ("TRIGGERED?") in the shell casing is ambiguous, an underarticulated argument, if an argument at all. I think the note reads quite clearly as a taunt directed at members of UT's community who object to the presence of guns on campus. Taken together with the writing on the flyer, the taunt also resonates as a threat. Here are the suppressed premises in the argument: "If you don't carry a gun, you're as vulnerable as a pig to a butcher. If that claim upsets you, you're too sensitive. You're too vulnerable. You could protect yourself—if you were carrying a gun." I suppose that is how the Texas state legislature would like you to compensate for your feelings of exposedness. The note in the shell casing (dare I say) weaponizes the jeering critique of sensitivity—a critique that in 2016 had been incubating in the trigger warnings debate for more than two years—and mobilizes its associated premises with the distinct aim of intimidating the display's targeted audience. Such intimidation presents a real threat to academic freedom—one that, though difficult to precisely measure, has begun to be explored in the courts.

THE CASE FOR ACADEMIC FREEDOM

In 2016, three professors at UT Austin sued the university, the board of regents, and the attorney general over SB 11; their main claim is that the campus carry law, and its specific implementation at UT, violates their First Amendment right to academic freedom. Although the case was dismissed by the district court, and again on appeal to the Fifth Circuit (Largey 2018), the claims in the suit are still worth examining. The complaint was brought to a district court in Texas before of the law took effect. Initially, the plaintiffs sought an injunction against the university's decision to allow guns in classrooms. In theory, UT might have opted to allow teachers to decide for themselves whether to allow guns in their classrooms. But while the law allowed schools to create their own rules for implementation, it does not allow rules that would "generally prohibit" guns on campus, a provision that has been understood to handcuff schools over the specific issue of classrooms. Despite its inability to recommend excluding guns from classrooms, the campus carry working group at UT unanimously expressed fear that the new law would chill the free speech of both students and faculty. The UT Austin Faculty Council also passed a resolution calling for a classroom exclusion.

Among the plaintiffs' other claims is an equal protection argument predicated on the fact that nearly all private colleges and universities, as well as many locations on the UT Austin campus *other than* classrooms, are excluded from the requirement to allow concealed carry; plaintiffs argue that no rational basis clearly divides those locations where guns are allowed from those where they are not. For example, private offices may be excluded, but shared offices, such as those often assigned to graduate teaching assistants, cannot be excluded, even if every occupant wants their office excluded. Plaintiffs also advance a due process claim based on the attorney general's threat to punish professors who do try to prohibit or even discourage CHL holders from bringing guns into the classroom. The suit also contains the novel claim of a Second Amendment violation, arguing that the licensure requirements in Texas, as well as in the forty-three other states from which Texas recognizes CHLs, are not "well-regulated," because "there has not been the imposition of proper discipline and training" (*Glass et al.* 2016, 5).

In 2017, the American Association of University Professors (AAUP) filed a brief in support of the professors' appeal (Flaherty 2017). The organization's review of the case law surrounding academic freedom, especially as it touches on speech in the classroom, argues that a law's chilling effect on free speech is determined by the standard of whether "a person of ordinary firmness" would be deterred from exercising his or her rights (Brief for the AAUP 2017, 18). The brief then presents social science research on the widespread opposition to campus carry among students, faculty, and staff, also citing a joint statement of opposition to such laws signed by the AAUP, the American Federation of Teachers, the Association of American Colleges and Universities, and the Association of Governing Boards of Universities and Colleges (20). Because all of the *Glass* plaintiffs teach courses involving controversial social issues, the AAUP argued that the court should recognize the professors as the experts on how the possible presence of handguns in their classrooms would alter the exercise of academic freedom in their courses: "Just as chemists best determine which chemicals are combustible, individual faculty must be able to decide that the ideas in their courses are particularly volatile, warranting the exclusion of guns" (24). The academic discussion of controversial topics, which often challenges students' dearly held beliefs, is only possible if the classroom is understood as a site reserved for the rhetorical practice of negotiating disagreement. Even the possibility that one's interlocutors may have a concealed handgun pierces this rhetorical space by placing a limit on one's willingness to risk provoking anger in someone who may have a lethal weapon. The *Glass* plaintiffs and the AAUP brief contend that guns and rhetoric can't coexist freely; the presence of guns in the classroom diminishes academic freedom.

It might seem strange for a court to adjudicate these claims about the rhetorical nature of a college classroom, and about the relationship between rhetoric and violence—especially since courts, like many other public sites of debate and deliberation in the United States, ban firearms. In a law review article entitled "Guns and Academic Freedom," Aurora Temple Barnes argues that two Supreme Court cases clearly indicate a First Amendment right to academic freedom (*Sweezy* and *Keyishian*), and that this right extends to both institutions and to individual professors (2017, 23). But Barnes cautions that the threshold for harm to academic freedom has not been clearly established. Patricia Somers and Nicholas Phelps, writing in the AAUP's *Journal of Academic Freedom*, report that "faculty have been injured psychologically and taken specific steps to avoid harm . . . They modify their classroom content and their delivery. They modify their interactions with students outside the classroom" (2018, 13). The antagonism of the state legislature and attorney general toward the public university and its faculty suggests that the fear, stress, and anxiety caused by SB 11 (10), and the exposure to intimidation and harassment caused by public opposition to the law (12), may be among its intended effects.

Somers and Phelps interviewed 140 faculty members around the time that SB 11 took effect, and they observed a shift in the tenor of even casual conversations between faculty members. Instead of talking about "research, vacations, or classes," one faculty member remarked, she and her colleagues were preoccupied with "issues such as the 'difference between a loaded weapon and chambered round,' 'the difference between prohibiting and discouraging weapons in the classroom,' and mourning the loss of academic freedom and faculty governance" (2018, 5). The respondents linked their concerns about safety to their own memories of UT Austin as a topos of violence in a way I found striking: "Many of the general comments about safety were punctuated by references to violent incidents on campus"—and here they go on to describe not only those incidents of gun violence which I have mentioned here, but also two murders committed on campus (one in 2016 and one in 2017), as well as an off-campus shooting at a fraternity party.[7] The authors remark, "As the participants related these scenarios we could visualize these 'flashbulb' memories perfectly" (5). A similar experience inflected my writing of this chapter, which at times felt as if it wanted to become a memorialization of gun traumas at my alma mater. These traumas are collective, inflicted on a campus community that spans many times, places, and relations to the university. They are not easily remembered, especially when the institution and the state wishes them to be forgotten. They are not easy to remember, because trauma is a flashbulb—sudden, blinding. But neither are they easy to forget.

These traumas should be remembered, remarked, and understood as the context for both gun policy and the practice (and limitation) of academic freedom at UT Austin. Texans had to mark the fiftieth anniversary of the first mass school shooting by welcoming concealed handguns into that school's classrooms. As teachers, we ought not to forget that a generation of our students has grown up rehearsing active shooter drills, watching as the accelerated frequency of mass shootings diminishes their purported mystery. Although the likelihood of facing a school shooting may remain statistically small, our students as well as our colleagues are affected by gun violence in myriad other places, too: in our neighborhoods and homes; in the forms of intimidation, abuse, accidents, and suicide. If academic freedom matters to us, we will have to embrace, in its defense, the sensitive nature of our classrooms and our communities. We are vulnerable to violence, and to the threat of violence, and to the limits inscribed on what can be thought, said, and heard by symbolic violence (see Eberly 2018, chapter 6). Yet this sensitivity to affection in language is also what makes it possible for us to study, teach, and learn.

CODA

I'm no longer a Longhorn but still a Texan: I became a Red Raider.[8] I stopped reflecting the school spirit "guns up" hand sign to the parking attendants on campus in 2017, after I was locked down in my office while teaching an online class. An armed student murdered an officer inside the campus police station, then fled across the campus. When it happened, my grad students and I were discussing Diane Davis's case for a rhetoric of responsibility. Davis argues that we are brought into being as subjects in language through a preoriginary responsibility for others. We can feel this responsibility, she suggests, through being faced with the possibility of death. The finitude of life—the fact that there are limits—is what makes it possible for me to be affected by others. I become a rhetorical subject, Davis argues, *in response* to the difference from me of those who affect me.

My students were talking about whether anything other than death could awaken us to this exposedness, this finitude, whether anything other than death could lead us to embrace our sensitivity to rhetorical affection and the responsibility that Davis argues comes with it.

I was saying, when a student alerted me to the lockdown order, that perhaps even spectacular violence *does not* awaken us. The possibility of death is a vulnerability, and when it confronts us, we may refuse to face it, and refuse to face the fact that we share this vulnerability, irreparably, with others.

Facing our own vulnerability is not easy, and for all the talk of how we need to work harder to understand each other across political differences, it's not actually that hard to understand wanting to arm yourself against your own vulnerability, or wanting to blame someone whose difference from you makes you feel affected and exposed. I don't think understanding is the rhetorical problem here. I think it's indifference. Davis writes that "[i]ndifference is the luxury of exposed existents who are not *faced* with the fact of their exposedness" (2010, 10). When the news came through, I shut my office door, turned off the light, and silently sent text messages to my wife, my parents, my colleagues in the building with me. Being exposed makes us responsible to one another. The violence was actually over already by the time the lockdown started; I hadn't *really* been in harm's way. But I'd lost the will, the next day or two, to wave even a symbolic hand gesture at others with whom I shared another Texas campus, where the law welcomes handguns so long as they're concealed.

NOTES

I would like to acknowledge Justin Hatch, whose doctoral research on Stokely Carmichael helped me think about the effect of his 1967 speech at UT, as well as the TTU graduate students whose insights helped me frame the coda.

1. For another reflection on the place of Parlin in memory and rhetoric, see Boyle 2018.

2. Only 22 percent of students support campus carry, if the results of a study of midwestern colleges hold in other regional contexts (Thompson et al. 2013).

3. For more on race and catachresis, see Calvin Warren's *Ontological Terror: Blackness, Nihilism, and Emancipation* (2018).

4. Psychoanalyst JoAnn Ponder (2018), who enrolled as a freshman at UT in 1972, reviews a variety of arguments surrounding the presence of a brain tumor compressing Whitman's amygdala that was discovered in his autopsy. Ponder, following the 1966 governor's report, contends that "the safest conclusion" is that "the tumor contributed to [Whitman's] problems, but was not the sole cause of his behavior" (242). Kristeen Cherney and Margaret Price (2018) remind us that while stigma about mental health and disability often increases in response to mass shootings, there is no consistent mental health profile that could be used to prevent acts of violence (103, 106). They also point out that people with mental health disabilities are far more likely to be victims of violence than its perpetrators (106).

5. I have not listed this work in my references because it was quickly discredited after its publication. For more on the author's manipulation of data to support his thesis, see Ludwig 1998 and Hemenway 1998.

6. Here I cite Ronell's insight into the way that stupidity implicates knowledge, because "stupidity . . . knows that it does not know," even as I am cognizant of a NYU

Title IX investigation finding her responsible for hostile environment harassment (made public in 2018).

7. Regarding the topos of violence, see Eberly (2018, chapter 2).

8. Much of the writing of this chapter was completed while I was at Texas Tech University. I've since joined the faculty at the University of Utah—in the first state to allow campus carry (in 2004).

REFERENCES

Barnes, Aurora Temple. 2017. "Guns and Academic Freedom." *Gonzaga Law Review* 53:1–42. Preprint, March 14.

Boggioni, Tom. 2015. "Armed Vet Destroys Gun Nuts' Argument on Mass Shooters by Explaining Why He Didn't Attack Oregon Killer." *RawStory*, October 2, 2015. https://www.rawstory.com/2015/10/armed-vet-destroys-gun-nuts-argument-on-mass-shooters-by-explaining-why-he-didnt-attack-oregon-killer/.

Boyle, Casey. 2018. "The Complete History of Parlin Hall (Abridged Version)." In *Inventing Place: Writing Lone Star Rhetorics*, edited by Casey Boyle and Jenny Rice, 59–72. Carbondale: Southern Illinois University Press.

Brief for the AAUP as Amicus Curiae, 2017. *Glass et al. v. Paxton et al.* United States Court of Appeals for the Fifth Circuit. https://www.aaup.org/file/Glass_campus_carry_0.pdf.

Britzky, Haley. 2019. "Young Military Hopefuls Are Willing to Go to War for Their Country. Instead, Many Are Losing Their Lives in School Shootings." *Task and Purpose*, May 8, 2019. https://taskandpurpose.com/military-students-school-shootings.

Burr, Beverly. 1988. "History of Student Activism at the University of Texas at Austin (1960–1988)." MA thesis, University of Texas at Austin.

Carter, Angela. 2015. "Teaching with Trauma: Trigger Warnings, Feminism, and Disability Pedagogy." *Disability Studies Quarterly* 35 (2). http://dsq-sds.org/article/view/4652.

Cherney, Kristeen, and Margaret Price. 2018. "Student Profiling and Negative Implications for Students with Disabilities." In *The Wiley Handbook on Violence in Education: Forms, Factors, and Preventions*, edited by Harvey Shapiro, 103–17. New York: Wiley.

Cokley, Kevin. 2016. "IUPRA Poll Results: Texas Voters' Attitudes about Gun Laws." *Institute for Urban Policy Research and Analysis*, April 26, 2016. https://liberalarts.utexas.edu/iupra/_files/pdf/memo_gun-laws.pdf.

Couch, Todd. 2014. "'Arming the Good Guys?' An Examination of Racial Framing in Students for Concealed Carry on Campus." PhD diss., Texas A&M University.

Daily Texan Editorial Board. 2013. "Regents, Powers and Lege Repeat History When They Fight." *Daily Texan*, April 1, 2013. http://www.dailytexanonline.com/opinion/2013/04/01/regents-powers-lege-repeat-history-when-they-fight.

Dart, Tom. 2016. "Cocks Not Glocks: Texas Students Carry Dildos on Campus to Protest Gun Law." *Guardian*, August 25, 2016. https://www.theguardian.com/us-news/2016/aug/25/cocks-not-glocks-texas-campus-carry-gun-law-protest.

Davis, Diane. 2010. *Inessential Solidarity: Rhetoric and Foreigner Relations*. Pittsburgh: University of Pittsburgh Press.

Eberly, Rosa A. 2016. "Texas Picked an Ominous Date to Arm Its Public Colleges." *Chronicle of Higher Education*, July 27, 2016. https://www.chronicle.com/article/Texas-Picked-an-Ominous-Date/237264.

Eberly, Rosa A. 2018. *Towers of Rhetoric: Memory and Reinvention*. Intermezzo. http://intermezzo.enculturation.net/05-eberly/eberly-tor-title.html.

Flaherty, Colleen. 2017. "AAUP Files Brief in Challenge to Campus Carry." *Insider Higher Ed*, November 22, 2017. https://www.insidehighered.com/quicktakes/2017/11/22/aaup-files-brief-challenge-campus-carry.

Gerdes, Kendall. 2019. "Trauma, Trigger Warnings, and the Rhetoric of Sensitivity." *Rhetoric Society Quarterly* 49 (1): 3–24.

Glass et al. v. Paxton et al. 2016. United States District Court for the Western District of Texas Austin Division. No. 1:16-cv-845.

Goldberg, Beverly. 2010. "UT Austin Shooting Rampage Ends Tragically in the Library." *American Libraries Magazine*, September 28, 2010. https://americanlibrariesmagazine .org/2010/09/28/ut-austin-shooting-rampage-ends-tragically-in-the-library/.

Hall, Katie. 2016. "UT Professors: 3 Bullet Casings, One with Note Inside, Left on Campus." *Statesman*, September 20. https://www.statesman.com/article/20160920/NEWS /309209832.

Hatch, Justin D. 2019. "Dissociating Power and Racism: Stokely Carmichael at Berkeley." *Advances in the History of Rhetoric* 22 (3): 303–25.

Hemenway, David. 1998. "Review." *New England Journal of Medicine* 339 (27): 2029–30.

Institute of Public Affairs. 1970. "The Sixty-First Texas Legislature: A Review of Its Work." University of Texas. https://lrl.texas.gov/scanned/sessionOverviews/review/61st.pdf.

Largey, Matt. 2018. "Appeals Court Blocks Bid to Revive UT-Austin Professors' Lawsuit over Campus Carry." *KUT*, August 16, 2018. https://www.kut.org/post/appeals-court-blocks -bid-revive-ut-austin-professors-lawsuit-over-campus-carry.

LaRotta, Alex. 2017. "The TSU Riot, 50 Years Later." *Houston Chronicle*, May 16, 2017. https://www.houstonchronicle.com/local/gray-matters/article/The-TSU-Riot-50 -years-later-11149852.php.

Ludwig, Jens. 1998. "Political Booknotes." *Washington Monthly* 30 (6): 50–51.

McGill, Kevin. 2018. "Appeals Court Hears Challenge to Texas Campus Carry Law." *Lubbock Avalanche Journal*, July 11, 2018. https://www.lubbockonline.com/news/2018 0711/appeals-court-hears-challenge-to-texas-campus-carry-law.

Nelson, Scott, et al. 2013. "Crossing Battle Lines: Teaching Multimodal Literacies through Alternate Reality Games." *Kairos: A Journal of Rhetoric, Technology, and Pedagogy* 17 (3). http://technorhetoric.net/17.3/praxis/nelson-et-al/index.html.

Ore, Ersula. 2017. "Pushback: A Pedagogy of Care." *Pedagogy: Critical Approaches to Teaching Literature, Language, Composition, and Culture* 17 (1): 9–33.

Orem, Sarah, and Neil Simpkins. 2015. "Weepy Rhetoric: Trigger Warnings and the Work of Making Mental Illness Visible in the Writing Classroom." *Enculturation* 20. http:// enculturation.net/weepy-rhetoric.

Patterson, Orlando. 1999. "When 'They' Are 'Us.'" *New York Times*, April 30, 1999. https:// www.nytimes.com/1999/04/30/opinion/when-they-are-us.html.

Pennie, Demetrick D. 2017. "Exploring College Leaders' Critical Incident Experiences Pursuant to Improving Campus Safety Policies during the Mass-Shooting Era." PhD diss., Texas Tech University.

Philipps, Dave. 2016. "What University of Texas Campus Is Saying about Concealed Guns." *New York Times*, August 28. https://www.nytimes.com/2016/08/28/us/university-of -texas-campus-concealed-guns.html.

Ponder, JoAnn. 2018. "From the Tower Shootings in 1966 to Campus Carry in 2016: Collective Trauma at the University of Texas at Austin." *International Journal of Applied Psychoanalytic Studies* 15 (4): 239–52.

Ronell, Avital. 2002. *Stupidity*. Champaign: University of Illinois Press.

Segalman, Bob, and Ralph Segalman. 1969. "The Riot That Did Not Happen—The Defused SDS National Conference (Austin, Texas)." Unpublished paper, cited by permission from the authors.

Somers, Patricia, and Nicholas Phelps. 2018. "Not Chilly Enough? Texas Campus Carry and Academic Freedom." *AAUP Journal of Academic Freedom* 9:1–15.

Steinem, Gloria. 1999. "Supremacy Crimes." *Ms.*, August/September 1999.

Texas Standard. 2016. "*Out of the Blue: 50 Years After the UT Tower Shooting.*" http://tower history.org/.

Thompson, Amy, et al. 2013. "Student Perceptions and Practices Regarding Carrying Concealed Handguns on University Campuses." *Journal of American College Health* 61 (5): 243–53.

Timmons, Patrick. 2016a. "Dildos on Campus, Gun in the Library: The *New York Times* and the Texas Gun War." *Counterpunch*, August 29, 2016. https://www.counterpunch.org /2016/08/29/dildos-on-campus-gun-in-the-library-the-new-york-times-and-the-texas -gun-war/.

Timmons, Patrick. 2016b. "Racism, Freedom of Expression and the Prohibition of Guns at Universities in Texas." *Counterpunch*, July 29, 2016. https://www.counterpunch.org /2016/07/29/racism-freedom-of-expression-and-the-prohibition-of-guns-at-uni versities-in-texas/.

Waller, Allyson. 2018. "Moving Forward: UT Professors Continue Legal Battle against Campus Carry Law." *Daily Texan*, April 20, 2018. https://www.dailytexanonline.com/2018 /04/19/moving-forward-ut-professors-continue-legal-battle-against-campus-carry-law.

Warren, Calvin. 2018. *Ontological Terror Blackness, Nihilism, and Emancipation.* Durham, NC: Duke University Press.

Weinstein, Adam. 2015. "The Secret History of the Campus Carry Movement." *The Trace*, July 5, 2015. https://www.thetrace.org/2015/07/the-making-of-the-campus-carry-move ment/.

10

NATIONAL NEWS COVERAGE OF WHITE MASS SHOOTERS
Perpetuating White Supremacy through Strategic Rhetoric

Scott Gage

National news coverage of mass shootings in the United States proceeds along a predictable pattern (Willis-Chun 2011; Park, Holody, and Zhang 2012). This predictability may tempt us, the audiences of that coverage, to overlook how the press represents mass shootings. However, examining national coverage of mass shootings and their perpetrators remains an important pursuit. Because most of us will never directly experience a mass shooting, news media play a critical role in shaping public perception of this form of violence (Schildkraut, Elssas, and Meredith 2018). As media shape public perception, they also shape audience subjectivity. According to Joshua Gunn and David Beard (2003), for example, the media evoke an apocalyptic sublime that attempts to transmute audiences into dazzled spectators of an unending tragedy. And as Cynthia Willis-Chun (2011) argues, the media also seek the production of an innocent, uncritical audience reassured in knowing that the social, cultural, and political problem of mass shootings "lies not with the dominant culture, but with those who fail to comply with it" (53). As these examples remind, the news media contribute in significant ways to "the social construction of society" (Schildkraut, Elssas, and Meredith 2018, 224). Moreover, the examples highlight an insidious relationship between national news coverage and mass shootings in the United States. Examining this relationship is essential to redressing this "uniquely American problem" (Dahmen 2018, 165).

I take up the relationship between news media and mass shootings in this chapter by examining representations of mass shooters whom media identify as white men.[1] Specifically, I argue that national news coverage of these shooters performs a strategic rhetoric (Nakayama and Krizek 1995) that perpetuates white supremacy, defined here as a form of direct, structural, and cultural violence (Galtung 1990) intended to

https://doi.org/10.7330/9781646422159.c010

maintain the subordination of groups and individuals not socially constructed as white. Enacted through visual-verbal displays (Prelli 2006), this rhetoric presents white supremacy to audiences as an interpersonal form of violence inflicted by deranged individuals. This rhetoric simultaneously attempts to conceal audience perception and critique of white supremacy in its structural and cultural forms. Presenting white supremacy in this way allows audiences, especially white audiences such as myself, to explain away the violence inflicted by white mass shooters and to avoid the difficult work of considering how white racial identity depends on, and is constitutive of, anti-Black violence, from slavery, lynching, and segregation to mass incarceration and, now, mass public violence wrought through gun, bullet, and wound (see also Corrigan's chapter 4 in this volume). It also allows white supremacy to persist as a multifaceted violence damaging social relations, exacerbating inequality, and taking life, all so often through the gun's pulled trigger.

I begin with violence and white supremacy, explaining both as a triad involving direct, structural, and cultural (Galtung 1990) manifestations of harm. I then discuss strategic rhetoric as a form of cultural violence supporting white supremacy, and I review its enactment in national news coverage of mass shootings in the United States. Importantly, the three parts of Johan Galtung's (1990) violence taxonomy are not entirely separate and distinguishable; where one part takes form, the other two are always already in play. I address strategic rhetoric specifically as a form of cultural violence in this chapter because the news media's depiction of mass shooters as deviant individuals protects hegemonic social structures, in particular, from implication in the violence of mass shooting. I focus my discussion of strategic rhetoric on Cynthia Willis-Chun's (2011) study of the Columbine and Virginia Tech tragedies. Next, I demonstrate the news media's enactment of strategic rhetoric when depicting mass shooters who are identified as white men. I do so through an examination of national news coverage of the gunman who murdered nine members of the Mother Emanuel church in Charleston, South Carolina, on June 17, 2015.[2] Analyzing news stories containing photographic images of the shooter, I argue that news media deploy image and word to highlight white supremacy as a form of direct violence enacted by deranged individuals. During this discussion, and across the chapter more broadly, I neither name nor show images of mass shooters such as the Charleston gunman. I do so both in respect to the No Notoriety campaign and in the hopes of containing any possible contagion effect (Dahmen 2011) produced by recirculating shooters' names and images. Lastly, I consider the implications of my chapter for the persistence of white supremacy, and gun violence, in the United States; for the rhetorics through which news media represent mass shootings; and for the audiences who consume those representations.

WHITE SUPREMACY, STRATEGIC RHETORIC, AND
MEDIA COVERAGE OF MASS SHOOTERS

Drawing from Johan Galtung, I understand violence to be an influence that limits the capacity of a living being, or a group of living beings, to thrive, flourish, and achieve full realization. As Galtung explains, violence is "the *cause of the difference between the potential and the actual*" (1969, 168; emphasis in the original); it increases the distance between what could be and what is in the well-being of a life and its surrounding environment. I turn to Galtung's definition of violence because it challenges us to "reject the narrow concept of violence—according to which violence is *somatic* incapacitation, or deprivation of health, alone (with killing as the extreme form), at the hands of an *actor* who *intends* this to be the consequence" (168, emphasis in the original; see also Allen's chapter 13 in this volume). Galtung (1990) demonstrates the nuance and complexity of violence in a three-part typology including direct, structural, and cultural violence. Direct violence involves instances of physical and/ or psychological harm inflicted by an agent or group of agents (Galtung 1969). It is usually overt and observable as an "*event*" (Galtung 1990, 294 emphasis in the original) and frequently erupts interpersonally. Less visible, but no less damaging, is structural violence. This violence emerges through disparate distributions of access, power, and resources within a system and often results in "unequal life chances" (Galtung 1969, 171). Supporting both direct and structural violence is cultural violence, through which the "symbolic sphere" of culture is used to "justify or legitimize" violence in its direct and structural forms (Galtung 1990, 291). Cultural violence, often taking form as speech, visual symbols, representation, and so on, presents direct and structural violence so they "look, even feel, right—or at least not wrong" (291). It can even mask direct and structural violence so that we see them "not as violent"—if we see them at all (291). As this chapter demonstrates, representation can function as an especially troubling form of cultural violence since it can protect direct and structural violence from interrogation and intervention without explicitly supporting or legitimizing either.

White supremacy is a form of violence. It seeks the diminishment of life, health, and opportunity for groups and individuals not socially constructed as white. It enacts "needs-deprivation" against those groups, negating claims to survival, well-being, identity/meaning, and freedom (Galtung 1990, 295). In its manifestations as direct violence, white supremacy exists along a continuum: on one side of the continuum, explicit physical harm and on the other side, subtle but observable exclusion and rejection, emotional and psychological injury. Expressed directly, white supremacy appears as an interpersonal violence between and among people and wounds immediately, although the wounds may not mark the corporeal body. Such expressions are easily recognizable and have tragically shaped American civic identity and belonging for centuries (Ore 2019). In its structural forms, white supremacy operates as a "racialized social system" that "shapes . . . life chances" (Bonilla-Silva 1997, 467). As a system, white supremacy places "actors in racial categories" (469) and wields influence over the access those actors gain to healthcare, education, wealth, and so on. Distributed across institutions, policies, and laws, white supremacy in its structural form operates covertly; it presents few discrete agents to observe and few, if any, individuals to blame. Lastly, in its cultural form, white supremacy manifests in language, in symbols, in epistemology (see also Gerdes's chapter 9 in this volume). It's the swastika, the noose, the Confederate flag. It's the hate speech and the whispered slur and the racially inflected joke. It's the rhetoric that sometimes argues for white supremacy and then sometimes denies it all. As a form of cultural violence, white supremacy persuades and influences, affirms and promotes; it reasserts the values of a world built by white superordination, and it makes claims to what can be seen, shared, and known about race. Strategic rhetoric provides but one example of white supremacy in its cultural form.

According to Thomas K. Nakayama and Robert L. Krizek (1995), strategic rhetoric provides a method of diversion through which whiteness retains power by eluding analysis and critique. Although centers of hegemony such as whiteness may resist "extensive characterization" through violence (291), they more effectively escape examination through strategic rhetorical maneuvering. For example, Nakayama and Krizek identify six discourses through which whiteness evades scrutiny; presents itself as a nebulous concept fluctuating between "universality and invisibility" (296); and causes difficulty in any effort to name, analyze, or understand it. This difficulty marks a strategic move toward rendering whiteness invisible, which "resecures" its central position as a hegemonic force (292). Hence the effectiveness of strategic rhetoric: if whiteness cannot be seen, then the power, influence, and violence it wields in everyday life becomes a "naturalized dominance" (299), both unnoticed and taken for granted. As a manifestation of white supremacy in its cultural form, strategic rhetoric reaffirms and protects whiteness as a center of social power. However, strategic rhetoric may also be deployed as cultural violence to legitimize, justify, and protect other aspects of a dominant culture. As Willis-Chun (2011) demonstrates in her study of the Columbine and Virginia Tech massacres, news media in the United State enact strategic rhetoric in their coverage of mass shootings and, through this rhetoric, obscure the relationship between gun violence and dominant social structures at the center of national life.

Willis-Chun's (2011) examination of the news media reveals that coverage of the Columbine and Virginia Tech tragedies enacts strategic rhetoric by depicting the perpetrators as individuals whose violence may be explained away as a function of their personal deviance. The media mark this deviance through reporting that positions the shooters both outside of and in opposition to the norms and expectations of the dominant culture, specifically norms and expectations involving class, heteronormative masculinity/sexuality, and American nationality. Representing the perpetrators as deviant in relation to those norms and expectations functions strategically to protect and preserve the social structures implicated in mass gun violence. To begin, the media's representations invite a distance, or a de-identification, between the shooters and the news media's audience; they "enabl[e] the public to see itself as apart from the gunmen" (Willis-Chun 2011, 58). This perception leaves audiences "secure in the knowledge that they are not monstrous, that they did not help to create the killers" (58). This impression focuses audience attention "on the aberrant nature of [the shooters]" (58) and obscures the influence the dominant culture may wield in the production of the shooters' violence. As Willis-Chun contends, diverting audience attention away from social structures "preserve[s] the innocence of the dominant culture" (47) by "allow[ing] [audiences] to avoid self or societal critique" and by assuring audiences that "the problem lies not with the dominant culture, but with those who fail to comply with it" (53). By directing the audience's attention toward the deviancy of mass shooters and away from "the social world that created and empowered these individuals," news coverage "allows power structures to continue unexamined" (59). Without such examination, components of the dominant culture that could be implicated in mass gun violence are reinforced as hegemonic forces influencing and structuring the social world; they are allowed to persist as the social world's difficult-to-see architecture—much as whiteness is allowed to persist as an invisible center of social power (Nakayama and Krizek 1995). By circumscribing critiques of social structures and their implication in mass gun violence, the news media's strategic rhetoric advances a narrow understanding of violence as overt physical and/or psychological harm inflicted by an individual actor or group of actors, or as what Galtung (1969) labels direct violence. This understanding privatizes violence; it reduces violence to harmful actions "authored by evil individuals" (Engels 2015, 188). Presented in this way, mass shootings become a function of the individual rather than a function of social structures or culture (and mass shootings, in turn, become easily narrativized, ideologically safe, and readily explained away). Media coverage representing mass shooters as "deviant monsters" (Willis-Chun 2011, 49), thus, undermines "vocabular[ies] for discussing structural violence" (Engels 2015, 118). Without that vocabulary, dominant social structures and cultures are protected and reinforced, and the status quo is maintained.

Importantly, the strategic rhetoric Willis-Chun (2011) reveals does not appear to extend to representations of race when shooters are identified as white men. For example, the media do not employ racial norms and expectations as a standard against which the Columbine shooters may be judged as socially aberrant. In fact, as Willis-Chun contends, media coverage of Columbine attempts to diminish considerations of race altogether. Audrey Kobayashi and Linda Peake (2000) advance a similar argument. According to them, the Columbine murderers are reported to have visited neo-Nazi websites, to have worn swastikas on their trench coats, and to have made racist and threatening statements about Black and Latinx communities; however, the killers' racial identities and motivations are written "out of the equation" (397). In contrast, media coverage of the Virginia Tech shooting "consistently exhibited . . . race" (Park, Holody, and Zhang 2012, 486). As these scholars demonstrate, the news media's coverage of mass shootings diminishes—if it doesn't altogether negate—race in its reporting when the perpetrator is identified as a white man. As part of this obfuscation of race, the media's strategic rhetoric obscures, protects, and perpetuates white supremacy, even when white supremacy is explicitly evident.

NEWS COVERAGE OF THE MOTHER EMANUEL SHOOTING

The violence at Mother Emanuel on June 17, 2015, is difficult to discuss. Words slip and escape, lose meaning. Grammar breaks down. I don't attempt here to offer understanding of the gunman's violence, to account for its specific reasoning or causation, including the long and tragic histories bearing on that horrific June evening. Others have already done that important work (Boyce and Brayda 2015; Egerton

2015; Bouie 2015; Demby 2015). Rather, I attempt here to account for the rhetorics through which national news media portray white mass shooters and for the ways that rhetoric perpetuates white supremacy. Importantly, I emphasize the contributions of both word and image in my discussion (see also Boedy's chapter 11 in this volume). I account for visual imagery because "photographs play a vital role in the transference of news to the public" (Dahmen 2011, 164). For example, the use of photographs in media coverage influences how audiences understand and remember particular events (Dahmen 2011). Additionally, photographs "influence which elements of a specific news story receive the most public interest and discussion" (164). My examination suggests the media's use of strategic rhetoric in its reporting of mass shootings emerges from a visual-verbal rhetoric of display (Prelli 2006). According to Lawrence J. Prelli, rhetorics of display arise from "particular, situated resolutions of the dynamic between revealing and concealing" (2). To display is to emphasize and reveal specific qualities or characteristics, specific meanings or possibilities, while simultaneously obscuring and concealing others. As rhetorics of display reveal and conceal, they both direct and divert audience attention, constraining what knowledge and understanding may be available. In the news media's coverage of the Mother Emanuel shooting, this dynamic between revealing and concealing functions strategically to protect and reinforce white supremacy by revealing it only as a form of direct violence inflicted by a deviant individual.

As in coverage of the Columbine and Virginia Tech massacres, media representations of the Mother Emanuel shooting present the murderer as deviant in terms of middle-class identity, heteronormative masculinity/sexuality, and American nationality.[3] However, the most prevalent strategies for presenting the Mother Emanuel shooter as deviant involve displaying the shooter's criminality, the shooter's mental health and, paradoxically, the shooter's explicit expressions of white supremacy. For example, news coverage of the shooting frequently emphasizes the killer's criminal history, specifically his two arrests at a shopping mall in Columbia, South Carolina, including one arrest at the mall for felony possession of the narcotic Suboxone (Seidman 2015; Flitter and Allen 2015). In addition, media coverage displays the Mother Emanuel shooter's criminality by focusing on the heinousness of his crime, labeling the shooting variously both as a hate crime and as an act of domestic terrorism (Berman 2015; Hanson 2015; Bierman, Mejia, and Serrano 2015; Makarechi 2015). Emphasizing the shooter's criminal history displays his criminality by presenting him as deviant regarding mainstream laws and legal standards of behavior. Such displays of criminality become amplified in reports labeling the shooting as a hate crime or as an act of terrorism. To be sure, the Mother Emanuel shooting warrants such labeling, and the media would be remiss not to include that language in its coverage. At the same time, terms such as *terrorism* position the killer far outside of the dominant culture. Such positioning magnifies the killer's criminality and with it, his deviance.

A range of images representing the Mother Emanuel shooter accompanies press reports emphasizing his criminality. One of the most common images depicts the shooter at his first court appearance. In the image, the shooter stands in the foreground of a closed circuit video feed wearing a prison uniform awash in blue-gray fluorescence. Two officers in dark paramilitary gear stand behind him. Both the prison uniform and the presence of the officers display the killer visually to audiences as a criminal. Such visual representation makes vivid the gunman's criminality and deviance. As Charles A. Hill (2004) explains, vivid information presents concrete, detailed representations that increase the reality of what is represented by positioning audiences closer to actual experience. Because photographic imagery is high in vividness (Hill 2004), the image of the Mother Emanuel shooter at his first court appearance brings audiences closer to the actual experience of seeing him in his prison uniform under the watchful eye of two police officers. In bringing audiences closer to this experience, the image increases the reality of the shooter's criminality and invites confirmation of his existence and identity as both criminal and deviant. Importantly, the shooter's position in the image plays a significant role. Appearing in the foreground, visually overlapping the officers behind him, the murderer is presented as the image's most focal element, for "foreground objects are more salient than background objects, and elements that overlap other elements are more salient than the elements they overlap" (Kress and van Leeuwen 2006, 202). Such positioning draws visual attention to the shooter and invites audiences to narrow their focus onto the person who has been displayed as a criminal. This narrowing of focus limits options for locating the criminality presented through the language of the news reports. Thus, the image locates criminality and deviance within the individual shooter, displaying him as an agent with full responsibility both for his criminality and for his position outside of the dominant culture.

A second strategy news media use to present the Mother Emanuel shooter as deviant involves displays of the shooter's mental health. Media coverage largely displays his health in terms revealing mental illness and abnormality. For example, reports frequently include language describing the murderer as "disturbed," "deranged," and "twisted" (Cary 2015; Sanchez and Smith-Spark 2015). Although news outlets and their journalists do not themselves present the Mother Emanuel shooter through such terminology, the inclusion of language such as *deranged* from sources they interview contributes to a display revealing the gunman's mental health as sick and abnormal. As with public discourse focusing on the mental instability of the shooter who attacked Gabby Giffords in Tucson, Arizona, coverage displaying the Mother Emanuel shooter's mental health in terms such as "disturbed" and "twisted" "disparag[ed] [the shooter] as fundamentally (and unforgivably) outside the realm of normal cognitive functionality" (Smith and Hollihan 2014, 599). Also like the discourse describing the Tucson gunman as mentally unstable, coverage labeling the Charleston shooter as "disturbed" "did more than just *describe* [the shooter] as . . . irrational: they in fact constituted him as such" (599; emphasis in the original). Thus, press reports engaging in this kind of display reveal the Mother Emanuel shooter to be deviant, opposing norms regarding mental health, situating the shooter once more outside of dominant mainstream culture.

Appearing frequently in press reports displaying the Charleston killer's mental health is an image of him in what appears to be a backyard, the blue evening sun setting in the darkening forest behind him. He sits atop a small wrought iron table encircled by potted flowers. Glaring at the camera over the lenses of aviator glasses, the shooter casually dangles a Glock pistol between his legs, loosely holds a Confederate flag over his left shoulder. Although the flag may be the image's most important element because of the salience it gains through color contrast (Kress and van Leeuwen 2006), I focus here on the gun, which amplifies the media's presentation of the shooter as deviant. Included in press reports displaying the killer's mental health, the presence of the gun associates his "deranged" mind with the potential of direct violence. This association displays the killer's mental health as a physical danger, a representation made more real through vividness and more tragic through the reality of the shooter's actions at Mother Emanuel. Correlating displays of the murderer's mental health with the gun appearing in the image intensifies his presentation in the news media as deviant; not only is he revealed as having a "disturbed" mind, that disturbance led him to extraordinary violence. This display situates the shooter even further outside of the mainstream; it renders him a psychotic aberration amid a world thought to be sane, rational, and nonviolent. As demonstrated by *USA Today*, media outlets frequently present the image of the shooter holding the gun and Confederate flag as the largest visual element in their reporting. In an article by Nathaniel Cary (2015), the image is situated in the middle of the report, assuming almost as much screen space as the verbal text appearing above and below it. The size and placement of the photograph in reports displaying the shooter's mental health is likely to have attracted audience awareness, for "larger photos . . . attract greater audience attention" (Dahmen 2011, 165). By directing audience attention toward the image, media outlets attempt to direct audience attention toward the presentation of the shooter as dangerous and mentally disturbed. Through their publication of the image, outlets also attempt to direct attention once more to the individual shooter. Although he does not appear in the foreground of this particular image, the killer does appear at the center of the visual field's x-y axis. This composition attempts to focus visual attention onto the shooter and to invite audiences to locate mental illness in him, the gun and Confederate flag only emblems of a deeper psychological disturbance, a deeper individual deviance.

Lastly, national media coverage of the Mother Emanuel shooter presents him as deviant through his explicit expressions of white supremacy. These displays introduce a paradox in the media's use of strategic rhetoric in coverage of the shooting. Whereas media coverage of perpetrators such as the Columbine murderers tend to divert attention away from their potential investments in white supremacy, coverage of the Mother Emanuel shooter draws explicit attention both to his investment in and enactment of white supremacy. Although press reports do not avoid white supremacy in their coverage of the tragedy in Charleston, they still attempt to divert attention away from white supremacy's structural and cultural functions. Media coverage does so by presenting the shooter as a deviant racist. For example, some news outlets quote liberally from the murderer's virulently racist manifesto (Robles 2015) while others attempt to explicate or decode the white supremacist symbols appearing on the shooter's website (Jeffery and West 2015). Similarly, publications such as the *Los Angeles Times* (Lee 2015) report on the murderer's activity on a neo-Nazi website while *Newsweek* (Mosendz 2015) quotes individuals who describe the shooter's explicit racism. This type of media coverage displays the shooter's explicit white supremacy and, in doing so, emphasizes his deviance, specifically his deviance of what Eduardo Bonilla-Silva (2015) refers to as the new racism, which advances racialized structures and practices in the United States through indirection, subtlety, and rearticulation. Key elements of this "color-blind" racism include "the increasingly covert nature of racial discourse and practices" and "the avoidance of direct racial terminology" (1362). Thus, the

Mother Emanuel shooter's explicit displays of white supremacy betray a more covert system of white racial dominance, a system that has established clandestine racism as a norm. Defying this norm, the shooter is revealed as deviant and aberrant and is separated out from the dominant racial culture of the United States.

The primary image associated with reports displaying the Charleston shooter's white supremacy depicts him standing alone on the edge of a swamp, a sparse environment of trees, branches, and moss behind him. Clad in a black jacket adorned with Rhodesian and apartheid-era South African flags, he glowers at the camera with dark eyes. This image further displays the gunman's explicit white supremacy, for the flags with which he poses, like other symbols presented on his website, "convey his appeal for a return to [w]hite dominance" (Boyce and Brayda 2015). Like the photographs previously discussed, this image also contributes to a media strategy individualizing the shooter's deviance. As in earlier examples, the photograph's composition attempts to narrow focus onto the shooter. Although the flags on his jacket gain salience through color contrast, the shooter is positioned just right of center in the visual field, creating a visual asymmetry that attempts to draw visual attention toward him (Kress and van Leeuwen 2006). This aspect of the image's design visually locates white supremacy within the shooter and in doing so, vividly reveals white supremacy as an individual deviance. Importantly, this image of the shooter appears most frequently in the reports I examined, making it a central component of a media environment emphasizing the killer's identity as a lone, deranged individual. Circulating through and forming the media environment in the days following the Mother Emanuel tragedy, stories and images such as those I've discussed here constructed displays revealing white supremacy as a form of direct violence enacted by deranged and deviant individuals, therefore contributing to a strategic rhetoric protecting and perpetuating white supremacy.

DE-INDIVIDUALIZING COVERAGE OF MASS SHOOTERS

At once recognizable and predictable, national news coverage of mass shootings in the United States risks normalizing this form of violence; as audiences grow accustomed to the reporting, we risk growing accustomed to the violence being reported. We also risk developing a taken-for-granted expectation that some aspects of each tragedy will be "highlighted at the expense of others" (Park, Holody, and Zhang 2012, 476). Specifically, as the news media's enactment of strategic rhetoric repeats and becomes more entrenched, audiences of that rhetoric risk habituation to displays of mass shooters as aberrant individuals, and with those displays, representations of gun violence as expressions of individual deviance rather than expressions of dominant social structures and cultures. Such displays are acutely dangerous when media display shooters who are identified as white, including those shooters whose motives are explicitly racist, as in the example of the Mother Emanuel gunman. In this reporting, national media strategically reveal white supremacy to be a form of direct violence inflicted by deranged individuals while simultaneously concealing white supremacy as a form of structural and cultural violence. Concealing white supremacy's structural and cultural functions attempts to curtail interrogations of its "systemic roots" (Bonilla-Silva 1997, 476). Without such interrogation, white supremacy, and its attendant gun violence, is allowed to persist, for white supremacy cannot be redressed if it is understood as a violence limited to individual actors.

If the rhetoric through which national news media report mass shootings is the problem, then a new rhetoric of reporting is needed. Following Adam Lankford and Eric Madfis (2018), I suggest an anonymized approach to coverage of mass shootings in which perpetrators remain unnamed and unseen. To that approach, I would add a rhetoric of de-invidualization, through which "consideration [could be] shifted from the killers as problems in themselves to the killers as symptomatic of pervasive social ills" (Willis-Chun 2011, 59). Through de-individualization, media could treat individual shooters as periphery by investigating social structures and cultural norms as sites of motivation for gun violence. Such an approach is not intended to absolve mass shooters of responsibility for their crimes, nor do I believe it is in any way a panacea for the problem of mass gun violence in the United States. Rather, de-individualizing media coverage of mass shootings presents an appeal to media outlets to "consider their ethical responsibility in covering mass shootings" (Dahmen 2011, 177) and to "balance seeking and reporting truth with minimizing harm in the reporting and publication process" (165).

Just as media bear ethical responsibility in their coverage of mass shootings, audiences bear responsibility in their consumption of that coverage. For example, audiences may resist the media's enactment of strategic rhetoric by de-individualizing interpretations of the media's reporting. Reports emphasizing shooters' individual deviances invite audiences not to look inwardly at ourselves or at the social world we've created but to look outwardly and to cast blame only onto individual shooters. This response can be easily rationalized since the rhetoric we generally use to discuss violence and criminality in the United States makes it "easier to blame individuals" than to "condemn a system" (Engels 2015, 18). However, blaming individual shooters prevents us from "get[ting] at the marrow of the problem" (3). To get at the problem, audiences could reject the easy explanations and interpretations available through media coverage of mass shootings and seek more complex and nuanced understandings of gun violence as a function of dominant social structures and cultures. Moreover, audiences in the United States could account for our own complicity in the persistence of gun violence as an intractable political and public health issue. Such an accounting could be especially valuable for undermining the persistence of white supremacy's violence. This approach could, for example, decrease the distance strategic rhetoric invites between white mass shooters and white audiences, who bear specific responsibility to acknowledge and eliminate white supremacy. If media coverage of white mass shooters displays white supremacy as an individual deviance from which white audiences are able to easily, and innocently, separate ourselves, then we bear responsibility to understand the shooters' violence not as an individual aberration but as constitutive of a structure and culture that has shaped our racial identities, our racial realities. Prelli (2006) argues that displays "comman[d] and sustai[n] attention" (9); however, that need not be inevitable, especially when we consume media displays of mass shooters and their violence. May we resist the "chilling script of deviance, violence, and containment" (Willis-Chun 2011, 59) through which media enact strategic rhetoric. May we shift our gaze beyond that rhetoric's display of individual shooters to the social worlds from which those shooters emerge. May we turn our gaze within.

POSTSCRIPT IN RAGE

I drafted this chapter before August 3, 2019, when another mass shooter enacted white supremacy's lethal racial fantasy at an El Paso Walmart, ultimately killing twenty-three people.[4] I could not speak that massacre into this chapter, could not yet look analytically at a horror that had forever altered the life of a student I was teaching at the time of the shooting. Indeed, this chapter was already difficult to speak. Difficult to unlock my tongue, thick with grief and anger, and stutter words at best inadequate. Difficult to dislodge the words I choke on for fear of unleashing a howl both primal and enraged. Difficult to voice rage and sorrow through a discourse that often feels in my clenched fists and jaws like an act of violence both layered over and interwoven with the deaths of Black and Brown people as authored by the hands, ropes, pyres, and guns of white men like me. As Brad Evans and Terrell Carver (2017) teach me, intellectualizing violence risks reducing, and perhaps exploiting and perpetuating, the visceral suffering violence inflicts, the traumas it forces bodies to bear. Risks severing the body speaking about violence from a living world in which violence continues to structure the possibilities of both who we are and who we could become. A living world in which white supremacy persists in killing, largely unabated, whether slowly through law and policy or quickly through weapon and wound.

How, then, to speak?

NOTES

1. This category of shooter is more frequently responsible for mass shootings than any other racial, ethnic, or gender group. In a study of 314 mass shootings from 1966 to 2016, Jason R. Silva and Joel A. Capellan (2019) discovered that 60.6 percent of all mass shooters were white and that 96.5 percent of those shooters were male (85).
2. Cynthia Hurd, Susie Jackson, Ethel Lee Lance, the Reverend DePayne Middleton-Doctor, the Reverend Clementa Pinckney, Tywanza Sanders, the Reverend Daniel L. Simmons Sr., the Reverend Sharonda Singleton, and Myra Thompson.
3. See Robles 2015; Berman 2015; Fieldstadt and Calabrese 2015; Flitter and Allen 2015; Makarechi 2015.
4. Andre Anchondo, Jordan Anchondo, Arturo Benavides, Leo Campos, Angelina Englisbee, Maria Flores, Raul Flores, Guillermo "Memo" Garcia, Jorge Calvillo García, Adolfo Cerros Hernández, Maribel Hernandez, Alexander Gerhard Hoffmann, David Johnson, Luis Juarez, Maria Eugenia Legarreta, Gloria Irma Márquez, Ivan Filiberto Manzano, Elsa Mendoza, Margie Reckard, Sara Esther Regalado, Javier Amir Rodriquez, Teresa Sanchez, Juan de Dios Velázquez.

REFERENCES

Berman, Mark. 2015. "'I Forgive You.' Relatives of Charleston Church Shooting Victims Address [name removed]." *Washington Post.* June 19, 2015. https://www.washingtonpost .com/news/post-nation/wp/2015/06/19/i-forgive-you-relatives-of-charleston-church -victims-address-dylann-roof/?utm_term=.c3b1adab5666.

Bierman, Noah, Brittny Mejia, and Richard A. Serrano. 2015. "Charleston Shooting Suspect . . . Said to Be 'a Classic Lone Wolf.'" *Los Angeles Times.* June 20, 2015. https://www .latimes.com/nation/la-na-charleston-lone-wolf-20150620-story.html.

Bonilla-Silva, Eduardo. 1997. "Rethinking Racism: Toward a Structural Interpretation." *American Sociological Review* 62 (3): 465–80.

Bonilla-Silva, Eduardo. 2015. "The Structure of Racism in Color-blind, 'Post-racial' America." *American Behavioral Scientist* 59 (11): 1358–76.

Bouie, Jamelle. 2015. "The Deadly History of 'They're Raping Our Women'." *Slate.* https://slate.com/news-and-politics/2015/06/the-deadly-history-of-theyre-raping-our -women-racists-have-long-defended-their-worst-crimes-in-the-name-of-defending-white -womens-honor.html.

Boyce, Travis D., and Winsome Chunnu Brayda. 2015. "In the Words of the 'Last Rhodesian': [name removed] and South Carolina's Long Tradition of White Supremacy,

Racial Rhetoric of Fear, and Vigilantism." *Present Tense: A Journal of Rhetoric in Society* 5 (2). https://www.presenttensejournal.org/volume-5/the-last-rhodesian/.

Cary, Nathaniel. 2015. "[name removed] Visited S.C. Confederate Museum." *USA Today*, June 22, 2015. https://www.usatoday.com/story/news/nation/2015/06/22/dylann-roof-visited-greenville-sc-confederate-museum/29130909/.

Dahmen, Nicole Smith. 2018. "Visually Reporting Mass Shootings: US Newspaper Photographic Coverage of Three Mass School Shootings." *American Behavioral Scientist* 62 (2): 163–80.

Demby, Gene. 2015. "[name removed] and the Stubborn Myth of the Colorblind Millennial." *NPR*. https://www.npr.org/sections/codeswitch/2015/06/20/415878789/dylann-roof-and-the-stubborn-myth-of-the-colorblind-millennial.

Egerton, Douglas R. 2015. "Before Charleston's Church Shooting, a Long History of Attacks." *New York Times*, June 18, 2015. https://www.nytimes.com/2015/06/18/magazine/before-charlestons-church-shooting-a-long-history-of-attacks.html.

Engels, Jeremy. 2015. *The Politics of Resentment: A Genealogy*. University Park: Pennsylvania State University Press.

Evans, Brad, and Terrell Carver. 2017. "The Subject of Violence." In *Histories of Violence: Post-war Critical Thought*, edited by Brad Evans and Terrell Carver, 1–13. London: Zed Books.

Fieldstadt, Elisha, and Erin Calabrese. 2015. "[name removed] Family Say He Was Loner Caught in 'Internet Evil.'" *MSNBC*, June 20, 2015. https://www.msnbc.com/msnbc/dylann-roofs-family-say-he-was-loner-caught-internet-evil-msna622791.

Flitter, Emily, and Jonathan Allen. 2015. "South Carolina Shooting Suspect Seemed Troubled, Drawn to White Supremacy." *Reuters*. https://www.reuters.com/article/us-usa-shooting-south-carolina-roof/south-carolina-shooting-suspect-seemed-troubled-drawn-to-white-supremacy-idUSKBN0OY28220150618.

Galtung, Johan. 1969. "Violence, Peace, and Peace Research." *Journal of Peace Research* 6 (3): 167–91.

Galtung, Johan. 1990. "Cultural Violence." *Journal of Peace Research* 27 (3): 291–305.

Gunn, Joshua, and David E. Beard. 2003. "On the Apocalyptic Columbine." *Southern Communication Journal* 68 (3): 198–216.

Hanson, Hilary. 2015. "[name removed] Identified as Charleston Shooting Suspect: Report." *Huffington Post*, June 18, 2015. https://www.huffingtonpost.com/2015/06/18/dylann-storm-roof-charleston-church-shooting-suspect_n_7612232.html.

Hill, Charles A. 2004. "The Psychology of Rhetorical Images." In *Defining Visual Rhetorics*, edited by Charles A. Hill and Marguerite Helmers, 25–40. Mahwah: Lawrence Erlbaum.

Jeffery, Clara, and James West. 2015. "The Deeply Racist References in . . . Apparent Manifesto, Decoded." *Mother Jones*, June 20, 2015. https://www.motherjones.com/politics/2015/06/references-dylann-roof-manifesto-explained-1488/.

Kobayashi, Audrey, and Linda Peake. 2000. "Racism out of Place: Thoughts on Whiteness and an Antiracist Geography in the New Millennium." *Annals of the Association of American Geographers* 90 (2): 392–403.

Kress, Gunther, and Theo van Leeuwen. 2006. *Reading Images: The Grammar of Visual Design*. London: Routledge.

Lankford, Adam, and Eric Madfis. 2018. "Don't Name Them, Don't Show Them, but Report Everything Else: A Pragmatic Proposal for Denying Mass Killers the Attention They Seek and Deterring Future Offenders." *American Behavioral Scientist* 62 (2): 260–79.

Lee, Kurtis. 2015. "[name removed] Manifesto Resembles Comments on Neo-Nazi Website." *Los Angeles Times*, June 22, 2015. https://www.latimes.com/nation/la-na-dylann-roof-web-20150622-story.html.

Makarechi, Kia. 2015. "Charleston Shooter's Apparent Manifesto Found Online." *Vanity Fair*, June 20, 2015. https://www.vanityfair.com/news/2015/06/dylan-roof-manifesto-charleston-shooter.

Mosendz, Polly. 2015. "[name removed] Confesses: Says He Wanted to Start 'Race War.'" *Newsweek*, June 19, 2015. https://www.newsweek.com/dylann-roof-confesses-church-shooting-says-he-wanted-start-race-war-344797.

Nakayama, Thomas K., and Robert L. Krizek. 1995. "Whiteness: A Strategic Rhetoric." *Quarterly Journal of Speech* 81 (3): 291–309.

Ore, Ersula J. 2019. *Lynching: Violence, Rhetoric, and American Identity*. Jackson: University Press of Mississippi.

Park, Sung-Yeon, Kyle J. Holody, and Xiaoqun Zhang. 2012. "Race in Media Coverage of School Shootings: A Parallel Application of Framing Theory and Attribute Agenda Setting." *Journalism & Mass Communication Quarterly* 89 (3): 475–94.

Prelli, Lawrence J. 2006. "Rhetorics of Display: An Introduction." In *Rhetorics of Display*, edited by Lawrence J. Prelli, 1–38. Columbia: University of South Carolina Press.

Robles, Frances. 2015. "[name removed] Photos and a Manifesto Are Posted on Website." *New York Times*, June 21, 2015. https://www.nytimes.com/2015/06/21/us/dylann-storm-roof-photos-website-charleston-church-shooting.html.

Sanchez, Ray, and Laura Smith-Spark. 2015. "Who Is the Charleston Church Shooting Suspect?" *CNN*, June 19, 2015. https://www.cnn.com/2015/06/18/us/charleston-church-shooting-suspect/index.html.

Schildkraut, Jaclyn, H. Jaymi Elsass, and Kimberly Meredith. 2018. "Mass Shootings and the Media: Why All Events Are Not Created Equal." *Journal of Crime and Justice* 41 (3): 223–43.

Seidman, Bianca. 2015. "What Was the Drug [name removed] Was Holding When Arrested in February?" *CBS News*, June 22, 2015. https://www.cbsnews.com/news/charleston-shooting-suspect-dylann-roof-drug-suboxone/.

Silva, Jason R., and Joel A. Capellan. 2019. "The Media's Coverage of Mass Public Shootings in America: Fifty Years of Newsworthiness." *International Journal of Comparative and Applied Criminal Justice* 43 (1): 77–97.

Smith, Francesca Marie, and Thomas A. Hollihan. 2014. "'Out of Chaos Breathes Creation': Human Agency, Mental Illness, and Conservative Arguments Locating Responsibility for the Tucson Massacre." *Rhetoric & Public Affairs* 17 (4): 585–618.

Willis-Chun, Cynthia. 2011. "Tales of Tragedy: Strategic Rhetoric in News Coverage of the Columbine and Virginia Tech Massacres." In *Critical Rhetorics of Race*, edited by Michael G. Lacy and Kent A. Ono, 47–64. New York: New York University Press.

11

GUNS AND FREEDOM
The Second Amendment Rhetoric of Turning Point USA

Matthew Boedy

This essay will analyze connections between white evangelical Christianity and gun rights, making the case for the inseparability of the rhetoric of guns and the rhetoric of religion. The analysis will center on Turning Point USA, a college student political advocacy group, and its campaign for gun rights.[1] Turning Point's founder and leader, Charlie Kirk, identifies as a white evangelical and his organization implicitly echoes him. The organization and Kirk rhetorically combine that religion and conservative-libertarian politics to create its value of "freedom," an amalgamation of religious and political independence that can be organized under the sociological concept of Christian nationalism. This freedom comes from God and is inherent in our rights, especially the Second Amendment. With that divine mandate in place, Turning Point attacks those who defy its call for freedom, those who advocate for more restrictive gun laws. This rhetoric from Turning Point and Kirk encourages detrimental effects on America's already sizeable partisan divide. It intensifies anger within the wider public gun debate and furthers mistrust among lawmakers who want to compromise. If one side claims God as the source for its policies, there can be no concession to the other side (see also Rood's chapter 6 in this volume). The question becomes how long this rhetoric can remain without irreparable damage to the republic.

Since its start in 2012, Turning Point has skyrocketed in funding and exposure, receiving praise from President Trump, who has singled it out for policy positions he has implemented. As of October 2021, Turning Point claims a "presence" on more than 2,500 college campuses and high schools across the country. It has published e-books on gun rights, capitalism, the value of fossil fuels, student loans, and American exceptionalism. Kirk has a history of supporting gun ownership. He also has written two books on the Second Amendment. *The Second Amendment and Hunting Heritage* was published in 2014 by a wildlife conservation

https://doi.org/10.7330/9781646422159.c011

and hunting enthusiast foundation.[2] The second book, *The Fight for America's Future: Defending the Second Amendment* (2018b), is available through Turning Point's website. Kirk has said he owns fifteen guns.[3]

Why a rhetorical criticism of guns and evangelical religion? Rhetorical scholars have shown a renewed interest in evangelicalism but have not tied guns to the religion debate. Evangelicals themselves are having the discussion now. Trump supporter and recently deposed president of the evangelical Liberty University Jerry Falwell Jr. opened his school to concealed guns and promotes gun ownership. However, other evangelical leaders like Russell Moore and the leading evangelical magazine, *Christianity Today*, have broached that relationship with a more critical eye (Moore 2016; *Christianity Today* 2017). Analysis of Turning Point and Kirk also offers a rhetorical link to evangelicals' political support for Trump, who campaigned on supporting the Second Amendment. More broadly, as debates over gun rights expand, this analysis offers the public a better understanding of how other contexts such as religion affects those discussions.

POLITICS, RELIGION, AND GUNS

Turning Point and Kirk's rhetorical link between white evangelical Christianity and guns is the ideology of Christian nationalism. In short, that -ism works through a series of assumptions. First, America is God's chosen nation, founded so the divine could grant its citizens inalienable rights. Therefore, gun rights as written in the Second Amendment are divinely protected. Turning Point and Kirk's use of these assumptions will be the heart of the analysis to follow.

These assumptions about rights and guns are clear in the broader scholarship of Christian nationalism. Scholars in religion argue, "Americans who subscribe to Christian nationalism believe that America has always been—and should always be—distinctively Christian in its national identity, sacred symbols and public policies" (Whitehead, Schnabel, and Perry 2018b). This leads to the belief that "America's historic statements about human liberties (e.g., the First and Second Amendments) are imbued with sacred, literal and absolute meaning." Specifically, on the Second Amendment, Christian nationalism claims that "the US Constitution was inspired by God [and] serves to elevate the gun, and the right to own it, to a sacred status bestowed by a Christian God." It is then not surprising that "Christian nationalism is an exceptionally strong predictor of opposition to the federal government's enacting stricter gun laws" (Whitehead, Schnabel, and Perry 2018a, 1).

Those who fall under the banner of Christian nationalism see anti-gun violence advocates threatening this right. This right is embedded in "a cultural style tied to deeply held senses" of identity and "attempts to revoke or even restrict this right could be interpreted as an attack on the wisdom and providence of the Christian God" (Whitehead, Schnabel, and Perry 2018a, 9). Sociologists have reported that evangelicals as a whole are more likely to own a gun compared to the general population, even more likely than mainline Protestants (Yamane 2016). And to make obvious the racial element, according to Pew research, 76 percent of evangelicals are white (2014).

Divine right is not the only basis for evangelical attachment to guns. Another basis is their "emphasis on individual autonomy and self-sufficiency" (Stroope and Tom 2017, 149). This often correlates to a conservative-libertarian political ideology summarized as "a preference for less government involvement and interference in individuals' and families' lives" (Merino 2018, 3). Evangelicals promote an armed individualism with divinely inspired gun rights as a defense against threats to individual freedom, including government. Consider Jerry Patterson, a former Texas state senator who helped pass the 1995 law that allowed Texans to carry concealed weapons. He told the *Deseret News* in 2018: "God-given [rights] goes back to the phrase in the Declaration of Independence that says 'all men . . . are endowed by their creator with certain unalienable Rights.' I believe that includes the right to self-defense" (Evans 2018). The National Rifle Association echoes the evangelical case for gun ownership. The same *Deseret News* article quoted NRA executive vice president Wayne LaPierre telling attendees at the 2018 Conservative Political Action Conference that the right to self-protection is "not bestowed by man but granted by God to all Americans as our American birthright" (Evans 2018). Some evangelicals cite Jesus's instruction to his first disciples to sell their cloak so they could buy a sword as a metaphor for gun ownership (Manseau 2016).

This kind of gun rhetoric is not new. But it was given tremendous support by the 2008 Supreme Court decision in *Heller v. District of Columbia.* The 5-4 decision "struck down a District of Columbia ban on handgun possession" and made it clear that "the Second Amendment protects an individual right to have a gun, at least in one's home" (Denniston 2008). While the court wrote the Second Amendment did not confer a "right to keep and carry any weapon whatsoever in any manner whatsoever and for whatever purpose" (Giffords Law Center 2018), the decision sparked new rhetoric from gun ownership advocates who began to argue that "the individual right protected by the Second Amendment was absolute and inviolable" (Long 2017).

Such rhetoric emboldened policy changes at the state level. After *Heller*, "at least twelve states extended and expanded laws to permit the open or concealed carry of weapons in public" including primary and secondary schools (Long 2017). This wave also provided an opening for at least two states to legislate the legality for some to carry concealed guns on college campuses, and prompted lawsuits by gun owners in other states to create this right. Texas and Georgia saw several years of such bills after 2008. Eventually each state's Republican governor signed this right into law, though both states faced stiff opposition from students, professors, and anti–gun violence organizations.[4]

The 2016 election of Donald Trump also gave a tremendous boost to Christian nationalism's link between God and gun. First, many evangelicals saw Trump as the divine choice for president. For example, Stephen Strang, a leading evangelical figure and publisher of a popular Pentecostal magazine, wrote a "spiritual hagiography" (Sullivan 2018) of the president called *God and Donald Trump*. The book "outlines a string of charismatics who had visions—or who now retroactively claim to have had visions—that Trump would one day win the White House" (Sullivan 2018). During the 2016 campaign, Trump promoted himself as a Second Amendment candidate. For example, asked in a January 2016 GOP primary debate "whether there were 'any circumstances' in which the government 'should be limiting gun sales of any kind in America,'" Trump replied: "No. I am a Second Amendment person" (Sullum 2018). Trump also said that several mass shootings would have turned out differently if "the bullets were flying in the other direction" (*Time* 2016). After taking office, Trump energized his base of voters by suggesting Democrats were trying to take away "your Second Amendment" (Berman 2018). Trump has said he has a concealed carry permit (Kruzel 2018) and as president supported "concealed carry reciprocity" legislation that would allow people like the president with a permit in one state to legally bring their firearms into other states, without abiding by that state's own laws for training. Anti–gun violence advocates have voiced strong opposition to the proposal (Alexander 2018).

KIRK, TURNING POINT, AND CHRISTIAN NATIONALISM

At the center of this religious and political context stands Charlie Kirk, a model Christian nationalist. Up until 2019, Kirk was a self-described "proud member" of the Chicagoland evangelical megachurch Harvest

Bible Chapel.[5] Kirk ties his religion to his nationalism through the rhetoric of freedom. In July 2018, Kirk sat down with Harvest Chapel's then executive pastor Luke MacDonald to record a "faith testimony." MacDonald told Kirk that his strong political beliefs and strong "spiritual faith" do not "seem to be in conflict" (MacDonald 2018). Kirk then described the gospel as a "gospel of liberation" and added that he would not "tell anyone else how to live their life." Kirk consistently promotes (usually by tweet) the idea that "America is the greatest country in the history of the world." He praises America for its freedom, especially its economic freedom in capitalism. He makes a brief biblical citation for "free markets" in chapter 5 of his 2016 manifesto *Time for a Turning Point*. There he links the opening of the Gospel of Luke and its story of how the Roman Empire taxed its whole realm to the spread of the Gutenberg Bible to today's ubiquitous Bible availability. He implies this last claim is an example of "free enterprise." The Luke reference is also an implicit attack on the "big government" of the Roman Empire.

Turning Point echoes this rhetoric of freedom. The *Weekly Standard*, in a 2018 profile of Kirk, noted he told one student rally that "there are three things all TPUSA-ers agree on" (Rubenstein 2018). The first is "America is the greatest country in the history of the world."[6] The organization has a publication titled *10 Ways America Is the Best Country in the History of the World* (Adams 2015). One of the "ways" listed in that book is America is the "most religious country." Not only are most Americans "fluent in their Christian faith," but "American experience is irrevocably connected through Christianity," according to the book. In short, "without religion, the government of a free people cannot be maintained" (13). More specifically, what is exceptional about American Christianity for Turning Point is its "correlation" to "the virtue of freedom" (16). Using descriptions from Alexis de Tocqueville, the book concludes: "The Creator is the source of American liberty . . . Americans believe that their fundamental rights come from God and are therefore inalienable." These words come just before a large picture of a small girl praying with her eyes closed with an American flag in the background (17).

Kirk and Turning Point also argue that this exceptionalism and its larger foundation, the "West," is in crisis, threatened by enemies both internal and external. In a video of one of his public appearances posted to his Twitter account in February 2018, Kirk says that as a Christian he is "very, very" worried that the United States is moving away from "our Judeo-Christian beliefs" that "created Western civilization" (2018c). In *Time for a Turning Point*, Kirk notes the "attack" on conservatives on college campuses "reflects a deep and abiding hatred of all that we have

been and all that we are" (2016, 174). This seems to be a political reference to the Constitution but also a religious reference to those "Judeo-
Christian" values. These two are inseparable for Kirk.

THE SECOND AMENDMENT AND GUN OWNERSHIP

Kirk and Turning Point tie gun ownership to Christianity through
nationalism. The Second Amendment is another of Turning Point's
10 Ways America Is the Best Country in the History of the World. The book
claims, "Nothing is more emblematic of the exceptionalism of America
than the Second Amendment" (Adams 2015, 35). It goes on to make
the "moral, legal, and philosophical case for the right of the people to
keep and bear arms."

Turning Point argues that the Second Amendment guarantees the
power and effect of the other amendments. In its 2016 book *The Case
against Gun Control,* Turning Point writes that the Second Amendment
"is arguably the most important, because it protects the sanctity of
all other amendments" (19). The group sells a sticker on its site that
says: "The 2nd Amendment protects the other 26," the text in the
shape of a gun. A poster at one point for sale on the site states the relationship more directly: "There is no First Amendment without the
Second Amendment."

For Turning Point and Kirk, the Second Amendment is under attack.
Kirk writes in the book's foreword that the work is "a direct response to
the agenda pushed by gun control advocates." He stressed that under
the Obama Administration "the right to bear arms is under attack and in
danger of being altered significantly or removed entirely" (2016, 1), not
offering any evidence to prove that claim. In the end, because "things
are happening" to end the Second Amendment, readers need to be
"proactive . . . while we have the ability to do so" (19).

Turning Point promotes gun ownership consistently through rhetorical acts of appropriation. In short, the organization takes phrases
from its political or religious opponents and revises them for its own
purposes. The first example is a sticker Turning Point sells on its website
that reinvents the pan-religious bumper sticker "Coexist." That sticker
uses symbols of major religions to spell the word. The Turning Point version includes guns, bullets, and a target as letters. This sticker implicitly
criticizes the pan-religious and global nature of the original message
and so implicitly supports America and its religion, Christianity.

It also moves that community aspect of that sticker to gun owners.
In short, as these religions exists in harmony, so too do all guns. This

sticker promotes not only a community or nation that normalizes gun ownership but also suggests that, like the unique and individual belief systems in the pan-religion sticker, "gun culture" is a unique and individual system, collectivizing a group so that its members can defend gun rights together. The absence of any gun control argument also suggests that Turning Point does not believe gun ownership and limits on gun ownership can coexist. There is no middle ground, especially if God grants us gun rights.

In another example of appropriation, Turning Point revises the "prochoice" mantra tied to abortion. It reuses the slogan in a poster that lists three types of firearms: a Glock handgun, an AR-15 rifle, and a 12-gauge shotgun. The first line, in bold black, reads, "I'm pro choice," which certainly might draw in viewers who are "pro-choice" when it comes to abortion. However, the opposing bold red of the second line, "Pick your gun," offers another definition of that phrase.

It is important to remember that in the abortion debate the rhetorical opposite of "pro-choice" is "pro-life." But Turning Point can't associate its "pro-life" position with gun violence, which of course creates death. In short, "pro-life" does not logically work as a mantra for gun ownership. Turning Point defers or wants its audience to ignore its hypocrisy here.

GUN OWNERSHIP AND FEMALE EMPOWERMENT

The Case against Gun Control is an appeal to white evangelicals. More specifically, Turning Point memes use conservative Christian ideologies of gender, particularly warrants of protection of "females," to urge more female gun ownership. First, *The Case against Gun Control* implies that women who face "violent assault" are "weak" and an "easier target" (2016, 13) and therefore need guns. How does this appeal to white evangelicals? There are two competing ideologies (or theologies) on gender in evangelical Christianity. The first, known as egalitarianism, argues there are no gender-based limits of what "functions or roles each [gender] can fulfill in the home, the church, and the society" (*Theopedia* n.d.). The other, known as complementarianism, is mainly found in conservative churches and argues that the man should be the leader in those areas and the two genders were "created to complement each other via different roles in life" (*Theopedia* n.d.). With its emphasis on the "headship" of the man, one of the central roles in complementarianism for men is as the protector of women, who are the "weaker vessel," to cite many translations of the first letter by Peter in the Christian scriptures (1 Peter 3:7). An appeal to gun owners as protectors of others is an appeal to men to get their women a gun, which serves as a substitute for the protective man.

Turning Point uses this implicit basis to argue for female empowerment, a call to women to assert "gun control."[7] This occurs in Turning Point memes originating on its Facebook page that use traditional gender stereotypes. For example, one meme shows a pink camouflage rifle aimed by a female. This meme argues for empowerment through its redefinition of "gun control." A powerful user, the woman, controls the powerful weapon. Arguing against "gun control" by anti–gun violence advocates who want more restrictions on purchases, training, and types of guns, the "control" in the hands of the woman is "a balanced stance and a smooth trigger pull." Yet, although the woman is holding her gun and aiming at an unseen target, there is no apparent threat, and the pink camouflage rifle would not normally be used to combat crime.

Self-defense is a common rhetorical element of gun ownership appeals in Turning Point memes and often situated in a larger context of a "purity" argument for white evangelical females. One meme shows a young white woman wearing an unzipped Abercrombie jacket and wide sunglasses holding what looks like an "assault rifle." But the text notes the woman doesn't "own any assault weapons. All my guns are defense weapons." One should note that the situation the woman is in—what seems like an open field, with a calm, even happy demeanor—does not indicate any need for self-defense. The woman also is not carrying the gun in a position of defense, its barrel angling to the ground.

Female empowerment appears in a third meme that depicts a young woman carrying a similar rifle. The claims, or "facts that destroy the anti-gun narrative," in the meme are highly debatable and are not just about preventing crime. Key here is that the female shares the same demeanor as the woman in the second meme. While this third woman carries on her hip a small firearm—a weapon commonly used in preventing crime victimization—she also carries a long rifle with a scope, a firearm not used in crime prevention. Pointing the gun barrel down and keeping the rifle's other end on her shoulder, she shows control like the other female. Both women also use a strong stance, and that power is applied figuratively to their gender.

The final way Turning Point argues for female empowerment is its anti-government principle. In one meme, we see a young woman with a handgun, tattooed with blue letters spelling NRA. Unlike the other three memes, this female is *not* a stock character. She is Antonia Okafor, founder of emPOWERed, a national student organization for female gun education.[8] This meme has a clear message: "government" as a possible enemy, aggressor, or abuser is a reason to carry a firearm. In short, owning a firearm can be freedom from government-based tyranny.

There is rhetorical confusion in this last meme, offering a moment to consider the conflicting messages of Turning Point USA. The group reveres America, its founding as a Christian nation, and its Constitution as example of divine inspiration. So then how do we come to understand Turning Point's anti-government principles evident in this meme? First, Turning Point often uses the qualifier *big* before *government*. The phrase "big government sucks" appears in its publications and as hashtags on social media. However, the Okafor meme crosses the line from suspicion of big government to distrust of all government. Turning Point crosses that line at other times, for example, using the phrase "Taxation is theft" in its materials. Turning Point has left unexplained this confusion.

Turning Point tries to use this anti-government appeal more broadly to persuade females they need a gun. In a chapter titled "Girls Just Want to Have Guns" in *The Case against Gun Control* Turning Point writes: "Gun control affects everybody, but it affects some more than others. In reality, women are disproportionately affected when politicians pass strict gun control laws" (2016, 13). Turning Point is playing fast and loose with words here. One could assume Turning Point is referring to the majority of women in the US population to make its case about disproportion. This elides the fact that the majority of gun owners are men (Horowitz 2017). This also may be a rhetorical ploy to avoid this fact: "Among Republican and Republican-leaning gun owners, women tend to be more supportive than men of policy proposals that would restrict gun ownership" (Horowitz 2017). And one should note the vagueness concerning "gun control laws," which are not defined, leaving open questions on which guns should be available, what training should be needed, or the issue of laws that limit gun ownership by age.[9]

Finally, what should be made of the fact that Okafor is Black? In other words, how does one explain an organization like Turning Point USA, which operates through appeals to white evangelicals and a call to Christian nationalism, using a Black female in its gun rhetoric? Slavery is another concept appropriated by Turning Point USA in its gun rhetoric. The central signifier of freedom includes freedom of body. The link becomes clear when one considers how Turning Point uses gun ownership to defy government tyranny. The chosen form of such tyranny to come in the rhetoric of Turning Point USA is socialism. Throughout its website, videos, and other texts, the group claims, "Socialism is slavery."

TURNING POINT, GUNS, AND ATTACKS ON FREEDOM

Kirk and Turning Point argue that freedom is the ability of any person to own any gun and carry it anywhere. *The Case against Gun Control* claims broadly that all "gun control" is bad. In his speech to the 2018 NRA convention Kirk said you cannot "pick and choose your freedoms; you either have freedom or you don't" (2018a). Such sweeping assertions are the rhetorical force the group uses to target opponents of "freedom." Turning Point attacks those it sees as attacking freedom through its Professor Watchlist, which claims to expose and document professors who "discriminate against conservative students" and "advance leftist propaganda in the classroom" (Professor Watchlist 2016a). The list links to articles from conservative "news" sites about these professors.

When the list first appeared in 2016, I was one of the original entries (Professor Watchlist 2016b) because I had advocated against a bill that became Georgia law allowing concealed firearms on campuses, a policy Turning Point supports.[10] This right had appeared only in a handful of states prior to Georgia becoming the tenth state to have it in 2017. Some states enacted this right legislatively; others were forced to by the courts deciding a lawsuit brought by gun owners against state universities. In short, this right is not in the Constitution, only interpreted from it in legal rulings over the years. The most powerful and important ruling was and remains the aforementioned 2008 *Heller v. D.C.*, which for the first time named an individual right—as opposed to the militia's or communal defense group's right—to carry firearms.

Turning Point's summary of my position on this law notes I believe "universities would be more dangerous if they had students legally carrying firearms" (Professor Watchlist 2016b). It adds that I "spoke out against a new bill, which allows for concealed carry on campus, claiming that he feared he would be shot by disgruntled students if concealed carry was legal at the university."[11] The conservative news site that Turning Point links to, *Campus Reform*, in its March 8, 2016, article quotes me directly three times and paraphrases me once (Ledtke). On those four occasions, I do not mention any classroom assignment, lecture, or practice in which I promote my opinion about campus carry.[12] The *Campus Reform* article came out four days after my first post about campus carry appeared on the *Atlanta Journal-Constitution*'s *Get Schooled* blog. In that blog post, I argued that education is best practiced without guns because "a gun becomes another way to avoid uncertainty, another way to evade learning" (Boedy 2016; see also Kreuter's chapter 2 in this volume).

How does my writing in a newspaper against a law "discriminate against conservative students and advance leftist propaganda in the classroom"? Let us start with what is important about Turning Point's summary: the repetition of "legal." Campus carry in my state would not become legal for another few months after another legislative session. While Turning Point jumps the gun on the passage of that law, the organization implies that my pedagogical stance against campus carry is an attempt to curtail the legal rights of conservative students. I am against something Turning Point thinks should be (and eventually became) legal and so I am both discriminating against some students and also advancing "propaganda"—which in this case means making a claim with which Turning Point disagrees. In short, I am against freedom and then am labeled as a propagandist, a term that negatively inflates the opinion I have and inflames those who disagree with that opinion. With any dictionary definition of *propaganda* in mind, implicitly I am curtailing the freedom of students to think for themselves by stating my own opinion from a position of power. To paraphrase Kirk from his NRA speech (2018a): I am against this one particular freedom, so I am against all freedom. And if I am against that freedom, I am against God, who granted this freedom.

According to Turning Point, for that I need to be exposed—my name, picture, employer, and salary permanently posted to a website.[13] I am to be "watched" or known by students as they decide whether to take my courses. This is not to imperil my freedom—Turning Point notes on its watch list website that it remains dedicated to professors saying "whatever they wish"—but to give the public (conservative parents and students) what they deserve to protect their own freedom, freedom from my indoctrination. That group must have freedom to decide for themselves. This nod toward individual freedom of choice uses the "market" of higher education against my institution and myself. In this rhetorical environment, one cannot find compromise or a balance of safety and rights. Those against freedom must be "watched" lest they spread their anti-freedom.

CONCLUSION

Turning Point is a clear example of the rhetorical connections between white evangelical Christianity and gun rights. The concepts God, guns, and nationalism strengthen one another so effectively none can be attacked without attacking them all. Freedom as a central signifier sits at the center of Turning Point's rhetoric, a node that leaves no room for compromise. While America has debated these central concepts throughout its history, Turning Point secures the commitment of its followers by using the strong appeal of religion, arguing that freedom is available only to those who would follow the organization's political ideology. It is a call to an unwelcoming Christian nation, an appeal to a divisive and dangerous crusade against critics and government. Eschewing compromise, it offers a rhetorical fiat unfit for democracy.

NOTES

1. Turning Point (n.d.) has aimed "to build the most organized, active, and powerful conservative grassroots activist network on college campuses across the country."

2. According to the organization's website, the book "dispelled myths many young people might have picked up" about hunting and gun ownership (Conklin Foundation 2019).

3. I personally heard this from him at a rally in Athens, Georgia, in April 2018.

4. Full disclosure: I participated in rallies with and gave money to anti-gun violence movements working to stop the Georgia bill, wrote several op-eds showing how concealed guns on campus would alter the atmosphere of college and, of course, contacted lawmakers to voice my concerns. Several of my colleagues in Texas and Georgia unsuccessfully sued to stop the law.

5. In 2019, Kirk moved his official residence to Sarasota, Florida. However, throughout 2020, as a pandemic ravaged the nation, Kirk spent considerable time in Arizona at the Turning Point USA headquarters in Phoenix. While there, he developed a relationship with Rob McCoy, the pastor of the Thousand Oaks, California, megachurch Godspeak Calvary Chapel. On Kirk's June 14, 2020, episode of his podcast, Kirk called McCoy his "personal pastor."

6. The other two: "The Constitution is the greatest political document ever written" and "Free market capitalism is the most moral and proven economic system to lift the most people out of poverty into prosperity."

7. This appeal to self-empowerment is noticeable in academic studies of gun rhetoric. "Marketing campaigns that limit the scope of female gun ownership to self-protection oversimplifies female gun ownership, failing to consider a multitude of ownership reasons for females including those who tie gun ownership itself to a sense of self-empowerment" (Koeppel and Nobels 2017, 48).

8. She is also part of Turning Point's "speakers bureau," which lists the speakers Turning Point will send to a campus (Turning Point 2019).

9. Absent also is any mention of banning guns from those with mental health issues. Kirk has on one occasion advocated to restrict access to guns for such people. After the Parkland High School massacre, Kirk said in a CNN interview that "psychopaths and crazy people" should not have access to guns or allowed to own them (*Amanpour*). He wrote an op-ed for *USA Today* on March 20, 2018, making the same case (Kirk 2018d). I have yet to find another moment where he has repeated these desired policies. Kirk's link between gun violence and mental health is also spurious. A 2015 National Institute of Health study that showed people diagnosed with mental illness committed less than 5 percent of gun-related killings in the United States (Tsilimparis 2018).

10. I am not the only rhetoric scholar on the list. Professor Kathleen Mack, chairwoman of the English department at the University of Colorado at Colorado Springs, was listed because she assigned a book critical of Trump's rhetoric. That book, *Post-Truth Rhetoric and Composition*, was written by rhetoric scholar Bruce McComiskey (2017). It has a chapter entitled "The Trump Effect."

11. This claim appears neither in what I wrote nor in the source linked on the watch list website.
12. I began doing so as part of a class on issues in higher education after this list came out. And that is protected by academic freedom. I also allowed legislators and gun ownership advocates who supported the bill to speak to my students.
13. My salary was added later as Turning Point began adding new names.

REFERENCES

Adams, Nick. 2015. *10 Ways America Is the Best Country in the History of the World.* Turning Point USA. https://tpusa.com/wp-content/uploads/2016/12/10WaysAmericaIsThe GreatestCountry.pdf.

Alexander, Ayanna. 2018. "Trump: Bill Combining Concealed Carry and Gun Background Checks Will 'Never Pass.'" *Politico*, February 28.

Amanpour: Sofie Whitney, Charlie Kirk and Joan Baez. 2018. PBS, February 22.

Berman, Russell. 2018. "Where the Gun-Control Movement Goes Silent." *Atlantic*, March 1.

Boedy, Matthew. 2016. "Nathan Deal: Colleges Should Focus on Education Rather Than Guns. But Aren't They Related?" *Atlanta Journal-Constitution Get Schooled* blog. https://www.ajc.com/blog/get-schooled/nathan-deal-colleges-should-focus-education-rather-than-guns-but-aren-they-related/coHQioD12q6Z5VnGEmprxJ/.

Christianity Today Editors. 2017. "The Christian History of America's Guns." *Christianity Today.* https://www.christianitytoday.com/ct/2017/november-web-only/christian-history-americas-guns-shooting-second-amendment.html.

Conklin Foundation. 2019. "Youth Projects." *The Conklin Foundation.* https://theconklin foundation.com/youth-projects.

Denniston, Lyle. 2008. "Court: A Constitutional Right to a Gun." SCOTUS blog, June 26.

Evans, Erika. 2018. "Is the Right to Bear Arms 'God-Given'?" *Deseret News*, April 19, 2018. https://www.deseret.com/2018/4/19/20643756/is-the-right-to-bear-arms-god-given#dave-larsen-speaks-with-a-customer-about-selling-firearms-at-dougs-shootn-sports-in-taylorsville-on-tuesday-april-17-2018.

Giffords Law Center to Prevent Gun Violence. 2018. "The *Heller* Decision and What It Means." https://lawcenter.giffords.org/gun-laws/the-second-amendment/the-supreme-court-the-second-amendment/dc-v-heller/.

Horowitz, Juliana M. 2017. "How Male and Female Gun Owners in the US Compare." Pew Research Center. http://www.pewresearch.org/fact-tank/2017/06/29/how-male-and-female-gun-owners-in-the-u-s-compare/.

Kirk, Charlie. 2014. *The Second Amendment and Hunting Heritage.* Houston: Conklin Endowment Fund.

Kirk, Charlie. 2016. *Time for a Turning Point.* New York: Post Hill.

Kirk, Charlie. 2018a. "Charlie Kirk: 2018 NRA-ILA Leadership Forum." NRA-ILA. https://www.nraila.org/media/20180504/video/charlie-kirk-2018-nra-ila-leadership-fo.

Kirk, Charlie. 2018b. *The Fight for America's Future: Defending the Second Amendment.* Self-published.

Kirk, Charlie. 2018c. "I don't have enough faith to be an atheist." Twitter, February 24, 8:54 p.m. https://twitter.com/charliekirk11/status/967608728282378240.

Kirk, Charlie. 2018d. "Parkland Shooting Spurs Information Age Solutions for Gun Violence." *USA Today*, March 20.

Koeppel, Maria D., and Matt R. Nobles. 2017. "Understanding Female Gun Ownership: 1973–2010." *Feminist Criminology* 12 (1): 43–71.

Kruzel, John. 2018. "Concealed Carry Bill Clears House, Faces Long Odds in Senate." *Politifact*, January 3.

Ledtke, Brian. 2016. "Georgia Profs. Worry They May be Shot by Students with Concealed Weapons." *Campus Reform*. https://www.campusreform.org/?ID=7361.

Long, Emma. 2017. "Why So Silent? The Supreme Court and the Second Amendment Debate After *DC v. Heller*." *European Journal of American Studies* 12 (2): n.p.

MacDonald, James. 2018. *Christianity and Politics w/Charlie Kirk*. YouTube. https://www.youtube.com/watch?v=SWFc7xafbTY.

Manseau, Peter. 2016. "Does the Bible Enshrine a 'God-Given Right' to Shoot in Self Defense?" *The Trace*. https://www.thetrace.org/2016/03/mississippi-guns-in-churches-self-defense-shootings/.

McComiskey, Bruce. 2017. *Post-Truth Rhetoric and Composition*. Logan: Utah State University Press.

Merino, Stephen. 2018. "God and Guns: Examining Religious Influences on Gun Control Attitudes in the United States." *Religions* 9 (6): 1–13.

Moore, Russell. 2016. "Is Gun Control a Christian Issue?" *RussellMoore*. https://www.russellmoore.com/2016/01/05/is-gun-control-a-christian-issue/.

Pew Research Center. 2014. "Evangelical Protestants." In *2014 Religious Landscape Study*. http://www.pewforum.org/religious-landscape-study/.

Professor Watchlist. 2016a. "About Us." https://www.professorwatchlist.org/about-us/.

Professor Watchlist. 2016b. "Matthew Boedy." https://www.professorwatchlist.org/index.php/component/content/article?id=201:matthew-boedy.

Rubenstein, Adam. 2018. "Kid Trump." *Weekly Standard*, August 2. https://www.weeklystandard.com/adam-rubenstein/kid-trump.

Stroope, Samuel, and Joshua C. Tom. 2017. "In-Home Firearm Access among US Adolescents and the Role of Religious Subculture: Results from a Nationally Representative Study." *Social Science Research* 67:147–59.

Sullivan, Amy. 2018. "Millions of Americans Believe God Made Trump President." *Politico*, January 27.

Sullum, Jacob. 2018. "Trump the 'Big Second Amendment Person' Becomes 'Trump the Gun Grabber.'" *Reason*, March 1.

Theopedia. n.d. "Egalitarianism." https://www.theopedia.com/egalitarianism.

Time Staff. 2016. "Read the Full Transcript of Donald Trump's 'Second Amendment' Speech." *Time*, August 9.

Tsilimparis, John. 2018. "The New Scapegoat for Gun Violence: Mental Illness." *Psych Central*. https://psychcentral.com/blog/the-new-scapegoat-for-gun-violence-mental-illness/.

Turning Point USA. 2016. *The Case against Gun Control*. https://tpusa.com/wp-content/uploads/2016/12/TheCaseAgainstGunControl.pdf (site discontinued).

Turning Point USA. 2019. "Speakers Bureau." https://www.tpusa.com/speakersbureau/.

Turning Point USA. n.d. "About Us." https://www.tpusa.com/aboutus/.

Whitehead, Andrew, Landon Schnabel, and Samuel Perry. 2018a. "Gun Control in the Crosshairs: Christian Nationalism and Opposition to Stricter Gun Laws." *Socius* 4:1–13.

Whitehead, Andrew, Landon Schnabel, and Samuel Perry. 2018b. "Why Some Christians Don't Believe in Gun Control: They Think God Handed Down the Second Amendment." *Washington Post*, July 25.

Yamane, Robert. 2016. "Awash in a Sea of Faith and Firearms: Rediscovering the Connection between Religion and Gun Ownership in America." *Journal for the Scientific Study of Religion* 55:622–36.

12

HIDING GUNS IN SCHOOLS
The Rhetoric of US Mass Shootings

Nathalie Kuroiwa-Lewis

US PUBLIC SPACES: WAR ZONES ANYTIME, ANYPLACE

In 2002, while pursuing my doctoral studies in rhetoric and composition at the University of Arizona in Tucson, I opened my computer one morning to find a flood of emails alerting me that a school shooter was present on campus (Broder 2002a). Soon, as the day progressed and into the next day, I would learn more.

The shooter was identified as Robert Stewart Flores Jr., a nursing student and former soldier in the Gulf War who, enraged by failing grades, had shot and killed three of his female teachers at the university's nursing school building (Holguin 2002, 3). He had reportedly carried an arsenal of weapons with him to the school, arming himself with over 200 ammunition rounds and five handguns (Broder 2002b, 1). Following the incident, the police chief of Tucson, Richard Miranda, intimated that things could have been far worse—Flores had intended to kill more people but, for whatever reason, had decided not to (Holguin 2002, 2).

Since that day, I have not forgotten the scope and magnitude of death that happened in the nursing building of the Tucson campus, nor have I been able to erase from my mind the many more such incidents that have come to be regularly reported in the news nationwide. Instead, I am only too keenly aware that gun violence in the United States happens to be a reality for all living in the country and that no one is exempt from it. Gun violence, by mere virtue of its continual presence (Lopez 2021; Lupkin 2013), is something people living in the United States, like myself, are asked to put up with, no matter the consequences. Yet, at what cost?

Years later in 2013, as a professor teaching at a small private liberal arts university in the Pacific Northwest, I was asked, like many teachers nationwide, to attend a mandatory emergency preparatory meeting falling on the heels of another shooting, that of Sandy Hook Elementary,

https://doi.org/10.7330/9781646422159.c012

where a young gunman, Adam Lanza, used a Bushmaster semiautomatic, firing 150 rounds and killing twenty first-graders, along with six other individuals (Altimari and Lender 2013, 1). At the meeting, which was led by a police detective, I raised my hand to ask him how anyone—staff, faculty, or students—could be expected to defend themselves against a campus shooter when a military-style weapon like the Bushmaster was involved.[1] Needless to say, my question could not be fully answered and many people in the room expressed different positions on the impact that such weapons wield in the public sphere. And yet my question at the meeting that day still stands and is testament to the problem of gun violence rendering everyday civilian spaces, such as US schools, potential war zones. I do not hesitate to ask it again.

Studies on gun violence show that from the year 2011, public mass shootings have been increasing in number across the United States (Follman 2014, 1–3). Schools, unfortunately, are not immune from public mass shootings. The Parkland massacre, where in 2018 fourteen students and three employees of Marjory Stoneman Douglas were killed (Stack 2019, 1) and fourteen others were injured (Chuck, Johnson, and Siemaszko 2018, 2), is but another example of many incidents, like the one at the University of Arizona, that have come to be known as active shooter/mass murder incidents (Carter 2017, 27) that, I assert, have succeeded in making war zones of countless civilian spaces in the United States—a telltale sign of the problem of American militarism in the wider culture.[2]

In their book *In/visible War: The Culture of War in Twenty-First-Century America,* Jon Simons and John Lucaites contend that the United States is in a state of full-blown war with other nations and yet has managed to give up very little (2017, 1). They argue that we are so steeped in a culture of militarism that our ability to see is obfuscated by paradox; we both see and do not see the US wars ubiquitous across the globe. They call this paradoxical state of affairs "displacement" and contend that psychologically our understanding of the presence of war around us is "displaced" or "normalized" to the extent that social problems such as gun violence or excessive police force in the United States have grown routine (2).

Taking the implications of their thesis further, I conclude that today's mass shootings are a natural by-product of a highly militarized culture; that anywhere in the United States, and at any given point in time, someone in the nation is fated to become the next victim of yet another mass shooting, for public spaces in the United States have become invisible, ready to be activated war zones hiding in plain sight.

Drawing on Franklin Zimring and Gordon Hawkins's landmark research concluding that lethal violence is a unique fact of living in the United States (1997, 3), much of my argument rests on the premise that language creates reality (Burke 1954) and that lethal violence shapes and is shaped by language about guns. To explain further, in what has now come to forecast the future, Zimring and Hawkins's early research showed that while the crime rate in the United States was similar to that of many countries in the West, incidents involving lethal force were excessive in the former, qualitatively setting the United States apart from other Western nations. According to them, the uniquely American reality, that of lethal violence, was "the real source of fear and anger in American life" (1997, 3). Although they did not entirely place blame on guns for the problem of lethal violence in the United States, they made a strong case that guns facilitate lethal violence by way of a gun's force of blow via the bullet's impact, ability to shoot long-range distances, and numerous strike capability (113). Recent studies on guns confirm the connection between guns and increased risk of death (Lopez 2021), attesting to the lethal nature of crime unique to the United States (8).

With these observations in mind, in this chapter, I explore the role that the language of the gun industry plays in ensuring and maintaining the presence of guns—dissociating guns from gun violence and promoting young people's use of guns in the civic sphere, particularly as it relates to school campuses nationwide.[3] I conduct a rhetorical analysis and study the public relations arguments of the Civilian Marksmanship Program's (CMP) information sheet titled "Air Rifle Marksmanship for Youth" (Civilian Marksmanship Program n.d.). I specifically choose to analyze the claims of the promotional material of the CMP, a nationwide JROTC- and NRA-backed program, because of the CMP's direct ties to Nikolas Cruz, the shooter of the Parkland Valentine's Day massacre. Little known to the public at large is the fact that Cruz had been, at one point, a member of the CMP at his school's campus, the scene of the massacre. This marksmanship program, which enrolls students in over 2,000 US schools (*Economist* 2018, 39), is an important site for my study of how the gun industry rhetorically attempts to recruit young people and advocate for guns in US schools in spite of the fact that school shootings occur in the country every year. That Cruz had been a participant of this very program, which provided him with shooting range training he used to shoot and kill seventeen people at the very school that had housed this program, makes the CMP an especially relevant program for study.

As I analyze the rhetoric of the CMP's information sheet (Civilian Marksmanship Program n.d.), I combine the theories of psychic numbing (Lifton and Mitchell 1995; Metz 1997; Gregory 2003) and rhetorical silence (Ott, Aoki, and Dickinson 2011; Glenn 2004) to assert that pro-gun organizations like the NRA and its affiliates speak to their audiences in ways that remove the causal link between guns and gun-related deaths and injuries, deflecting attention away from their social effects.[4] In doing this, I argue that the language of the gun industry mutes the audience's perception of risk, encouraging one to see guns as mere objects of recreation—ahistorical and value-free, and therefore to be used for recreational (benevolent) purposes only.

CRUZ AND THE DEREGULATION OF GUNS

As a starting point for understanding how the gun industry tends to frame the use of guns in the civilian sphere, it is important to know that many of today's standard, mainstream guns available for purchase throughout the United States are military-style guns—essentially weapons of war—and that numerous active shooter incidents in the United States involve guns and gear with militaristic characteristics (Diaz 2013, 11; Carter 2017, 115–16). To illustrate this fact, take as an example the Parkland incident that occurred on Valentine's Day in 2018 when Nikolas Cruz, an expelled high school student of Marjorie Stoneman Douglas, walked into the building of his former high school and armed with an AR-15, began shooting, killing seventeen people and injuring fourteen, five of whom were reported to be in critical condition (Chuck, Johnson, and Siemaszko 2018, 2). News accounts reveal that Cruz was an experienced marksman, having participated in his school's JROTC gun club shooting competitions (Elder 2018a, 2018b; Kirby 2018; Biesecker and Binkley 2018). At the time of the incident, Cruz wore a gas mask and was carrying 330 rounds of ammunition. Inscribed on a magazine in his semiautomatic was a symbol of the Nazi Party (Baynes 2018, 2–3). Officials report that 180 cartridges were found untouched when he fled the premises (2), abandoning his rifle. Also reported was that on this day, Cruz had been seen wearing a JROTC emblem on his shirt (Biesecker and Binkley 2018) and that three JROTC members, including Peter Wang, who opened the door to help his classmates escape, were killed in the shooting. Wang was accepted into West Point after his death (Neuman 2018; Rozsa 2018). Further news accounts indicate that prior to the massacre, Cruz had had a history of run-ins with the police and was known as a threat in the area. Documents indicate that over an eight-year period, the sheriff's office of Broward County had received forty-five phone calls about him or his brother. The FBI had also been notified of Cruz and even specifically told he might shoot others (Baynes 2018, 4).

In addition to these reports, a significant detail worth examining is the fact that Cruz's weapon of choice in the incident was a Smith & Wesson M&P15.223, an AR-15 he had legally purchased at the Sunrise Tactical Supply store in Coral Springs, Florida (Jansen 2018). A semiautomatic rifle based on the military model of the M-16 used in Vietnam, the AR-15 is appropriately called by gun scholar Tom Diaz an ideal weapon meant for "shooting as many people as one can" (2013, 12). While gun advocates may laud the technical features of highly militarized weapons like the AR-15, it is precisely their sophisticated lethal power that should be cause for concern, for the militaristic nature of their design is deliberate, focused on perfecting lethality over time (Diaz 1999, 5). As some have noted, guns in today's marketplace are inherently lethal, posing an existential threat to those around them (9). Gun violence, as such, can be seen to be the direct result of what Tom Diaz claims is a "virtually unregulated distribution of an inherently dangerous consumer product" (9). The fact that the AR-15, like many military-style guns of its kind, remains widely available in the civilian market despite its innate lethality is what makes it so dangerous.

Take, for example, the AR-15's superior targeting capabilities. Although the rifle is not fully automatic and therefore won't fire in sprays of bullets like a machine gun once a trigger is pulled, it is nonetheless designed to shoot several rounds during a matter of seconds (Vitkovskaya and Martin 2018, 1). Its recoil and muzzle velocity allow the user to shoot with extreme precision, causing excessive ricochet when striking the bone of an animal (2). Estimated to shoot up to forty-five rounds in a single minute and accurately target an object at a distance of a quarter of a mile (Wing and Reilly 2016), the AR-15 is designed to shoot at speeds much faster than that of handguns; hence the injuries they cause are outsized and, for many, fatal.

Not surprisingly, then, given the AR-15's lethal design, an injured organ of one of Cruz's victims was described as "look[ing] like an over-ripe melon smashed by a sledgehammer" that "was bleeding extensively" (Sher 2018, 2). That Cruz was able to kill seventeen people and injure fourteen more with this weapon (Chuck, Johnson, and Siemaszko 2018, 2) is indicative of its outsized and multiple target killing powers. For today's guns, available for anyone to purchase throughout US gun stores nationwide, are not mere neutral commodities but often military-style weapons—a killing technology designed to wreak the kind of carnage that soldiers and unwitting civilians might encounter on the battlefield.

Underreported and unacknowledged in this vast landscape of American gun violence are the injured and the high costs of medical bills society must bear (Bernstein 2017). Year after year, throughout America's mass shootings, little, if any, information is made public about the injuries that the survivors of gun violence suffer and are hospitalized for as a result. As David Bernstein summarizes this problem, those who are injured are erased from public memory, their wounds mainly "unnoticed, unnumbered, and unstudied" (2).

Coinciding with the lack of attention to the injured is knowledge of the enormous cost of their medical care. Although figures vary according to studies completed on this issue, one particular study notes that for the years 2006–2010, medical bills totaled an estimated $88.6 billion for the survivors of gun violence alone who visited an emergency department (Lee et al. 2014, 896). Compare this cost to the $174 billion estimated for both the surviving and the dead in 2010. Such an estimate was triple the funding for the US Department of Homeland Security Budget and twice the budget allocation for the US Department of Education in that year alone (897). Significant here is the fact that costs for medical care tied to gun violence exceed many US federal budget allocations. In addition to lack of knowledge about the cost of medical care tied to those injured and killed from gun injuries, some research indicates that gun ownership may in actuality lead to increasing one's chances of dying by homicide or suicide (Anglemyer, Horvath, and Rutherford 2014, 105; Lopez 2021).

Nationwide research on guns remains severely restricted, the result of years of structural impediments imposed by Congress over time. In 1996, for example, Jay Dickey, an Arkansas politician, persuaded Congress to endorse an amendment (known as the Dickey amendment) that cut funding to the Centers for Disease Control and Prevention (CDC) for any efforts deemed to "advocate or promote gun control," curtailing the CDC's ability to study the gun issue and gather information (Zhang 2018, 1–2).

In 2005, the NRA succeeded in passing the Lawful Commerce in Arms Act through Congress, preventing tort litigation against the gun industry (Diaz 2013, 12). The cumulative effects of these achievements have made it exceedingly difficult, if not impossible, for any federal body to seriously gather information on guns or for the gun industry to be seriously challenged. There is currently no nationwide registry responsible for tracking gun deaths in the United States (as can be found in other industries, such as the Fatality Analysis Reporting System that exists to keep record of vehicular deaths) (Zhang 2018, 2). Consequently, because the ability of federal agencies to track and disseminate nation-wide data is hampered, the public's knowledge of the realities of gun violence remains seriously limited.

Just like the proponents of the tobacco industry, which decades ago refused to acknowledge the connection between cigarette smoking and cancer (Proctor and Schiebinger, 2008, 11), it is my contention that the gun industry operates along similar lines, denying the causal rela-tionship between guns and gun deaths. Like big tobacco of years past, the culture of today's gun industry is one of secrecy where tremendous effort is exerted to hide the facts on the health effects of guns (Diaz 2013, 11). Such secrecy and lack of information results in a distorted, almost benevolent view of guns, where the public is asked to see many of today's militarized guns as objects only—mere artifacts for display, as Brian Ott, Erik Aoki, and Greg Dickinson (2011) have noted, and not technologies of war uniquely designed for the battlefield.

PSYCHIC NUMBING AND THE COLLECTIVE INABILITY TO FEEL PAIN

How has gun violence, of the scope and caliber found in a field of battle, come to be sanctioned through language in the United States? How is it that American public spaces everywhere have become potential zones of warfare? To understand in greater depth just how gun industry lobbies such as the NRA and affiliated pro-gun organizations use language to shape the public's perceptions of guns, I turn to Robert Jay Lifton and Greg Mitchell's theory of psychic numbing.[5] Psychic numbing, which Lifton and Mitchell define "as a diminished capacity or inclination to feel" (1995, 337) and as an emotional dissociation that occurs in the individual (130), explains in large part what they see as the nation's problematic psychological response to the US bombing of Hiroshima and Nagasaki during World War II. For Lifton and Mitchell, who apply this theory particularly to the case of Hiroshima, the US decision to drop the bomb led to a collective inability to understand the pain of its victims, resulting in a national lack of feeling (337–40). According to them, once numbing is spread out in society, people can become desensitized to acts of murder and violence as well as to larger societal problems afflicting the homeless and the poor (339–40). In their view, numbing can lead to more and more extreme acts of violence as a means of compensating for lack of feeling (340).

Drawing on their thesis, I assert that the problem of psychic numb-ing, that is, desensitivity to violence, is prevalent in the pro-gun rhetoric of the industry where the link between guns and gun violence is denied and guns are distanced from the lethal results they produce. Moreover, the discourse removes the sense of risk associated with them and ignores the fact that guns endow those who access them the power to kill others (Taubes 1992).

Robert Gregory, like Lifton and Mitchell, concerns himself with the problem of psychic numbing and centers his attention on the bomb (2003). He discusses the findings of scholars who reviewed survey results of people's perceptions of the Chernobyl accident and argues that people conceded to the use of nuclear power, unable to comprehend the gravity of the danger it presents. He gleans from the research of these scholars that in general, the characteristics of nuclear power are such that people remain uncritical regarding the problem of radiation, agreeing to what they are told and disavowing the unpleasant, while those in power exercise increasing authority, and media elements work together to obscure information (234). For Gregory, the public is unable to deal with the problem (235) and remains unknowing in the face of nuclear dangers, incapable of exercising their critical faculties. Most important, he points to the very real socioeconomic factors at work that function to, as he puts it, "lull populations into consumerism and ignorance-based acceptance of the pronouncements of vested interests." He calls for more truthful information to be made available to the public (236).

In addition to this perspective, Walter Metz, who applies a film studies approach to psychic numbing, claims that in the wider US culture, many Americans refuse to acknowledge the implications of bombing Hiroshima and that this "has produced a pattern of distancing and denial about nuclear trauma" (1997, 46). Throughout his article, Metz analyzes themes of the Cold War he sees emerging in select Hollywood films as he focuses on the fact of nuclear trauma. He stresses Lifton and Mitchell's ideas on "denial and deferral of the cultural consequences of Hiroshima which began in 1945 and continues to this day" (63) and shows how disavowal of the bomb permeates many Cold War themes in film. Although Metz concerns himself mainly with the subject of nuclear trauma in film, his point that censorship or lack of access to information is one of the effects of psychic numbing (46) is relevant to understanding the psychology of psychic numbing from a cultural perspective. Metz observes further what he points out is the tendency for people to participate in rituals of "cultural distancing" and "cultural denial" (47).

While Lifton and Mitchell, Gregory, and Metz focus on psychic numbing as it specifically relates to the nuclear bomb/culture, it is my contention that the dynamics of psychic numbing operate in similar ways in the gun industry. Like the PR language of the nuclear sector, one finds in the discourse of the gun industry a tendency to omit the question of risk associated with the technology. Instead, the audience is encouraged to view guns as risk-free, mere objects in an ahistorical sense, unconnected to the wider world of the living, the flesh and the body. To a large extent, Brian Ott, Eric Aoki, and Greg Dickinson come to this conclusion in their observations that visitors to the Cody Firearms Museum are being asked to interact and view guns as artifacts, and therefore in a distanced, aesthetic way (2011, 217).

In their analysis of the way guns are presented to the public at the Cody Firearms museum, Ott, Aoki, and Dickinson remark that visitors are directed throughout the museum to see guns "as inert objects of visual pleasure" and that the link between guns and gun violence is rendered invisible (2011, 216). They call this invisibility an "absence" imbued with meaning and assert it "is a fully embodied rhetorical experience." They compare the visitor's experience of seeing guns exhibited to observing the text of a speech, contending the museum space "is a material space with effect" (217). In comparing the site of the museum to a speech text, they argue that the absence of any acknowledgment of gun violence in the exhibits functions just like a text endowed with persuasive effects. In this sense, the lack of attention to gun violence in the physical space can be interpreted as a way of swaying the visitor to see guns as objects of recreation, mere things to be gazed at and enjoyed for their aesthetic appeal and not objects that can cause injury or death.

Moreover, they observe that the word *weapon* is omitted from the museum, its website, and associated material. They remark that viewers in the museum are led from display to display of guns, not asked to see the broader social context beyond the gun as an object for display, and that this kind of looking imposes "a desensitizing and decontextualizing effect" on the visitor. Divorcing the gun from its sociohistorical context, according to them, serves to inculcate "a discrete, finite and a-contextual view of firearms" (Ott, Aoki, and Dickinson 2011, 219) where viewers are persuaded to perceive guns as things within a vacuum, not as technologies contingent on and inextricably bound to larger sociohistorical forces at work.

This kind of seeing, which essentially erases the material impact of guns, is, I contend, a silence created in a physical space. By silence, I draw here on what Cheryl Glenn calls "a specific rhetorical art" (2004, 2); like speech, silence performs a "complementary rhetoric" (3).[6] For Glenn, silence and speech are connected and work in tandem (7). Comparing silence to the mathematical significance of the number zero, Glenn contends that "silence is an absence with a function, and a rhetorical one at that" (4). Such silence therefore is one with rhetorical purpose, motive, and intent, demonstrating that silences imbued in a text can be read for rhetorical effect. Such an effect draws on what Glenn claims is "silence *as a rhetoric*, as a constellation of symbolic strategies that (like spoken language) serves many functions" (xi). Silence, then, similar to spoken language, can serve multiple purposes (xi). In this context, Glenn makes the case that silence is strategic and can be used in acquiescence to power (xi).

THE LANGUAGE OF THE CMP: GUNS ARE
GOOD FOR YOU AND OTHER MANTRAS

To explore how the language of psychic numbing and rhetorical silence works in the gun industry, I turn now to the information sheet "Air Rifle Marksmanship for Youth" by the CMP. My interest in this document is tied to a larger interest in the CMP, a JROTC- and NRA-led marksmanship program that Nikolas Cruz participated in when enrolled as a student at Marjory Stoneman Douglas High School. As one of four members of this program, Cruz practiced target shooting and trained for school shooting competitions after school hours (Elder 2018a; Kirby 2018; Biesecker and Binkley 2018). This program may not be known to many Americans, but it is housed in many schools throughout the United States, allowing students to register for target shooting practice in lieu of credit for select courses (Elder 2018b; Project Censored 2018).

Motivating my inquiry is how the CMP's information sheet uses persuasive language to promote an NRA program on US campuses. Insightful here are its rhetorical strategies designed to inform schools, parents, and club organizations about its nationwide after-school sports program with the goal of persuading young people to join. In analyzing these strategies, it's important to understand the JROTC's desired target population.

Marvin Berlowitz argues that the JROTC seeks to recruit at-risk populations in urban schools. He also claims that the JROTC contends its training in leadership skills is beneficial to schools, but doesn't provide the data to prove this (2000, 394). Lesley Bartlett and Catherine Lutz conduct a historical study of the JROTC origins, rooted in World War I, and compare its origins to the growth of the organization, especially in the 1990s (1998, 120). They assert that in the 1990s the JROTC concentrated its efforts in prioritizing middle-class and white values, emphasizing allegiance to the state over race (119–20).[7] They also claim that the

JROTC targets students who are at risk (127) and that schools housing JROTC programs tend to be poor (126). They argue that the language of the JROTC program in the 1990s emphasizes the teaching of life skills needed for a wide range of jobs, especially for those in the middle-class sector (125). They claim that self-esteem for populations at risk is a strong aspect of the rhetoric (125).

With this perspective in mind, upon first analyzing the rhetoric of the CMP information sheet, which provides the reader with a list of the advantages of joining the air rifle marksmanship program, the reader will observe a key feature of psychic numbing—the overall removal of a sense of risk, threat, and danger associated with guns. Although the text focuses on air rifles and not other gun types such as firearms or handguns, the central message of the text—that participating in air rifle marksmanship is a safe school activity—is worthy of examination in that its line of reasoning reveals a pro-gun ideology that emphasizes the gun as a neutral tool, allowing one to deflect attention away from larger sociohistorical problems tied to gun culture in the United States.[8] Subheadings such as "Air Rifle Marksmanship Is One of the Safest Youth Sports," "Shooting Is a Sport for All," "Target Rifle Shooting Teaches Valuable Life Skills," and "Target Shooting Is a Sport of Discipline, Control and Non-violence" (Civilian Marksmanship Program. n.d.) are but some of the examples of the language demonstrating the tool metaphor.

Given that not everyone in the audience may be aware of the distinctions between air rifles and other guns, and that the information sheet argues, in general ways, that air rifle marksmanship can lead users to handle guns more safely, it is my contention that the text creates a rhetorical space for the audience to potentially conflate generalizable claims made about air rifles to other gun types. This conflation of claims demonstrates numbing in that the audience may potentially be asked to identify with the argument that all guns are neutral tools and that all gun types are on an equal footing in terms of lethality.

Applying Walter Metz's theory that people take part in the rites of "cultural denial" (1997, 47) to the language of the CMP information sheet, I assert that another feature of psychic numbing emerges in the language in the elevation of marksmanship to the status of a mainstream sport. This is done through a listing of positive facts about air rifles that occludes any negative references to guns. In this way, the document succeeds in framing them in a highly charismatic light—as something that is good for you—while omitting or creating silent spaces on potentially controversial questions related to the sport. The text does this by framing air rifle marksmanship as a commonplace sport on the same level as other sports. We are told, for example, that "air rifle marksmanship is part of the Olympic sport of shooting" and that it "is practiced as a sport in more than 150 countries" (Civilian Marksmanship Program n.d., 1). Moreover, we are told that "in the US, air rifle is a popular high school and youth club sport as well as NCAA championship sport" (1). In this way, we are led to view the air rifle marksmanship program as a serious activity, associating it with elite sports competitions.

We further see psychic numbing taking place in that the language of the text frames rifle marksmanship as a sport similar to that of other sports, downplaying or rendering absent a sense of threat associated with the activity. The notion that marksmanship could potentially be different from other sports, involving dangers unique to handling rifles, is effaced. Rather, the text emphasizes the sport's shared likeness with other sports, classifying it as a sport that "may well be the safest of all youth sports," minimizing the perception of risk.

While we are led to conclude that risk in this sport is similar to or on the same level of that of other sports, the text attempts to reach out to individuals who deviate from an athletic ideal or standard. This rhetorical move is emphasized through the subheading titled "Shooting Is a Sport for All," suggesting that air rifle shooting is an inclusive and democratic sport, available to young people of various backgrounds and skills who may not necessarily see themselves as athletes in a traditional sense.

It is here that the text attempts to appeal to diverse audiences in that it claims to be "a sport where sex, size, speed or 'natural ability' do not determine success" (Civilian Marksmanship Program n.d., 1). This appeal to difference is reiterated in that we are told marksmanship is an ideal activity for "an exceptionally wide variety of youth" that "do not have the size, height, strength or speed to succeed in many sports" (1). By framing marksmanship in this way, the text creates an opening for appealing in highly positive ways to people who may see themselves as on the margins, unable to conform to the traditional ideals of the athlete in society.

Beyond the appeal to a sense of difference in the audience, safety is a theme that emerges as the document repeatedly makes claims that air rifles are safe, removing any notion of danger or peril from the text and thereby deflecting the reader's attention away from questions about the risks involved in handling a rifle. As such, the language establishes a favorable, threat-free view of air rifles. To give this impression, the information sheet defines air rifles in highly positive ways, highlighting only the benefits of the sport. Drawing on Lifton and Mitchell's (1995) thesis that psychic numbing desensitizes the individual to violence, the text's singular stress on the positive aspects of the program serves to minimize the perception of threat, as air rifle injuries are described as minor and the problem of bodily harm remains largely unaddressed and silent.

The text makes this case stating that "in the last 10 years, these organizations and competitions reported only six minor injuries resulting from the improper handling of air rifles" (Civilian Marksmanship Program n.d., 1). This claim suggests that an individual's lack of skill or knowledge in operating an air rifle may be at fault for any gun injuries that occur. The injuries of the user are not specified, nor are we told how they came about—most important, we are asked to believe at face value that the injuries were small and therefore not asked to identify or empathize with the pain of those injured, suggesting that the guns in and of themselves don't pose serious bodily harm. The question of whether or not serious injuries have occurred throughout the program's duration is not addressed, remaining a silent space embedded in the text.

Moreover, through the use of intensifiers in language, the document further attempts to heighten or bolster the impression that marksmanship is a safe school activity, appealing to the audience's needs for security. By doing this, the text omits any mention of the negative effects of riles, remaining silent on the issue of lethality. The program is described as "extraordinarily safe" due to the "rigorous safety rules and training" in place. The theme of safety is stressed to such a degree that the article claims, "Air rifle marksmanship may well be the safest of all youth sports" (Civilian Marksmanship Program n.d., 1), with little context or evidence in support as this is made absent in the text. Blame for injury is allocated on the lack of skill of the user and not the weapon.

Not only does the text/article purport that the program is safe, it largely defines the program as one providing training in gun safety, contending a causal link between air rifle firing range experience and accident prevention and low accident rate without data for support. This draws our attention away from the lethal nature of guns, requiring us to focus on safety training rather than the risks tied to handling a gun. For example, it claims that young people "who learn rifle safety" through "range firing opportunities" are "much less likely to ever be involved in a firearm accident than youth who have no gun safety training" and that "[t]he most effective gun safety training is to give youth supervised gun handling experiences" (Civilian Marksmanship Program n.d., 3). By arguing this position, the authors of the informational sheet equate target shooting experience with prevention, asking the audience to accept their claims at face value, though no evidence is provided. The reader here is merely asked to consent to this claim. The notion that gun use can lead to injury and bodily pain is absent from the text.

In line with its stress on the program's safety record, the text links air rifle firing range experience with the virtues of cultivating an improved sense of self. Target shooting is defined as "teach[ing] valuable life skills," leading to "enhance[d] student performances in schoolwork as well as in home, family, social and work-related activities." Though no concrete or factual evidence is provided to support this argument, the article assumes students who are target shooting will achieve specific life skills, presented in a bulleted list. Selected items among these skills are "[s]elf-control, selfdiscipline and emotional control," along with "[r]esponsibility" and "[s]elf-image enhancement" (Civilian Marksmanship Program n.d., 2). Such a list suggests that by participating in the program, young people can improve as students and as citizens of their community.

While the informational article doesn't directly address national incidents of gun violence, such as mass shootings, for example, it does allude to them in vague and euphemistic language that serves to make such incidents less real in the mind's eye, removing emotion connected to the question of peril. Violence—injuries and deaths from guns—is described in a highly abstract, impersonal context as "negative interests," something far removed from the material world and therefore presented as less consequential (Civilian Marksmanship Program n.d., 4). By addressing gun violence as "negative interests," the language succeeds in alienating guns from the fact of gun violence and directing the reader's gaze away from the lethal design and function of guns. Incidents of mass shootings are not addressed, only hinted at in round-about fashion through abstract language that shields the audience from the realities of lethal violence occurring nationwide.

That the air rifle program is described as an antidote to gun violence demonstrates a major persuasive appeal in the organization's advocacy efforts. The text claims that its marksmanship activities "can counteract potential negative interests that might grow out of dangerous images of guns that are conveyed by popular culture and the media." In this context, the text invites the reader to assume that exposing young people to air rifle marksmanship training will eliminate someone's motivation to misuse guns. Deaths and injuries due to guns are blamed on the media and pop culture, and gun training programs are described as ideal activities for channeling young people's energies in nonviolent ways. This is emphasized by the fact that we are told that "[t]arget shooting prevents such interests from becoming destructive or dangerous." Moreover, the article assumes, without supporting evidence, that there is no causal relationship between gun shooting as a hobby and gun violence, asserting instead that gun shooting as a hobby can counter gun violence. It claims that young people participating in marksmanship programs are "extremely unlikely to commit acts of violence of any kind," assuming that participants in such programs shoot for competitive or recreational purposes only and have no motives to use their skills to commit acts of gun violence against others. This argument assumes that target shooting training in these programs prevents incidents of gun violence from happening and that members have no ill intentions in participating in the program. Moreover, gun practice is defined as a hobby that "guide[s]" young people "into positive, structured, disciplined, sports-oriented activities" (Civilian Marksmanship Program n.d., 4). Such a view suggests that young people are being led to participate in activities beneficial to their well-being, socializing them to become productive, and not violent, members of society.

A LOTTERY OF DEATH? WHAT IS TO BE DONE?

It is a fact of life that in the United States countless lives have been lost to gun violence. Guns have taken the lives of 1.5 million US citizens since 1968, killing more citizens than soldiers killed in all combined US wars (Bailey 2017, 1). Couple this with the extraordinary fact that in 2017, approximately 40,000 people died from gun violence (Violence Policy Center n.d.), compared to only 5,586 people killed in terrorist incidents from 1969 to 2009 (Diaz 2013, 1). In this chapter, I ask the question: how are such astounding conditions of gun violence made possible through language? In analyzing the language of the CMP, a program closely tied to the shooter Nikolas Cruz, one discovers a highly incentivized rhetoric designed to recruit young people by framing guns as objects of recreation, divorced from their social effects. In this light, the language of the CMP information sheet masks the role that guns play in gun violence, avoiding any inquiry into the relationship between guns and gun incidents. The lethal technology of guns, whose unique function is to kill or at the very least maim, is ignored, while guns and target shooting are depicted as positive outlets. Unfortunately, research on gun violence today shows that the phenomenon of what is called "active-shooter/mass murder" violence (Carter 2017, 27) is accelerating at a quickening pace (26–27), with the FBI reporting a jump from 6.4 active shooter incidents occurring every year from 2000 to 2006 to 16.4 shootings every year from 2007 to 2013 (27). The Great Lottery of

Death, as some have observed (Cienski 2002), is now upon us, and one must ask, when does the worship of Moloch stop?[9] How many more lives must be sacrificed before the full implications of the link between guns and gun violence are fully recognized?

NOTES

1. The Bushmaster is the object of a lawsuit brought by families of the victims of the Sandy Hook Elementary shooting, which charges the Bushmaster's maker with promoting it as a combat weapon (Barbash 2019). For further details on the Bushmaster's military origins, see Hunter 2002.

2. Richard Kohn formulates his definition of militarism as "the degree to which a society's institutions, policies, behaviors, thoughts, and values are devoted to military power and shaped by war" (2009, 182). Kohn claims that militarism can lead to "the domination of war values and frameworks in American thinking, public policy, institutions, and society to the point of dominating rather than influencing or simply shaping American foreign relations and domestic life" (196). Following this logic, one can conclude that a war mindset in aspects of everyday life may result in war-related behaviors in the civilian sphere.

3. Matthew Lacombe studies the language of the NRA's magazine *Rifleman*, contending that the NRA is successful in creating social identity and portraying itself as instilling values by "tying gun ownership to personal responsibility, good citizenship and civic virtue" (2019, 1352).

4. For an in-depth discussion of many of the NRA's pro-gun arguments, see Duerringer and Justus 2016 and Medlock 2005.

5. In an earlier article, Lifton defines numbing as "an overall category that includes the standard psychoanalytic defense mechanisms of denial, suppression, and repression. It's an overall tendency to diminish feeling by unconscious impulse or even by conscious will or with the mix of the two" (1982, 628).

6. "Employed as a tactical strategy or inhabited in deference to authority," writes Glenn, "silence resonates loudly along the corridors of purposeful language use. Whether choice or im/position, silence can reveal positive or negative abilities, fulfilling or withholding traits, harmony or disharmony, success or failure. Silence can deploy power; it can defer to power. It all depends" (2004, 18).

7. In this decade, JROTC serves white, middle-class desires to "discipline" minority students and subordinate racial difference to an identification with the nation (Bartlett and Lutz 1998, 119).

8. For a rich discussion on how the NRA employs the tool metaphor in speaking about guns, see Duerringer and Justus 2016.

9. Cienski called the Washington, DC, sniper case shooting incident "a lottery of death." Cienski's allusion is an apt metaphor for mass shootings that can happen virtually any time and any place in the United States.

REFERENCES

Altimari, Dave, and Jon Lender. 2013. "Sandy Hook Shooter Adam Lanza Wore Earplugs." *Hartford Courant,* January 6, 2013. https://www.courant.com/news/connecticut/newtown-sandy-hook-school-shooting/hc-sandyhook-lanza-earplugs-20130106-story.html.

Anglemyer, Andrew, Tara Horvath, and George Rutherford. 2014. "The Accessibility of Firearms and Risk for Suicide and Homicide Victimization among Household Members." *Annals of Internal Medicine* 160 (2): 101–10.

Bailey, Chelsea. 2017. "More Americans Killed by Guns since 1968 Than in All US Wars—Combined." *NBC News*, October 4. https://www.nbcnews.com/storyline/las-vegas -shooting/more-americans-killed-guns-1968-all-u-s-wars-combined-n807156.

Barbash, Fred. 2019. "Families of Sandy Hook Shooting Victims Can Sue Gunmaker Remington over 2012 Attack, Court Says." *The Washington Post*, March 14, 2019. https://www .washingtonpost.com/world/national-security/families-of-sandy-hook-shooting-victims -can-sue-gunmaker-remington-over-2012-attack-court-says/2019/03/14/4222b1ec -4671-11e9-aaf8-4512a6fe3439_story.html.

Bartlett, Lesley, and Catherine Lutz. 1998. "Disciplining Social Difference: Some Cultural Politics of Military Training in Public High Schools." *Urban Review* 30 (2): 119–36.

Baynes, Chris. 2018. "Florida Shooting Suspect Nikolas Cruz 'Etched Swastikas into Ammunition Magazines Used in Massacre.'" *The Independent*, February 28, 2018. https:// www.independent.co.uk/news/world/americas/florida-shooting-nikolas-cruz-swas tikas-ammunition-magazines-parkland-massacre-a8232916.html.

Berlowitz, Marvin. 2000. "Racism and Conscription in the JROTC." *Peace Review* 12 (3): 393–98.

Bernstein, David. 2017. "Americans Don't Really Understand Gun Violence." *The Atlantic*, December 14, 2017. https://www.theatlantic.com/politics/archive/2017/12/guns-non fatal-shooting-newtown-las-vegas/548372/.

Biesecker, Michael, and Collin Binkley. 2018. "Shooting Suspect Was on School Rifle Team That Got NRA Grant." *AP*, February 16, 2018. https://apnews.com/article/shootings -north-america-us-news-ap-top-news-nikolas-cruz-87b429399f774064beefd7a7dff3a41a.

Broder, John, M. 2002a. "Arizona Gunman Chose Victims in Advance." *The New York Times*, October 30, 2002. https://www.nytimes.com/2002/10/30/us/arizona-gunman-chose -victims-in-advance.html.

Broder, John, M. 2002b. "Student Kills 3 Instructors and Himself at U of Arizona." *The New York Times*, October 29, 2002. https://www.nytimes.com/2002/10/29/us/student-kills -3-instructors-and-himself-at-u-of-arizona.html.

Burke, Kenneth. 1954. *Permanence and Change: An Anatomy of Purpose.* Berkeley: University of California Press.

Carter, Gregg Lee. 2017. *Gun Control in the United States: A Reference Handbook.* 2nd ed. Santa Barbara: ABC-CLIO.

Chuck, Elizabeth, Alex Johnson, and Corky Siemaszko. 2018. "17 Killed in Mass Shooting at High School in Parkland, Florida." *NBC News*, February 14, 2018. https://www .nbcnews.com/news/us-news/police-respond-shooting-parkland-florida-high-school -n848101.

Cienski, Jan. 2002. "Sniper Makes Everyone Feel Like a Target: 'If There Is Any Message, It Is for This Individual to Turn Himself in, to Stop This Insane Killing.' A Lottery of Death: Residents Avoiding Outdoors Chores in Wake of Shootings." *National Post*, October 9, 2002.

Civilian Marksmanship Program. n.d. "Air Rifle Marksmanship for Youth." https:// thecmp.org/wp-content/uploads/AirForYouth.pdf.

Diaz, Tom. 1999. *Making a Killing: The Business of Guns in America.* New York: New Press.

Diaz, Tom. 2013. *The Last Gun: How Changes in the Gun Industry Are Killing Americans and What It Will Take to Stop It.* New York: New Press.

Duerringer, Christopher, and Z. S. Justus. 2016. "Tropes in the Rhetoric of Gun Rights: A Pragma-Dialectic Analysis." *Argumentation and Advocacy* 52 (3): 181–98.

Economist. 2018. "Should the Army Subsidize High-School Soldiering?" (March 1, 2018) 31.

Elder, Pat. 2018a. "Florida Gunman Nikolas Cruz Knew How to Use a Gun, Thanks to the NRA and the US Army." *Democracy Now*, February 23, 2018. https://www.democracynow.org/2018/2/23/florida_gunman_nikolas_cruz_knew_how.

Elder, Pat. 2018b. "Shooter Cruz, JROTC and the NRA." *Institute for Public Accuracy*, February 20, 2018. http://accuracy.org/release/shooter-cruz-jrotc-and-the-nra/.

Follman, Mark. 2014. "Yes, Mass Shootings Are Occurring More Often." *Mother Jones*, October 21, 2014. https://www.motherjones.com/politics/2014/10/mass-shootings-rising-harvard/.

Glenn, Cheryl. 2004. *Unspoken: A Rhetoric of Silence*. Carbondale: Southern Illinois University Press.

Gregory, Robert J. 2003. "Venturing Past Psychic Numbing: Facing the Issues." *Journal for the Psychoanalysis of Culture and Society* 8 (2): 232–37.

Holguin, Jaime. 2002. "Arizona Gunman Had Threatened School." *CBS News*, October 30, 2002. https://www.cbsnews.com/news/arizona-gunman-had-threatened-school/.

Hunter, Stephen. 2002. "The Bushmaster XM15: A Rifle Known for Its Accuracy." *The Washington Post*, October 25, 2002. https://www.washingtonpost.com/archive/politics/2002/10/25/the-bushmaster-xm15-a-rifle-known-for-its-accuracy/52e537a2-4e19-4bad-b732-db4f8183973d/.

Jansen, Bart. 2018. "Florida Shooting Suspect Bought Gun Legally, Authorities Say." *USA Today*, February 15, 2018. https://www.usatoday.com/story/news/2018/02/15/florida-shooting-suspect-bought-gun-legally-authorities-say/340606002/.

Kirby, Jen. 2018. "Nikolas Cruz Was Reportedly on an NRA-Funded Rifle Team in High School." *Vox*, February 16, 2018. https://www.vox.com/2018/2/16/17021874/report-nikolas-cruz-florida-rifle-team-nra-grant.

Kohn, Richard, H. 2009. "The Danger of Militarization in an Endless 'War' on Terrorism." *Journal of Military History* 73 (1): 177–208.

Lacombe, Matthew J. 2019. "The Political Weaponization of Gun Owners: The National Rifle Association's Cultivation, Dissemination, and Use of a Group Social Identity." *Journal of Politics* 81 (4): 1342–56.

Lee, Jarone, Sadeq A. Quraishi, Saurabha Bhatnagar, Ross D. Zafonte, and Peter T. Masiakos. 2014. "The Economic Cost of Firearm-Related Injuries in the United States from 2006 to 2010." *Surgery* 155 (5): 894–98. http://dx.doi.org/10.1016/j.surg.2014.02.011.

Lifton, Robert Jay. 1982. "Beyond Psychic Numbing: A Call to Awareness." *American Orthopsychiatric Association* 52 (4): 619–29.

Lifton, Robert Jay, and Greg Mitchell. 1995. *Hiroshima in America: A Half Century of Denial*. New York: Avon.

Lopez, German. 2021. "America's Gun Problem, Explained." *Vox*. https://www.vox.com/2015/10/3/9444417/fedex-indianapolis-mass-shooting-gun-violence-america-usa.

Lucaites, John L., and Jon Simons. 2017. "Introduction: The Paradox of War's In/visibility." In *In/visible War: The Culture of War in Twenty-First-Century America*, edited by Jon Simons and John L. Lucaites, 1–24. New Brunswick: Rutgers University Press.

Lupkin, Sydney. 2013. "US Has More Guns and Gun Deaths than Any Other Country, Study Finds." *ABC News*, September 19. https://abcnews.go.com/blogs/health/2013/09/19/u-s-has-more-guns-and-gun-deaths-than-any-other-country-study-finds.

Medlock, Scott. 2005. "NRA = No Rational Argument? How the National Rifle Association Exploits Public Irrationality." *Texas Journal on Civil Liberties and Civil Rights* 11 (1): 39–63.

Metz, Walter. 1997. "'Keep the Coffee Hot, Hugo': Nuclear Trauma in Lang's *The Big Heat*." *Film Criticism* 21 (3): 43–65.

Neuman, Scott. 2018. "Army Awards Medal for Heroism to 3 JROTC Cadets Killed in Florida Shooting." *NPR: The Two-Way*, February 21, 2018. https://www.opb.org/news/article/npr-army-awards-medal-for-heroism-to-3-jrotc-cadets-killed-in-florida-shooting/.

Ott, Brian, Eric Aoki, and Greg Dickinson. 2011. "Ways of (Not) Seeing Guns: Presence and Absence at the Cody Firearms Museum." *Communication and Critical/Cultural Studies* 8 (3): 215–39.

Proctor, Robert, and Londa Schiebinger, eds. 2008. *Agnotology: The Making and Unmaking of Ignorance.* Stanford: Stanford University Press.

Project Censored. 2018. "Parkland Shooter Belonged to Group Advocating Marksmanship as Substitute for Science." April 6, 2018. https://www.projectcensored.org/parkland -shooter-belonged-group-advocating-marksmanship-substitute-science/.

Rozsa, Lori. 2018. " 'Selfless Service': JROTC Remembers Three Slain in Florida High School Shooting." *The Washington Post,* February 19, 2018. https://www.washingtonpost.com /national/selfless-service-jrotc-remembers-three-slain-in-florida-high-school-shooting /2018/02/19/1e3138f2-158b-11e8-8b08-027a6ccb38eb_story.html.

Sher, Heather. 2018. "What I Saw Treating the Victims from Parkland Should Change the Debate on Guns." *The Atlantic,* February 22, 2018. https://www.theatlantic.com/politics /archive/2018/02/what-i-saw-treating-the-victims-from-parkland-should-change -the-debate-on-guns/553937/.

Stack, Liam. 2019. "Parkland Shooting Suspect Is Getting $430,000 from Life Insurance and May Lose His Lawyers." *The New York Times,* April 24, 2019. https://www.nytimes .com/2019/04/24/us/nikolas-cruz-insurance-policy.html.

Taubes, Gary. 1992. "Violence Epidemiologists Test the Hazards of Gun Ownership." *Science* 258 (5080): 213–15.

Violence Policy Center. n.d. "Revealing the Impacts of Gun Violence." http://vpc.org /revealing-the-impacts-of-gun-violence/.

Vitkovskaya, Julie, and Patrick Martin. 2018. "4 Basic Questions about the AR-15." *The Washington Post,* February 16, 2018. https://www.washingtonpost.com/news/checkpoint/wp /2018/02/15/4-basic-questions-about-the-ar-15/?utm_term=.425807a04a55.

Wing, Nick, and Mollie Reilly. 2016. "Here's What You Need to Know about the Weapons of War Used in Mass Shootings." *Huffpost,* June 13, 2016. https://www.huffpost.com /entry/mass-shootings-weapons-ar-15_n_575ec6b7e4b00f97fba8de0c.

Zhang, Sarah. 2018. "Why Can't the US Treat Gun Violence as a Public-Health Problem?" *The Atlantic,* February 15. https://www.theatlantic.com/health/archive/2018/02/gun -violence-public-health/553430/.

Zimring, Franklin, and Gordon Hawkins. 1997. *Crime Is Not the Problem: Lethal Violence in America.* New York: Oxford University Press.

13

A NON-DEFENSIVE GUN
Violence, Climate Catastrophe, and Rhetorical Education

Ira J. Allen

When I mention my shotgun, some people nod knowingly and say, "Good home defense gun." And I explain, "No, not exactly," or "Really, no, not at all." I keep it locked up, unloaded, inaccessible. If somebody wants to break into my home while I'm there, I have a baseball bat. If they only want my stuff, well, that's not worth killing or dying for. My gun's not a defensive gun. It's not a gun for the present, though I do shoot clay pigeons to keep in practice and because it's fun. My gun isn't for shooting people, at least in these times. (For shooting people in other times? Maybe; one hopes not; maybe.) This is an end-of-one-world gun, and it is nice to think that the circumstances that would make owning such a gun rational will never arrive. (It is very white to think they are not already here, but also very white to ward them off by collecting and displaying guns like talismans).[1] My non-defensive gun is, in short, a response to climate change. My own experiences of acquiring and learning to use effectively a "non-defensive gun" are a form of uncomfortable bet-hedging on a catastrophic future, but they also suggest a useful lens on the violences of the present, which spin out in a web around the *topos* of a "defensive gun."

When people think of gun violence in the United States, they often think of mass shootings. Mass shootings in the United States, however, are a vanishingly small element in the far larger wildfire of US gun violence (to say nothing of our still greater problems).[2] In contradistinction to mass shootings, which are terrifying because they are imagined as "attacks," the ubiquitous gun violences we more quietly live with are framed, at least somewhat effectively, as defensive.[3] The topos of "a defensive gun" at once undergirds the formation of American statehood itself and creates the organizing discursive background against which "an epidemic of gun violence" *pops*. Acceptable "defensive" violence is the cultural condition for spectacular aggressive violence. And a cultural

https://doi.org/10.7330/9781646422159.c013

obsession with spectacular aggressive violence is one condition of possibility for maintaining the ubiquity of "defensive" violence.

This is not new. As Roxanne Dunbar-Ortiz has shown in *Loaded: A Disarming History of the Second Amendment* (2018), it is a story that traces its arc in American history back to the "self-defensive" European genocide of native peoples in the Americas that served as one cause for the United States' "defensive" founding revolution and ensured the constitutional protection of organized "collectively defensive" violence in the Second Amendment. Dunbar-Ortiz painfully demonstrates that "killing, looting, burning, raping, and terrorizing Indians were traditions in each of the colonies long before the Constitutional Convention," such that it was an enshrinement of tradition for "the Second Amendment's language [to] specifically g[i]ve individuals and families the right to form volunteer militias to attack Indians and take their land" (18). Recall that the US constitutional justification of these militias is that they are "necessary to the security of a free State." American militias are conceived, constitutionally speaking, as defensive bodies committed to gun violence in the name of security. They were organized at founding and have been since—from genocide to slave patrols and the policing they spawned—along racist lines.

The defensive (thus imagined as not) violence carried forward by the Second Amendment and embodied in such post-independence genocides as Andrew Jackson's and other "Indian Wars" foregrounds *protection* of white supremacy. Dunbar-Ortiz notes, "What distinguishes the US experience is not the amount or type of violence involved, but rather the historical narratives attached to that violence and their political uses, even today" (2018, 42). American violence, articulated as part of the colonizers' "civilizing" mission, was genocidal from well before the country's founding—and yet special constitutional care is taken to present the right to bear arms as a function of security, that is, of defense rather than aggression. (What is to be "protected," it goes unstated, is whiteness, Europeanness. Society must be defended.) Meanwhile, guns themselves are *of course* tools of violence. Placing US history within the historiographical context of her own experiences of "gun-love," Dunbar-Ortiz writes, "Guns are made for killing, and while nearly anything, including human hands, may be used to kill, only the gun is created for the specific purpose of killing a living creature" (15).[4] We know that guns are *for* violence, but guns' place in US culture remains based in a concept of defensive, necessary force that would be somehow *no longer violence.* Ultimately, Dunbar-Ortiz argues, there is no way of truly grasping the significance of gun aggression in contemporary life without insight into the offensive character of the Second Amendment.

The US Second Amendment organizes gun violence in America, and there is no amount of thoughtful or bipartisan rhetorical collocation that can sidestep its genocidal marriage of aggression and self-justificatory claims to defense. In this light, it looks unsurprising that so much American gun policy discourse is organized around the phrase "assault rifles" as correlative to the *obvious* attacks of mass shootings—which are "vicious" and "shocking"—rather than around the handguns with which the overwhelming majority of gun violence within the country is enacted. In the formation of the US American state, both initially and still today, political-rhetorical possibilities hinge on the pretense that organized gun violence can be defensive without *also* being aggressive. The aggression that we disavow in focusing overmuch on mass shootings allows us to avoid working through our own ongoing investments in state violence on a mass scale. The result is a national habit of gun violence (domestic and global) against abject, raced, and gendered others.[5]

Taking Dunbar-Ortiz's argument as a watchword, the rest of this essay hovers elsewhere in time: not in the US past that lends current constitutional language its significance, nor even in contemporary globalized US violence against abject non-white others, but over a possible future liable to be both hotter and darker than our present. My hope is to get a different view of what responsibility for gun violence can look like by understanding the violence that *makes states as such* in tandem with the rhetorical education that makes political communities.[6] When we think of gun violence not from the vantage point of a past that has led to the specific "us" of the present moment, but from the perspective of the aleatory future anterior—what might have come to have been at a stabilized future moment—the political waters of gun violence appear muddier than ever. The distinction between aggressive and defensive gun violence does not hold well at the level of social formation.

Our complicity in and reliance on violence (past, present, and future) is particularly clear when we imagine ourselves in spaces of climate catastrophe–driven social collapse. Territory- or property-based *we*-making entails violence; where there are guns, the violence will be gun violence. This essay is an attempt to get away from both the cupidity and the bloodthirstiness of most American discussions of gun violence. Our very lives are built on and in violence. At the same time, any us-to-come in the ruins of climate disaster will only be an inhabitable political community to the extent that it *also has* some way of abjuring violence. There is a kind of *dissoi logoi* mentality to simultaneously taking ownership of and marking as impermissible our founding and maintaining violences. One way of at once taking responsibility for and abjuring violence, I suggest in closing, is rhetorical education.

Following recent reports by the Intergovernmental Panel on Climate Change (2018, 2019) and *No Immediate Danger,* the first book of William T. Vollman's massive two-volume *Carbon Ideologies* (2018), this essay moves forward with acceptance that the future will be hotter and darker than the present—and that the time to begin work on making that hotter, darker future better is now. I do not say "averting that future" (we are inundated with increasingly desperate reports that say we can, but we cannot actually do so).[7] Making our hotter, darker future better (better than it would otherwise be, that is) means in equal parts preparing for it and working to conserve what we take to be best, culturally speaking, about our own time.[8] After touching on current predictions regarding climate change, social collapse, and deep adaptation, I return to discuss rhetorical education as a complement to a non-defensive gun. Taken together, these offer interweaving ways of preparing for a world to come that shed light on our conceptual and practical investments in gun violence in the present. By "a world to come," I mean whatever set of social structures will replace—in whole or in part, and likely through what is frequently called "staggered collapse," at least for a time—the interimbricated collection of systems constituting "our" world.

My aim is not to say what the future *will* look like, but only that it will likely be hotter and darker than our present—and that (gun) violence may well be differently distributed while rhetorical education will be no less vital. At stake is a way of approaching future catastrophe that valorizes what we take to be best in our present moment, while also accepting due responsibility for what we take to be worst. To see the violences of the future as *our own*, as violence properly so called (not imposed upon us by a fully legitimated need for defense), is to recognize the violences of the present as equally so. In either temporality, as preparation for flexible meaning-making under conditions of uncertainty, with an eye to tradition and an eye to utility, rhetorical education is an important way of hedging the hedge-bet that is a non-defensive gun. To help one another become enthymematic is as valuable a way of preparing for worlds to come as any other more immediately practical or obviously instrumental ones. Together with feelingly integrating visceral knowledge of our own aggressivity—in rhetoric as in gun violence—rhetorical education is vital to negotiating the specter and substance of violence constituting our world in the present. Understanding the endoxic possibilities of the future induces greater realism about the endemic violences of the present. Our climate emergency in particular suggests possible futures that align with redistributions of world-making violence.

CONFRONTING A HOTTER, DARKER FUTURE

The Intergovernmental Panel on Climate Change (IPCC) is in many ways a conservative body. Established in 1988 by the United Nations and the World Meteorological Association, it is comprised of representatives selected by national governments: political actors and climate scientists alike. All the more striking, then, that its 2018 "Special Report" paints such a dire picture of both short- and mid-term human and nonhuman futures on Earth. Keeping global temperature rise to 1.5°C above pre-industrial levels, the number widely seen as most compatible with only moderately disastrous outcomes for hundreds of millions of people around the globe, appears in this report as all but impossible. Jim Skea, co-chair of IPCC Working Group III (on climate change mitigation), highlights the gravity of our situation in the report's summary: "Limiting warming to 1.5°C is possible within the laws of chemistry and physics but doing so would require unprecedented changes" (Intergovernmental Panel 2018). Similarly dire framing appears throughout both the executive summary and the many hundreds of pages of the report itself. And that was in 2018. Not only have the "unprecedented changes" called for in that report not occurred, but two of the world's largest contributors to climate catastrophe—the United States and China—have increased emissions in the past year (UN Environment Programme 2019). As I conclude this essay in November 2019, the IPCC has recently released two further reports: one on the impacts of climate change on the ocean and cryosphere and one on its effects on land around the world. Both are catastrophic, so I stay only a moment with the latter. It is a representative anecdote for our moment.

"Climate Change and Land" lays out an array of possible mitigation strategies (from changing diets to large-scale shifts in land use and economic patterns) (Intergovernmental Panel 2019). It highlights that useful action in the near term *remains possible*. The report's undertones, however, are consistently catastrophic. Acknowledging that temperatures over land have already risen 1.41°C over pre-industrial levels, the IPCC seems to have revised its orientation from a preferred limit of 1.5°C to the less ambitious (though likely still unachievable) goal of "restrict[ing] warming to '*well-below*' 2°C" (1-3 and passim).[9] Here, "well below" is set off in the inverted commas of skepticism. The goal of 1.5°C has all but disappeared from current climate change discourse, replaced by 2°C (hopefully below, but with decreasing confidence). This latter number, which many regard as itself unduly optimistic (given feedback loops like, for instance, virtually unstoppable permafrost melting and Arctic sea ice loss), is all but synonymous with widespread social decay and collapse.[10] And indeed, though underscoring that real possibility remains, the "Climate Change and Land" report is bearish on our prospects for avoiding dramatic negative outcomes: "*Confidence* is *very high* that the window of opportunity, the period when significant change can be made, for limiting climate change within tolerable boundaries is rapidly narrowing" (1-4). We are, in other words, approaching the end of that period within which we might avert many of the anticipated catastrophic impacts of climate change on large-scale human social organization.

In 2018, we were aiming still at 1.5°C. As I finish this essay in 2019, we are mostly aiming to stay below 2°C, and even the "well below" is falling away. Indeed, the United Nations' "Emissions Gap Report" of 2019 leads with the observation that "to get in line with the Paris Agreement, emissions must drop 7.6 per cent per year from 2020 to 2030 for the 1.5°C goal and 2.7 per cent per year for the 2°C goal," and acknowledges that "the size of these annual cuts may seem shocking" and "they may also seem impossible, at least for next year" (UN Environment Programme 2019, xiii). We are, in other words, neither on a path to effectively mitigating climate catastrophe nor, for the most part, even cognitively or emotionally well equipped to imagine such a path. Much of the rest of the report assumes 3°C as a horizon for the twenty-first century. What will we be hoping for when this essay goes to print, in early 2022? Without going further into the many specifics of our climate catastrophe, suffice to say that humans' future as a species organized in large-scale, complex societies is not looking promising.[11]

And yet, October 2018 saw a flood of efforts at optimism, hot on the heels of the direst report of the IPCC to date. Each bleak news moment since has done the same. Efforts not to have to think about climate catastrophe and the accompanying possibility of large-scale social breakdown, of "unprecedented changes" that are reactive rather than proactive, have along the way become increasingly detached from reality. See, for instance, the bright-eyed remonstrations of Christopher Smith et al. in *Nature Communications*: "Current fossil fuel infrastructure does not yet commit us to 1.5°C warming" (2019). Unfortunately, Smith et al.'s wan hope would have required immediate cessation of all fossil fuel–based new production (dear reader: new production did not cease). And their model offered only a 64 percent probability of maintaining temperature below catastrophic levels as reward for that politically implausible undertaking, while also excluding the virtually certain (though as yet largely unrealized at their time of writing) contributions to warming due to permafrost melting and forest dieback. Even as that *Nature Communications* study came out, so too did reports that Arctic permafrost had seen a 0.3°C temperature rise in the last ten years alone (Biskaborn et al. 2019).

Noble as the effort to salvage a certain kind of climate hope may be, it is representative of the self-disabling intellectual contortions required—and undertaken often by exceptionally smart people—to imagine ourselves to be doing much better than in fact we are. Such effortful, defensive optimism is not unlike the work of those who try, in a United States structured constitutively by racist gun violence, to introduce bans on some optional rifle accessories (bump stocks, for instance). The flowing together of public energy for movements to decrease gun violence without fundamentally altering the constitutional landscape (the youth-led March for Our Lives, for example) with unfounded climate optimism is noteworthy. As Dunbar-Ortiz (2018) has shown, the Second Amendment presents a hard limit on the amelioration of gun violence—the US polity is rooted in the trope, understood from the get-go in racist terms, of a non-defensive gun. While it may well be possible to cut down on the comparatively very low casualties of mass shootings, just as it may well be possible to modestly reduce fossil fuel emissions, these are anti-radical aims. Their proponents assume the continuation of the very system that massively overshadows any hoped-for effectuation of those aims, which consume massive amounts of public attention and emotional energy but amount to a sort of running in place. There are times for hopeful efforts at small-scale reform, of course, but not all economies of attention are equally propitious for meliorist optimism.

Still, trying to believe in a future that redeems the ruins of the present is not without virtues. The present essay is in its way such an effort. We need to believe that we can do *something*. The problem is that when we imagine positive outcomes of present action that misalign with the realistic possible trajectories of the past into our contiguous future, we disable our own capacity for effective action. And in the same stroke, we diminish our ability to prepare for futures marked by radical change that exceeds our intentions in various directions. Believing ourselves to be more capable than our structuring conditions allow for (constitutional and environmental feedback loops alike) prompts a sort of frenetic inactivity. Our *special* concern about mass shootings, like our more and less obvious forms of hopeful climate denialism, is a disavowal of real responsibility. Not for nothing does novelist Kim Stanley Robinson imagine a future historian describing our era as "the Dithering" (2013). We live in the period in which we knew the catastrophic consequences of our lifeways but hesitated decade after decade at the threshold of the radical forms of action that would be necessary to foster different consequences.

When we think of the climate catastrophic future today, and when we think about the roles of gun violence in the ongoing world-making of the United States, *dithering* describes most of what we do with that thinking. I am suggesting that a focus on mass shootings, like an increasingly desperate search for climate optimism, is effectively a form of dithering. In some ways, at least at the level of known solutions, addressing climate change is counterintuitively *easier* than addressing gun violence. We have a pretty good idea of what it would take to radically reduce carbon emissions, though little or no political will to take the necessary steps. By contrast, our species has *very little idea* of how to actually build political communities not founded and maintained in violence. A cultural obsession with the spectacle of "mass shootings" is, in effect, a disavowal of responsibility for the extent to which gun violence is written into the constitution of American life. Taking responsibility for our climate emergency suggests a different understanding of world-making violence than we often maintain. And such responsibility models a more potentially effective approach to gun violence than that taken by well-meaning meliorism focused on spectacular moments of gun violence. Paired with rhetorical education, I am suggesting, knowing and owning our own violences may be a way of making more meaningfully democratic political community.

Responsibility, in general, starts with honesty about our ability to negotiate constraints. In a vein similar to Robinson's work, Vollman's *Carbon Ideologies* sets out from a realistic acceptance that radical climate change is locked in. We *will* live in a hotter, darker world, or our descendants will, and we in the present bear responsibility for that. In such a world, the violence that forms all societies will be closer to hand. Vollman, seeking if not forgiveness then at least understanding of our current dithering from inhabitants of a difficult future we have failed to avert, writes:

> Now that we are all gone, someone from the future is turning this book's brittle yellow pages. Unimpressed with what I have written so far, he wishes to know why I didn't do more, because when I was alive there were elephants and honeybees; in the Persian Gulf people survived the summers without protective suits; the Arctic permafrost had only begun to sizzle out methane; San Francisco towered above water, and there were

still even Marshall Islands; Japan was barely radioactive, Africa not entirely desertified. (2018, 12–13)

Vollman writes to a future that will, at best, *understand* our present dithering. To inhabitants of such a future, living lives far harder than those of most present-day readers of this essay, our dithering will be the source of their darkness. For Vollman, that future is the unavoidable outcome of our equally (almost) unavoidable dithering. The point, of course, is not that Vollman knows precisely what the future will bring. No one does. Rather, it is that extrapolating realistically forward from our present circumstances suggests a future whose forgiveness we might wish. We might even reasonably hope for such forgiveness, given that we are far more stuck in a heating trajectory than we often prefer to believe.

This essay does not exactly urge that a reader assume the unavoidability of Vollman's hotter, darker future, though. My aim here is only to think our present through the lens of that future's *plausibility*, its realistic possibility. We need to confront a very possible future in which large-scale social systems (with their concomitant violences, from the interpersonal to the structural to the ecological, and distributions of awareness of those structuring violences) will have broken down and been replaced by smaller-scale societies—with their own violences. As sustainability management scholar Jem Bendell notes in a meticulously sourced, now widely circulating repudiation of his own successful career, "The field of climate adaptation is oriented around ways to maintain our current societies as they face manageable climactic perturbations," but what all the available data suggests is that adaptation needs to take "as its starting point the inevitability of social collapse" (2018, 5). We do not know where we, collectively, are heading, but it seems likely to be very bad—and significantly worse than the present for most people pretty soon.

Bendell may be right or wrong about the *inevitability* of social collapse. Its plausibility, however, is beyond argument for anyone who acknowledges the realistically possible social impacts of a climate emergency that threatens pandemics, unresolved "natural" disasters of fire and flood, disrupted power grids and supply chains, and diminishing food security for billions worldwide.[12] Living with less, fighting for survival and over more limited resources than we currently enjoy, squander, and transform into our own undoing, the inhabitants of our ruins might well be hoped to understand why we did not change now, though perhaps not to forgive us for our dithering. In the visions of a hotter, darker future offered by Bendell and Vollman (and increasingly many sober climate scientists), direct participation in world-making violence is nearly inescapable.[13] In smaller societies operating with limited resources, it is all but impossible to imagine policing and military actions as having nothing to do with one's own life. The state monopoly on violence, always more nominal than actual, recedes in such a future.

PREPARATION FOR VIOLENCE AND RHETORICAL EDUCATION

So, how do you prepare for a future that will be very different from the present? It matters quite a bit *what* will be different. One increasingly common vision of the future is that suggested by "preppers," who have in the space of ten or fifteen years gone from lunatic fringe Ted Kaczynski throwbacks to television stars to the very wealthy and even your neighbors.[14] Prepper stances on violences and the future are instructive. For many preppers' visions of the hotter, darker future, guns are especially important—a personal capacity for violence is central to preparation for self-sufficiency under conditions of radical uncertainty. "Better stock up on ammo" is accordingly, among preppers, a common enough sentiment to be both deadly serious and periodically self-ironized. On the Reddit forum r/Preppers, for instance, a search in any given month will turn up multiple hits for people asking about ammunition prices, sharing favorite websites and apps for buying ammo, and urging one another to Buy Now!

User dankpickle01 begins one representative thread in April 2019 by urging, "Now is the time you should be stacking this stuff knee high . . . If you don't already have a nice inventory, now is the time to buy cheap and stack deep" (dankpickle01 et al. 2019).[15] Guns here, of course, appear as *defensive* responses to extraordinary circumstances. As another user, Dasneal, responds in the thread, having more guns and ammo than one could realistically ever need is—for both training and catastrophe purposes—"a reasonable approach to take for defensive prepping." Other users on this thread, however, question whether preparing for violence is really more useful than building community. Reasoning that "humans by nature are a communal species," ConstipatedUnicorn argues that it is better to "work with [one's] neighbors to help build a solid foundation of people who, even in the event of needing to bug in [i.e., shelter in place, as opposed to 'bugging out'], can rely on one another for supplies, security and an overall community." These posts offer a representative, if swift, overview of the gamut run by "preppers." Even while many preppers are basically decent people, concerned with community building in and for uncertain times, the trope of the "defensive gun" recurs often as a foundation for discussion. Here as elsewhere in US society, gun violence is conceived of in the anticipatorily justified terms of "defense" and "security." Prepping, rather than being somehow outside the norms of general society, is in this regard at least cleanly within the endoxic space demarcated by the constitutional trope of a defensive gun.

So what is it, exactly, that preppers are preparing for? What is "very different" about the futures toward which prepping orients? Broadly speaking, at stake are various ends of a (nominal) state monopoly on violence, the end of large-scale social order.[16] Acronymized as SHTF, the ubiquitous (among preppers) trope "shit hits the fan" names a dizzying array of possible negative futures: from the astronomically unlikely (sudden-onset totalitarian rule) or virtually impossible (zombie apocalypse) to the entirely plausible (large-scale pandemic and accompanying social disarray) to the historically almost certain (periods of social unrest in which the world-making character of violence is redistributed, no longer outsourced to the state with recurrent individual interruptions).[17] Rather than writing off such dark visions as mere apocalyptic fantasy, the anxieties of loser sons and white supremacists (though, as Casey Kelly demonstrates in *Apocalypse Man* [2020], there's plenty of both in the mix), it's worth underlining again that these visions have some basis in reality.

Our climate emergency *does* threaten broad-spectrum social instability or collapse, as even such stolid institutions as the US military establishment now freely recognize.[18] And make no mistake: social collapse of a complex society *entails* redistribution of the means and enactments of violence. Violence, as Walter Benjamin observed, is both the making and unmaking of the state (1986). Taking responsibility for a world of at least partially or temporarily unmade states and more widely distributed violence while refusing our own psychic and social organization along the racist, genocidal lines associated with the trope of the defensive gun starts by owning our own capacities for (gun) violence as aggression. We owe it to our future and present selves alike to know that our gun violence, while it may indeed be world-making, cannot be "defensive" in a strong or exculpatory sense. There is something to be said for learning to shoot a gun and for knowing that, in so doing, one is preparing for fundamentally impermissible violence against other people on behalf of a world-making one prefers. And there is something to be said, by contrast with normative attitudes toward state violence as acceptable and the doxa of "defensive prepping" alike, for regarding such learning as always and intrinsically a moral failure—even if it might not always be a terrible idea.

Assuming a future of less stably organized violence in which one is oneself prepared to do violence, even if only as a thought experiment about the social meanings of climate change, it is not immediately obvious that rhetorical education must be conserved.[19] Is there a role for rhetorical education in preparing for worlds after warming? After all, rhetoric is often contrasted with violence: the open hand as against the closed fist relies rather a lot on the outsourcing of the closed fist to violent agents of the state. We rhetoricians have a number of well-worn stories about rhetoric and democratic societies; the idea that rhetoric and democracy fit tongue and groove is one of our oldest conceits about either.[20] What use for rhetorical education, then, in preparing future worlds ordered by the disorder of institutional decay and social break-down, in the capitalist ruins of democracy? Hell, what real use for rhetorical education in our own (or any other) wildly undemocratic, even anti-democratic present? Such pessimistic questions presuppose the loss of constituted democracies that have always been more fantastically than actually stable. We kid ourselves if we think we have lost democracy, which we never had in the first place; rhetorical education is, now as ever, a tool for increasing access to voice in a spirit of democratic hope. Or, at least, it *can be* such a tool.[21]

It is not for nothing that our oldest rhetorical models derive from martial cultures with mixed records as regards rule of law and state form (no less so in the Warring States period of Guiguzi than during the Peloponnesian War that shaped Isocrates' vision of the ends and means of rhetorical education). Though contemporary rhetoricians are entranced by the image of rhetoric's persuasion (or invitation) as an open hand rather than the closed fist of violence, rhetoric and violence name interlocking forces. As Megan Foley notes, "The ethical antithesis between persuasion and violence hinges on the question of necessity. Acts done out of necessity, Aristotle writes, are beyond the scope of ethics—only voluntary acts are praised or blamed" (2013, 192). We are able to suppose rhetoric to exist within the domain of ethics because we stipulate its distinctness from necessity. Necessity here resonates with a framing of gun violence as "defensive" rather than "aggressive," of *some* violence as not really our responsibility. As so often, matters are murkier than that.

Rhetorical education emerged at sites not merely of some direct democracy (Attic Greece) or influential advisors to rulers (pre-Qin China), but also of widespread war.[22] Rhetorical education is a form of sense-making, constraint-negotiation on behalf of fuller political community, developed in and for contexts of frequent violence. The trouble with seeing persuasion and violence as cleanly separate entities is, as Foley argues elsewhere, that "the rhetorical tradition is built upon a simultaneous denial and retention of violence," with the result that, "unable to admit rhetoric's complicity with violence but equally unable to give it up, violence remains as the disavowed center of rhetoric's definition" (2012, 175). Believing necessity to free us from blame, as in the trope of the defensive gun, we at once disavow rhetoric's violence and reinscribe that violence as the force of persuasion. We do better, then, not to disavow but rather to consciously negotiate the violences at the heart of rhetoric. For Foley, this is a matter of apprehending rhetoric's "interior threshold that renders [persuasion and force] simultaneously distinct and distinguishable from one another" (180). On this reading, the virtue of rhetorical education lies precisely in the possibility of *knowing* and still *refusing* violence at the heart of rhetoric. Rhetorical education offers us a way of knowing, owning, and abjuring our own violences. In urging rhetorical education as a complement to violence, I am offering not a solution to (gun or any other) violence, but rather a way of living better with the—habitually disavowed, but strictly unavoidable—fact of violence as an element of human world-making.

The tense vibration of persuasion and violence at the heart of rhetorical education is nicely adumbrated in Cheryl Glenn's "Rhetorical Education in America." For Glenn, rhetorical education *both* "inscribes the relations of language and power at a particular moment" (2009, x), that is, upholds the doxastic violences of a given political community, *and* "enable[s] students to govern knowledgeably and virtuously both their own households and the commonwealth" (vii). The promise of rhetorical education is not only to grant more of us access to better positions along rhetorical gradients, but also to enable us all to negotiate the constraints of cultures we at once inherit and pass on—with an anticipatory eye to ever fuller, more epistemically (and so materially) equal, less violent political communities. John Duffy's recent *Provocations of Virtue* is one of the finer works to consider this promise at the nexus of rhetorical theory and classroom practice. His vision of a helplessly ethically oriented rhetorical education aligns with Glenn's, Foley's, and my own, offering an extensive framework for cashing out rhetoric's troubled virtues in teaching contexts. It is in "the ordinary work of teaching students to frame their claims truthfully, demonstrate accountability in supporting those claims with evidence, and consider opposing arguments thoughtfully, fairly, and fearlessly" (2019, 145), as Duffy has it, that rhetorical education's virtues take root. Such virtues are a necessary complement to knowing and owning our violence. They are what allow us to abjure without disavowing what we *are*, and so perhaps to become more than merely violent.

Seen in this light, rhetorical education is a social tool for both conservation and invention.[23] It is, as I argue throughout *The Ethical Fantasy of Rhetorical Theory*, a way of being troubled by and actively negotiating the inequalities and violences of our becoming together in symbols. Rhetorical theory and education, in my framing there, is "*an iterative bet that a self-conscious, quasisystematic articulation of enabling constraints*—something like foundations to be taught—*better enables us and any who become our students to negotiate constraint*" (2018, 278). The aim of rhetorical education is to increase the troubled freedom of its students. Increasing that freedom entails serious and ongoing negotiation of our violence, including both a core violence at the heart of rhetoric and the constituted violences at the heart of the political communities we maintain. Taking full responsibility for violence means surrendering the trope of the defensive gun. And it means refusing ourselves the substitutive satisfaction of being *especially* concerned by violent spectacles such as mass shootings. Substantive responsibility calls upon us to focus attention especially on the core structures that constrain our possibilities of democratic becoming. If we can imagine taking responsibility for our own world-making violences in the hotter, darker future we have already prepared, can we afford anything less in the violent maelstrom of the present?

NOTES

1. An "end-of-the-world" gun presumes the world has not yet ended, but which world? Survivability in this one is deeply raced, gendered, classed, and so on. Correcting a media narrative of misogyny within the Black Panther Party, for instance, Linda Lumsden (2009) highlights the centrality of guns to the BPP's development of a Black feminist vision of agency—the point was *control of* means of violence that were going to be used by *somebody* no matter what. Merits of violent/nonviolent approaches to social change are of course contested, but see August Nimtz's important "Violence and/or Nonviolence in the Success of the Civil Rights Movement" (2016), which convincingly establishes the role of both violence and nonviolence in forcing change. At the same time, exactly *how* white a "defensive gun" may be is detailed throughout Dunbar-Ortiz's *Loaded* (2018). See also Casey Kelly's *Apocalypse Man*. Kelly notes of the "open carry" movement that "the public display of firearms militarizes public space and normalizes the threat of violence as a substitute for civic norms, all to procure for white men an illusory sense of self-mastery and coherence" (2020, 129).

2. As of early December 2019, of 36,168 recorded gun deaths and 27,216 reported gun injuries in the United States (of which roughly two-thirds were suicides), a scant 603 deaths and 1,673 injuries are attributable to mass shootings or mass murders (in the expansive definitions used by the Gun Violence Archive [2019]). These 1.7 and 6.1 percent of gun deaths and injuries, respectively, are far from

trivial for anyone touched by those shootings, and there is no denying the psychological impact of mass-mediated vicarious witnessing. Still: within the vast burning forest of gun-enabled violence and self-harm in the United States, mass shootings are brightly crowning individual trees.

3. The security-promising, US-prosecuted "war on terror," in addition to costing at least $6.4 trillion over the past eighteen years, has directly killed more than 800,000 people, including hundreds of thousands of civilian noncombatants (Crawford and Lutz 2019). Rosa Eberly, especially in chapter 2 of her monumental *Towers of Rhetoric* (2018), makes the link between the "defensive" violence of endless war and the violence of men killing women, cops killing poor people and people of color, and yes, also mass shooters.

4. Strictly speaking, this is not quite true. Swords purpose-made for killing were developed at around the same time, in the Western world at least, as nomadic peoples were settling into agricultural habits defined by private property. Equally, plenty of real guns are made explicitly as toys: finnicky tools for hobbyists who shoot at paper or spinning metal targets and never intend to shoot at anything else. Hyperbole notwithstanding, the general principle holds.

5. Recognition of the raced and racializing character of "defensive" violence in the ongoing formation of an American state is a driving force in the police and prison abolition movement. See, for instance, Davis 2005 or Olson 2004.

6. Recall Walter Benjamin's articulation of the tension between violence that founds and violence that maintains the state: "All law-preserving violence, in its duration, indirectly weakens the lawmaking violence it represents, by suppressing hostile counterviolence" (1986, 251). On the consequences of this insight for law in general, consider James Martel's vision of a Benjaminian *faithless leap* through and beyond the violence of states (2014). See also Eli Friedlander's "Assuming Violence" (2015) for interpretive consequences of various possible translations of *Gewalt* and understandings of *Kritik* in this crucial essay of Benjamin's.

7. As Vollman puts his unhappily realistic and at times hopeful, but withal both apologetic and sympathetic vision, "Well, in the end I did nothing just the same, and the same went for most everyone I knew. This book may help you in the hot dark future to understand why" (2018, 13). In the time since this essay was completed, matters have significantly worsened—and that worsening, and with it the darkness and heat of our future—has been captured in a number of further IPCC reports.

8. I devote significant attention to this practice in a recent essay titled "Beginning Again" (2020).

9. This IPCC report marks the difference between pre-industrial and contemporary temperatures by comparing the over-land average of 1881–1900 with that of 1999–2018 (Intergovernmental Panel 2019).

10. On the extreme risk associated with these feedback loops and tipping points, see Lenton et al. 2019.

11. A recent quantitative modeling study in the *Nature* journal *Scientific Reports* suggests a less than 10 percent probability—in the optimistic scenario—of avoiding large-scale civilizational collapse in the relatively near term (Bologna and Aquino 2020).

12. Consider the pictures painted by David Wallace-Wells 2019 and Dahr Jamail 2019. These, in turn, do no more than touch on the devastating impacts of human activity in general and anthropogenic climate change in particular on nonhuman species (with feedback loops for human life as well). See especially Kolbert 2014.

13. Published in no less an organ than *BioScience* and signed by over 11,000 scientists, the "World Scientists' Warning of a Climate Emergency" could hardly sound the klaxon louder (Ripple et al. 2019). Citing a "moral obligation to clearly warn humanity of any catastrophic threat" (1), William Ripple et al. note that "despite

40 years of global climate negotiations . . . we have generally conducted business as usual and have largely failed to address this predicament" (1–2). The result is that "the climate crisis has arrived and is accelerating faster than most scientists expected" and "is more severe than anticipated, threatening natural ecosystems and the future of humanity" (2).

14. On the development of an industry (both culture and cottage) around those who prepare for catastrophe and on the ways in which "apocalyptic gloom sells," see Gwendolyn Foster's *Hoarders, Doomsday Preppers, and the Culture of Apocalypse* (2014, 2). Foster remains too attached, though, to the notion that violence *in* the United States *returns from abroad*, as though violent, racist world-making were not part and parcel of the domestic American experiment. Meanwhile, CNN and Bloomberg run gushing yearly roundups of luxury bunkers, and a de-identified Google search for "1% bunkers" turns up hundreds of breathless articles about how *terrific* the conditions available to discerning doomsday preppers have become these days. For one among many essays on the phenomenon, see "Who Gets to Survive Climate Change?" (Penny 2019). For more relatable or everyday takes on prepping, see for instance Stacy Murison's beautiful essay "Pinterest Prepping" (2018) and Alan Feuer's "The Preppers Next Door" (2013).

15. This poster, dankpickle01, responds to others suggesting that prices have been lower in the past and easily could be again: "All I'm trying to say is you will probably not be able to find prices this low on guns and ammo ever again. Buy now, as inflation and political climate increases the cost of ammo" (dankpickle01 et al. 2019).

16. Jodi Dean's "Communism or Neofeudalism" (2020) offers a darker still view of how the *maintenance* of state forms and social order, and corresponding violences, might play out in coming years.

17. On this last, see especially Walter Scheidel's *The Great Leveler* (2017). His sanguinity about social order going forward, however, borders on the absurd. It is more than a little noteworthy that this exceptional history of violence, though published in 2017, has nothing to say about climate change in the present.

18. See, e.g., "Implications of Climate Change for the US Army" (United States Army War College 2019). The document has an unusual (though par for the course in the Trump era) circulation history, first appearing in and then disappearing from the digital archives of the US Army War College in July 2019. It is housed online by the Center for Climate and Security, a deeply defense establishment–connected policy shop.

19. Bendell's deep adaptation may be seen as such a thought experiment. It is, as he puts it in a subsequent work, meant to "provide a way for people to have generative conversations about what to do, and what to stop doing, in light of our predicament . . . based on the assumption that a breakdown or collapse in our society is likely, inevitable, or unfolding" (2019, 8). I find deep adaptation a helpful framework on the whole, but am troubled by its frequent presumption that climate collapse *can* proceed without violence.

20. For one example among hundreds, perhaps thousands, see George Kennedy's introduction to his translation of Aristotle's *Rhetoric* (2007).

21. In so saying, I am somewhat at odds with Susan Miller's *Trust in Texts* (2007), which offers a realistic—but I think a step too pessimistic—reappraisal of standard accounts, treating rhetorical education as merely training in the systems of trust-making associated with privileged elites.

22. On this historical nexus of the West and China, not yet widely apprehended by Western rhetoricians, see especially You 2010 and Wu 2016.

23. For an especially clear articulation of rhetorical education's conservational uses under catastrophic conditions, see Cryer 2018.

REFERENCES

Allen, Ira J. 2018. *The Ethical Fantasy of Rhetorical Theory*. Pittsburgh: University of Pittsburgh Press.

Allen, Ira J. 2020. "Beginning Again: *Jericho, Revolution*, and Catastrophic Originalism." In *Representations of Political Resistance and Emancipation in Science Fiction*, edited by Judith Grant and Sean Parson, 61–77. Lanham, MD: Lexington.

Bendell, Jem. 2018. "Deep Adaptation: A Map for Navigating Climate Tragedy." *IFLAS Occasional Paper 2*, 27 July.

Bendell, Jem. 2019. "Because It's Not a Drill: Technologies for Deep Adaptation to Climate Chaos." *Connect University Conference on Climate Change*, May 13. DG Connect: European Commission, Brussels, Belgium.

Benjamin, Walter. 1986. "Critique of Violence." In *Reflections: Essays, Aphorisms, Autobiographical Writings*, translated by Edmund Jephcott, 277–300. New York: Schocken.

Biskaborn, Boris K., et al. 2019. "Permafrost Is Warming at a Global Scale." *Nature Communications* 10 (264): n.p. doi: 10.1038/s41467-018-08240-4.

Bologna, Mauro, and Gerardo Aquino. 2020. "Deforestation and World Population Sustainability: A Quantitative Analysis." *Scientific Reports* 10 (7631): n.p. doi: 10.1038/s41598-020-63657-6.

Crawford, Neta, and Catherine Lutz. 2019. "Human Cost of Post-9/11 Wars: Direct War Deaths in Major War Zones, Afghanistan and Pakistan (October 2001–October 2019); Iraq (March 2003–October 2019); Syria (September 2014–October 2019); Yemen (October 2002–October 2019); and Other." *Costs of War: Watson Institute, Brown University*, November 13.

Cryer, Daniel A. 2018. "Withdrawal without Retreat: Responsible Conservation in a Doomed Age." *Rhetoric Society Quarterly* 48 (5): 459–78.

dankpickle01 et al. 2019. "Now Is the Time US Preppers for Guns and Ammo." In r/Preppers. Reddit, April 5. https://www.reddit.com/r/preppers/comments/b9u6xs/now_is_the_time_us_preppers_for_guns_and_ammo/.

Davis, Angela. 2005. *Abolition Democracy: Beyond Empire, Prisons, and Torture*. New York: Seven Stories.

Dean, Jodi. 2020. "Communism or Neofeudalism." *New Political Science* 42 (20): 1–17.

Duffy, John. 2019. *Provocations of Virtue: Rhetoric, Ethics, and the Teaching of Writing*. Logan: Utah State University Press.

Dunbar-Ortiz, Roxanne. 2018. *Loaded: A Disarming History of the Second Amendment*. San Francisco: City Light Books.

Eberly, Rosa. 2018. *Towers of Rhetoric: Memory and Reinvention*. Intermezzo/Enculturation.

Feuer, Alan. 2013. "The Preppers Next Door." *New York Times*, January 26.

Foley, Megan. 2012. "*Peitho* and *Bia*: The Force of Language." *symplokē* 20 (1–2): 173–81.

Foley, Megan. 2013. "Of Violence and Rhetoric: An Ethical Aporia." *Quarterly Journal of Speech* 99 (2): 191–99.

Foster, Gwendolyn Audrey. 2014. *Hoarders, Doomsday Preppers, and the Culture of Apocalypse*. New York: Palgrave.

Friedlander, Eli. 2015. "Assuming Violence: A Commentary on Walter Benjamin's 'Critique of Violence.'" *boundary 2* 42 (4): 159–85.

Glenn, Cheryl. 2009. "Rhetorical Education in America (A Broad Stroke Introduction)." In *Rhetorical Education in America*, edited by Cheryl Glenn, Margaret M. Lyday, and Wendy B. Sharer, vii–xvi. Tuscaloosa: University of Alabama Press.

Gun Violence Archive. 2019. *Gun Violence Archive 2019*.

Intergovernmental Panel on Climate Change. 2018. "Summary for Policymakers of IPCC Special Report on Global Warming of 1.5°C Approved by Governments." *IPCC*, October 8.

Intergovernmental Panel on Climate Change. 2019. "Climate Change and Land." *IPCC*, August 7.

Jamail, Dahr. 2019. *The End of Ice: Bearing Witness and Finding Meaning in the Path of Climate Disruption.* New York: New Press.

Kelly, Casey Ryan. 2020. *Apocalypse Man: The Death Drive and the Rhetoric of White Masculine Victimhood.* Columbus: Ohio State University Press.

Kennedy, George A. 1997. Introduction to *On Rhetoric: A Theory of Civic Discourse,* by Aristotle, translated by George A. Kennedy, 1–25. New York: Oxford University Press.

Kolbert, Elizabeth. 2014. *The Sixth Extinction: An Unnatural History.* New York: Henry Holt.

Lenton, Timothy, et al. 2019. "Climate Tipping Points—Too Risky to Bet Against." *Nature* 575:592–95.

Lumsden, Linda. 2009. "Good Mothers with Guns: Framing Black Womanhood in the *Black Panther,* 1960–1980." *Journalism & Mass Communication Quarterly* 86 (4): 900–922.

Martel, James. 2014. *The One and Only Law: Walter Benjamin and the Second Commandment.* Ann Arbor: University of Michigan Press.

Miller, Susan. 2007. *Trust in Texts: A Different History of Rhetoric.* Carbondale: Southern Illinois University Press.

Murison, Stacy. 2018. "Pinterest Prepping." *Rumpus,* July 4.

Nimtz, August H. 2016. "Violence and/or Nonviolence in the Success of the Civil Rights Movement: The Malcolm X–Martin Luther King, Jr. Nexus." *New Political Science* 38 (1): 1–22.

Olson, Joel. 2004. *The Abolition of White Democracy.* Minneapolis: University of Minnesota Press.

Penny, Eleanor. 2019. "Who Gets to Survive Climate Change?" *New Statesman America,* March 19, 2019 (updated July 25, 2021).

Ripple, William J., et al. 2019. "World Scientists' Warning of a Climate Emergency," *BioScience,* November 5.

Robinson, Kim Stanley. 2013. *2312.* London: Orbit.

Scheidel, Walter. 2017. *The Great Leveler: Violence and the History of Inequality from the Stone Age to the Twenty-First Century.* Princeton: Princeton University Press.

Smith, Christopher J., et al. 2019. "Current Fossil Fuel Infrastructure Does Not Yet Commit Us to 1.5 C Warming." *Nature Communications* 10 (101): n.p. doi: 10.1038/s41467-018-07999.

UN Environment Programme. November 26, 2019. "Emissions Gap Report 2019." *UN Environment Programme.*

United States Army War College. 2019. "Implications of Climate Change for the US Army." Accessed at Center for Climate and Security, "UPDATE: Chronology of US Military Statements and Actions on Climate Change and Security: Jan 2017–Oct 2019."

Vollman, William T. 2018. *No Immediate Danger.* Vol. 1 of *Carbon Ideologies.* New York: Viking.

Wallace-Wells, David. 2019. *The Uninhabitable Earth: Life After Warming.* New York: Penguin.

Wu, Hui, trans. and ed. 2016. *Guiguzi, China's First Treatise on Rhetoric.* Carbondale: Southern Illinois University Press.

You, Xiaoye. 2010. "Building Empire through Argumentation: Debating Salt and Iron in Western Han China." *College English* 72 (4): 467–84.

14

TALKING TOGETHER ABOUT GUNS
TTAG and Sustainable Publics

Peter D. Buck, Bradley A. Serber, and Rosa A. Eberly

During the 2016–2017 academic year, a small group of Penn State–University Park faculty collaborated to bring programming about the US gun violence epidemic to campus and much of central and northern Pennsylvania. At the time, Peter Buck was the academic programs manager for Penn State's Sustainability Institute, Rosa Eberly was an associate professor in communication arts and sciences and English and the incoming director of Penn State's intercollege minor in civic and community engagement (CIVCM), and Brad Serber, who was one of Eberly's former doctoral advisees, was a postdoc in communication arts and sciences as well as the assistant director for that minor. Buck and his family have been friends with Eberly for about thirty years. The goal of their series, Talking Together about Guns (TTAG), was to generate conversations across differences, particularly given how politicians, law enforcement officials, activists, lobbyists, and citizens regularly assume the intractability of gun debates in the United States (see also Serber's chapter 8 in this volume). This chapter describes the thinking behind the eleven events that comprised TTAG and sketches its possible legacy. The authors believe TTAG serves as a potential model for grassroots collaboration among faculty, students, staff, and local organizations to address issues of public concern (see also Rood's chapter 6 in this volume). What follows is a far-ranging conversational representation from February 1, 2019, of their thoughts on what compelled them to create TTAG and what they hope it can do for our public(s)—that is, for people who share direct or indirect consequences of gun violence. Following the dialogue, the chapter concludes with the authors' recommendations for those who wish to continue talking together about guns and other contentious public problems on their campuses.

https://doi.org/10.7330/9781646422159.c014

PETER BUCK: It's been a little while since we worked on Talking Together about Guns, and so much has happened since we concluded that program. Whether it's related to gun violence, structural racism, environmental degradation, or political rancor, there's so much. One week ago, there was a mass shooting in State College (Pallotto and Paez 2019), just a few miles from Penn State's main campus, where we've worked together. And, in my mind, Talking Together about Guns was, at its heart, a way for people to confront, talk, and listen about some of the most entrenched beliefs we have in the United States. So, I thought it would be good to talk about that program, both root and shoot. Sound good to you?

ROSA EBERLY: Sounds good.

BRAD SERBER: Sounds good to me, too.

PB: Can I say something about this first? We all agree that scholars today have a role to play in civil society and democracy. For us, the work of democracy and work in public or with publics, as Dewey (1927) might say, isn't abstract. It's real. We are approaching the work of civic life in the spirit of Frank Fischer, as—we hope—humble participants in the endeavor of advancing well-informed and genuine shared decision-making.[1] Sound okay?

RE: Yes. I think about this work as a kind of democratic capacity-building, what Jeremy Cohen and I wrote about in *A Laboratory for Public Scholarship and Democracy* (Eberly and Cohen 2006).

PB: Rosa, why don't you tell us about the beginnings of TTAG?

RE: I had just had a commentary published in the *Chronicle of Higher Education* on the ominous date that the Texas legislature was going to pass their campus carry law (Eberly 2016b). It was fifty years to the day after Charles Whitman murdered fourteen people and injured thirty more from the Tower at the University of Texas at Austin. Peter, you asked me to have lunch with our colleague Jill Wood because you wanted to get people talking about guns and gun violence. Jill was particularly concerned about the connection between gun availability and domestic violence. I'm sorry, I don't remember which mass shooting had prompted you two to start thinking and talking together.

PB: It was the Umpqua shooting. After Virginia Tech and my own experience with the Hetzel Union Building (HUB) lawn shooting at Penn State in 1996, I felt I had to do something. Just about anything.

RE: Maybe you should say something about that. What prompted you to want to do this?

PB: I guess it was a few things, really. I went to high school with two people who were deeply affected by gun violence, one as the family of a victim and the other as a shooter. My friend and actually my senior prom date was the daughter of a labor rights activist. In 1979, he was supporting Black textile workers in Greensboro, North Carolina. The Ku Klux Klan drove in and shot down five people in plain sight, including my friend's father, Dr. Michael Nathan (Remembrance n.d.). I'll never forget the afternoon we were in class years later, watching a video on hate groups. Footage from that day came on. Can you imagine seeing footage of your father's death . . . while you're in school? Her family is so strong.

I also knew the HUB lawn shooter, Jillian Robbins. Not really well. We were in math class together in high school. I remember her as a quiet and quirky girl who wore flannel shirts. She drew pictures of fairies and robots. After I graduated from high school, I saw her at a restaurant in town where she worked with friends of mine. Then, on the cool, damp morning of September 17, 1996, she hid herself in a cluster of thick shrubs and trees armed with a 7-mm Mauser rifle she'd taken from her dad. She had been an army reservist but was discharged after failing to graduate from high school. When she woke up that day, she decided she couldn't handle her hallucinations and delusions anymore and resolved to die. She shot and killed Penn State student Melanie Spalla, injured student Nick Mensah, and hit some backpacks and buildings. She incapacitated herself when she attacked student Brendon Malovrh with a knife. He disarmed her.

I don't mean to be dramatic, but I had been going to the HUB with a classmate almost every day after my music theory classes early in the semester. And I just wasn't there for whatever reason that day. It left a mark on me to know a shooter and to have had a shooting on the campus where my parents got married, where I spent a lot of my child-hood, and where I was then in college.

From 2016 to 2019, I served as an elected official, too—chair of the Ferguson Township Board of Supervisors—and a staff member at the university. I'm just really worried about how we talk about guns and gun violence and what the incredible number of guns in our nation does to our other rights. Early in 2020, I decided to run for the Pennsylvania House of Representatives. My opponent has an A rating from the NRA, while I am a Moms Demand Action Candidate of Distinction because of my commitment to using the law to create a culture of gun safety.

As you once asked us, Rosa, "What's the space between the First and Second Amendments?"[2] It seems to me that speech has to win. So, after Umpqua and Virginia Tech, I thought that we had to get people to talk about this. Jill and I worked with an intern who looked into models of deliberation and gave us a report that said, "Yeah. We can do this." And your name was in her report because of your years of work.

RE: And you're so shy.

PB: [*Laughs*] That's me. Never pushy either.

RE: Not in the least.

PB: Anyway, that's some of what motivated me to get people talking about guns. What about the two of you? What connections do you have to guns?

RE: My dad was a Marine in World War II and, while he kept an M-1 in the house, I never saw it until after I left for college, after he started going to Marine Corps reunions. What I did see—and did

experience daily growing up—were the consequences of the trauma
he experienced fighting in the South Pacific in the 1940s. But the
UT Tower and Public Memory course is definitely what got me
into doing research about guns, gun violence, and guns as a public
health issue in the mid-1990s. I saw while living on the South Side of
Chicago in the 1980s and in Austin in the 1990s and early 2000s that
gun violence was a very different issue depending on skin color and
neighborhood.

Yet something that happened in my family in 2002—I've not talked
much about this and have not written about it before—made me sure
that I would continue to educate people about the consequences of gun
culture in the United States. A few weeks after I moved back to Pennsylvania from Austin in 2002, my sister called early on a Saturday morning
to tell me that she and her two children were okay, but that her husband, from whom she had recently separated, had shot himself to death
while he was on the phone with her and the kids the night before. All
three of them—my sister and my niece and nephew—pleaded with him
from the other end of the phone line . . . only to hear the blast from a
pistol and then silence. And then the aftermath. As I again recall what
happened, trauma time (Edkins 2003) divides my judgment: observing
an immensely selfish act made possible only by the presence of a gun.
And feeling gratitude that he did not kill my sister and her children, too.

PB: That's awful, Rosa. As a dad and son, that story hits me on both
sides. "The sins of the father," you know? What about you, Brad?

BS: Yes, I can relate to that on both sides as well. It's very hard to think
about. I suppose I come at this from a different perspective. I don't
really have a direct connection to guns. To my knowledge, only two
families that I knew growing up kept guns in their houses. Both
families did lots of hunting, and one of them also had several family
members in the military. One of them is one of my best friends, and
for his bachelor party, he decided that he wanted to have an Alcohol,
Tobacco, and Firearms–themed weekend. That's about as close as I
have ever been to guns.

But I was in fifth grade when the Columbine High School shooting
happened, and that event hit me really hard. I can't remember if we
had regular lockdown drills every year after that, but I do remember
everyone being really scared. I also remember my middle school and
high school implementing lots of new security measures. My classmates and I weren't quite what the March for Our Lives organizers
from Parkland refer to as "the school shooting generation," but we
were precursors to it (Founders of March for Our Lives 2018, 7).

PB: That event is such an interesting hinge in American life. People cite
it as being a wake-up call, something that made us all aware of the
potential of mass shootings, but then nothing happened. Just shock
and horror followed by going about your day. Speaking for myself, I
was tired of that doldrum of political-with-a-small-p action and the do-
nothing rhetoric hindering it in the years since. So, as often happens

with me, I got fed up and needed to just do something about it, even if small. So, Rosa, I turned to you because of your years of work. You brought so much, including Brad. Will the two of you talk about your work before we started?

RE: Well, in 2011, John Gastil was my new department head. He gave me a reason to return to work I had done on a project about the 1966 University of Texas Tower shootings and public memory, a project that I'd set aside in a combination of bewilderment and despair a few years after moving from UT to Penn State. Gastil assigned one of my advisees to be my research assistant during the summer of 2011, and I assigned that research assistant, Sarah Kornfield, now at Hope College, to make a definitive list of all the campus shootings that had happened since 1966. One of the hardest-working people I have ever known, she reluctantly told me partway through the summer that the cataloguing was taking a toll on her wellness. Her reflection was a harbinger of what Brad later called his "dissertation crying log," a catalogue of the news reports that made him cry while writing his dissertation and, insofar as he could identify them, his associated triggers (Serber 2018). Having been away from the topic and the work for a number of years, I had neglected to prepare Sarah for the psychological toll that studying gun violence can take. While that toll is small compared with the traumatizing effects of actual violence, it is real (Pettit 2016). The next summer, I assigned my research assistant and advisee Craig Rood, now at Iowa State, to read what I'd written so far about the 1966 UT Tower shootings and materials from the class I had taught in the Division of Rhetoric and Composition at UT Austin. Craig's dissertation idea came in part out of that reading; if you haven't read Rood, do (Rood 2015, 2019). The next year Brad read the same materials Craig had. Additionally, I had decided to offer a new course, Contemporary US Political Rhetoric, about school shootings, and Brad sat in on and guest-lectured for the course and contributed mightily (Eberly and Serber 2013). Based also on work he had done with Jim Aune and Jen Mercieca during his master's at Texas A&M, Brad's dissertation broadened the scope to what he calls "targeted violence."

PB: Brad, do you want to talk about that?

BS: Sure. I suppose I should lead into that with the story of Jim Aune's memorial. Jim was my master's thesis advisor at Texas A&M and a good friend of Rosa's. Sadly, he committed suicide just a few months after I had left A&M to complete my doctoral work at Penn State. Rosa and I later learned that his suicide happened during the very first meeting of the school shootings class. A few weeks later, she and I traveled together to Texas for his memorial service. Without yet having a term for it, that trip was where some of my earliest thoughts about targeted violence began. On the way to the memorial, I came down with a terrible head cold. My nose would not stop leaking. In the meantime, our eyes would not stop leaking from the grief. Our bodies were rejecting Jim's death. "Leaking, leaking" became our euphemism for the visceral, uncontrollable tears that follow loss and trauma.

En route to College Station, Rosa tried to cheer me up, pointing to a billboard in the distance: "Not just turkey . . . and more!" Struck by the redundancy and awkward syntax, we laughed as a brief respite from all the leaking. It was one of those goofy moments that rhetoric's road trips are known for, and we continued to joke about it from time to time.

PB: Wow. The humor of rhetoricians.

BS: Yep. Anyway, I remember that shortly after I defended my thesis, and just a few months before Aune died, he asked me if I had any thoughts about my dissertation. Having recently seen the film adaptation of Lionel Shriver's *We Need to Talk about Kevin* (2003) and reflecting on the Tucson and Aurora shootings, I told him that I was thinking I might write about school shootings.

I was surprised when he shook his head in disapproval. I never asked why, but he told me that he did not think it was a good idea. Perhaps, just months before the Sandy Hook shooting, Aune had figured that the country was just going through a phase with mass shootings and did not think it would be wise for me to stake my research program on a topic that might not be "sustainable." Perhaps, after directing my master's thesis on the aftermath of the Rwandan genocide, he was trying to protect me from the years of emotional labor that inevitably accompany the study of such graphic violence.

Despite his cryptic warning to me not to write about school shootings for my dissertation, I went to Penn State to work with Rosa in order to do just that—or so I thought. It was during the Q&A session after a panel discussion with her and one of our former students from the school shootings class that I had an epiphany. Our colleague Steve Browne asked the three panelists to reflect on school shootings as a genre. I realized while listening to the student's response to Browne that the events I was interested in studying did not all happen in schools and did not all involve guns. Put simply, I realized then that my dissertation would be about "not just guns . . . and more!"

When I mentioned that I was looking to broaden my dissertation's scope, another colleague, Kirt Wilson, then directed me to Robert Fein, Bryan Vossekuil, and Gwen Holden's National Institute of Justice article about "targeted violence" (1995). When they coined the term, it included a wide variety of crimes, such as stalking, harassment, robberies, assault, and murder. Various US government agencies have since taken up the term to refer to mass homicide attacks in public places where "unsuspecting victims believed themselves to be safe" (Fein, Vossekuil, and Holden 1995, 2). Targeted violence thus encompasses not only school shootings, but also mass shootings in other locations as well as non-shooting attacks like the Boston Marathon bombing, Xinjiang knife attacks in China, and Germanwings plane crash. In response to Browne and Wilson, I argued in my dissertation that widening the genre from school shootings to targeted violence "allows those who study these attacks to see broader patterns across them" and also "allows them to make different claims about why and how targeted violence happens and what, if anything, politicians, law enforcement officials, and citizens can do to prevent" such attacks (Serber 2016, 9).

PB: So, we have personal experiences at our campuses with mass shootings, threats to public discourse, and rhetoric. Why then? I had my own reasons. But Rosa . . . ?

RE: In June 2016, I was nearing the completion of what would become my book *Towers of Rhetoric* (2018), and I was, frankly, hoping that I might finally put the topic of gun violence behind me as a scholarly focus. Then-editor Susan Jarratt invited me to do a "Counterpoint" essay for *Rhetoric Society Quarterly,* and I could not ignore that kind of platform to talk about gun violence (Eberly 2016a). I had learned from Black Lives Matter that focusing on violence in educational contexts risks obscuring how racism and police militarization combine to escalate brutality. Limiting scholarly focus to school shootings can also overshadow the fact that mass shootings are consistently preceded by domestic violence and distract attention from the problem of urban gun violence, especially police brutality. The *Rhetoric Society Quarterly* counterpoint allowed me explicitly to connect gun violence with white supremacist heteropatriarchy. After I submitted that counterpoint, I thought that surely I would be able to write about something else for a change.

And here we get to campus carry and Talking Together about Guns. About that time, I traveled back to Austin for the Southern States Communication Association conference. I was invited to talk about the fiftieth anniversary of the Tower shootings. I had heard a few months earlier that the Texas law allowing campus carry was to take effect on August 1, 2016, the fiftieth anniversary of the UT Tower shootings, an act of public forgetting so audacious that I could not shake it.

PB: I see this purposeful forgetting on other issues too. Around the time that we were putting on TTAG, I had a number of discussions about the Confederate flag and Confederate monuments with some guys I've known for fifteen or twenty years. They would use the dual notions of state's rights and heritage to defend people flying the Stars and Bars right here in central Pennsylvania. These two ideas were sanitized of slavery, of secession and treason, of lynchings, and of Jim Crow. Later, it was as if the Confederate flag hadn't been put front and center at the Charlottesville protests or played an essential part in the identity badging of white supremacists all over the world. Nevertheless, I would agree with these guys. "Sure. They are defending states' rights and heritage: Mississippi's explicitly invoked state right in its secession document and the heritage of white men being granted a constitutional ancillary right to own African people and dispose of them as they pleased, a right not reciprocated to Black men to own white people and dispose of them as they see fit." Sadly, that was waved away—and the idea that our Black neighbors should be offended by the symbol was waved away as missing the point. Those folks were choosing to be hurt and taking it the wrong way, as if forced illiteracy, whipping, murder, and being treated like a commodity are just little things.

In the intervening years, and especially since the murders of Breonna Taylor, Ahmaud Arbery, and George Floyd, we are seeing people acknowledge this deliberate "forgetting." I hope we do not forget again and more. But I digress.

RE: As I recounted in my commentary in the *Chronicle of Higher Education*, I called the UT Texas System Office and the Governor's Office, only to be told by both that the co-incidence was a coincidence (Eberly 2016b). As I wrote in that commentary, however—and as I argue at much greater length in *Towers of Rhetoric*—the fact that campus carry was legalized only on public college and university campuses demonstrates that campus carry is part of an attack on public higher education specifically, and by extension, an attack on the very idea of publics and publicity (Eberly 2018).

PB: I can't agree more. I've thought about this a lot since you raised it early in our conversations about TTAG. Campus carry attacks both the First Amendment's freedoms of speech and assembly and the freedom of inquiry that is foundational to colleges and universities. The threat of immediate lethal force chills our questions, our expression of those questions, and our gathering together to ask those questions.

BS: You've experienced that firsthand, haven't you?

PB: I have. As I said, I'm a former township supervisor. About three years ago, a man came to a series of meetings to allege that his Second Amendment rights had been violated. A gun that he possessed had been seized by the police and he wanted us to fire the chief of police. Incidentally, I learned later that he was a convicted felon, so he had lost his right to carry a firearm. The first time he spoke, he became agitated, especially as he talked about guns and his (now lapsed) right to them. The second and third times he spoke his agitation built up, such that he came very close to threatening us, dangling the possibility that our actions or lack thereof on his requests could lead to some kind of violence. Whether he has a right to a gun or not, the mere threat of the gun was chilling.

Each of the nights that he spoke, he remained in the audience as we deliberated. I watched him. I wondered to myself, *Am I going to have to grab Janet, my fellow supervisor, and run?* Jill Wood was actually there with her then five-year-old son because she was advocating for an ordinance to allow backyard chickens. As he spoke, I thought, *Am I going to have to tackle him so they can escape? Will I die doing that?* These are not the thoughts of someone who can deliberate well. These are the thoughts of a stressed person narrowing their decisions because they can't attend to all of the details. That's bad for deliberation. It's bad for teaching.

RE: So, we had lunch and began a year-long conversation about how to help our community prepare for what we feared would be coming from the Pennsylvania legislature, as it has in many other states: a proposal that campus carry be explicitly legalized on Penn State's and other public universities' campuses in the Commonwealth. More generally, we wanted to facilitate conversations that might help people from very different backgrounds find common purpose around issues related to gun violence. Using topical invention and focusing on public memory and academic and public communities, we ended up with eleven events across an academic year.

BS: And you were already doing things. We had started working on Constitution Day and decided to use your question about the space between the First and Second Amendments as the theme for that year.

RE: September 17 that year was the twentieth anniversary of the fatal Penn State shooting that Peter talked about earlier. And I had consulted early in the process of producing a rotoscopic documentary called *TOWER* (Maitland 2016), one that was based in part on work students and I did in the Tower course at UT to refocus attention away from the shooter and onto the victims. I was able to arrange for the film to be shown on campus just a few weeks after its international premiere. Penn State Libraries collaborated to purchase a copy of the film for its collections. Always involve librarians!

A late-night phone call from a beloved friend in Austin, Olin Clemons, alerted me to two other films that had recently aired on PBS: *Armor of Light* (Disney and Hughes 2015), which asks whether one can be pro-gun *and* pro-life, and *Peace Officer* (Barber and Christopherson 2016), which chronicles how a former law enforcement officer became concerned about the militarization of police and the use of excessive force across the United States. These films reminded me of my activist hero and filmmaker friend Angela Aguayo and her stunning public memory documentary *778 Bullets* (2012), which tells the story of a 1970 police raid on a Black Panther house in Carbondale, Illinois.

All these films required that someone local with expertise on film join our team, and we were lucky that Matt Jordan, an associate professor of film studies, said yes. I had just learned to run the radio boards at WPSU-FM, but television and I are allergic to one another. With Matt on our team we were able to persuade WPSU-TV to air *Armor of Light* and *Peace Officer* and to hold a live town hall on the air after the latter film, reaching nearly 1 million rural Pennsylvania households.

WPSU thus became a co-sponsor of TTAG, as had the university libraries. My new department head, Denise Solomon, the best department head in the universe, supported the series generously, as did Marie Hardin, dean of the College of Communications. English professor Debbie Hawhee, who was directing the Center for Democratic Deliberation, helped with funds from her named professorship, and other centers pitched in what they could. Webster's Bookstore and Café was one of a handful of businesses in downtown State College that supported TTAG as well. I am well aware that not all universities have these kinds of resources. But what all colleges do have are colleagues and courses.

We surveyed our colleagues and our courses, and students, faculty, and staff were our greatest collaborators. Brad, you and CAS graduate student Morgan Johnson were invaluable in this effort—as were many other graduate student and faculty colleagues. And when you went to the University of North Dakota, you continued this work.

BS: Thank you. And yes, I did. When I started at UND, I was surprised to see a call for an internal grant explicitly devoted to research on targeted violence from Emeritus Professor Aqueil Ahmad. Following our success with TTAG, I proposed a similar series that would consist of eight events during the fall 2018 semester that focused on "not just guns . . . and more." The event series, entitled Target: Nonviolence, consisted of four films and four related brown bag lunch discussions. Only the last week of the series focused on mass shootings. The other three weeks focused on white supremacy and hate speech, sexual violence, and racism. Simultaneously with the series, my graduate students read Frank Meeink and Jody Roy's *Autobiography of a Recovering Skinhead* (2009), Susan Brison's *Aftermath* (2003), and several visual rhetoric journal articles about racism, homophobia, and lynching, and my dissertation (Ott and Aoki 2002; Dunn 2010; Ehrenhaus and Owen 2004; Owen and Ehrenhaus 2011; Thornton 2013; Ore 2015; Serber 2016).

The expansion from "talking together about guns" to "talking together about targeted violence" enabled participants to broaden their conversation to a variety of local issues. I chose the topics and films based on local incidents that I had heard about in my first year in North Dakota. I chose the first film, *Welcome to Leith*, because it chronicles an attempt by white supremacists to take over a small town near Bismarck in 2012 (Nichols and Walker 2016). The second film, *The Hunting Ground*, explores sexual violence on college campuses (Dick 2015). I included it not only because of the high statistics around that particular issue on college campuses, but also because of the problem of missing and murdered Indigenous women, many of whom are victims of human trafficking. The third film, *3½ Minutes, 10 Bullets*, was one that we included in TTAG (Silver 2015). North Dakota's gun culture and lax hate crime laws, the firebombing of a local Somali-owned café in 2015, a racist incident at a Fargo Walmart that garnered national attention in 2017, and police brutality and Black Lives Matter activism in Minneapolis all made that one an easy choice. Finally, I chose *It Can Happen Here* because it discusses how mass shootings have happened across urban, suburban, and rural settings (Squilla 2010). I dedicated the series to the memories of Savanna Greywind and Olivia Lone Bear, two Indigenous women who went missing in separate incidents in North Dakota and later were found dead during my first year at UND.

Like my dissertation, I wanted Target: Nonviolence to be about "not just guns" and "not just schools," but also about other kinds of violence that take place in other settings. Much like at Penn State, the "town and gown" divide that plagues many college towns pushed me to open these events to more than faculty, staff, and students, so we also invited local community members. Representatives from each of those categories attended the event series, many of them more than once. Rather than viewing Target: Nonviolence as a one-and-done event series, the point was to plant seeds for sustained conversations between those directly affiliated with the university and local residents about violent issues that affect their community.

Despite what appears to be the macabre "sustainability" of mass shootings and other kinds of targeted violence, both TTAG and Target: Nonviolence have shown me that there is something holy and wholly sustainable about the public dialogue and deliberation that appears in their wake.

PB: That's an interesting way of putting it. Can you say more about that?

BS: Sure. For me, the holiness is in the unpredictable—but, at least in my experience, productive—nature of people with different back-grounds, perspectives, and interests coming to talk about difficult subjects. Both TTAG and Target: Nonviolence brought different audiences to each event. Some people only attended one or two events, and some attended most or all of them. Nevertheless, the discussions were always deep, remained mostly civil, and were full of gratitude. As for wholeness, there was something really powerful in replicating and expanding TTAG in a new environment. Happy Valley in Pennsylvania and the Red River Valley in North Dakota have some things in common, but there are many differences between them as well. If the premise behind *It Can Happen Here* is that mass shootings and other kinds of targeted violence can happen anywhere, TTAG and Target: Nonviolence have shown me that quality public deliberation also can and should happen anywhere.

PB: We've each taken the original idea of TTAG down other avenues. In the course of running for the Pennsylvania legislature, I responded to the Moms Demand Action questionnaire. Part of my response included my commitment to the slow and deliberative model in TTAG versus the fast and reactive discourse that dominates social media and public gatherings like the "Reopen the Economy" protests in Michigan and Pennsylvania in the midst of the coronavirus pandemic. You look at those protests and you see armed white men with red faces draped in American and Confederate flags, yelling in capitol police officers' faces. These false and distorted expressions of patriotism are perfect examples of the problem before us: hot emotions and inflammatory rhetorical spaces. I want to create spaces where we can feel what we feel, but work through those feelings in a way that requires patience and recognition of one another, what Dr. King (1965) called *agape*. It also requires a certain kind of "expertise" to set up.

This is where I see us as academics using our skills and knowledge to work for both the public good and our publics that I referred to earlier. I'm reminded once again of the work of Frank Fischer (2000), who writes about experts and expertise, primarily in environmentally and scientifically complex issues. But he proposes that people with expertise need to play humble roles as citizens, as equals in the ongoing work of democracy, as have our colleagues Scott Peters, Theodore Alter, and Timothy Shaffer (2018), who have examined the work of agricultural extension agents and their role in community decision-making and civic life. Maybe we three and our partners in these discussions are like democracy extension agents.

BS: And maybe even more than that. At UND, I began each event with a discussion of voluntary and captive audiences. I reminded those who attended each event that they were free to come and go at any time but that they should not process heavy subjects alone. Only a few of the participants from the events left early, and most wished to stay long after the discussions had subsided. The biggest recurring theme was that the structural conditions of racism, sexism, xenophobia, and other power imbalances enable targeted violence. Those who regularly attended the series discussed how it was easy for politicians, journalists, and citizens to get caught up in the physical violence of attacks and to ignore or downplay those structural conditions. In order to create large-scale change, they insisted, different groups needed to work together to dismantle those conditions.

PB: I think it's interesting how much you have both focused on the combination of discussion toward some goal and processing together to cope with the heaviness. By talking more slowly and carefully, we can deal with personal and collective emotions and move toward solutions, or at least ways to manage these forms of targeted violence.

BS: As I started saying regularly to my students during my work with Rosa on the CIVCM minor, "We can't solve difficult problems if we can't talk about them."

RE: Just as the best classroom discussion rarely happens on the first day of class, individuals and communities do not enter discursive spaces ready to do productive collaborative work without some collective preparation, particularly around such charged issues as gun violence, police brutality, and campus carry. Do you think we can confidently say that TTAG made a difference in the ability of campus and other publics' ability to talk together about guns?

PB: I'm not sure.

BS: I would like to think so.

PB: Part of me says it probably did and certainly for us and the folks we connected with over the course of doing it.

RE: With the number of events and their reach, the series remains in public memory, at least for now. Perhaps it will serve as a resource if and when campus carry comes to Penn State's twenty-three campuses. While I wasn't able to get to the vigil for the victims of the mass shooting last week, a handful of people—at my yoga class, at the Y, and in the waiting room of a medical office—mentioned that they thought of TTAG at some time after hearing the news of the shootings. Maybe the series helped people talk more easily about something that is so very hard to talk about.

PB: I'm reminded of a finding by Nathaniel Geiger, Janet Swim, and John Fraser (2017) regarding why people don't talk about climate change. They think that other people don't want to talk about it, so they may not talk about it even if they want to. But when they are informed through evidence-based interventions, their efficacy to talk about climate change increases. That can promote community-level discussions. And I mean talk. Not shout. People are good at shouting about guns or targeted violence—or climate change—but they aren't so good at talking and listening about it. So, these slowed-down discussions do that. And if we talk and listen, informed by good evidence again and again, we can at least get to a place of understanding.

BS: And that is good for us.

RE: And good for democracy.

RECOMMENDATIONS FOR CONTINUING TO TALK TOGETHER ABOUT GUNS . . . AND MORE

It is our hope that we and others will continue to talk together about guns and other difficult subjects on our campuses and in our local communities. Based on our experience with Talking Together about Guns and Target: Nonviolence, here are our recommendations for others who wish to continue talking together.

1. *Talk together about not just guns . . . and more!* As Brad mentioned, we can't solve difficult problems if we can't talk about them. Guns are an important part of conversations around targeted violence, but so are other weapons, mental health, cultural violence, security measures, and other concerns.

2. *Research local issues and current events, and tie events to local exigences.* Local issues bring communities together to solve collective problems. Tying broader issues to local concerns is also a good way to make conversations more meaningful and more memorable.

3. *Invite people from many different backgrounds and perspectives.* Brad's department chair, Tim Pasch, wisely recommended on an early draft of his grant application that he pitch the events as explicitly nonpartisan. It seemed so obvious to Brad that he initially didn't think to put it in the proposal or promotional materials, but several participants thanked him for framing the series that way. The whole point of "talking together" is to get out of our usual echo chambers, whether they are personal, political, professional, or institutional. Invite people from across and beyond campus. And, as Rosa mentioned, always involve librarians!

4. *When you do this, consider who and what you might have to guard against.* Unfortunately, there are important safety considerations to account for when planning events like this. Talking together about guns sometimes risks having gun-owning participants who want to talk with their guns. It's the same concern that Peter mentioned about the space between the First and Second Amendments in his township board meeting. We had quite a few discussions about the possibility that someone might show up with a gun. Outside of Philadelphia, Pennsylvania permits people to open carry without a permit. North Dakota allows unloaded open carry during the day and concealed carry day and night. We also talked a fair amount about vociferous gun rights fundamentalists who could hijack a discussion. And what if we faced both? In the end, we thought that the first was very unlikely but much more frightening and the second was a possibility that we could work through with some difficulty.

5. *Involve your campus and local law enforcement or other relevant professionals and experts.* We encourage hosts to speak with mental health professionals, mediators, and law enforcement to ensure that you are well informed and safe. Although different people (rightly) have different reactions to police presence in the context of police brutality, getting the police involved in both the planning and implementation of events can have several advantages. Not only can they provide security if events get out of hand, but police officers also can bring a unique perspective on gun violence. We brought in a few police officers to respond to TTAG and Target: Nonviolence films, and they made several insightful comments in the panel discussions. One important recommendation here is to consider the optics of having an officer in uniform at your events and what that might signal to participants. Based on a commanding officer's suggestion that Brad received for Target: Nonviolence, he recommends plainclothes officers over uniformed ones. There are other experts who can be of aid, for example, mental health professionals, clergy, and media professionals.

6. *Connect the learning happening inside and outside of the classroom.* Some of the best learning takes place outside of the classroom. Not only do programs like these reinforce content, they are also a great way to bring people from the university and other members of the local community together.

ACKNOWLEDGMENTS

Bradley Serber would like to thank Emeritus Professor Aqueil Ahmad for his generous support of the deliberation series mentioned in this chapter.

NOTES

Serber is now at Penn State University, but this conversation took place while he was working as an assistant professor at the University of North Dakota.

1. In *Citizens, Experts, and the Environment,* Fischer recognizes that experts have important roles to play, especially if they can establish means for citizen engagement. While TTAG was not a governmental body with policy-changing or policy-crafting authority, it created venues that functioned to "offer citizens an opportunity to deliberate more directly in the decisions affecting their own lives" (2000, 37).
2. That question was the theme of Constitution Day 2016 at Penn State: http://civcm .psu.edu/constitution-day/past-constitution-days/2016-2/.

REFERENCES

Aguayo, Angela. 2012. *778 Bullets.* New Filmmakers. http://www.newfilmmakersonline .com/movie-download/58831,5232/Angela-Aguayo-778-Bullets.

Barber, Brad, and Scott Christopherson. 2016. *Peace Officer.* Independent Lens. PBS. http://www.pbs.org/independentlens/films/peace-officer/.

Brison, Susan J. 2003. *Aftermath: Violence and the Remaking of a Self.* Princeton: Princeton University Press.

Dewey, John. 1927. *The Public and Its Problems.* New York: Henry Holt.

Dick, Kirby. 2015. *The Hunting Ground.* Chain Camera Pictures. http://thehuntinggroundfilm .com/.

Disney, Abigail, and Kathleen Hughes. 2015. *The Armor of Light.* Independent Lens. PBS. http://www.pbs.org/independentlens/films/the-armor-of-light/.

Dunn, Thomas R. 2010. "Remembering Matthew Shepard: Violence, Identity, and Queer Counterpublic Memories." *Rhetoric and Public Affairs* 13 (4): 611–51.

Eberly, Rosa A. 2016a. "Counterpoint: Essay on Criticism in the Face of Campus Carry." *Rhetoric Society Quarterly* 46 (4): 351–57. https://doi.org/10.1080/02773945.2016 .1203202.

Eberly, Rosa A. 2016b. "Texas Picked an Ominous Date to Arm Its Public Colleges." *Chronicle of Higher Education,* July 27. https://www.chronicle.com/article/Texas-Picked-an -Ominous-Date/237264.

Eberly, Rosa A. 2018. *Towers of Rhetoric: Memory and Reinvention.* Intermezzo. http:// intermezzo.enculturation.net/05-eberly.htm.

Eberly, Rosa A., and Jeremy Cohen, eds. 2006. *A Laboratory for Public Scholarship and Democracy.* San Francisco: Wiley.

Eberly, Rosa A., and Brad Serber. 2013. "Life, Liberty, and the Pursuit Of . . ." *Journal of General Education* 62 (4): 277–96. https://doi.org/10.1353/jge.2013.0028.

Edkins, Jenny. 2003. *Trauma and the Memory of Politics.* New York: Cambridge University Press.

Ehrenhaus, Peter, and A. Susan Owen. 2004. "Race Lynching and Christian Evangelicalism: Performances of Faith." *Text and Performance Quarterly* 24 (3–4): 276–301.

Fein, Robert A., Bryan Vossekuil, and Gwen A. Holden. 1995. "Threat Assessment: An Approach to Prevent Targeted Violence." Washington, DC: US Department of Justice. https://www.ncjrs.gov/pdffiles/threat.pdf.

Fischer, Frank. 2000. *Citizens, Experts, and the Environment: The Politics of Local Knowledge.* Durham, NC: Duke University Press.

Founders of March for Our Lives. 2018. *Glimmer of Hope.* New York: Penguin.

Geiger, Nathaniel, Janet Swim, and John Fraser. 2017. "Creating a Climate for Change: Interventions, Efficacy and Public Discussion about Climate Change." *Journal of Environmental Psychology* 51:104–16. https://doi.org/10.1016/j.jenvp.2017.03.010.

King, Martin Luther, Jr. 1965. "Remarks at Penn State University." University Park, January 21. https://cecr.ed.psu.edu/sites/default/files/African_American_Chronicles _MLK_1965Speech.pdf.

Maitland, Keith. 2016. *TOWER.* Independent Lens. PBS. http://www.towerdocumentary .com/.

Meeink, Frank, and Jody M. Roy. 2009. *Autobiography of a Recovering Skinhead.* Portland, OR: Hawthorne.

Nichols, Michael Beach, and Christopher K. Walker. 2016. *Welcome to Leith.* Independent Lens. PBS. http://www.pbs.org/independentlens/films/welcome-to-leith/.

Ore, Ersula J. 2015. "'They Call Me Dr. Ore.'" *Present Tense: A Journal of Rhetoric in Society* 5 (2): 1–6.

Ott, Brian L., and Eric Aoki. 2002. "The Politics of Negotiating Public Tragedy: Media Framing of the Matthew Shepard Murder." *Rhetoric & Public Affairs* 5 (3): 483–505. https://doi.org/10.1353/rap.2002.0060.

Owen, A. Susan, and Peter Ehrenhaus. 2011. "Looking at Lynching: Spectacle, Resistance and Contemporary Transformations." *Quarterly Journal of Speech* 97 (1): 100–113.

Pallotto, Bret, and Sarah Paez. 2019. "4 People Now Dead in State College Shootings, Police Say." *Centre Daily Times,* January 27, 2019. https://www.centredaily.com/news/local/com munity/state-college/article225068910.html.

Peters, Scott, Theodore Alter, and Timothy Shaffer, eds. 2018. *Jumping into Civic Life: Stories of Public Work from Extension Professionals.* Dayton: Kettering Foundation.

Pettit, Emma. 2016. "The New Gun-Violence Scholars." *Chronicle of Higher Education,* August 22. https://www.chronicle.com/article/The-New-Gun-Violence-Scholars/237 521.

Remembrance of Michael R. Nathan from Duke University Medical School. n.d. https:// fmch.duke.edu/education/michael-r-nathan-memorial-fund.

Rood, Craig. 2015. "Deliberating in the Aftermath of Mass Shootings." PhD diss., Pennsylvania State University.

Rood, Craig. 2019. *After Gun Violence: Deliberation and Memory in an Age of Political Gridlock.* University Park: Pennsylvania State University Press.

Serber, Bradley A. 2016. "Reaction Rhetorics: Targeted Violence and Public Security." PhD diss., Pennsylvania State University.

Serber, Bradley A. 2018. "The Dissertation Crying Log: Research, Pedagogy, and the Ethics of Care." Gershman-Ahler Distinguished Lecture in Qualitative Research, University of North Dakota, April 4. https://www.youtube.com/watch?v=fP-be8Zc3B4.

Shriver, Lionel. 2003. *We Need to Talk about Kevin.* New York: Counterpoint.

Silver, Marc. 2015. *3 1/2 Minutes, 10 Bullets.* Candescent Films. https://www.participantmedia .com/film/3-12-minutes-ten-bullets.

Squilla, Lynne. 2010. *It Can Happen Here.* University Park: Pennsylvania State University Applied Research Lab, Institute for Non-Lethal Defense Technologies. https://www .youtube.com/watch?v=u32GH3-w4IU.

Thornton, Davi Johnson. 2013. "The Rhetoric of Civil Rights Photographs: James Meredith's March against Fear." *Rhetoric & Public Affairs* 16 (3): 457–87. https://doi.org /10.1353/rap.2013.0023.

AFTERWORD

Catherine R. Squires

In 2005, Angela Davis asked *"How do we imagine a better world and raise the questions that permit us to see beyond the given?"* In 2020, I sit here wondering, gathering my thoughts, imagining, and writing, as my black tea brews: *Why did the world react to the 2020 murder of George Floyd so differently than to the 2015 mass shooting of the Mother Emanuel congregants?*

What else did we need to see, hear, feel in order to have one white supremacist murder spark urgency more than others? What is it about the gun, the distance, the speed, the belief that perhaps suffering wasn't as great because the power of the almighty gun strikes people down so fast, so mercilessly?

I start a list:

> *Guns and distance.*
> *Velocity.*
> *Time.*
> *How long does it take to kill someone?*
> *How far do you have to go?*
> *How far before you care?*
> *How far before you dehumanize?*
> *Does regret ever close in?*

Guns reinforce and extend what Resmaa Menakem calls white body supremacy (2017).[1] Guns make exceptionally, spectacularly deadly the reach of white body supremacy. Multiply its victims with breathtaking speed. The gun allows an individual to socially distance from their target.

In a summer of pandemic, a summer of social distancing, to witness a white supremacist execute a Black man not with his gun, but using his knee. As Derek Chauvin crushed George Floyd's neck, taking his breath away in a slow, deliberate, incremental act of murder, it collapsed the myth of distance between killer and killed, murderer and murdered. The world heard George Floyd's last words. Witnesses heard and saw the officers listen to George Floyd's final cries. As seventeen-year old

https://doi.org/10.7330/9781646422159.c015

Darnella Frazier pointed her cell phone camera and started recording, still the police continued to drain breath from his body, deny blood and oxygen to his brain, caused his heart to stop beating. Witnessed in real time and then circulated online, millions saw it happen. It was witnessed in human-scaled time, not the sped-up time of video games and multiple magazines, reloading and resuming sprees of shooting with immediate death as bullet hits brain, heart, artery, lung.

In 2020, the immensity and the intimacy of death are almost inescapable. The air is suffused with stories of loved ones unable to sit at the bedside to comfort the dying, of overwhelmed doctors and nurses driven into the ground by holding the weight of all the grief. In this context, the murder of a Black man in broad daylight mattered in a way that changed something.

COVID-19 has compelled many of us think about death in new registers, new scales, new intimacies, new risk assessments, new horrors. To think about our own vulnerabilities, the vulnerabilities built into systems not ready for a complex and fast-changing world. Which deaths are "inevitable" or "preventable"? How many deaths are "acceptable"? For what reasons?

I felt in the streets, saw in the haggard faces of doctors interviewed on TV, heard in the voices of loved ones and friends who desperately waited for a test result and a reason to hope for the best, echoed in the cries within overwhelmed and underequipped hospitals a desire to reclaim dignity for the dying, for their loved ones, for their caretakers. These elements put a charge in the air of 2020 that I didn't perceive or feel when I wrote about online mourning of the Mother Emanuel victims in 2015.

Thinking about death, something that dominant US culture is loathe to do, had to be done.[2] Bodies in refrigerated trucks. Morgues full. A wildly uncontrolled virus that could strike anyone at any time. Jobs lost, food scarce, forest fires burning out of control, hurricane surges blasting away coastlines and dragging neighborhoods into the sea.

Watching George Floyd's funeral, we had to stop, to catch our breaths. We felt grateful that we still could breathe.

The mass shooting, despite its obscene increasing recurrence in the past three decades, still seems to many something that is unique, an aberrance. Though our children are drilled to shelter from active shooters, the resignation noted in this volume speaks to the ways it is easy to rationalize that it won't happen to me/us; if it does, there is nothing I/we can do to stop it.

But over 225,000 deaths from COVID-19? A knee on a neck, inflicting over eight minutes of pain and agony ending in death? Those things could have been prevented.

Had there not been four other officers with guns, with ultimate authority for death standing by, perhaps bystanders could have done more than plead, than record, than witness. They could have banded together without, at least, fear of death by the guns held in the brutal hands of those policemen.

But the witnesses had already been taught otherwise—by Philando's death a few years earlier, by Jamar's death, by Breonna's death, by Cece's incarceration, by Sandra's despair in the cell, by all of the hashtagged names—they knew in their bones that Black witnesses would be blamed for their own murders if they tried to intervene, to save George Floyd from the ultimate "good guys with guns."

> In the past, [Black] people adapted the way they lived in the world as a response to the traumatic experience of slavery. Some of these adaptations included resistance and resilience, but they also included . . . the use of invisibility because it provides protection, secrecy to protect the lives of others who cannot expect fair treatment, and hiding hope because it leads to disappointment . . . Jim Crow and continued acts of race-based violence meant the adaptive behaviors remained useful and were passed down from one generation to the next. (Jacobs and Davis, 2017, 202)

Where do we go from here? If we want to speak of a society where eulogies for gun victims are a distant memory, we need to step into the speculative, the imaginative realm, for we don't know what such a society looks or feels like.

I suggest we turn to the issues of trauma and bodies, harm and repair. I think it is important to include these terms in our work moving forward as rhetoric and communication scholars invested in alternatives to the dominant discourses of guns and reform that have not brought an end to the violence. I suggest explorations of systemic forms of trauma as well as abolitionist thought as pathways to imagining otherwise, to being ready for miracles.

> We have learned that trauma is not just an event that took place sometime in the past; it is also the imprint left by that experience on mind, brain, and body . . . We have discovered that helping trauma victims find the words to describe what has happened to them is profoundly meaningful, but usually it is not enough. (van der Kolk, 2014, 21)

Trauma is now understood to have individual and systemic dimensions, but most public discussions still focus on trauma caused by singular violent events, like those suffered by soldiers in war. Indeed, the definition of PTSD, the only trauma-related disorder recognized in the *Diagnostic and Statistical Manual of Mental Disorders*, is based on someone surviving a "life-threatening event" followed by specific symptoms: flashbacks, avoidance, and hyper-vigilance. But trauma experts recognize two other types of trauma: intergenerational trauma and complex trauma.[3]

Recent groundbreaking work on racial disparities in public health recognizes the impact of intergenerational trauma, cyclical harms that are byproducts of struggling to survive in a white supremacist society. Trauma responses can be passed down across generations, and the cascading, ever-present assaults of micro- and macroaggressions, deprivations caused by structural inequities, and other harms literally wear down Black, Brown, and Indigenous bodies. This "weathering" makes us more susceptible to a variety of chronic diseases, like hypertension (see Geronimous et al. 2006).

Complex trauma occurs when you experience chronically violent and/or neglectful, chaotic, unpredictable relationships with others. Complex trauma arises when you do not experience consistent caring or protective responses from others who witness these harms. When the people who are supposed to be there for you—colleagues, friends, doctors, nurses, police—stand by or ignore what is happening, complex trauma can arise.

Gaslighting, microaggressions, redlining, stereotyping, profiling: are these not chronic, neglectful, chaotic, and unpredictable elements of negotiating life in a racist world? Trying to breathe freely, all the while knowing that at any moment, any white person with a gun can stand their ground and take your life (or the lives of other people who look like you). The pain is compounded by a justice system that has repeatedly ruled that white people's fear of Black bodies matters more than keeping Black bodies safe. This is a society that keeps you on guard all the time, makes you not trust your surroundings, unsure about how people will see you.

And then when you try to speak to that experience, you're told that it's all in your head, you're exaggerating. You're making people uncomfortable.

I do not know the name of the genius was who coined this hashtag, but they did us a service in cleverly linking the historical and structural violence that has produced the unequal racial and traumatic outcomes of the year 2020: #Covid-1619.

When we look at the history of the slave patrols, soldiers on the frontier, police, vigilantes, all gunning down Black people, Brown people, and Indigenous people, we see that guns are part of the chain of intergenerational trauma. Concealed carry statutes, Stand Your Ground laws, and qualified immunity reinforce the fears that drive complex trauma. Witnessing, whether live or recorded, another legal execution of a Black person, a Brown person, or an Indigenous person, hearing the stories of disappeared Indigenous women and having no one take responsibility, and having no idea when this organized chaos will end: these things are part and parcel of intergenerational trauma and complex trauma. When a cop shoots another Black person, Brown person, or Indigenous person, all of that history and complexity is part of the landscape, even if witnesses don't see it.

They feel it. *The body keeps the score.*

We must be mindful of what van der Kolk calls the "miracle and tyranny" of language (2014, 232): people who experience trauma cannot always narrate their trauma, or what trauma feels like, or when it started, particularly in the cases of complex and intergenerational trauma. Trauma is an embodied phenomenon, interwoven into one's tissues and nerves. Trauma can override the brain's language and memory centers. Acknowledging these facts of neurobiology is crucial to future explorations of rhetoric and gun violence. What kinds of interdisciplinary partnerships might we seek to learn from the embodied experiences of BIPOC folks who are more likely to be targets of gun violence, more likely to be stereotyped as the bad guys with guns?

> "For people trying to solve their everyday problems, behaving in a violent and life-annihilating way is not a solution . . . Where life is precious, life is precious . . . Why do we feel every day that here life is not precious?" (Ruth Wilson Gilmore, quoted in Kushner 2019).

The year 2020 introduced many Americans to discussions of police and prison abolition in a whole new light. Many of these discussions center on the need to imagine and implement new systems for repairing harms, systems that are built by and for the communities experiencing harm. To rethink "criminal justice" by moving away from punishment-oriented approaches to repair of harm.

The evidence abounds: the criminal justice system is racist and has failed to create safety and security for all. Incarceration, the death penalty, digital and bio-surveillance—none of these offer real restitution to victims or deter criminal acts. Instead, the criminal justice system itself often traumatizes survivors of violence and their communities as "bad guys" are hunted down. Beth Ritchie, Michelle Wallace, Angela Davis, Kimberlé Crenshaw, Miriam Kaba, and other scholars and activists have shown with clarity how the criminal system is set up to maximize exposure of Black, Brown, and Indigenous communities to police violence and surveillance, to incarceration and indebtedness.

The abolitionist idea is this: imagine society into one where there are no jails, are no police. Imagine a society where victims are offered healing and reparation instead of state-sanctioned vengeance. Where those who inflict harm are held accountable not by being caged but through reparative, restorative processes that help make communities whole and greatly reduce future harming behavior.

> Historical, intersectional analysis of the prison recognizes that "punishment" does not follow from "crime" in the neat and logical sequence offered by [dominant] discourses that insist on the justice of imprisonment, but rather punishment . . . is linked to the agendas of politicians, the profit drive of corporations, and media representations of crime. (Davis, 2003, 112), p.112

I'd like to suggest that demystifying the discourses of incarceration and policing may also help to demystify the gun's taken-for-granted necessity as a feature of modern life. Gun rights advocates insist that guns provide essential safety: the police can never catch or lock up *all* the bad guys; the dregs of society continue to birth bad guys. Personal arsenals are needed because policing and carceral systems don't keep us safe.

The abolitionist answers: *That's what we've been telling you. Safety isn't generated by policing and violence. Safety is about establishing human relationships of care and trust, not punishment and shame. We change the conditions that produce violence to reduce violence instead of acting violently.* This approach throws into question the utility of the gun: what is the need for every citizen to pack a stand-your-ground pistol if the goal is to end violence as a means of problem-solving?

We would do well to continue investigating how the gun acts in public memory and imagination, to ask why there are so many people who cannot imagine life without the gun—either the threat of its power or its alleged protection against imagined enemies. Indeed, the transcontinental expansion of the United States without the gun is hard to imagine, since guns and control of their manufacture and distribution gave distinct advantages to white settlers in assaults on Indigenous peoples, in campaigns to recapture the enslaved, in practices to restrict and terrorize Asian and Latinx migrants.

The gun helps to ensure that cycles of punishment and trauma continue. Current gun discourses make the cycle of violence seem like an infinity loop rather than something that can be transformed by human intentions.

What if we focused our attention on rhetorics of imagining otherwise and invited people to talk about a world without guns, a world where there aren't "bad guys" because everyone has food, shelter, clothing, meaningful employment, healthcare, art, and a sense of wonder about the world?

What if we started our explorations in the Speculative instead of the Here and Now? Both, of course, are important, but what are we missing when we neglect opportunities to imagine the future?

There are people now reweaving the world, creating rhetorics that make nonviolence real, that make communal support and mutual aid viable options and reduce exposure to police brutality. There are visionaries who will help speak us into a society based in repair of harm, fostering resilience to thrive, not just survive. I would be eager to see what comes from interdisciplinary engagements of scholars, youth, activists, artists, and others imagining gun abolition together.

The essays in this book make a compelling case that gun culture is locked in a deadly embrace with white supremacy. White supremacy can't be reformed: it must be abolished. And so, like the abolitionists who imagine a world without the prison industrial complex, can we imagine a world without guns? It may not happen in our lifetimes, but the work starts now.

NOTES

1. Menakem argues that white supremacy is not only comprised of political and ideological systems of oppression, but also rests on the belief that the white body itself is superior, the norm against which all other bodies are measured. Importantly, the white body is a body empowered to inflict pain on and otherwise physically dominate Black, Brown, and Indigenous bodies.
2. For US reluctance to speak about death, see, for example, anthropologist Anita Hannig's article about why she teaches a class on death to college students (2017).
3. Research with Indigenous and Black people, as well as survivors of the Holocaust, have provided these broader understandings of trauma. See, e.g., van der Kolk 2014; Menakem 2017; Jacobs and Davis 2017.

REFERENCES

Davis, Angela Y. 2003. *Are Prisons Obsolete?* New York: Seven Stories.
Davis, Angela Y. 2005. *Abolition Democracy: Beyond Empire, Prisons, and Torture.* New York: Seven Stories.
Geronimous, Arline, et al. 2006. "'Weathering' and Age Patterns of Allostatic Load among Blacks and Whites in the United States." *American Journal of Public Health* 96 (5): 826–33.
Hannig, Anita. 2017. "Talking about Death in America: An Anthropologist's View." *Undark. org.* https://undark.org/2017/10/19/death-dying-america-anthropologist/.

Jacobs, Simone, and Chandra Davis. 2017. "Challenging the Myths of Black Women—A Short Term, Structured Art Experience Group: Exploring the Intersections of Race, Gender and Intergenerational Trauma." *Smith College Studies in Social Work* 87 (2–3): 200–219.

Kushner, Rachel. 2019. "Is Prison Necessary? Ruth Wilson Gilmore Might Change Your Mind." *New York Times Magazine*, April 14, 2019. https://www.nytimes.com/2019/04/17/magazine/prison-abolition-ruth-wilson-gilmore.html.

Menakem, Resmaa. 2017. *My Grandmother's Hands: Racialized Trauma and the Pathway to Mending Our Hearts and Bodies*. Las Vegas: Central Recovery.

Squires, Catherine R. 2015. "Making Visible Victimhood, Bringing Intersectionality to a Mass Shooting: #SAYHERNAME, Black Women, and Charleston." In *Dangerous Discourses: Feminism, Gun Violence and Civic Life*, edited by Catherine R. Squires, 121–44. New York: Peter Lang.

van der Kolk, Bessel. 2014. *The Body Keeps the Score: Brain, Mind and Body in the Healing of Trauma*. New York: Penguin.

INDEX

CONTRIBUTORS

Ira J. Allen is associate professor of rhetoric, writing, and digital media studies at Northern Arizona University. His writing and translations appear in such journals as *Advances in the History of Rhetoric, SubStance, Modern Language Notes, College Composition and Communication, Theory & Event,* and *Political Research Quarterly.* His book *The Ethical Fantasy of Rhetorical Theory* (University of Pittsburgh Press, 2018) explores the meanings and utility of rhetorical theory for scholars across the humanistic disciplines. He has recently edited or coedited (with Elizabeth A. Flynn) special issues of *Screen Bodies* and *Rhetoric Review* on ubiquitous surveillance and rhetorical witnessing, respectively.

Brian Ballentine is a professor and the chair of the department of English at West Virginia University. He completed his PhD at Case Western Reserve University, specializing in technical and professional communication. His research has appeared in journals such as *Technical Communication, IEEE Transactions on Professional Communication, Technical Communication Quarterly, Computers and Composition,* and the *Journal of Technical Writing and Communication.* In addition to program administration, his most current research interests are at the intersections of environmental rhetoric and digital representations of the environment. His article on hydraulic fracturing appeared recently in a special issue of *Communication Design Quarterly* dedicated to environmental communication.

Matthew Boedy is an associate professor of rhetoric and composition at the University of North Georgia. He lives in Gainesville, Georgia. He is the author of *Speaking of Evil: Rhetoric and the Responsibility to and for Language,* published by an imprint of Rowman & Littlefield in 2018. He has written for public audiences about gun violence. He also fought against a Georgia law allowing guns on campus.

Peter D. Buck's academic and civic work resides at the nexus of sustainability, risk, democracy, and expression. He manages academic programming for Penn State's Sustainability Institute and holds an affiliate position in educational theory and policy. His most recent work appears in *Clinics of North America,* Routledge's volume *Teaching Climate Change in America,* and Springer's *Universities and Sustainable Communities.* Peter serves as chair or co-chair of two intergovernmental climate working groups and as president of the Pennsylvania Environmental Resource Consortium. In 2020, he was the Democratic candidate for Pennsylvania's House District 171. He lives in State College, Pennsylvania.

Lisa M. Corrigan is a professor of communication, director of the gender studies program, and affiliate faculty in both African and African American studies and Latin American and Latino studies at the University of Arkansas. Her first book, *Prison Power: How Prison Politics Influenced the Movement for Black Liberation* (University Press of Mississippi, 2016), was the recipient of the 2017 Diamond Anniversary Book Award and the 2017 African American Communication and Culture Division Outstanding Book Award, both from the National Communication Association. Her second book is titled *Black Feelings: Race and Affect in the Long Sixties* (University Press of Mississippi, 2020).

Rosa A. Eberly is an associate professor of rhetoric in the department of communication arts and sciences and the department of English at Penn State. Since 1996 she has taught courses on rhetoric, violence, and public memory, with emphasis on violence in educational settings. Eberly directs the intercollege minor in civic and community engagement and teaches graduate seminars on publics theory, rhetoric and poetics, and sound character(s). She is author of *Towers of Rhetoric: Memory and Reinvention* and *Citizen Critics: Literary Public Spheres*; coeditor of *A Laboratory for Public Scholarship and Democracy* and *The Sage Handbook of Rhetoric*; and coauthor of *The Elements of Reasoning*, 2nd ed.

Scott Gage is an associate professor of English and director of first-year composition at Texas A&M University–San Antonio. His writing addresses the intersections of rhetoric, violence, and white supremacy and may be found in *Computers and Composition, College English*, and *Present Tense*.

Kendall Gerdes is an assistant professor in the department of writing and rhetoric studies at the University of Utah. Her writing has been published in *Rhetoric Society Quarterly, Philosophy & Rhetoric, Transgender Studies Quarterly*, and *Kairos*, and she coedited the book *Reinventing (with) Theory in Rhetoric and Writing Studies: Essays in Honor of Sharon Crowley* (Utah State University Press, 2019).

Ian E. J. Hill is an associate professor in the history and theory of rhetoric in the department of English language and literatures at the University of British Columbia, where he is also affiliated with UBC's graduate program in science and technology studies. In addition to the history and theory of rhetoric, his research and teaching focus on rhetoric and technology—the ways people advocate, resist, design, and otherwise argue and debate machines and systems, as well as how technologies themselves are persuasive. He published *Advocating Weapons, War, and Terrorism: Technological and Rhetorical Paradox* (Pennsylvania State University Press, 2018), and his work has also appeared in *Quarterly Journal of Speech, Advances in the History of Rhetoric, African Yearbook of Rhetoric, Western Journal of Communication, Communication and Critical/Cultural Studies, Philosophy & Rhetoric, Rethinking Marxism, Kenneth Burke Journal, Communication Teacher*, and the edited collections *Handbook of Communication and Security* and *Burke in the Archives*.

Nate Kreuter is an associate professor of English at the University of Georgia, where he is also the director of first-year writing. He has written a variety of articles on rhetoric in the US intelligence community and the rhetorical canon of style. Nate is a gun-owning hunter and fisherman who believes that the rights afforded by the Second Amendment and sensible firearms regulation can be balanced. As both a scholar and a citizen, he is concerned with the ongoing American epidemics of suicide and gun violence, as well as the emergence of unregulated militias.

Nathalie Kuroiwa-Lewis is an associate professor of English at Saint Martin's University in Lacey, Washington. She has a PhD in rhetoric and composition and works in two distinct areas: critical rhetoric and creative writing. In her scholarship, she uses critical rhetoric to analyze the rhetoric of American militarism. In her creative work, Nathalie writes poetry focusing on socioeconomic, environmental, and feminist themes. She is passionate about teaching writing, and her areas of expertise in her academic writing include rhetorical theory and criticism, expressivism, interdisciplinary rhetoric, environmental rhetoric, political rhetoric, the rhetoric of literature, and the rhetoric of war.

Patricia Roberts-Miller, professor emerita of rhetoric and writing and recently director of the University of Texas at Austin University Writing Center, is the author of *Speaking of Race: How to Have Antiracist Conversations That Bring Us Together* (The Experiment, 2021),

Rhetoric and Demagoguery (Southern Illinois University Press, 2019), *Demagoguery and Democracy* (The Experiment, 2017), *Fanatical Schemes: Proslavery Rhetoric and the Tragedy of Consensus* (University of Alabama Press, 2009), *Deliberate Conflict: Argument, Political Theory, and Composition Classes* (Southern Illinois University Press, 2007), and *Voices in the Wilderness: The Paradox of the Puritan Public Sphere* (University of Alabama Press, 1999).

Craig Rood is assistant professor of rhetoric in the department of English and the program in speech communication at Iowa State University. His essays on public deliberation and gun violence have been published in the *Quarterly Journal of Speech, Rhetoric & Public Affairs,* and *Rhetoric Society Quarterly.* He is the author of *After Gun Violence: Deliberation and Memory in an Age of Political Gridlock* (Pennsylvania State University Press, 2019).

Bradley A. Serber is an assistant teaching professor at Penn State University. His research focuses on the rhetorics of violence and abnormality, and he has taught courses on argumentation, persuasion, intercultural conflict, rhetoric and violence, and civic and community engagement, among other things. His research has been published in the *Journal of General Education, Argumentation & Advocacy,* the *Oxford Encyclopedia of Health and Risk Message Design and Processing,* and *Citizen Critics.* He is currently working on a book manuscript that explores public deliberation in the aftermath of targeted violence. He was also the 2018 recipient of the Joyce and Aqueil Ahmad Endowment for the Promotion of Peace and Nonviolence at the University of North Dakota.

Ryan Skinnell is an associate professor of rhetoric and writing at San José State University. He is the author or editor of six books, including *Conceding Composition: A Crooked History of Composition's Institutional Fortunes* (Utah State University Press, 2016), *Faking the News: What Rhetoric Can Teach Us about Donald J. Trump* (Societas, 2018), and *Reinventing (with) Theory in Rhetoric and Writing Studies: Essays in Honor of Sharon Crowley* (Utah State University Press, 2019). In 2019, he edited a special issue of *Rhetoric Society Quarterly* about rhetoric and demagoguery. Dr. Skinnell has also published numerous essays in academic and popular outlets on rhetoric, political speech, and writing instruction.

Catherine R. Squires is associate dean of the University of Minnesota's Humphrey School of Public Affairs. She has authored multiple books and articles about race, media, and power, including *The Post-racial Mystique* (2014). Currently, her work focuses on intergenerational storytelling and healing. Dr. Squires earned her PhD from Northwestern University in 1999. She is always on the lookout for interesting birds.

Lydia Wilkes is an assistant professor and writing program administrator at Auburn University. Her research interests include how rhetoric and violence manifest in public and educational spaces and how they affect possibilities for human flourishing. Her scholarship has appeared in *Composition Forum, The Proceedings of the Computers and Writing Conference 2016–2017,* and the *Journal of Veterans Studies.*